FLASH OF SILVER

...the leap that changed my world

GRAHAM KERR
The Former Galloping Gourmet

Flash of Silver: The Leap That Changed My World
© 2015 by Graham Kerr
ISBN: 978-0-692-53566-0

Audio Read by the Author and eBook Versions Available at www.grahamkerr.com

Dedicated to...

TREENA

Without whom very little of all this would have been possible. I shall be forever grateful.
Upstreaming on my own now, I'm on my way. Rest well, you earned it.

About the Cover

"You have to be the most unutterably boring man in the entire world!"

Treena had just watched one of my early television programs in New Zealand when I was about 27 years old.

"Well," I responded, *"If you are so clever, why don't you produce the show."* I was not convinced.

"Okay...I will!" And with that she set off for Broadcasting House.

Later, as producer for the Galloping Gourmet, she gave me my first instruction.

"You want to teach people, to get them into the kitchen and share food with those they love... that's all good stuff but first of all you have to entertain them. TV is first and foremost an entertainment!"

"Give me the first six minutes...I need you to run into a live audience and jump over a chair holding a glass of wine. Talk about a film location and tell a funny story. Then it's all yours!"

"Jumping the chair may look like a gimmick but trust me, that leap is going to change everything."

Eventually, I did as I was "commanded" and gradually became less boring; or so I am told.

It was that tension between us that made the program what it turned out to be, a game changer in the communication of practical information...

Treena was nominated for two daytime Emmy awards as "producer of the year", whilst I leapt over five hundred and thirty chairs in my hot pursuit of peace.

The rest, as they say, is history. Or, as in this case, a book for you to enjoy! And to find out what happened when I landed in a more peace-filled place.

Contents

Acknowledgements

I hope that this entire story will express my thanks to so many people. Each and every person has made a significant contribution to my life.

The account itself needed some very consistent help. Since I wrote every single word with a mechanical pencil I shall be forever grateful for that instrument given to me by my beloved

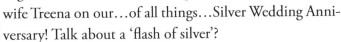

wife Treena on our…of all things…Silver Wedding Anniversary! Talk about a 'flash of silver'?

This pencil script was translated into type by Laurie Glaspy and passed through my very long-term secretary Wendy Pilcher, who did the original basic layout. Treena and our daughter Tessa Fulton then endured a reading over afternoon tea day after day after day…(The tea helped!).

Our teatime included the notes introduced by our salmon expert—the co-author of "May The Rivers Never Sleep" Mr. Bill MacMillan, who kept my imagination submerged in good marine science…for the most part!

Our son Andy then began to imagine the method of distribution and layout with his good friend Josh Rathke. They eventually handed this on to Ryan and Cynthia Malane who surveyed the newly emerging e-publishing business for us and made several inspired observations, becoming good friends, as a result.

My Editor over a great many years, John Duff, raised the issue of Charles Dickens and his many classics that began their lives in serial form. It was this *nudge* that started me thinking of our initial method of distribution…

I have been greatly blessed to have Sandy Silverthorne provide delightfully good-humored 'whimsies' to garnish and explain my words. Once again he has exceeded my fondest hopes. For the cover, credit goes to Ryann Entwistle…an extremely talented young lady.

Pictures of the Galloping Gourmet were shot by Robert Peterson in 1970 for Life Magazine.

Our audio version was made possible by Jeff Rex of KAPPS Radio Station in Mount Vernon, Washington, with Treena's help as its producer.

The very detailed editorial process was kindly provided by Professor Donna Lee Brien and her Doctoral candidate Jillian Adams of Central Queensland University, Australia.

We also want to thank the team at Constant Contact, for their invaluable help in creating our newsletter and teaching us how to navigate the process of maintaining our email subscriptions.

Daniel Livengood (how's *that* for a name?!) designed our Reflective Readers Club and my www.GrahamKerr.com website – a brilliant young web designer.

Finally we have received "big picture" web "understanding" from Brad Clure that has brought all this work into your "reflective" life.

Throughout this entire process Treena and Tessa have been an enormous source of encouragement and comfort. They, above countless others, have my undying gratitude for putting up with all the time and focus that it takes to assemble a whole life story.

Now it is you that I want to acknowledge. You are the reason for it all, the individual who may eventually having spent over 20 hours of reading/listening, decide to jump into the river of resilience and head upstream on purpose. Because of your potential contribution we may have a better chance at survival in this season into which we have been born.

Heading upstream (with you?) on purpose!
Graham Kerr
Mount Vernon, Washington, US

1

FLASH OF SILVER

...the leap that changed my world.

BOOK ONE: DOWNSTREAM DISCOVERIES

Introduction to the Trilogy
A "Memoir & Metaphor"

At a recent appearance, I told my audience that, whilst some people suffer from allergies, that I suffered from allegories, acronyms and metaphors.

At that moment, my wife Treena cried out for all to hear,

"You don't suffer, your audience does!"

Much laughter, much truth! You are about to enter the first of many acronyms. **M&M** goes beyond the small colorful candy and the Rap Artist and represents...**M**emoir and **M**etaphor.

This Trilogy is a mix of the two. The memoir is about my entire life of over eighty years and its remaining hopes. The metaphor compares my life and especially my lifelong love affair and partnership in purpose with Treena, with that of two Wild Pacific Chinook salmon and their life cycle of about seven years.

Each chapter will be called a "Rite of Passage" and will begin with the voice of the male salmon, called (eventually) a "buck" and will also include the female voice of the "hen". It is here that imagination must meet science with a degree of poetic license and engage with your willing acceptance as our audience of one.

I have read many excellent books about the Chinook and have had the great good fortune to have my manuscript read by Bill McMillan who has spent his life in the study of the Pacific North West Rivers and their "inhabitants". His book *May The Rivers Never Sleep* by Bill and John McMillan (a father and son collaboration and Frank Amato Publication) is a splendid example of Bill's love for the subject. He has allowed me a measure of poetic license that follows the story but drew the line when my imaginings flew in the face of good science. Rather than finding his input restrictive I actually found it very helpful in understanding my own life and journey with greater clarity.

It is my belief that all creation is connected and that, through metaphor and shared imagination it may be possible that I, as the author and you as my reader or listener, may find ourselves in the same river of revelation from time to time. I do hope so, for that is my intent.

Our fondest hope is that we might join with you and possibly your friends, as we reflect upon the powerful resilience of these splendid fish. They are no doubt "driven" to reach their final resting place so that their species may survive.

May we too, as modern humans, in our own fight upstream against many man-made obstacles, overcome them all as a "flash of silver" example that we can keep on going...we can survive and even *thrive*!

Welcome to the river of resilience!

Preface to "Flash of Silver"

Any change that reduces consumption will threaten some segment of the global society. Relinquishment is counter-intuitive in a consumer-based culture.

It is, however, the lifecycle of the Pacific salmon. The salmon leaves its ocean of opportunity in prime condition and begins its journey upstream against continual downstream pressures, obstacles and predators, driven to achieve its natural task to preserve the species.

A Chinook salmon that succeeds in its life goal may reach the age of seven, or even eight years and beyond.

We humans, avoiding the multiple obstacles in our lives may live seventy or eighty years and beyond.

Some of us have the "stamp of the salmon" as our motivation. We have experienced the early days of downstream growth. We have taken time to adjust to the salty world ahead of us and then taken the competitive plunge of self-interest through acquisition to own more for one's self.

It has taken my wife, Treena and I, over eighty years to journey this far and these sixty-four segments are not so much chapters as rites of passage through which both salmon and mankind can often pass in their natural response to our modern world.

It is my great desire that, no matter your age or occupation, you may somehow decide that you too have the stamp of the salmon on your life, and that there is within you the hunger to eventually go beyond immediate self-interest so that our species may survive and even thrive! The choices you make will be observed as a "flash of silver" as you leap over the many obstacles that will stand in your way as you journey upstream.

I need, therefore, at this very early stage, to ask you to join me as I submerge both of us in the "river of imagination" as I attempt to use the faculty of imagination to "provide meaning to experience and understanding to knowledge."

I shall ask you, therefore, to imagine a conversation with a wild Pacific salmon. Its egg lies in a scooped out redd amid quite large clean gravel over which runs a reasonably deep ripple of fresh, clear, cold, oxygenated water. The milt from the male salmon has settled upon the egg, and the massive effort of these parent fish is now resulting in...life! Here now is the Buck Chinook wild salmon who will, with a hearty dose of our shared imagination, address you, direct.

Rite of Passage One
"The Journey Begins...The End Is In Sight"

I am alive!

Flash...flash...it's almost a rhythm and I'm being lifted off a large round stone surface with each brilliant glance of light. I can see nothing other than the bursts of light but I can feel the rapid rise and fall of whatever surrounds me. I am curled upon myself and have an inner urge to grow to take hold of that which is life.

An Understanding

A female Chinook salmon will lay about five thousand eggs in a gravel nest called a redd, which is composed of a series of depressions made by sweeping her powerful tail against quite large gravel in a swiftly flowing shallow river bed. It is entirely possible that she began her life in this same reach of the river, perhaps as long as seven, even eight years ago. Less plausible, but still just as possible, could be that the male salmon who has fertilized her eggs with his milt also began life in the same river and the same season of the same year. Let us imagine it so?

I am twelve weeks old

At first all is blurred, and then suddenly I can see. I am surrounded by a mass of bright orange globes, like the one to which I am still attached, but my eyes are free, and I see many other clouded eyes around me; some begin to struggle and others lay silent and unmoved.

I'm attached to a kind of energy, at least for a while, as the yolk drains. I grow and wriggle almost free. My tiny body has uncurled and straightened.

As the yolk falls away I am free at last. Along with those around me, I swiftly move downstream and I find I am no longer simply an egg. I will never know what others call me or even care.

I am moving, I am aware, I am hungry...I am alive and I'm only one-inch long (or so I'm told!)

An Understanding

The egg that hatches and remains attached to its birth yolk is already a survivor. Less than ten percent will advance to the new name we have for them, alevin –from the old French a lever, to lift up or rear, as in offspring. From the time of spawning in the fall to hatching in the spring, the emerging fish gather nourishment from what is called a "yolk sac" that contains proteins, minerals and vitamins, a kind of breast feeding. When the yolk is exhausted, the alevin change their name for the second time from baby (alevin) to infant (button up fry). It is then that they leave their gravel birthplace and hunt for their own food.

Add on another six weeks

So now, as I said, I am hungry and only an inch long, and am being carried away from my birthplace that I have fixed carefully in my memory. I know exactly what it smells like and I shall never forget.

After another two weeks

Right now...I'm hungry. Since I am a pretty small fry (no pun intended) I am looking for something very small...oh...and nourishing. I really don't want to bite off more than I can chew! There is a tiny speck of a thing. It's also alive. Should I? Couldn't I get by with plants?

I know absolutely nothing about vegan, and dismiss the blades of bank grass as incidental camouflage and shade for a warm day. It moves...it's smaller than me...therefore it's FOOD! I gulp it down; it protests for a brief, tickling moment. It has a small crisp texture and then it's gone...not so bad. I need more and more and more. I grow and grow as I'm swept downstream.

I am forty weeks old!

I glanced over my gills yesterday to discover that I've picked up my own camouflage. Not unlike the grass-covered banks, they are short, dark bars down my three-inch flanks and I'm now entitled to what some people call me now, "Parr".

...and now for a brief "flash" in my imagination.

My Mother sits up in her turned-down bed, her knees drawn up with arms tightly wrapped about. She seems not to be pleased. My Father stands at the open window, a light breeze billows the cotton curtains. He is silent and unmoved, drawn in upon himself?

I see a sudden flash of light, as if a drop of water has disturbed a perfectly flat pool. The droplet subsides and sets up a ripple, and each tiny wave catches the same source of light with moving rings of liquid fire. In the very depths of my imagination I believe I have seen the moment that my earthly body received its eternal spirit.

"We are not human beings having a spiritual experience.
We are spiritual beings having a human experience."

Pierre Teilhard de Chardin

The energy-filled ripples were, in my still emerging consciousness, the response to my human creation; one of expanding "joy" that is identical to the same emotion experienced at the moment at which all life begins, whether it is within egg or seed.

22 January 1934. *I am born!*

I am told by mother that at age three I liberated her treasured silk underwear through an upper window of my parent's apartment. They were picked up by a brisk breeze and managed to garnish the street lamps. Following this attempt at gaining public attention, I spent several hours making a colorful mural on the bedroom wall using all her makeup –rouge, lipstick, powder...the works. She was, once again, not amused.

All this simply to lead up to the devastation of war with Germany on September 3, 1939. I was five. It is at this time that my memory begins its takeover bid.

1939 -I am five years old

She is kindly but distant, a little like my maternal Grandmother. She is being patient. My foot is on a large round stone. I'm sitting on a low garden bench.

My parents John and Marjory (Mardi) Kerr

I have brown shoes with laces and I am being taught how to tie them. "So that is how you make a single bow," she explained as we looked down upon my fumbled knot.

"But never leave it at that," she cautioned. "Before the bow is tightened it needs to be turned once again within itself, then it won't come undone and cause you to stumble."

I just stopped writing and made the double knot in my much larger, but still brown, shoes. I needed to know how to describe this, my very first experience with a learned response that had a practical, useful outcome.

It was second nature to tie the double knot. I must have now done it thousands of times...yet it is almost impossible to describe.

Is it, I wonder, to be like this on the whole journey with any or all accomplishments that I now take for granted? I strongly hope not!

I learned this shoelace lesson from an unknown mentor in a cottage garden in the English countryside where I was briefly billeted to get me, and thousands of young children like me, out of London and its bombs to a place of relative temporary safety. Both my parents were in the Armed Forces, which certainly prompted their decision to find me a safe house in the countryside.

Within months they became convinced that my mother should resign from active service in order to be with me.

Our return to London is my next vivid flash of memory. Heavy anti-aircraft fire blossomed against the smoky sky. Great circles followed as shell after shell screamed into the air. Shrapnel clattered on the taxi roof as the driver steered around debris on the roadway, lit poorly by his shielded headlights. I felt my mother's rough serge uniform against my bare legs as she drew me close.

We arrived at her parent's home in Golders Green, unscathed by that evening's raid.

I was given her old room, its windows taped to reduce the risk of flying glass. I was told to get under the bed if bombs began to fall, and to undress and get to bed and they would be up later. Searchlights waved back and forth across the night sky probing for planes. Guns fired and bombs exploded...all in the distance. I folded my clothes on a side chair, as taught by my shoelace instructor, and got into a cold bed and looked out on my new noisy world.

My mother and grandmother came up the stairs and I pretended that I was already asleep.

"Look at him, he must have been tired," my mother said as she tucked me in.

"Such a good little boy," my grandmother whispered. "Look how neatly he has folded his clothes."

The curtains of my memory fall back into place following that briefly lit scene, an experience that fashioned a powerful foundation for what I now call the desires of my heart. I had been taught to do a small thing and do it well. What I had done was observed and had received approval that had been shared.

I was encouraged and it felt good to be me.

Authors note: At the conclusion of each Rite of Passage (Chapter) you will find a means by which you can go directly to our Reflective Readers Club. In order that you can get the best possible use of this unique opportunity I have inserted a full description of how we hope this will work. That will ultimately be up to you.

—Graham

Welcome to the Reflective Readers Club (RRC)

Both Treena and I are avid readers. We cancelled over the air TV in 1999 and are members of Netflix for DVD watching which is restricted to usually no more that 90 minutes a day.

Our news comes in on NPR and The Week magazine. We do our own research, when needed, on the web. This leaves us free to pick up a book and read in order to become better informed, inspired and entertained. For us, this "input" management works really well.

When a book sets out to encourage some form of change I use a pencil to write my presuppositions on the subject matter on one of the blank pages. I do this so that, if the author succeeds in convincing me to take action, then I know why I changed my mind, or was moved to join a "cause".

One of the best ways to benefit from a good book is to read it in the company of others, as in BOOK CLUBS. Unfortunately, in our fast paced and crowded world, these are now harder to find.

This, then, is the reason why I created the REFLECTIVE READERS CLUB, so that you, as my reader, might use each Rite of Passage to reflect upon your own life at these important and influential periods.

At the end of each Rite of Passage there is an icon (for eBook) or the web address (for print) or a verbal cue (for the audio). If you follow these directions it will bring you directly to a listing of all the Rites of Passage. Click the number you have just read and you are immediately in the ebb and flow of members' comments.

I have asked three relevant questions at the head of all the comments, you can use these to REFLECT or simply add your own observations.

It is my great hope that you would take the time to plunge into this river of resilient discussion. By doing so you will join a movement of thinking people who, by their very words and experience, can help to slow the present decline into ruin that is so apparent in the time into which we have been born and for which we have direct responsibility as stewards.

I very much look forward to your company
Graham Kerr

Please join us in the Reflective Readers Club
www.grahamkerr.com/rrc

Rite of Passage Two
"Acquisition" Year One 1940

I was never on my own during my time as a fry. We were a small shoal, all hatched about the same time in the same stretch of river. I'm less than four months old and already over two inches long, and yes, I've been able to shift my protein diet of what some call zooplankton, to include small insects.

My camouflage has been deepened and widened, and at times I am almost invisible, especially in the quiet, deeper general stretches of river. It is not always eating and floating quietly downstream. There are frequent rapid, flashing tumblings over large stones and rocks. Once or twice the bottom simply dropped out of our world and my companions and I found ourselves in midair surrounded by foaming water that pushed us deeper down onto the riverbed.

It was during the second of these sudden descents that I caught sight of a huge version of myself going in the opposite direction. It seemed so odd, and yet at the same time, so right, but nothing that made me even think about following.

Some of these rapid movements were bruising and some of my shoal didn't make it. There was one who always seemed to get my attention...

1940
I am six years old
"Acquisition" Year One

In the very early days of the war, my father, who served as a member of the London Scottish Territorial Army (not unlike the United States Reservists and National Guard), was commissioned as an officer and shipped overseas to Egypt where he served as a munitions expert for its North African campaigns. During his absence, my mother worked in an insurance office in Brighton, Sussex, on the south coast. She found an apartment on Cromwell Road in the neighboring town of Hove. I joined a small group of other children for the first time. It seems that our immediate circle had absent fathers serving in the war effort.

Me and my bicycle outside our apartment on Cromwell Road

It was in Hove that I joined the local Scout troop. Along with a rather large wide-brimmed hat, I was issued a stave (walking stick) that measured just five feet, slightly taller than I was at seven.

It was my first understanding of ownership, or rather pride of ownership. The stave was mine and it could, within reason, be cut, drilled and bound for specific purposes from the bottom up. For this I was given a ruler, some heavy twine, a hand-operated wood drill and bit, and best prize of all...a penknife!

I meticulously cut even rings every one inch from the bottom until I reached one foot, and then bands at each foot until the top where I drilled a hole. I made a loop through the hole with an old (yes, you've guessed it) leather shoelace. I bound the twine around the middle to mark the *carry at the balance point* and the job was done.

I loved that stave; it was my rifle in a time of war, my weapon, and even a mark of some authority that set me apart from my companions. I vividly remember dressing up in my khaki shirt and shorts, cramming the hat on my head, taking up my staff in the walking stick position, and marching down Wilbury Road, a left on Eaton and first right on Selborne. It was about there that Sylvia lived, a flaxen-haired six-year-old who, I reasoned, might be impressed by my newly whittled stave and general outward appearance in uniform. I stood outside her house for a while, hoping to be recognized and admired.

I was not...

Later, I was to have my own Raleigh bike. It was green with white-walled tires. That bike morphed into a Bown Auto cycle 98 cc, maroon with gold pin striping, and eventually to an MG "M" type with a Bugatti styled rear end. Oh, how I *loved* each of these easily seen acquisitions, they were mine, all mine, and each of them got me places.

As I enjoyed my brand new scouting uniform, another uniform reentered my life. My father came home from Egypt, where his efficient handling of munitions had found favor. He was posted back to the War Office in London, to assist with the European Campaign.

His return blended with a sudden tumult of whitewater emotions that was so sudden, painful and profound that I added two and two and came up with five. It was a self-deceit that remained for over fifty years, and shall be revealed in my story at the proper time.

My father, in my original imagination at the time of my conception, was distant and withdrawn. This did not make him in the least cold and unwelcoming; he was to all outward appearances a *jolly good chap*. He was hale and hearty, warmly welcoming and decent...on the outside and to outsiders. It was beyond the obvious that the less understood Major John Douglas Kerr lived out his lonely life.

My father was the youngest of four sons. My grandfather, whom I don't remember at all, was a very conservative Scottish architect from a famous architectural family. He was, I am told, quite a dour disciplinarian who often crept downstairs in the middle of the night for a "wee dram of Scotch." He had to deal with a squeaking hinge on the liquor cabinet and oiled it often to avoid my grandmother's displeasure at these *nocturnal nips*. My grandmother cleaned out the hinge as often as he oiled it. This is the only human-interest story passed down to me about my father's family...a distant group indeed, that made little show of their emotions.

My grandfather; and my father, the youngest of four

My simple addition of two plus two was to put my father's reappearance together with our move away from my young friends to the other side of Brighton to the East, halfway to Rottingdean. At the same time as the move, I was sent to a preparatory school for boys as a boarder. I was eight years old and the bottom dropped out of my world for the very first time.

My parents were reunited and I was sent off to school to board when my new home was less than two miles away. Had school been a happy experience all would have been fine...but it wasn't. At nine, I was moved up into the then upper school that normally received eleven-year-olds, but the war had somehow caused an overflow to take place. I was reasonably tall for my age and quite good at sports, so I was considered the right size to be advanced before my time. All I can recall about this savage experience is no doubt colored by my apparent failure to catch up in the classroom.

In the French class, I was made to stand on a stool and recite the verbs that came before (or after) the noun. I remember that list to this day because it was beaten into my leg (we wore shorts) by the French teacher who had heavy gold rings on a large, hard hand.

The combination of pain and humiliation drove me to do my best for the masters. I struggled with every subject.

My classmates interpreted this as "sucking up to the Masters", and I was arraigned before a jury of my peers in the "courts" held above the stone and flint Gothic entrance to the school. They found me guilty and I was sentenced to be beaten with the *plank*.

I had to live between the rock of abusive teachers and the hard place of judgmental fellow students.

In my extreme youth I was a "fag" (a forerunner to a "batman"/servant to Army officers) to the Head Boy, a public school Squash champion. One day, I carried his diminutive butter ration (less than one ounce) in its small glass-covered dish to the dining room, tripped over the sandstone step, lost my grip...and it smashed. As a penance, I handed over a prized one-pound tin of Tate and Lyles Golden Syrup, sent by my mother. This was accepted...but in addition I had earned "six of the best". Remember that my prefect was a Squash champion... and his best was better than most. They were almost up to those of the school's chaplain, my housemaster, who added another "six" for my being late for chapel.

"You" he thundered as he raised the stick "will not...THWACK...be late...THWACK... for GOD...THWACK!"

I added both of those sixes together and made thirteen out of them!

I could, as is said often in memoirs, go on, but I will say that I was driven to the bottom of my young and inexperienced life, so much so that I ran away. I didn't have far to run; my parents lived at the midway point along that day's long-distance run.

The custom in those wartime days was to prepare us as future Junior Officers who would be *happy* to die for King and country! As part of this conditioning, the rule was "last boy back gets beaten." I was a sprinter and helpless at a distance, and I was dead last...so I turned right around and ran back home. My distant dad was home and before long he took me back to school with the then pretense that I'd had a toothache.

I had now nowhere to go and no respite from both pain and humiliation, well, perhaps there was always track and field and my ability to sprint? I worked harder than most to win. My academic teachers would sigh at my struggles in the classroom. "Kerr, go and do what you do best...hit the track", and so I trained to win the 100-yard dash for my age group.

On Sports Day I wound up side-by-side with a new boy, tall, thin and...fast! I got a great start and at 50 yards was well ahead. That is when I heard him coming up behind...I simply could NOT fail again; I couldn't lose the only thing I could do...so I deliberately tripped myself up and hit the track with a screeching thud. "Too bad Kerr" one of the boys yelled, "you had it in the bag."

I lived for almost fifty years before I came to understand what I lost that day, and how strangely what the throwing of the race was to cost me.

Please join us in the Reflective Readers Club

www.grahamkerr.com/rrc

I had a good sense of smell, even when I was just a buttonup fry I made a very careful note of how my birthplace felt to my new sensing of the world about me. As I was swept downstream, eating quite well and putting on length and weight, I was still aware of that special scent. True, it was getting weaker and it now and again startled me with quite strong clouds of acrid, stinking density, not as much a slime but on its way!

Recently, a whole new rush of aromas seemed to join my singular river. It came in on my right fin side. Along with these new waters came more of...me.

Some feel, looking upon us from above, that we often look alike, at least in our various families. I am a Chinook—sometimes called a King—although I don't look upon myself in that way; I quite like Chinook, even though in my parr state of one to two years I'm more like a prince in camouflage? One new arrival, another Chinook, came into my side of the river and got my attention in the midst of all its own shoal. Up until now, I really haven't been interested in female fish, called hens. As a young buck, I am more interested in chasing after...food. But this hen is different! Her body has a much smaller fin (adipose) between the upper one (dorsal) and the one I swish for direction (caudal). She has a smaller nose than mine and a beauty spot near her caudal fin.

This hen was shorter than me and rounded, nicely rounded! She came closer and our eyes met...lovely eyes! Something yet unformed within me wanted to leap out of the water into the air and...splash!

24

Understanding

Most natal rivers that have salmon runs are fed by many tributaries. As they join the main river they come complete with the new season's young salmon.

You might call this poetic license or even mere human conceit, but my earlier aquatic imagination suggested that there might be an entire lifecycle relationship between a male buck and a female hen. Both would be of the same species, Chinook, both from the same river basin, born in the same season in the same year.

Less plausible, but still just possible, is how I saw such an event and now, in my story, it has happened. **Would you, dear reader, stretch your imagination to match mine and join us for the relational journey of a lifetime!**

I recall a much later experience that plays into my feelings on this monogamous relationship and for this I fast forward to 1974, while we lived on the Eastern shore of the Chesapeake Bay in Maryland, USA. Our son, Andy, had become a keen hunter and was an exceptional shot. He and his good friend Ned were planning to hunt wild geese. I was invited to join them. I took my camera, preferring not to shoot at a living creature.

Sometime later, they fired at, and wounded, a large goose. It spiraled out of the sky into Peach Blossom Creek and was clearly not dead. We motored quickly to the spot and Ned expertly reached for its head and swung it in a violent, blood-splattering circle so that its neck broke, ending the bird's pain.

I asked to be put ashore where I sat watching the dead goose's mate continue to circle, quite high up, apparently looking down for signs from its lifelong partner, and as it did so, crying out for over an hour.

I understood, on that crisp autumn day, what creation intended for whole-life partners and the central security it offers for family; the building block for community.

1944
I am ten years old

My sudden series of crushing descents into the turmoil and confusion of my schooling had so disoriented me that I suspect my memories have been garnished by the pain and humiliation I experienced. I have no recourse to my fellow students of 1944, at least, none that I can find. I'm certain about the clear memories I have already shared. However, there is more that I should not exclude because they are the shadows that occupy the foundations set down in my early life.

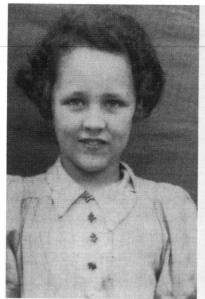

"Treena at ten, took my mind off soccer...completely!"

Our Housemaster's name is not important; that I recall him as sadistic...is. After lights out, he would wait in the hallways for a child to speak, which was forbidden. In a brilliant second of time he would snap on the lights and demand, "who spoke?" Silence – shocked, terrified silence...because we knew what would follow. "Own up, or I'll beat the lot of you," and with scarcely room for a breath he added, "out of bed, all of you, bend over!"

He then did his *rounds* with a large leather-soled slipper; loud thwacks, a few tight whimpers but seldom tears...that, too, was forbidden!

In the pitch darkness of my mind I recall, without evidence for or against, that a boy soaped the steep steps outside of our room and our nocturnal enemy, hell-bent on his abusive mission, slipped and fell. He broke his neck in the fall.

The school paraded in front of his coffin, set out in the school chapel, with a police inspector who studied each child's response to seeing the results of his possible mischief. I recall, darkly, that each child shared a common delight to see him dead.

Later, one member of our house, in an unrelated incident, was savagely beaten up in the school latrines with mops soaked in urine; his crime was being...Jewish! His attackers came from another house, in an unrelated incident, so I and many others declared ourselves to be members of the "anti-beating up society". We stormed the other house, breaking its windows with stones until firehoses were turned on us to quell the riot.

IMAGINATION? I truly do not know, but each is firmly fixed in the memory of a fragile ten-year-old whose life laid about him in suspect ruins.

My parents had moved. The war ended in May 1945 and I was now 11.

I had a temperature of over 103°F (this is my mother's evidence). The sick wards at the school were full and I was sitting it out in the midst of a dangerous flu epidemic. My mother, who had come for a brief visit, was furious and that day, reminiscent of her earlier "rescue" during the Blitz had come to take me home; again.

My father had been demobilized and chose to enter the hotel business. Their first appointment as management was the Dorset Arms Hotel in East Grinstead, Sussex, on the south coast of England, roughly 2.8 miles from the school. I was transferred to Michael Hall (coeducational school), a Rudolf Steiner educational system that began in Germany in 1911. It could not have been more different…

An old Scripture describes such a shift as "coming out of darkness into his wonderful light." For me, it was just such a move and my next few years were to pour real substance and eagerness into the shadowy vacuums of despair upon which my life had been precariously balanced.

When I arrived in Michael Hall, I was eleven. Not only did I now find myself amongst girls, but I also had a teacher, Ms. Dawson, who would remain my class teacher until I was due to leave school. I had entered into an extended, creative family of young people who were utterly unaware of measured competition.

Michael Hall class picture

There were no marks or grades on papers, no exams, and no position in the class. The first exam we would take would be on school leaving, and a great many students passed that first test with flying colors. There were also no scores for sports; even tennis was simply the joy of getting the ball over the net and serving when you felt like it! I introduced cricket, which we also played without counting the runs. You might well ask...so what's the point... surely someone *has* to win? The point was that we were enjoying each other's achievement, and when we said "well held," we actually meant it as an unconditional encouragement.

Oh, how I loved that school and how I thrived with my academic classes, woodwork and knitting (yes, we all did the same classes).

If there was to me a single problem it was the food. At boarding school it had been macaroni cheese tainted by the aroma of rotting grass clippings from the sports field. Here the dining room smelled of cabbage and beans.

It was in late summer of 1945 that I was sitting at my desk during a break and I saw a young girl in one class below mine.

She had tight black curly hair, and a face that shone with pure joy. She held a pair of castanets, which she crisply clapped to the beat of her feet as they scampered up dust. She had an audience of classmates surrounding her clapping to the same measure, delighting in the dance. I grabbed my Kodak box camera and gained the inner circle. I bent over the viewfinder and centered her. "Can I take your picture?" I cried.

She posed with hands circled about her castanets and looked straight at me.

Our eyes met through the camera lens...lovely eyes. *Click.*

I wish I could share that picture with you now but I had no film in the camera, as film was beyond my pay scale!

Over fifty years later we returned to that exact spot and went through the same original motions for the Biography TV Series.

Please join us in the Reflective Readers Club
www.grahamkerr.com/rrc

**It was then, on that autumn day that
I had begun to fall in love...with Treena.**

Rite of Passage Four
"First Love"

Year two and six months

The young hen's eyes were what I noticed first and what drew me to her side in the midst of our merged shoals. It was later that our fins touched. Usually it meant that I was close to something solid, a warning to keep me off jagged rocks. This time it was different and welcome. I wanted it to continue. I swam a little closer and so did she, as we made our way downstream for one season in our early lives.

And then, one day, she was gone, nowhere to be found, but like the aromas of my birthplace I had set the feel of her fin firmly in my memory and I continued on my way...to the oceans that lay beyond my then understanding.

An Enquiry

Seventy three million sharks are hunted and killed each year by cutting off their dorsal fin, a traditional delicacy that has more to do with the host's apparent social status than actual taste, which is negligible.

Without its dorsal, the shark simply bleeds to death and may, in some cases, be eaten alive by its own kind; not a good way to go, regardless of which way you consider it!

Sharks have senses, including an ability to sense through their skin vibrations in the water.

Does this mean that the fin itself can...*feel*, and does it have the sense of touch?

I needed to know because of how I have come to *imagine* the salmon's ability to use its pectoral fins to somehow hold hands.

1945 to 1949
I am eleven to fifteen years old

"Treena"

Girls, up until Treena, were of no real consequence. Soccer held much greater interest. Treena was different and my life changed with that brief encounter.

My parents had noticed the change. My bedroom was in the annex to the main hotel, overlooking the gardens. I had doodled Treena's name next to a heart on the bedroom wall, a more advanced decorative feel than my earlier use of my mother's makeup.

"You can't draw on the wall," my father was quite stern, "we don't own the hotel...so don't mess with it!"

The maintenance man was called in and my record of first love was permanently covered in cream-colored paint.

My mother, on the other hand, was helpful. She arranged for badminton and a strawberries-and-cream tea party on the lower lawn. She asked my school friends and Treena. The parents gathered in the bar, and we kids in a garden flanked by large, old rhododendron bushes over ten feet tall. During that warm English summer afternoon, I took a wild swipe at the shuttlecock and it arced over and into the pink flowering bushes. Treena and I went hunting for it and in the cool shade of that hundred-year-old English Roseum rhododendron, our hands touched for the first time.

I was now twelve and I had fallen in love! There was nothing I could think of that was more thrilling than the touch of our hands. At first simply brushing, but later...reaching out and holding, even with fingers interlaced. We went to movies and held hands. My mother took us to Brighton on a Greenline bus...and we held hands. I used the hotel line to phone her...and read poetry and talked almost endlessly until my father, wondering why guests complained of difficulty making reservations, discovered that, once again, I needed to know my place in the "hotel business."

This might have simply continued to develop seamlessly into a lifelong love affair had it not been for Steven Cole, the chemist's son, who could afford film at a discounted price for *his* camera. Steven was my best friend at school and therefore had some contact with Treena, but he went totally beyond all reason, as they both did; they went to see a movie together...on their own and even, I fantasized, perhaps had an ice cream! Surely their hands didn't touch? It was more than my young heart could bear, and I *almost* drew upon my bedroom wall to somehow spell out and find release for my anguish.

This time, my distant dad came to the rescue. I explained my serious situation, to which he listened wisely.

"Does she have a good friend, a girl?" he asked.

"Yes, her name is Joyce," I replied.

"Then invite Joyce to go to the cinema with you," he suggested, with a knowing smile. "That should do it." So, I did.

I had shared a small hardbound book with Treena *"Three Men in a Boat"* by Jerome K. Jerome. A day or two after my invitation to Joyce, which she had accepted, Treena had my book returned to me. Within its pages was a short letter and a press-dried flower...a purple pansy.

The note read: *"If you keep this flower I know everything is okay between us. If you give it back to me I will know that it is over and I will never go the pictures with another boy all my life."* *Treena*

In a loud burst of joy, I threw the pansy into the ditch!

Now, I needed to let Dad know that his wisdom had worked.

"So…" he seemed to hesitate...for effect?

"So...what do you intend to do about Joyce?" He asked.

"What do you mean?" I questioned.

"You have asked her to go to the cinema, so what should you do?" He had an emerging smile.

"I can't take both of them!" I burst out.

"Why not? Are they not friends?"

And so I took both Joyce and Treena. I bought them both an ice cream with the last of my pocket money and I sat between them, holding my own empty hands. My father had said that this is what is meant to grow up as a young gentleman, and to treat young women with the good manners to which they were, as the fairer (not weaker) sex, entitled.

Then, one day, she was gone. She, her parents, and her two younger brothers just vanished. Treena's father was a fine artist and a portrait painter who could occasionally put food on the table and send his daughter to a good school. Also occasionally, he was unable to obtain a commission and simply *had* to move. There were times when creditors remained unpaid and his move was sudden, with no forwarding address. Treena had gone, and nobody could find out where.

I was now left to my own devices as a child without siblings in a home where I could neither use the phone nor draw on the walls. It was, however, a home where I could eat early with my parents, who would then work until long after I would go to bed. Such is the life for Hotel Management who live on site. Some call it a "champagne lifestyle on a beer income." My father was technically, if not clinically, an alcoholic. He was definitely

drinking alcohol, but not once did I ever see him "the worse for wear." If anything, his good diction became more precise, accompanied by an admirable ability to be, as I have already described him, a jolly good fellow. The staff and customers referred to him as *The Major*, which suited his upright military posture and bristling moustache.

My father was a distant dad, possibly because his father and grandfather had modeled such a relationship. He had helped me with Treena, but otherwise we had little contact. I did, however, want to be like him. I would do what I observed that he did so well.

I was an only child, and our odd family hours were utterly different from those enjoyed by my school friends whose parents were off duty when mine were on. Because of this deep divide, my life was singular. The kitchen became my place of interest. It was there that I was allowed to play and learn, and so I did. At no time did I look upon food with awe or reverence...it was...food. It was at times challenging and also hot *work*. What I remember loving most was being seen and accepted as a kind of *kitchen mascot*. The cooks would cry out "come and see what the little Master can do now." At least, I think they called me a little Master, but I've never been sure. I was indeed tolerated because I was the Manager's son, but in due time I could chop and stir well enough to be useful. I enjoyed the atmosphere of a busy kitchen, the flames, noise and the friendly banter, but I never, ever imagined that cooking might become a lifelong pursuit. My vision of the future was to do what my father did, and do it so well that I might become the Managing Director of the Dorchester Hotel in London. This would allow me to wear a frock coat (cut-away morning jacket with striped trousers, a grey silk tie secured by one good pearl tie pin...oh, and a perfect red carnation)!

It was the outward appearance that appealed and the opportunity to greet the world's most famous people as my customers...just as my father greeted his local country town celebrities. I was so certain of this career pathway that I moved very early from Michael Hall to a "crammers" in Brighton who prepared me for the one exam required to leave school, which in turn would help me to attend the two year Hotel Management course at Brighton Technical College. I entered that course close to my fifteenth birthday, perhaps the youngest student they had ever had?

I had several culinary "events" that attracted the Chef instructor's attention.

"When you graduate, we will have to give you a Fireman's helmet instead of a Chef's hat," he said, *almost* laughing. I found commercial-sized gas cook tops as challenging in those days as I do even now! There were also good moments. I recall having made Coquilles St. Jacques, a dish of scallops cooked in a cream sauce, served in a scallop shell decorated with piped "duchesse" potatoes. The dish was simple enough to cook and garnish, but we also had to serve it in the college dining room, which was open each day to the public. The Maitre D' Hotel of the restaurant, another instructor, required that the dish be "silver service". To do this, we had to loosen the garland of potato from the shell (it had been placed under a radiant grill to brown lightly), and slide the whole contents from the shell to the customer's plate… and still keep its perfectly round shape. I actually did this several times and it stands to this day as a very encouraging example of risk and reward.

Without a degree of risk, there is little chance for the enormous mixture of relief and achievement that follows in its steps. It is the *leap* that goes on to support even greater attempts at the seemingly impossible challenges that the world often uses to sort the men from the boys, and of course, the women from the girls!

My parents were offered a new job in a hotel in what is now called the "English Riviera" in Torquay, Devonshire. I transferred to South Devon Technical College that taught the same Hotel Management courses and continued to soak up my culinary foundation. In the midst of this early training, two things stand out…I had made what our instructor had called a passable Quiche Lorraine (eggs, bacon, and Gruyere cheese in a bread dough crust similar to the original German dish). I needed my father to see it and join in its approval. I wrapped it carefully, slid it in my backpack, and took off for home on the local bus. We gathered about the table with some interest—it had disintegrated into a pile of sodden custard and crumbs. My father pinched together a wad of the mixture, sniffed it and popped it into his mouth.

"Mmm…mmm" he intoned, chewing (unnecessarily) and swallowed.

"Good job," he said, "must have looked so good."

This was pure *rebar* in my foundation. Our contacts were few and far between, but when the light came on it was WONDERFUL!

Later that year, as the early summer set in, our kitchen garden began, quite literally, to bear fruit…a copious crop of raspberries. I was employed for the first time, and actually paid to do meaningful work. I was a fruit picker. I earned enough in that short season to buy myself a much longed for pair of light grey flannel trousers, my first good pair of slacks.

Please join us in the Reflective Readers Club
www.grahamkerr.com/rrc

Rite of Passage Five: "lower case gourmet" (1949–1951)

I continue to be carried along by the river current, which is full of twists, turns and the occasional big surprise. The scent of my birthplace remains, though it is weaker all the time and strange new aromas seem to get stronger close to the banks. I try to stay midstream.

I'm increasingly aware of my size and rather pleased about it. I tried a piece of the green stuff that fell into the water – it was actually good, but doesn't happen often. I no longer bother with the tiny wriggly things and have been eating up bigger prey that live out of the water and even flap their fins and fly! Even tiny fish, smaller than me!

Yesterday, I came upon a whole cluster of red globes, like the ones in my birthplace. They were not moving so I tried one...not bad, in fact quite filling. I admit it felt a little troubling, but I couldn't see the eyes moving, so, well...let's face it, I know I need to grow and so I eat.

An Understanding

The salmon doesn't seem to mind what it eats, even its own kind as eggs, alevin, even fry. It clearly has a considerable appetite. This eventually can prove to be its downfall when, buried within a tempting morsel, is a sharp hook.

1949 to 1951
I am fifteen to seventeen years old

When I was a child of about six (1940) the government introduced food rationing that lasted through and beyond the end of World War II in 1945 when I was eleven. During this time, food was really quite restricted. For example, these rations were meant to last an adult for *one entire week.*

Bacon/ham 4 oz. (100 g) (Other meats were measured by cost with a maximum of 1 shilling and 4 pence per week)

Butter 2 oz. (50 g)

Cheese 2 oz. (50 g)

Milk 3 pints (1800 ml)

Sugar 8 oz. (225 g)

Eggs 1 egg (down to 1 egg for 2 weeks on occasion)

Candy 3 oz. (87 g)

There was also a points system; sixteen points were given per person with which you could buy a tin of meat or fish, or two pounds of dried fruit or eight pounds of split peas, etc.

It was during these lean years that school meals were started because many mothers were working in support of the war effort. I mention this because it strongly affected the way the entire country viewed food.

British people, upon winning a war (with more than a little help from our friends) do not generally celebrate with conspicuous consumption. Oh, a few beers at the pub, an extra serving of chips with the fish...but that's about it.

My training at the hotel school was probably affected by the gradual resumption of regular amounts of food. Our instructors had been chefs before the war, during the 1920s and beyond, when the living was easy and generous to those who could afford it. They clearly longed for the good old days to return and so they set up our curriculum to cover the French kitchen, organized by Auguste Escoffier (1846–1935). He died at 88 years of age, when I was age 1. He wrote *Le Guide Culinaire* in 1903, that was later released as *"The Guide to Modern Cooking."* It became my textbook bible alongside Saulnier's *"Le Repertoire de la Cuisine."*

Louis Saulnier worked directly with Escoffier, whom he regarded as his mentor. His *Repertoire* is unusual as a culinary work because it contains no actual quantitative recipes. What it did and does, to a lesser extent nowadays, is provide an association of ingredients, which in the experienced chef's mind come together as a *sensually imagined* dish. This was extremely important in these earlier days when the practice of taking good wine with good food was almost an art form practiced, albeit, by a favored few. Nonetheless, it had its well understood boundaries, for good reasons.

Assume, with me please, that you are dining at the Savoy Grill in London before Escoffier left to go to the Ritz. The great wines of France lay in its cellars, wines that commanded high prices. Since they would be drunk alongside food, it followed that they should compliment and not override the other. We still live with the same idea in a far too simplistic sense with the rule…

> *Red wine with red meat.*
> *White wine with white meat.*

In those days, however, the match was often well enough known so that if a menu had, for example, a "Blanquette ris d'Agneau en Croustade" you would know that these tender lamb sweetbreads would be coated in a cream sauce with button mushrooms and served in an open bread "box" that had been deep-fried. In other words, rich but delicately flavored. With this you might order a Pouilly-Fuisse from the Maconnais region of Burgundy in France. We know this wine by its grape variety nowadays as Chardonnay. The big difference is the cost. While the Pouilly was reasonable when compared with a Chassagne-Montrachet from further south, they were both much more expensive than a pretty good Chardonnay from the Napa Valley in California, and, some might still argue…of greater intrinsic value than just the name and its status appeal.

My point here is that menus used to be written using well-known names that would be understood, as to content, by the customer. They would think then, if experienced, to order an expensive wine as an extension to the dish itself.

I have been told that Louis XVI had a lesser official of his court named Gourmet le Picquer that sprung from the word "grommet" used for a vintner's assistant. Apparently this official would taste the wines of various vintages and recommend to the chef what he thought might be a balanced association of flavors.

If this is true, then it suggests that the wine comes first, or used to, especially when both rare and expensive.

Now…fast-forward and we have some excellent fresh (some would say eager) wines that are readily available at reasonable prices. So…now the food comes first and the wine follows.

Naturally then, the need to know special dishes by odd place or personality names has almost disappeared. We now have chefs create dishes on-the-spot and simply list the ingredients, as did Saulnier, in his Repertoire.

However, I grew up back at the end of food rationing, at a time of simple celebration and a cultural desire not to show off. This was not helpful for the reemergence of fine dining.

One famous casualty in this return to normalcy was André Simon, a charming Frenchman who sold champagne before World War I in 1933. He established the Wine and Food Society, and in the year of my birth (1934), went on to found the International Wine and Food Society in New York, which in turn went on worldwide.

André Simon

When my parents moved back to Sussex, to the Roebuck Hotel at Wych Cross in the Ashdown Forest, we moved quite close to André Simon's home at "Little Hedgecourt." It was at this time, in my 16th year, that André Simon became my occasional mentor and went on to be a considerable influence in my future career.

André had lived through the turbulent slipstream of two world wars. As someone who was deeply involved in the French wine trade activities in England, he was intimately aware of the need to revive the understanding of the art of fine dining. André wrote a simple paragraph that laid out his vision for the society he founded when I was born.

"To bring together and serve all who believe that a right understanding of good food and wine is an essential part of personal contentment and health, and that an intelligent approach to the pleasures and problems of the table offers far greater rewards than the mere satisfaction of appetite."

Such a "right understanding" would, quite reasonably, result in the increased sale of *good wines* in restaurants that served...*good food*. In other words, it revived the *good old days* for all concerned.

My parents now managed a hotel that made it to the top 20 list of "Great Country Hotels of England." (It was number 14, as I recall). Our clientele enjoyed the revival of gastronomy; our chef had arrived from France, our maître d' from Poland, our cuisine was classic French, as was the mode of service. I was therefore *raised up* in the rapid flow of this return to better times, a return that meant economic survival as well as a heady sense of achievement.

I was back in the kitchen, mostly in Garde Manger, where all the incoming food (including game from the forest) was inspected, cleaned and prepared ready for the pan. I also handled some of the cold buffet work for which we were becoming famous.

The Sous Chef (second in command) was an excitable Spaniard. "Chop me some parsley, QUICK!" he ordered. I began to pick at the tight curly head from that day's herb garden delivery. "I said chop it, not fiddle with it," he shouted for everyone to hear.

"This is the way we did it at the food school," I replied defensively!

SWOOSH!

A 10 inch, or so, Sabatier steel chef's knife flew past my head into the painted wood plank wall of the prep area. I stopped picking and started chopping...stalks and all. The Spanish chef, I learned later, had been a knife thrower in a carnival! Much later, in my 60s, I returned to that very kitchen, drew a circle around the deep scar in the painted wooden wall...and signed it. I suspect that also has now been covered by another coat of cream-colored high-gloss latex! Such is life?

Soon after my 16th birthday I was to transition to the dining room and come into direct contact with our customers.

I would lay aside the white cook's coverings and put on the black and white outward appearance of a servant.

Strangely...I was to find this surprisingly difficult.

Please join us in the Reflective Readers Club
www.grahamkerr.com/rrc

Rite of Passage Six:
"Early Tumult!" (1949–1951)

I am getting larger and longer. The bars on my sides are dark and I think them quite handsome. Recently I had another jolt, it's the only way I can describe it. One moment it was all pretty normal, only the banks had become quite far apart and slowly the river got much deeper.

Then, quite suddenly, parts of the stream quickened alarmingly and I was sucked up with dozens of my shoal into a vortex of water.

I've never gone so fast. It was so scary. The water seemed to narrow into a darkened hole.

Then down —down —hurtling down and around and around in a crazy spinning chaos. Members of my shoal pressed bleeding against me and then flung aside.

Blood in the water...and foam and falling, then the foam began to ease its rose-tinted fury, and as suddenly as it started...it stopped.

It was hard to see clearly, the river had become thick with blood and mud. Severed bodies with bars like mine drifted by my side, the current almost gone.

Some, like me, had survived but many perished.

An Understanding

On many salmon runs, dams have been put in place to generate electricity for domestic and industrial energy. Salmon must pass through those dams and their turbines; giant blades pushed by the weight of steeply descending water.

*Many fish die in these energy plants before they make it fully downstream. Others are prevented from regaining their birth river by these vast concrete barriers. A great deal of money is spent every single year trying to transport both the young and older returning wild salmon around these **very green low carbon footprint** energy resources.*

So far, it has been somewhat ineffective and the once teeming rivers are greatly depleted. Some, however, still get through...and even back; those are the amazing salmon survivors.

1950 to 1951
I am sixteen to seventeen years old

I had wanted to go directly from the kitchen to the front office as a Trainee Manager. I dressed in my best charcoal gray three-piece suit and my old school tie and went down to begin the journey that I had planned, in my youthful conceit, would end at the Dorchester Hotel in London.

"Why" my father queried, "have you changed?"

"I'm ready to go, to learn to – manage – like you, Dad."

"Well, if that's what you want – go change – something older and – lighter," he added.

"I really need to be ready to greet customers."

"Not quite yet, go change," he gestured to the door.

I returned several minutes later in my old grey slacks, now obviously too short, and a T-shirt.

"That's good" he smiled, "now come with me."

We went into the quite ornate men's room

"This is where you learn management, it begins here. It's about service, service, service."

I attacked that *necessary* room with a mix of humiliation, anger and ambition. If I had to do this menial task, I would do it well enough to be released to do *anything*! I can still visualize that Mosaic marble floor, the caustic chemicals, gleaming white china...and my reflection in those revealing mirrors. I was a long way from the frock coat, striped trousers, silver grey silk tie, and the perfect carnation.

My lowest rung didn't last long. A week or so and I was released to the Maître d'. Teddy was a delightful, elegant, perfectly suited prince of a man, born in Poland who fought with the allies in the war.

For some reason that still remains well outside of my understanding, I did not start at the bottom rung of his ladder. He placed me halfway up for a short while before I descended to my proper level of experience.

I was an intern Chef-de-Rang, usually second only to the Maître d'. In our case, my duties were restricted to cooking tableside on a small trolley called a gueridon equipped with a silver flambé lamp and a lovely copper pan, coated inside with silver!

Since my years in the kitchen had given me some ability to cook, it was this that was to allow me to try my emerging gift on actual customers, who, for the first time, would pay for and additionally reward a good performance.

My first couple were quite young, as I recall, in their mid-20s. He wore a dark suit and a regimental tie, which looked like the Royal Artillery. She wore a blue frock with an emerald clasp, and she had light brown curly hair. They were not married.

Should you wonder about my memory being so detailed, I should let you know that in those days it was really that accurate. I literally memorized my customers, where they sat, and what they ate and drank. It wasn't just for the added tip; it actually thrilled me to see how much they enjoyed being remembered.

I approached the couple on that night with my trolley equipped to cook and serve a Crêpes Suzette for their dessert. Everything is *mise en place;* it must be! That is the classic French (and logical) method of *putting everything in place* before the cooking starts. There are four lacy thin French pancakes, so thin that you can read a newspaper headline through them! Six cubes of sugar had been rubbed vigorously in the zest of an orange and a lemon, three of each. There were two ounces of butter, a bottle of Grand Marnier and a small wine glass each of fresh orange and lemon juice.

The dish is quite simple...light the methylated spirit wick in its handsome silver tableside lamp, and warm the silvered copper pan. Add the butter, let it melt and just froth. Add the lump sugar and crush it into the butter to become a very light fudge. Add the orange and lemon juice. Stir to a boil. Add 2 ounces of Grand Marnier. Now, lift the delicate crepes with a spoon or fork and lay them, one at a time, to soak up the sauce. Fold in half, and then half again, and lay against the pan side while turning the rest.

The pan is then tipped to expose the surface to the flame and become hot. A glass of about 2 ounces more Grand Marnier is then added (never from the bottle directly, it can cause a flashback into the bottle with potentially explosive results). The alcohol will naturally catch fire and caramelize the sauce coatings on the crepes.

The portion is two each with a couple of spoons full of the sauce.

I performed that night and told both stories that are classically told as you work. There was the stage version –where the crepes were cooked as part of a play, and then there was my preferred story of a very young waiter (age 14?) called Henri Charpentier who accidentally caught some crepes on fire while serving the future King Edward of England, when he was Prince of Wales.

The Prince was dining with a most attractive young woman friend named, Suzette. The accident was served, the Prince delighted, and the lovely lady immortalized. Just how a 14 year old came to be cooking for royalty is a bit of a stretch for some historians, but hey…here I was with a young couple in a country hotel, making a less accidental dish and I was only two years older!

That occasion remains vivid because it was the formal start of my public career.

I delighted in having the opportunity to serve directly, and I had a story to tell. I had made a dish for them to taste and enjoy. How else would you describe the many episodes I was to do on television?

After several of these great memories, I was put rather firmly back in my place at the foot of the dining room ladder…a *Commis*…not short for communist; but French for assistant or "agent" of the waiter. It's a cool title for a busboy.

The Waiter waits…the Commis runs and puts plates down first before the "silver" service, and removes the plates afterward…never EVER speaks and seldom gets more than a snippet of the eventual tip. Not a fun job, especially for me!

It was here that I came face to face with a problem that would stay with me for years, perhaps, to be honest, for my entire life in the *oceans of opportunity.* You will recall that I am an only child. I played and grew up alongside my friends whose parents visited the hotel as customers. It was often these self-same parents whom I served as *Commis*.

It was fine when I could tell stories and set pancakes on fire, but now I took away their dirty plates and was not allowed to say a word! I did not like being THAT kind of servant. I wanted the frock coat, striped trousers, grey silk tie and the perfect red carnation. I wanted to greet royalty and have them call me "Graham."

All this came as a bit of a shock. Cleaning restrooms was not a public task, and neither was my kitchen time, but here is where I came to see myself as a *servant,* and my parents also as servants.

Status was important. There was a sharp division between classes in those days and the two seldom mixed, even in warfare! It was upstairs/downstairs and regardless of my public school education and county accent favored by the BBC Radio in the postwar days, I was still a *servant*, even to my friends whose parents were customers.

My parents afforded to dress me so that I would "blend in" with my friends from the *upper* customer class. I owned a Houndstooth Harris Tweed jacket, riding boots and britches, and a pair of cavalry twill trousers for less equestrian moments. One evening, I was invited to the "Hunt Ball" at which men were to wear full evening dress of "white tie and tails." My mother helped with the tie and wing collar, stood back and admired her now almost six-foot, rail-thin son and announced proudly "you will knock them dead!"

That was my first real experience at feeling set apart. Not only did I not knock them dead, but rather it was I that died...acutely aware of being mutton dressed up as lamb. I exchanged my white tie and tails for a white waiter's jacket and got back to my proper calling!

My first customer as a full-fledged waiter was Lord Shawcross, then Chief Justice of the British Isles. He ordered, "the largest Dover sole you have, drenched in butter."

"Would you like me to fillet that for you my Lord?" I asked. I was hoping he would say no because the task had to be achieved tableside and took considerable dexterity.

"No, no, I'll wrestle with it, that's fine."

Much relieved, I placed the order and the Chef found a plump denizen of the deep and grilled it perfectly with copious layers of butter. I hastened to the table with the silver oval salver sizzling hot. I inserted two flat silver fish knives, splayed out in a V-shape, held in my right hand and carefully lifted this buttery monster to check on the point of balance. It looked perfect! Swiftly I transferred it directly to the...*tablecloth!*

As a Commis, I had always placed the hot china plate down just before the waiter served the dish. I had not waited. The fish sat there in front of his Lordship, as butter slowly began to spread out over the starched white Irish damask tablecloth.

His Lordship looked up and in a kindly voice said "do you think I might trouble you for a plate?"

I scraped the fish back to the salver, replaced the tablecloth, reheated the fish (tableside) all the while with a face that would easily have matched a perfect carnation.

More time sped by and I continued to climb the restaurant ladder until, still as a trainee manager. I was, under serious supervision, attempting to be the Restaurant Manager at seventeen!

I'm not being guarded by keeping the name of our most famous guest a secret. I came to understand that our customer's lives were theirs to live, and not mine to reveal. Mr. X was a "hugely wealthy oil baron" who was thrifty to the point of meanness. In his huge mansion he had installed a very British bright red phone booth. If his guests wanted to use a phone, they could feed the meter and do so!

One night, we closed the dining room to accommodate an almost regal private party. He had spared no expense. The bill, that night, was an astonishing two thousand pounds sterling.

Our Maître d', Teddy, took the bill for this amount to be signed on a perfectly polished silver tray. Mr. X gave it a cursory glance, signed it with a flourish, felt in his pocket, retrieved some small change, selected a sixpence and dropped it with a slight clatter on the tray. "That's for the staff," he told Teddy conversationally.

I waited as Teddy backed away from the table and began to take on the red carnation blush that I had known so well. He went to his bureau at the door, removed his white gloves very deliberately and returned to the table with the tray and…the tip. Attracting Mr. X's attention, he bent low and close to Mr. X's right ear. It was then that he told Mr. X exactly where he could put his sixpence, and apparently he described its destination with admirable anatomical correctness. I was unable to hear the exchange, but moved forward to try to save the day when Mr. X broke into an extremely hearty laugh. "Well done! Well done indeed!"

He reached into an inner pocket, withdrew his checkbook and wrote a huge check. "There now," he looked up at a wide-eyed Teddy, "that's for the staff with my thanks for a splendid evening." His guests applauded.

Restaurants, I had learned, were pure theater. We were not so much servants as actors, and our customers were the audience…or was it also, occasionally, the other way around… Shades of things to come?

Please join us in the Reflective Readers Club
www.grahamkerr.com/rrc

Rite of Passage Seven: "A Fate Worse Than Death" (1951–1953)

After the nasty jolt, the ugly clouded river cleared but remains ominously deep, wide and slow moving. I'm apprehensive now, no longer simply going along for the ride and enjoying the hunt for tasty treats. I know nothing about innocence but whatever that is, I now lack it.

Large members of my shoal are no longer my eager, adventurous companions. We are fewer and further apart, not suspicious of each other, just somehow moving forward with less... wonder? I have noticed, however, that my dark markings are fading and a rather nice silver is taking their place. So all, perhaps, is not lost?

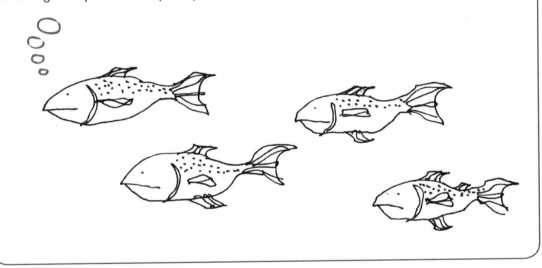

An Understanding

In some rivers the extremely logical use of dams to produce hydroelectricity has had the equally obvious "unintended consequences" of disrupting the migration of salmon, well...hardly **unintended**. *It was pretty obvious, but somehow many people planned to give nature a hand and somehow bypass the obstruction with fish ladders, transports, all manner of human assists, because salmon were not only part of the ecology, but also valuable to both culture and commerce. Notwithstanding every effort, the typical salmon runs before the dams were put in place outnumbered those today by about 100 to 1!*

Older dams are now being removed, the streams rehabilitated with natural implants and many of us now await the miracle of resilience to take place as the salmon rediscover their birthplaces. It is happening at the Elwha and Glines Canyon dams near Port Angeles in Washington State; where large salmon have already been spotted in the previously barricaded upper reaches of the Elwha River.

Imagine, a natural stream without man-made barriers for the salmon?

1951 to 1953
I am seventeen to nineteen years old

"My boy," Dad beckoned me into his office and shut the door.

"We need to talk, sit down." I sat in the old leather chair with the row of brass studs that held the cracked hide in place.

"You have just over seven months before you get called up for your National Service." He was stating the obvious because everyone was more than aware of the start dates for the mandated compulsory Armed Forces service that began at age 18.

"I want you to avoid a fate worse than death." He was deadly serious!

"What's that?" I exclaimed, feeling a little apprehensive.

"Your work here and training will almost certainly mean that you will go to the Army Catering Corp. and that (he paused for emphasis) is a fate worse than death. You must avoid being an Army cook."

My father had clearly been abused during his earlier years by British Army cooking and wanted to help me to avoid spending two fruitless years of continuing that culinary tradition!

"I suggest we get you a job in the local garage in East Grinstead instead," he suggested.

"The owner is a customer. We've already talked it over," he continued with his plan.

"On your forms we will leave out the kitchen years and put in garage mechanic for your 17th year. That should get you into REME (Royal Electrical and Mechanical Engineers) and then at least you can pick up *something* useful during your two years."

I agreed and spent six somewhat cold and grimy months out in the mechanical world with which I was not exactly enamored after my comfortable life of borderline luxury.

My father was right! I did get my posting to the REME in Honiton, Devonshire.

Very soon after my 18th birthday, my father took me by train to the country town of Honiton where we stayed the night in a small hotel before my call-up reporting time.

"You are to report from 0900 hours up to 1700 hours," he explained, "so you will be there at exactly 0900 hours. That will give you a head start, which is always wise," he added gruffly.

"Now, let's go out and get drunk; I want to see how you handle it."

He drank large Scottish whiskeys and I had a beer. After two pints I was no longer thirsty and didn't want to further the experiment, so we had an early night without solving whether or not I was able to be drunk and still well mannered.

At *precisely* 0900 hours, my father shook my hand, wished me "good luck, my boy," wheeled about smartly and literally marched off down the road, with back straight and arms swinging at exactly thirty degrees. I watched him go...he never looked back. I turned, less carefully, to the guardhouse and reported. The Regimental Sergeant Major (Senior non-com) just happened to be there.

"What do you want sonny," he barked!

"Reporting for National Service...er...Sir," I replied, as my father had briefed.

"Ah then, another bleedin' two-year wonder...well, at least you're right on time." He checked a list, marked me off and handed me a map of the base.

"Count yourself as number one...that's the last you'll ever be at the top of any other Army list, so make the most if it."

He looked past me at my rapidly disappearing father.

"That your dad?" he asked.

"Yes...Sir."

"Army?"

"Yes...Sir."

"Good start!" With that, he left me to my induction where I was indeed number one, for just one day!

By the time my fellow *shoal* of recruits had made the rounds receiving jabs, collecting their kit and eating a remarkably tasteless meal, I had found the best bed in the empty barrack room. I made my bed as instructed, again by my father, balanco-d my webbing belt and gaiters, polished the brass, and had begun to polish my boots. I had almost a whole day's head start, all because of my father.

We had never been close. Perhaps he'd never seen or experienced anything remotely emotional and close? He had gone as far as he knew how. He was an enormous help on that day. Oh, how I wish we had had a closer, less rigid, relationship.

The Army proved to be entirely predictable and, looking at my motor vehicle experience, decided that I should be a radar mechanic. They also decided that, due to my accent and public school background, I should be a potential officer. I was given a white flash to wear in my epaulet and a round white plastic disc behind my REME badge.

You will remember, I'm sure, my deep commitment to my outward appearance. I loved those white decorations!

I attended W. O. S. B. (War Office Selection Board) for junior officers and had been coached to be both positive and confident when interviewed. Against my father's best advice, I applied for a commission in the Army Catering Corp. The "fate worse than death" was to be a cook, surely not an officer, I reasoned.

The General Officer at the Selection Board sat behind a green baize covered table, tapping my file as he read my application.

"How tall are you," he demanded.

"Six feet three inches...SIR!"

"Good height for the Brigade of Guards...why don't you want to be in the Guards?" He leaned forward to better hear my answer.

"Don't have the personal or family income, SIR."

"Mmm...but why the Catering Corp.?" He sounded just like my father.

This is where I had to play confident.

"Sir, because the food is so awful and I think I could help to make it better – SIR."

He looked at me, a rail-thin 18-year-old.

Then he brushed his hand in dismissal and said, "The British Army is not yet ready for you." I was returned to my unit without acceptance as officer potential to await my Radar Mechanics course in ten to twelve weeks.

I was now on a huge training base, also in Devonshire. It was midsummer and uncharacteristically hot for England. All the new arrivals were paraded in front of the Headquarters building. We had been "sized" with the right marker being the tallest man.

I was it!

The short and somewhat rotund Staff Sergeant shouted...

"All those who think themselves qualified for special jobs, one step forward, MARCH!"

I was the only one on parade that moved.

My father had not warned me that, in the British Army, you volunteer for NOTHING but certain death!

"Oh – so what 'ave we 're?" He looked up into my face.

"What's your name then?" He asked with mocking interest.

"KERR, 22657960 Staff." I shouted energetically. He found me on his clipboard.

"Potential officer, I see 'ere. Didn't want you, I see 'ere!" He grinned with flat, unfeeling eyes.

"So – what can you do that's – special?"

"Oh – I don't know – perhaps the Commander's Clerk?" I replied with a sinking feeling that all was not well.

He consulted his list again.

"Says 'ere you wanted to be a 'Caterin' Officer?"

"That's right Staff."

"How would you like to 'elp him?" He asked almost kindly.

"Fine – Staff." I agreed.

"Change into your denims (Army fatigues) and report to the cookhouse."

I was dismissed.

I knocked on the Catering Officer's door and was told to enter.

He was an untidy man in his mid thirties with strands of hair swept over a large bald patch. It was tightly slicked in place, but needing a trim. Hanging on the wall behind him like a piece of gross art deco was an enormous aluminum fry pan with an uneven hole almost in the middle.

My eyes flicked back and forth from the barely covered baldness and the hole in the pan.

"Private Kerr reporting...Sir?"

"Ah yes...Staff Sergeant tells me you want to help me do my job for – let's see– at least ten weeks, is that so?" he questioned.

"Yes Sir...delighted to help if I can. I've done Hotel School, worked in classic French cuisine and as a Trainee Manager," I recited this quickly.

"Good – I've got just the job for you. Follow me, I'll show you to your office."

He led the way down a dingy, sour-smelling corridor over a rough concrete floor with green and yellow painted walls. He turned left as he stood back so that I could see clearly where I was to – help him do his job.

It was the pan wash.

The pan wash was designed to deal with a two-thousand-man kitchen, it contained four enormous stainless steel sinks, each about three feet long, two feet wide and two feet deep. Against two walls were giant racks filled with deeply pitted aluminum saucepans of various sizes, mostly very large and seriously discolored at their base. A very short young man turned from one of the sinks, and wiped the sweat and steam from his face.

"Sir?" He questioned.

"McDuff – this is your new assistant." The catering officer gestured to me.

"He's waiting for a radar course, and he's all yours for at least ten weeks." He patted me on the shoulder.

"Enjoy." He smiled as he left.

Andy McDuff was nineteen and from Glasgow with an accent as broad Scots as mine was BBC Southern Counties.

What a pair!

I *sweated* that job alongside him and encountered a fate even beyond that which was worse than death. I scraped my way through layers of baked on mutton fats, oatmeal and scorched rice pudding. Every imaginable culinary insult known to saucepans had been perpetrated and were mine to somehow correct and clean. My flesh pores opened up and absorbed the rich variety of awful smells. No matter how long the showers…the stench remained. I shared a small room with Andy, as nobody else wanted us near.

Then one day the Staff Sergeant came to visit.

"So – ow's it going," he asked.

"Fine – Staff." I stood to attention, eyes front.

"Seems you've lost your toff accent," he observed.

"Yes Staff."

"Well now. The Officer's Mess wants to 'ave a party to celebrate the tenth anniversary of the REME. Their cooks ain't up to much – so 'ow would you like to 'elp them out?"

"Yes – Staff – er – delighted," I added.

Who wouldn't be delighted, *anything* but these giant abused pots.

The dinner went very well. Well enough for the Command Catering Advisor, a Major, to come out after the meal to "compliment its Chef."

"When did you pass through St. Omer?" he asked.

St. Omer was in Aldershot in Hampshire, a huge sprawling military city. It was the HQ Army School of Cooking.

"Never been Sir…I'm REME, waiting for a radar course," I replied.

"Amazing!" He paused for a moment remembering perhaps the Sole Veronique or the Rhum Baba he had just consumed.

"How would you like to be transferred to the ACC (Army Catering Corp.) and be a Corporal Chef instructor at St. Omer?"

"I think I can swing it," he added.

I didn't even think once… "Sir, I'll take it."

If it was to be a fate worse than death…it was going to be better than the pan wash…and who needs radar in my future career as an Hotelier anyway?

Please join us in the Reflective Readers Club
www.grahamkerr.com/rrc

Rite of Passage Eight: "A Taste of Things to Come" (1954–1956)

One year and three months...

I'm pretty used to my ever-depleting shoal; not what some would call on speaking terms, but you get to know each one by differences in camouflage and the way each turns after a new food opportunity. There are bucks like me, although as a smolt I hardly warrant that as a title yet...but I'm almost there.

Then there are hens...and that rounder shape and flatter slope to the forehead. Like the scent of my birthplace...there are none like my first touch…way back upstream. I can still feel her fin against mine.

Then, quite suddenly, a silvery flash caught my eye through the gloomy water.

Was that her...so much larger and, well, rounder?

And then, no matter how fast I swam in her direction, all I ever got was that distant flash of silver.

 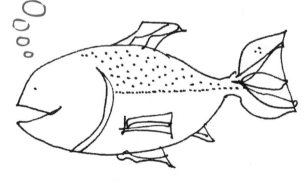

An Understanding

The young salmon's life is lived in fresh water and it isn't until osmoregulation begins that the silver scales begin to appear. It is during this stage, which can take the Chinook past its first year, that the parr quite suddenly becomes a smolt. Osmoregulation is the way in which the totally fresh water fish gradually adjust to salt water. Obviously, this means that the natal river is now within the upper tidal reaches of the ocean. It is in this increasingly salt water that the smolt can live for as long as seven years.

Yet more of year one plus three months. . .

The next stretch of the river has been quite strange. With the water running slower and still deep, it is now cloudy and smells really bad.

The banks are streaked with stained mud. The scent of my birth river is almost overwhelmed, and there is much less food.

I'm really unhappy, and the rest of my shoal are finding it hard going. It's actually difficult to let the water in and out, and it is sickening most of us.

Along with the water, there is no shade from the banks. The tall green things have gone and sometimes it gets quite warm.

This is not a good time to be alive.

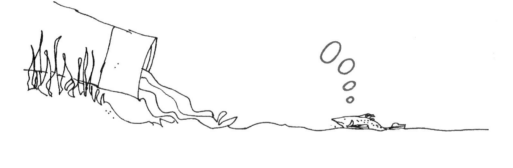

An Understanding

The lower sections of many rivers have been greatly degraded from pristine former times by amongst many causes, heavy industry, commercial agriculture and outlets for pollution.

1954 to 1956
I am twenty to twenty two years old

Treena, Miss Jersey Battle of Flowers

"The Daily Mirror" is a popular British tabloid, which in the middle 1950s, had just begun to grant a little space to bathing suited (not bikini) beauties. There she was, smiling that smile directly at me. She was taller and pleasantly rounder...just lovely. Treena was eight months younger, so she must have turned nineteen. She had won the "Miss Jersey Battle Of Flowers"–the first ever to do so.

It isn't easy to connect with people through a newspaper, but since I was in quarantine with Rubella, which sounds so much better than "in bed with Rubella", I was able to focus on the task. My letter got through and amazingly I got an answer, though not as warm as I wanted. I had confessed that I was a British Army Officer, so far so good, and that I served in the Army Catering Corps. Treena's father clearly shared my father's disdain for my occupation and prompted a line in her letter. "I suppose," she wrote, "this means you will defend Britain with a fish slice?" I carried that small wound for years. It played directly into my continuing trouble with being seen as "servant class". I was not, however, dissuaded, and we began, in a desultory way, to correspond. Then, once again, the family simply vanished with no forwarding address.

This brief encounter prompted me to begin a card system on my series of brushes with young women. Card number one was *Treena*. I listed her attributes and personality, and the degree of contact. In her case, the card read, Level Two...*held hands at movies*. By the time I had passed into my twenties I had got up to card number thirty-one. That card listed my contact as Level Ten, *engaged to be married!*

And so it was on a dull, rainy day in Wales that I received a curious envelope in the post; curious because it had been readdressed four times by the hotels where my father had served until it found him...who sent it to me.

I wish I had saved that envelope; it was to mean so much!

Her letter was much warmer and so welcome because her family had either moved (or escaped) from the Channel Islands to Folkestone in Kent, which was less than thirty miles from my parent's hotel in Tenterden. This meant that, while I was over 300 miles away in Wales, Treena was less than an hour's drive from my family home.

I applied immediately for five days' leave. It would take me ten hours to reach home in my very small MG "M" type sports car. At twenty years old it was a challenge and an adventure with a tremendous reward at the end. I remember making it in eight hours virtually nonstop...only for gas and the odd sandwich. I had arranged to pick Treena up in the evening of my second day on leave.

I had previously invested in a sheep's wool and leather bomber jacket made popular during the war, and was trying to grow a moustache to go with it...not so successful!

Treena's parents greeted me kindly enough and said that she wasn't ready yet. We sat together and attempted to cover some of the intervening nine years; it wasn't easy...or especially welcoming. Then the door to the living room opened and Treena walked in. She stood still for a moment...just looking at me with quiet interest.

It is described by some as a moment when the world stops moving...it did just that for me. I knew before she said one word or made a single movement, that our lives would begin to dissolve into each other...we would never part again. This was not love at first sight, but rather second. I had fallen in love at eleven; now I was twenty and now all things were possible.

We ate that night in my uncle's inn about twenty miles from Tenterden. It remains almost dream-like in my memory. I'm sure we talked but I cannot remember a word...or, for that matter, what we ate!

The next morning we took a typical English country walk over footpaths with rights of way guaranteed in some cases for hundreds of years. Ours took us, as we walked hand-in-hand, to a rather muddy cattle crossing. Ever apparently gallant, I offered to carry her over this quite ripe compost. It was a marvelous opportunity to hold her in my arms and display my masculine strength. She agreed and placed one hand on my shoulder...her face coming close enough to kiss. I swept her up in my arms, held her securely and strode out into the crossing. I sank immediately up to my knees in manure!

Many cattle had passed and paused long enough to make this morass possible. I retained my grip...but couldn't pull my leg free. Treena, now very close to my ear, whispered...

"So, what do we do now?"

My response went beyond the obvious distraction to what had completely taken over my mind.

"Will you marry me?" I asked.

"Well...yes," she replied, and it was then, up to my knees in it, that we kissed for the first time. My leg came free and we retreated from the crossing laughing helplessly and loving with all our hearts.

There was to be so much more manure that we needed to somehow cross.

I had to break my prior engagement. Treena had already done the same in the Channel Islands. Both of our parents were unhappy. We were too young, too inexperienced, and too poor...but we were too much in love to listen.

On September 22, 1955, we were married in St. Mildred's church in Tenterden, originally built in the 13th and 14th centuries. Treena was radiantly beautiful in white, and I was highly polished in No. 1 Dress Uniform with Sam Browne belt and sword, white gloves and the single "pip" on my epaulet that showed the world that I had received the Queen's Commission, albeit in a non "Royal" Corps. Only the cap badge on my dress hat showed to whom my service belonged. It was a Grecian Urn with flames rising from it, the official symbol for the Catering Corps. Everyone I knew referred to it affectionately as the "flaming piss pot."

On that day, everything was magical. My sword chattered along with my limbs as I waited on several hundreds of years of old flagstones for her to arrive at my side. We kissed, as required, we cut the cake, we brushed off confetti, and we took a car to London to the Rembrandt Hotel...

We began to find out *eventually* what love is meant to be.

Please join us in the Reflective Readers Club
www.grahamkerr.com/rrc

55

Rite of Passage Nine:
"A Shoal of Two" (1955–1957)

Remarkably like my earliest memory of life, the flash –flash of light was now repeated as I glimpsed brief flickers amidst the gloom. That flash persisted. This time, it was a few scales of silver and a shadowy glimpse through increasingly cloudy water. And then, quite suddenly, there she was. She slowly swam a little upstream, against the current, to meet me. Our heads almost touched, our eyes were quite close and observant. We turned about each other, and again our fins touched. It was the same thrilling moment as we settled down to swim through murky, stale-tasting, deep green waters. I was content to be a shoal of two as we began to adjust to the increasing saltiness of the river.

An Understanding

There is no science-based research that shows anything like monogamy within migratory fish species and, as has been suggested before, there is only my author's conceit to propose such a lasting aquatic relationship, and yet…it is well known that "buck salmon" develop a jaw formation complete with teeth that is entirely different from the "hen," and biologists conjecture that it is with these fearsome jaws that bucks repel other bucks who presume to move in when the hen begins to lay her eggs. It is this protective "maleness" that has led me to embrace the idea that a relatively monogamous relationship might actually start in the natal river with roots in clean water gravel beds upon which we were conceived. This has now gone beyond mere conceit to be this author's conviction, not solely because it seems better as a metaphor, but because it has become quite real and even touching.

And so "the two became one...fish."

1955 to 1957
I am twenty one to twenty three years old

I had ordered champagne from room service on our wedding night, as it seemed the right thing to do. We had one glass each and washed our faces in it the next morning. It was flat and stale and lingered throughout the day as we journeyed by train to Portmeirion in North Wales.

Portmeirion is a fanciful collection of architectural nostalgia built by Sir Clough Williams-Ellis. He had visited and fallen in love with Portofino, Italy, and wanted to blend his memories with a magnificent site at the mouth of the River Dwyryd that spills out onto miles of hard packed sandy beaches.

The main building and three cottages had been built in the 1850s and we occupied "The Mermaid". We had been preceded by Noel Coward who wrote Blithe Spirit while on retreat. Frank Lloyd Wright thought it worth a visit, as did Gregory Peck, Ingrid Bergman and Paul McCartney. There is no mention of Treena and I, but then at that time why refer to an Army Catering Advisor...although Miss Jersey Battle of the Flowers, a budding film actress, well... perhaps? This perfectly reasonable omission does, however, allow me to reveal the first of a great many ways in which Treena stepped aside from opportunity in order to stay alongside me...*as one flesh.*

It was in the spring of 1955, just six months before our September wedding, when we stood together in the small garden behind the Woolpack Hotel in Tenterden, Kent...my parent's hotel and my new home base for visiting Treena on every leave I had. It was an awkward moment, as I pushed away at the grassy-edged flowerbed with my foot, trying to find the way to explain my feelings to her.

"I know you had the J. Arthur Rank screen test and you did so well with the Jersey Repertory Company – and, and" – I found it hard to finish the sentence.

"Yes," Treena enquired. She was holding my hand and gave it an encouraging squeeze.

"Well, you see," I blurted out the rest, "I don't think I could be the husband of a star... and I so want for us to be married." I stopped pushing at the earth with my shoes and took her other hand in mine. Our eyes were now open and questioning each other.

"Would you, could you, consider giving it all up to be my wife?" This was as tough as it gets; what right had I to ask such a thing!

Treena paused, looked down for a thoughtful moment and then gave me that impossible smile of hers.

"Why yes...of course." That was all she said, but it didn't stop there. It was as if this scene would keep on and on repeating itself until she herself had unwittingly become the very *substance in shadow* that I had feared for myself.

One day following our honeymoon I had to report for Regular Army Officers Selection Board, since I had applied to be admitted into the Regular Army so that I could possibly afford to be married. A little like the cart before the horse?

My fellow officers had filled my denims with confetti and I shed stray pieces of it on the assault course.

"What's going on here?" Enquired the testing officer as he inspected several pink heart-shaped pieces.

"Just married, Sir," I replied sheepishly. "Fellow officers...bit of a prank," I explained.

"When were you married?" he asked.

"Ten days ago." I replied proudly.

"Good God man, did your CO know this?" He exploded!

"Yes Sir."

"Then just coast through the tests, you won't fail or pass, and come back when you've sorted yourself out, okay?"

He gave me an encouraging pat on the back and moved on.

It was an *almost* closed door. I wondered how we would manage. I had sold the MG to have enough for our honeymoon and still owed over 100 dollars to my tailors in London, Flights of Saville Row. How grateful I am for that prank, the confetti and the outcome. I had no way of anticipating how, with Treena's amazing help; I was to become *almost*...famous!

Colonel Horsfall, RASC, was actually famous and became so during World War II during the North African Campaign. He was a Corporal when the war started and one of the first to arrive in Alexandria, Egypt.

His then Senior Officer, a capable Regular Army Major, ordered him into the desert to "deal with the locusts." That was it, just four words. It was all that Corporal Horsfall needed. He obeyed. At the end of the war he reported back to his, by then, quite senior officer who was a Brigadier (one star) General. "Where have you been Horsfall?" He enquired.

"Dealin' with the locusts, SIR." Corporal Horsfall replied with his usual energy.

"But...that was over three years ago!"

"Yes Sir."

"How did it go?"

"Quite well Sir, pesky things, but we made a difference I think!"

"Amazing...and you did it all yourself?"

"Well, I had a team of four good lads, Sir."

Corporal Horsfall became famous. His story made the rounds and he was granted a field commission for his "consistency during the war against...locusts." That wasn't the end of it. In the peacetime Army it wasn't easy to reach higher and highest ranks, but this forceful Yorkshire Officer wound up as a full Colonel with red tabs and a red band around his hat... and quite a reputation.

These were the days in 1956 when Armed Forces had become something of a political football. One of the contentious issues was the Army Emergency Reserve (AER) where former National Servicemen had to report for two week's training each year to...upgrade their skills? They were called "fourteen day wonders."

Colonel Horsfall oversaw the training of thousands of these "wonders" at the Bedford Army Barracks in Bedfordshire. It was a hotbed of possible political inquiries and the good Colonel wanted the Food Services to be the least of his worries. Using his "locust" reputation shamelessly, he got permission to tour the entire British Army, looking for a catering advisor who could help him avoid such challenges and might actually add to his fame?

Shortly after my marriage to Treena, I instituted a form of "self service" in the other ranks' mess hall in Tonfanau, Wales. After a somewhat "rocky" start it actually worked, and I added a modified a la carte menu with varied main dishes that were served, in small quantity, at ten-minute intervals in an attempt to be fair. It also worked. These very small attempts of mine gained enough attention to bring Colonel Horsfall on a visit to see for himself.

Lieutenant "Dickie" Bird was the Base Administrative Officer and a good pal who told us the "locust" story. "Behind his back, he's affectionately known as *donkey drop*, for Horsfall," he laughed.

The Officer's Mess put on a dinner to welcome the good Colonel, and he put in a full day inspecting my little empire. At the "cocktail party" before dinner our Colonel introduced Treena to Colonel Horsfall.

"Oh," Treena replied brightly, giving him her amazing smile, "you're the one they call donkey drop?"

I stood frozen in that moment, imagining that the floor had suddenly opened and that my future had disintegrated. Colonel Horsfall immediately erupted in gales of laughter!

From that moment on, my service to Queen and Country, and my very new marriage, were secure. Throughout our time with "donkey drop" he insisted on calling Treena "Tina", and remained beyond correction. We moved to Bedford and began to innovate in a big way. I believe that I was the first to introduce self-service in the British Army, but still stand to be corrected if anyone would be kind enough to let me know of a similar service before April of 1956?

There were two additional events that are considered by some to be the reason why I apparently earned the title..."Maitre D' to the Army".

Shrove Tuesday is often celebrated in the British Isles with a pancake breakfast. This has even become an international event between the towns of Liberal in Kansas (USA) and Olney (UK). A race, over a measured distance, is marked out in both locations and participants run, complete with pancakes and pans, with a flip at the start and finish. This began five years before my spectacular event in Bedford (UK). There have been no repeats, of my own experience, anywhere! It began with my orders to the usually amiable Corporal Chef who "lorded it" over the bakery section.

"I want a pancake for everyone next Tuesday."

"But...Sir, you see..." The Corporal appeared concerned.

"But *nothing* Corporal, it is tradition and we *shall* celebrate it." I was going to have my way.

The pancake was to be served at lunch and as I made my rounds of the dining room a large, beefy private held up a loose pancake on his fork and said . . .

"Look at this, Sir...it's bloody raw!" He pleaded.

It was indeed pallid, misshapen and untouched. I reached over and snagged the offending pancake on my "swagger stick" (a short stick carried by officers). I carried it to the kitchen where I was greeted with an impressive site that should have carried a warning. The Bakery Corporal's back was toward me, the floor was littered with eggshells, the front and top of the coal-fired stove was heavily streaked in batter. He had his hat on the back of his head and his jacket was soaked in sweat. I came in at his right side, extended the pancake-coated stick between his heavily perspiring face and the stove and explained...

"Look here Corporal, this pancake appears to be...raw?"

"Raw...RAW...I'll give you bloody RAW!" And with that he turned to his left and threw two crepe pans the length of the kitchen, one crashing through an outdoor window.

I kept my cool and a little shakily I asked, "Is something wrong?"

"I tried to tell you but you wouldn't listen...we got twelve hundred men for lunch and all I got is two bleedin' pancake pans!"

I understood from that day until now to listen carefully when I come up with yet another *apparently* bright idea!

My second amazing deed resulted in several questions being asked in the Houses of Parliament where the Labor Party was at odds with the Army Emergency Reserve; they considered it a waste of money. I had been told to provide a Grand Party for some of the Colonel's very senior officer friends. It was to take place in Officer's Mess. I thought it would be fun to have "costermonger barrows" – painted cardboard fronts with striped awnings and mock wheels. The idea was that each "barrow" would display, in cold buffet form, a particular dish...whole poached salmon on one, a cold roast Baron of Beef on another, ham, salads, desserts on others...They were all built upon six-foot wooden tables.

I asked two "fourteen day wonders" what they were doing. They were painting rocks white at the time.

"We're here for typing training." One of them replied.

"So, what's your speed?" I asked.

"One twenty." He replied.

"Seems fast enough. How would you like to do something more creative than paint rocks?"

"Great Sir...is it indoors?"

They did such a fine job that I gave them two pounds each out of my own pocket (about $10 in today's money).

It was a HUGE success, that is, until the following Monday when a leading national newspaper had a major centerfold titled:

"THEY MADE ME A BARROW BOY
FOR MY FOURTEEN-DAY TRAINING"

I had chosen, of all people, a newspaper reporter and cameraman to make my barrows. The Labor Party pounced on it as a perfect example of waste. I was right up to my neck in it. If it had not been for a parliamentary backbencher who cried out on a point of order, my

career would have been *toast!*

"Mr. Speaker," he gained attention.

"Is it not true that this officer gave these men a couple of pounds each out of his own pockets?"

"That is so," he replied.

"Damn blackguards," yelled the backbencher.

"HEAR HEAR" chorused the members.

And that was as far as it went, leaving me with the description...

Maitre D' to the Army

Please join us in the Reflective Readers Club
www.grahamkerr.com/rrc

Rite of Passage Ten:
"The Oceans Beckon" (1957–1958)

It was easier to notice and the further downstream we swam, the more pronounced it became. There was a decided tang to the water and the ever-present downstream flow had become uneven. At times, it seemed to go in the opposite direction and gain strength, only to slow down, stop, and then do what it had always done. Our birthplace aromas were still just there but the incoming tang had certainly got our attention because along with its arrival had come some very tasty new treats.

This seemed a safe place to hang out and grow.

An Understanding

Our Chinook duo had finally arrived in the downstream stretch of the river that could be reached by saltwater tides. It is in this increasingly saline solution that the young "smolt" must spend time adjusting to the huge change that lay ahead. It is called **osmoregulation** and allows their freshwater system to gradually switch over to seawater. These blended waters also provide a natural crossroads in the life of salmon. As the young smolt adjust to the ocean, their elders return, drawn by the same scent of their natal river.

For a brief period they can come face to face with each other and their respective futures.

1957 to 1958
I am twenty three to twenty seven years old

One way or another, I had now spent eight years with food. Certainly I had had the "odd" breaks connected to my failed avoidance of the Army Catering Corps coupled with several months dedicated to teaching and being taught to kill my fellow man, should my government so order.

To be absolutely truthful, my hands-on food experiences totaled about six years.

It was just after my 23rd birthday, early in February 1957, that we left the British Army and its constant, predictable downstream current of employment. Opening up before us was a world of opportunity. What would we choose to do?

My parent's hotel in Tenterden, Kent, was doing quite well and it was they that suggested we take over the food side of the business live in the hotel and share in the profits as a family business. The Woolpack Inn was built in the 15th century in the shadows of St. Mildred's Church, where we had married. It had fond romantic memories for us both and since we were now a family of three, having been joined by our first child Theresa Jane (Tess) within one hour of our first anniversary, we were overjoyed at this ongoing security.

It became my first experience of selling what I did to others and living off that income... not just me, but Treena and Tess were to be sustained by my choices and personal effort. You may recall that I had several brushes with innovation where I was very eager to improve methods of serving. My past motives had been to somehow gain status for both myself and those under my command. Now it was different; I still wanted improvement, but now it entailed competition. What could I do to get folks to come and eat, return as regular customers, and hopefully to tell others how good it was?

Our small, low ceiling, dark oak beam restaurant could seat forty at a pinch. We also had an oyster bar off the saloon bar, and the occasional function at the town hall that was our next-door neighbor.

We settled into two rooms above the kitchen and purchased a Morphy Richards Electric Fire that had a red bulb in the base and gave off

The Woolpack Inn

comforting warmth. You may wonder why I mention this. It is because that fire and the warmth it generated in those cold, damp, tiny rooms remain one of my most prized early possessions. To this day I am ever on the hunt for something like it!

By the spring of 1957 I had settled enough to try something new. Best of all, our cook was willing! The menu was typical for those postwar days, very conservative and somewhat French, mostly grilled to order. I laid out a small table with a large tray of crushed ice and presented that day's menu items in small glass-covered dishes. There were steaks, lamb chops, chicken and fish, but there were also the vegetables that were local and seasonal, including fresh herbs. And this was in 1957!

I invited my customers to choose what they enjoyed eating and select the vegetables as both side dishes and, if they wished, incorporated in a garnish or sauce. It was an immediate success and with one small decision I had begun a lifelong journey in the use of local ingredients for which people had natural preferences.

Somewhat flushed by this early *triumph*, I began the Saturday Evening Candlelight Buffet. It was here that I spent altogether too much time and experienced the first pushback amongst the many that must be encountered by innovators! The problem with my cold buffet was its appearance.

With the Morphy Richards Electric Fire, and Tess

I loved to fiddle with decoration, be it aspics or chaud-froid...lobster as a mousse...even a boars head glazed almost black and decorated with hearts in descending size from forehead to snout with sprays of Lilly of the Valley butter-cream caught up to encircle the cheeks.

It was summer by now, and we were very busy. Treena was assisting in the kitchen while I took orders and "fiddled with the cold boars head". When the head responded to the unusually warm weather by erupting with a major outbreak of tiny "grubs" and had to be incinerated in the backyard, causing a far from pleasant aroma, well, you might imagine there was an accounting! I retreated into relative simplicity to bide my time; there were to be spectacular boars heads in my future, but none of which ever led to success.

It was during this new season of our life that the unexpected happened. Egypt decided to claim the Suez Canal as its own, and Britain decided it shouldn't.

Suddenly, our new success ground miserably to a halt. There was petrol (gas) rationing and we were in the country, and out of our customer's range. There was an 8 percent interest rate on bank loans and literally overnight we were unable to continue. The Woolpack was sold at a substantial loss and my parents were engaged to manage the quite famous Royal Ascot Hotel, built on lands owned by the Queen, quite close to the Windsor Great Park and across the road from the Ascot Racetrack that was featured in "My Fair Lady" and numerous newsreels of spectacular hats!

We came as a packaged deal. Once again, I was the food man and my parents were General Managers. The Royal Ascot had recently been purchased by a well-known Hotelier, Alex Taylor. Alex had made a small fortune during the war by selling mock crocodile skin gasmask cases in the Burlington Arcade in London. Nowhere else on earth would there have been such fashionable protection!

When the war ended, Alex, who had changed his name from Schneiderman, began buying up some of the grand old houses that had been "requisitioned" during the war. He swiftly divided the huge rooms, installed simple bathrooms, and gave the outside a coat of paint. Bingo...yet another Boutique Hotel was ready to be run by a returning officer with no other immediate prospects.

Alex sold out his share in the very profitable business in order to, in part, distance himself from this *get rich moderately quickly* routine. He bought a lovely Victorian mansion called Burleigh Bushes, just down the road from the hotel and settled down to the good life. My parents were his gracious "front" who came complete with many old and faithful customers and, of course, Treena and I.

Within a few months, my parents were offered one of the most prestigious of all small hotel management, the famous Gravetye Manor, near East Grinstead...quite close to his first managerial appointment at Ye Dorset Arms. That left Treena and I on our own. I received a call from Alex Taylor to come down to Burleigh Bushes and "discuss the future."

I was now twenty-three years old and had *trained* as management but had never actually held the reins of a hotel of any size.

"I'm going to take a risk with you Graham." Alex sat comfortably in his grand personal office, the sun slanting across a large walnut desk.

I sat nervously facing him.

"I'm offering you the General Management of the Royal Ascot...along with Treena, of course.

"Your parents have done a great job and have provided you with a good example of how a hotel should be run...so let's see if you can do it?"

"Mr. Taylor, I'm grateful...however, I really don't think I have sufficient years of experience..."

"Let me judge that." He cut me off abruptly.

"How much do you want to be paid?" He enquired.

"I really don't know...I haven't thought it through."

"If you don't know what you're worth, then you're worth nothing." He advised sternly.

And so I experienced my first leap up the ladder to my goal as a senior hotelier. From a Junior Assistant Manager to a General Manager is like being plucked off of a ladder just a few steps up and hung out to dry half the way up with no rungs in-between. The problem with this is there really is no way down, at least no way that either feels good or looks good, especially on a resume. Mr. Taylor decided to use this transition to close the hotel completely for renovations, and to detail the way in which it would be run. I shall always be grateful for those months of preparation.

I was given a clipboard and many sheets of graph paper and commanded to follow him as he traced every single step of every pathway that any guest was likely to take. He began the assessment about one mile away from the hotel in all directions, which included good visual signs and an easier entry to the car park. I made notes and from the notes and wrote a job description and qualification for every single member of the oncoming staff. My earlier attempts were *savaged* by Alex but each was also a learning curve. What I lacked, I was now learning with hypothetical customers. When the paperwork was complete I then interviewed an almost brand new staff for the entire hotel. It worked so well and made the reopening a truly *grand* affair that went off without a hitch.

And so began a very steep journey to the top...at least to the top of this small hill. It wasn't easy. In fact, it was grim. What we lacked in experience we made up for in sheer hard work. At one stage we had gone sixteen weeks without a single day off and many of those were over twelve hour days.

Taylor demanded perfection—perhaps he desired to put as much distance between himself and his early faux crocodile skin gasmask cases as he could? For whatever reasons he had, we became his target to blame.

Several months in, during the famous race week when we were extremely busy, the Duke of Norfolk came in for luncheon. He asked for a Sole Veronique, which was not on the menu. I took the order personally from His Grace to the Head Chef.

"Tell them 've do not 'ave the provisions." The Chef was French and not in the least impressed by English Nobility.

This I repeated to the Duke who replied..."Nonsense my good man, you have Dover Sole and there are black grapes over there (he waved at a large decorative fruit bowl), so be a good chap. I'm not in a hurry."

I took the grapes on a small silver plate down to the kitchen.

"Chef, he's wise to us." I explained and handed over the grapes to be peeled.

"I tol' you, 've 'ave not the provisions!" He shouted excitedly (he was very busy). He then grabbed the grapes and screwed them into a juicy pulp to prove his point. I returned with my empty silver plate to the fruit bowl and selected a fresh bunch of grapes. Returning to the noisy, bustling kitchen, I stood in front of a now red-faced, agitated 280 pound, six foot Chef and as calmly as I could, said...

"Chef, this is now an order, and you will make the Sole Veronique."

This time he brushed the grapes aside, the silver clanged to the floor, he spun me around and grabbed me by the scruff of my morning coat and the seat of my striped trousers and frog marched me to the dining room door. He then pushed me through it, much to the customers' surprise, and my total confusion and embarrassment. I made it to my office, called the Chef on the phone and sacked him. He was already in full "retreat." Down to the kitchen I sped, got the grapes off the floor and eventually made the Sole Veronique for our most senior Duke, who by this time, had had several large Scotch's and didn't seem to mind the rather long wait.

And so it went, from crisis to crisis. No amount of job description would ever equip one for life in the fast lane of a busy hotel in search of perfection.

Our career launching came to an abrupt end in the spring of 1958. Treena was now seven months pregnant with our second child and we desperately needed just a little time to ourselves. We took the *whole day* off during a relatively quiet period. We had a good lunch in Windsor and saw two separate main movies back to back. Quite tired, we returned early to have a sandwich in our apartment over the stables. I went to the hotel to fetch them and ran into our receptionist.

"There's hell to pay." She was quite pale.

"Taylor's in the dining room, Mrs. Taylor is managing the room..." she hurried on... "You gave the Maitre D' the day off and you weren't here."

That was enough; it was a rule that we *never* left the main dining room so *unattended.*

"Oh," she added, "and Mr. Taylor is dining with the Chairman of British (overseas) Airways."

I reported to Mr. Taylor who was now quite inebriated.

"Stand over by the door," he ordered without even looking up.

I did so...sending a message to Treena that I shouldn't be too long. Half an hour went by...a clanking knife on glass got my attention. On my way over, the glass shattered.

"See what you've done now!" He thundered.

"Clean it up...bring more Brandy!"

Another half hour elapsed and they began to leave.

"Get the Chairman's Rolls to the courtyard door," ordered Alex.

The huge Rolls crunched forward over the gravel, its large lights cutting through a thickening ground mist between the trees. I held open the main doors as they said their farewells.

Suddenly out of the mist ran my beloved in a white blur of nightgown...like a moth toward a candle she ran toward the headlights. There she stopped, perfectly lit, and faced Mr. Taylor.

She then addressed him directly.

"You **********..." She has always had a great command of the English language but even I had no idea where she had gathered such a string of obscenities, at least in any other situation they might have been judged obscene but in this case...apt?

She then fainted.

I bowed slightly and said...

"Good night Sir, Madam...if you might excuse me."

I scooped her up as best I could in her *condition* and walked off into the night, accompanied only by the soft purring of the Rolls Royce and the crunch of gravel underfoot.

Treena and Tess. Picture taken while Treena was pregnant with our second child.

Please join us in the Reflective Readers Club
www.grahamkerr.com/rrc

Rite of Passage Eleven:
"Off to the Unknown" (1958)

We seem to be the early explorers among our cohorts. I say that because we see so many who appear, at first sight, to be like us—but smaller, that are left behind. For a week or two we gain our "sea legs" and then...swish...we are gone! But, not without a near fatal encounter with a creature suddenly exploding the brightness and streaking toward us before we lost ourselves in the shoreline weeds.

An Understanding

Not all salmon move quickly from their birth river to the ocean. What are called "ocean type" Chinook who migrate out at a much smaller size, a year earlier, may remain in the estuary a considerable time before moving into the ocean. But when "stream type" Chinook, such as our pair, have reached sufficient size prior to migrating they don't remain long in the estuary for additional growth. The estuary is a dangerous place that can be packed with predators.

Entire nesting colonies of Caspian terns and double crested cormorants await the less wary during the downstream flood of smolts in spring. Hatchery fish particularly attract them due to their lack of savvy after release from protective ponds. From this point onward they will increasingly pack on Omega-3's from the rich ocean environment as stored energy and as a result are more highly prized since their "fat carries flavor."

Our pair of Chinook may now spend only a couple of weeks in this transition as they experience the ebb and flow of the blended salt and fresh waters. Then it is off to the vast unknown of ocean travels.

1958
I am twenty four years old

The very next day Mr. Taylor appeared to have not the slightest memory of the previous nights shocking confrontation. He was charming, affable, and enthusiastically plunged into planning the immediate future success of the Royal Ascot Hotel with me (and could it now also include Treena?) as its General Management.

I was stunned...*almost* speechless!

How could such an attack go unnoticed and beyond some sort of reconciliation? I was ready to offer our resignation before being fired but...*nothing* like this had been considered.

Our future, however, was sealed. Treena found it impossible to live with the unspoken barrier and refused to speak another word to Taylor. I continued to serve, but was actively seeking another management position while trying somehow to keep the peace! We interviewed for two truly awful jobs, neither of which would have made a positive contribution to *anyone's* resume.

I began to realize that I had advanced too early in the normal ladder of success. I was hanging onto a "good" rung way ahead of my years, but had no rungs beneath me. I could *not* descend into such unsavory circumstances.

We discussed the possibility of a "complete break", to literally start over again in some far off land.

As we thought this through, Treena, in the seventh month of her pregnancy, had a miscarriage and the baby boy was lost to us. I was advised by our very senior physician to "be quiet about it, don't dwell on it...don't discuss it...just get on with your lives." This could not have been worse advice. What Treena needed was to grieve, be comforted and loved tenderly, but all she got from me was more and more chat about when we would move and where!

It was in the midst of these troubles that we both thought of either Canada...or even New Zealand.

The Canadians offered us an Assistant Manager's post in the Canadian Pacific Railway hotel chain.

The New Zealanders' asked me to come to New Zealand House in London for interviews. This I did; it was in May 1958, a year that would radically change our lives.

I commuted for my interviews in driving rain, when London can seem so bleak and uncomfortable. The interviewer was cheerful and seemed impressed by my dress black jacket and striped trousers...and, of course, the pearl gray tie; a carnation seemed inappropriate!

She explained that my present job had no match yet "back home." "We only have one independent restaurant with a wine license in the whole nation it's called *The Gourmet* in Auckland. The rest are tourist hotels."

"I really don't mind what I do." I replied. "I just need to get as far away from here as possible."

She scanned my short resume and the form I had completed at her request.

"I see you have had Army service...as a Catering Advisor?"

I nodded.

"How does working with the Navy appeal?"

I didn't want to go back to the Armed Forces and remained silent, thinking it through.

"Oh," she sighed. "That seems to have gone."

"Ah, just a moment," she continued.

"How about the Chief Catering Advisor to the Air Force?"

Immediately I felt like I was reaching way too high on the ladder yet again.

"That's a big job for a man with my experience," I replied.

"Well, actually," she explained, "it's a pretty small Air Force."

"Tell you what," she said brightly. "There are several members of the Air Board here for a conference and they are meeting as we speak." She rushed on. "They want a cup of tea at three o'clock...so why don't I see if you can join them?"

I had come to town, and I had nothing to lose...

"Might as well."

Promptly at three o'clock in the afternoon, I was ushered into a moderate size conference room. At a table were seated five senior Air Force Officers, all Air Commodores (Two-Star Generals).

"G'day," they chorused heartily. "Come and sit down...have some tea and a biscuit."

They were all in their mid fifties and well garnished with campaign medal ribbons.

"We've had a quick look at your record," said the more senior officer. "We like what we see...so far."

Then followed the most bizarre interview of my life with questions that seemed to have little or no bearing on my culinary or administrative ability.

"What we want to know is if you will fit in with the New Zealand way of life." The older officer was genuinely concerned and leaned in toward me as though to emphasize his need to know me better.

Since I had no prior expectation, there was no fear of rejection, and so I spoke confidently with the deference I had learned addressing my famous customers at the Royal Ascot.

In less than one hour, these five officers seemed to have used up their tea break and went into a brief huddle with each other...they didn't even ask me to leave the room.

"So, what do you think mate?"

"He's got what it takes!"

"Good enough—think he's right!"

"All agreed?"

"Sure, yes, right, good."

They turned to me and gave their instant verdict.

"You've got the job if you want it. It has the rank of Squadron Leader (Major). You may have to wait a couple of years until you're twenty six to qualify...can you start in September?"

It was breathtaking. I just sat there for a moment. My tea had remained untouched, as was the biscuit (cookie).

"Thank you for your time," I replied weakly, "and the tea," I added hurriedly.

"Yes, I think that can work. I'll let you know." I wondered what Treena was going to say.

"Okay then," said the Senior Air Commodore. "We shall look forward to some good dinners at the Headquarters Officer's Mess at Shelly Bay," and laughed with the others as he shook me by the hand and patted me on the back.

I had a job offer. It was over 16,000 miles away from our pain-filled home.

What would Treena think?

This I considered in the long, wet drive back to Ascot.

Quite apart from the job offer and the obvious dislocation, they had introduced an unusually touchy condition. I was to go ahead and become "acclimated" to New Zealand life six months before my family could join me.

Six months separation...and it wasn't a wartime posting!

"Well, how did it go?" Treena greeted me at the door of our apartment. She had long ago made tea, which like my earlier one had gone cold.

"We have a job...*confirmed*." I replied, as brightly as I could.

"Really? Wow, what is it? When do we get out of this mess?" She was immediately excited at any prospect of moving.

"It's Chief Catering Advisor for the Royal New Zealand Air Force...it's quite a small Air Force." I added with a smile.

"They want me to leave in September."

"They want *you* to leave...what about *us*?" She asked sharply.

"I'm to go ahead to make a place for us, and you will follow with Tess by sea, leaving in February next year." This was the clincher.

"Next year," she exploded, "but that's one, two, three...that's *six* months!"

"I know, I hate it too, but we have nothing, no furniture or savings, and I need to find us a place to live and save hard...and...oh, I shall miss you." It sounded like a lame afterthought to all the obvious practical issues. Treena just stood there and looked directly into my eyes; it seemed that she was searching for some kind of assurance.

"I'll reheat the tea." She turned abruptly to find some measure of relief in our British answer to all things.

No matter how we examined it, the answer was the same. We had to leave and soon...and this was the only bird in the hand!

When it was reluctantly settled between us, I set out to see Taylor.

He greeted me with his usual bustling enthusiasm. After awhile he paused long enough for me to tell him about the New Zealand offer.

He remained silent, a large glass of gin in one hand.

"I had high hopes for you," he started slowly.

"Your dream was the Dorchester...I shared that with you and just wanted to get you started on the fast track. You could still make it, you know?" He began to negotiate which was his custom, anything to get his way.

"Actually, that dream has faded," I explained. "All I really need now is to find a new life where I can close the door after a working day...and be a family."

"If you insist on leaving," Taylor's eyes narrowed as he put his glass down firmly on the desk, "then," he continued severely, "I shall see to it that you never get another job in the British Hotel business...ever!"

I sat there watching the bridges burning behind me, literally blazing out of his wounded eyes.

And so, it was over. It is all very well to be an early achiever, but not so pleasant when one is locked into virtual slavery to the one person who has offered such an immediate opportunity. He wanted a "no notice" departure, and so we packed and left the next day.

My parents came to the rescue with jobs for Treena and I at Gravetye Manor, the famous small hotel near East Grinstead in Sussex where they served as General Managers. I became the Restaurant Manager, and Treena a kind of "maid of all trades," often called a GA for General Assistant.

We had just over three months before we were to be parted.

It was during this "odd" season in Gravetye that I observed once again my parents and their extraordinary gift of hospitality and administration.

It was important to overlap in such a close environment. Treena and I were about to, quite literally, go out into the oceans of opportunity and here were my parents on their way back upstream toward a successful retirement. My old mentor Andre Simon, the founder and World President of the Wine and Food Society chose to have a luncheon for several of Europe's foremost food writers.

I supervised that event and helped serve the amazing wines from our vast cellars.

One bottle was especially valuable, an 1896 Cockburn Special Reserve Port with a heavy wax seal over the cork.

I took this very seriously, standing the bottle upright for two days to let the sediment settle after very gently moving it from its cool, horizontal, dusty bed. I chipped off the wax with great care and probed the old cork with a fine steel corkscrew. It gave way easily, too easily...*it crumbled!* No matter how tenderly I pushed and turned, it continued to mash into small, damp pieces. Eventually I managed to scoop the remains from the bottle and decant the old wine through a fine mesh sieve, using a candle flame to help me spot the sediment as it approached the shoulders of the ancient bottle.

The port was perfect...perhaps the wax seal had saved it.

The *mighty* food writers sniffed at their tiny portions and savored this spectacular wine.

"Gentlemen," Andre addressed the all-male gathering. "This bottle is magnificent...the cork must have saved it," he pronounced in his very French manner.

"Graham," he beckoned to me, "let us see the cork."

I rushed to the still room and turned out the waste bin into which I had tipped the crumbled cork.

Swiftly I assembled a small pile of damp, deep purple stained cork on a pure white Irish damask linen serviette set on a small silver tray and took it to him, allowing him to be the first to see the evidence...just in case.

"Ah ha!" he said. He took a good pinch of the moist crumbles in his fingers, raised them to his fine nose and inhaled carefully.

"As I said...the cork is perfect."

Such is the business of fine dining and the age of the true Gourmand.

My other truly notable customer during this waiting period was Winston Churchill.

Yes...*the* Winston Churchill.

He was dining alone and I presented the huge wine list; there were over 600 wines in the large cellars at that time. He riffled the pages, snapped it shut, handed it back and said gruffly in that famous almost lisp...

"Bring me something in the largest bottle with the greatest alcoholic content at the lowest conceivable price."

Mr. Churchill remains an unusual example of how a grand old age can be achieved in spite of somewhat questionable lifestyle choices.

September arrived all too soon, and it came time for me to depart from the land of my birth...never, as a resident, to return. I boarded the almost vintage four-gas-engined Hastings aircraft, a larger version of the DC3 at Lyneham Air Force Base. We rumbled down the runway, only to come to a stop in order to receive a telegram...for me. "Safe trip...I love you. See you soon...Your Treena".

The fuselage door was closed, and the steps removed. We turned into the wind and very slowly rolled down the runway, lifting off into a cool gray sky with the green fields of England gradually fading from sight.

I was on my way to a whole new life.

Please join us in the Reflective Readers Club
www.grahamkerr.com/rrc

Rite of Passage Twelve: "Flying Solo" (1958)

I have been here long enough. The strange tang in the water has grown stronger and my hen and I have ventured further into the strangely moving waters.

My appetite has grown and something compels me to move out into that dark, deep, blue-green expanse as if pulled by the strings of an unseen puppeteer.

Drawn by this irresistible desire to simply move, I take a last long look at my constant companion...knowing deeply that we would reconnect out there, and brushing lightly against her flank I turned towards the open place...and rushed ahead in a shoal of silver.

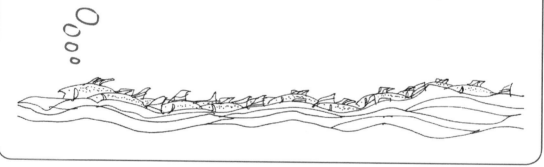

An Understanding

Our smolt, as he is now known, having grown larger in the added year of freshwater rearing is ready for the ocean. He will make that move in a great company that may be millions of little salmon moving in clouds of silver. Subgroups moving off in gatherings of their own as their migrations mysteriously diverge to take them to dispersed ocean feeding grounds that will not be over-exploited by any one single group.

1958
I am now twenty four years old

Our flight plan was to take us across the North Atlantic to Iceland, then on to Montreal, down to Omaha Nebraska and San Francisco, over the Pacific to Hawaii, then on to Canton Island in the middle of nowhere (thanks to the excellent navigator because this was long before GPS!), then on to Fiji and finally into Whenuapai, near Auckland, New Zealand.

Our plane was a four-engined gas powered propeller transport, originally built for the Royal Air Force in the UK in 1948 and was used to deliver coal to Berlin up until 1949.

There were four that were especially built for the Royal New Zealand Air Force, called the H.P. 95 Hastings C3 which had Bristol Hercules 737 engines that had pretty frequent lubrication problems; so much so that aircrew used to call it "the best three engined aircraft in the world."

Since it was equipped to fly troops, the seats were facing to the rear. It was noisy, deafeningly so, and cold. The seat headrests were designed for paratroopers *with* helmets!

All of this was perfectly reasonable when compared to the in-flight meals provided in soggy boxes! This was my first encounter with the Air Force Catering Services and I swore over every tired and tasteless bite that "something needed to be done, and soon!" Whenever I'm tempted to complain about air travel since that early experience, I remind myself that it could only have been worse had we crashed!

Our arrival at the RNZAF base in Whenuapai, near Auckland in the North Island could not have been more spectacular. We came in quite low (we never got very high) over the Bay of Islands; perfectly green, ringed with golden sands in a bright blue sea. The islands gave way to the mainland that looked as though it had been somehow painted and that they had got the colors altogether too vivid to be natural!

I sent off a telegram to let Treena and Tessa know that "daddy has landed in our new home."

I had flown about 12,890 miles and had now to face another 400 miles on the Limited Express, a curious overnight sleeper train to the capital city of Wellington. I was now home away from home...alone!

It took ten days to reach New Zealand with engine lubrication problems in San Francisco, Hawaii and Fiji...amazing coincidences with attractive places!

Keflavik in Iceland was shrouded in low gray clouds with an early snow that covered practically everything in a dirty white. For some obscure reason the U.S. Army had posted a Colonel in the U.S. Cavalry to this out-of-the way spot. He had come on his own and without anything that resembled a tank. Quite possibly this had given rise to a certain kind of melancholia that was only relieved by shooting bottles with his chrome-plated Colt 45 that he wore strapped to his thigh. I knew this because he insisted that I go out beyond the city into the drifting snow and watch him find solace by shooting sundry whiskey bottles that he had only recently drained. Though unsteady, he was remarkably accurate. It is amazing how the smell of cordite, wet snow and scotch lingers in the memory...

Our longest flight seemed to take forever, just over 2,330 miles from Iceland to Montreal, 15 hours at about 12,000 feet through clouds that were not exactly hospitable.

The trip to Omaha was to be our shortest, and we made quite a splash on landing at the S.A.C. Airbase (Strategic Air Force Command) with its vast array of B52 jet bombers lined up and ready to go.

We touched down like a large DC3, our gas engines roaring and with rusted exhaust streaks down the cowlings.

The ever-ready S.A.C. Aircrews tumbled out to see us, apparently in awe of our heirloom status and the fact that it could still fly!

That evening, my first on U.S. soil ever, was an amazing experience. We dined in the U.S. Air Force Officer's Club that had a special on that very day

"32 ounce Porterhouse on the plank.
Eat it all, you keep the plank!"

I cannot recall the price, but I was now on day three consuming my inflight box meals and since I had never eaten more than a 4 ounce steak, I simply had no way of imagining what it would look like. Surprisingly, it was the *plank* that I really wanted...a kind of trophy to record my first taste of the United States. It was a struggle, but I won the prize...thank God there was a good deal of bone! I had that plank for years.

It was in San Francisco that the entire trip took on a new twist. We had landed at Travis Air Force Base just fifty three miles out of San Francisco (when you go over the Oakland Bay Bridge) and sixty seven miles on 101 that goes over the Golden Gate Bridge; this I *had* to do!

The Hastings aircraft had engine lubrication problems that allowed a small group of us the opportunity to rent a car and drive to San Francisco. I became the designated driver because I had experience driving on the *wrong side of the road* in France.

A quick word here about what is *right* and *wrong* for traffic use...

In early Britain, most men were right-handed and kept their swords on their left side. It was, as a result, much easier to mount a horse on its left side. It was also sensible to have the *drawn* sword on the right; so they kept to the left for perfectly obvious reasons that were... *right*. There are seventy four nations that still keep to this rule. Swords are now less obvious!

It seems that the French Revolution turned things about in the remaining world, beginning with Napoleon's conquests. Apparently, the French aristocracy preferred the left side and forced "peasants" to use the right. After the revolution, those of the deposed "upper class" stopped using the left for fear of being discovered and beheaded. Again, these were excellent reasons for *keeping one's head* and opting for a change!

All of this is simply necessary for you to understand so that what happened in San Francisco is perhaps reasonable?

We rented from the Hertz Company, who accepted my British license to drive without question. The friendly, tousle-haired young man at the desk asked, "did you want comprehensive insurance?" We conferred amongst ourselves, and being young, confident and almost penniless, we decided to go without.

Our vehicle was a Chevrolet Bel Air 4-door sedan of truly enormous (to me) size. It was easily twice the length of my MG! It also came with a turboglide transmission that apparently *changed itself without a clutch.*

We set off on Interstate 80 and connected to 680 down into Oakland and over the Oakland Bay Bridge. All was well because the traffic was on the freeway and obviously going one way. I began to settle down.

As the tallest city I had ever seen loomed closer I came off the bridge and continued on 80 until it met up with the off ramp to 5th Street. I had been told that this would take us up to the famous Nob Hill and a great view of the city.

I found Geary and went down to Jones to make a right, only to find it was a one way. I backed off, in some confusion now, and took the next right at Leavenworth...I should have seen its name as an omen!

As Leavenworth went steeply uphill I had to stop at Clay and turn right.

Yes, there really is a point to all this!

I had noticed the abbreviation GR on the gearshift indicator on the steering column just behind the enormously distracting dash mirror that reflected the traffic lights that were obscured by the Chevy's overhanging roof.

GR, I had been told, meant *grade* or perhaps even *grope.* It had been used to replace HR, which stood for hill retarder, which was often misunderstood. GR actually meant *grade retarder*, but to this day for my purposes it means *grope.*

It was at this very intersection that I saw the light change in the angled visor mirror. I chose GR to handle the grade ahead and accelerated...changing the gear with my foot on my habitual clutch, which of course had been morphed by modernity into a power brake!

We stopped as designed, suddenly...right in the intersection.

The car behind slammed into our uninsured trunk.

I froze...my youthful confidence evaporated.

Traffic on Clay, yet another one-way street coming from my left, began to honk. Now in complete confusion I took off up Leavenworth, which was completely empty...until I came bumper-to-bumper with a large police car.

I managed this by choosing, in my panic, the *British side of the road!*

The policeman got out slowly. He was large and black; he wore dark glasses and his hand rested on a huge revolver. My window was down. He leaned into the car and turned his head to take in six very scared members of the British Commonwealth of Nations.

Since he chose not to speak...but simply to observe...I found my voice.

"I'm terribly sorry Constable...new here, you know," I croaked and tried to smile.

"Are you a limey?" He asked.

Why yes...indeed...a limey," I replied hopefully, "and these men are...Kiwis," I added.

"If you get to kill anyone today...you're for the hot seat," he responded. "I strongly suggest you park...NOW!"

I found the nearest space and after considerable effort managed to get the boat-shaped vehicle alongside. We exchanged license numbers with the car that had rammed us from behind. I had no insurance you may recall!

The rest of the day was ruined. We tied the trunk together and contemplated fearfully the return trip that we had planned on taking over the Golden Gate Bridge. As we crossed, I performed an extraordinarily anti-American act.

In a strong crosswind I actually hit the bridge, scraping the entire side of the Bel Air. Neither my companions nor I said a word until we pulled into the Hertz drop off where the tousle-haired agent was still on duty.

"So...how did it go?" He asked brightly. "Have a good day? Great city, isn't it? Any damage?" He enquired, all without really stopping for, or expecting, an answer.

"Well," I said haltingly, "there are a couple of issues."

I then proceeded to explain with a few small embellishments, largely in response to his apparent delight with our tale of woe.

In the end, he simply stood there laughing with tears rolling down his face.

"Hell! That's amazing!" He cried. "What a story! I'm going to dine out on that for months!"

And then he added...

"Have that on me!" He did this without actually seeing the almost totaled Bel Air.

We left that same evening and had seemingly disappeared without a trace...until now, that is? After fifty six years, does it still matter?

Please join us in the Reflective Readers Club
www.grahamkerr.com/rrc

FLASH OF SILVER

2

...the leap that changed my world.

BOOK TWO:
THE OCEANS OF
OPPORTUNITY

Rite of Passage Thirteen: "An *Almost* Whole New Way of Living" (1958-1971)

The water about me has almost completely changed.

There is just that hint of my birthplace, but it gets less and less as I plunge forward. The tang is now strong and constant, but it's the bottom that has changed and become so deep there are times it disappears in darkness.

Above has become like some of the rapids on my way downriver, except the riffles are deeper and come in a rhythm.

The biggest change came with the food. I had my first full meal of tiny crunchy "snacks." Great texture, these could become a favorite...but alas, I am growing and begin to target prey of increasing size. Other species of fish of an age and size small enough for me to swallow have the added thrill of providing a chase to catch...and I am becoming quite proficient at it.

A part of me grieved at leaving my hen behind, but this open water was so new in so many ways that I simply settled down to finding my way, with so much to experience for the first time.

An Understanding

The North Pacific has abundant supplies of plankton, which are small to microscopic individual sea creatures. They lack the power to go against a tide...and so they live and drift in the major oceanic currents. But our growing salmon is now beyond the size to target such small creatures. Nevertheless, the bait fish that our Chinook will increasingly target for rapid sustained growth— such as sand lance, sardines, and herring—all partially or completely depend on abundant zooplankton as the basic ingredient of the productive ocean food chain.

Our salmon were consuming a tiny organism called krill (euphausiids), quite like a very small shrimp...about 2 to 20 mm long, and about 2 inches at maturity.

Typically, according to its salmon species, there are about thirty different forms of marine life that the salmon enjoys, and these kinds often alter during their ocean migration. In the case of Chinook that grow to an exceptionally large size, their choice of targeted prey quickly shifts. This is particularly so for our Chinook that has been reared in the river long enough to begin eating other fish that can be as large as a third to a half of its own 7-8 inch long body size. He will soon be near the top of the ocean food chain.

Our Chinook appears to have an especially ravenous appetite and grows fast in strength, speed and size.

1958
"Down Under"
I am still twenty four years old

If you turn a geographically correct model of earth, keeping the equator level with the floor and stop each 90 degrees, starting with the Americas and rotating to the left...you will see the Atlantic and all of Europe and Africa with a glimpse of the Middle East.

Turn another 90 degrees and there is the Indian Ocean, Middle and Far East, including Australia.

The last turn is the most surprising. It is mostly the Pacific Ocean with Japan at the top, Australia off to the left, and Hawaii all on its own, mid right.

At the bottom of all this blue is New Zealand.

Surely this is a *place apart* in our crowded world and it was to be our home for the next seven years.

My task as CAT.1 (Catering One) or the Chief Catering Advisor to the Royal New Zealand Air Force was to oversee all aspects of feeding the nation's Air Force, which was spread out from Fiji in the north to McMurdo Sound in Antarctica.

I was based in Wellington, the capital city that is strategically situated at the extreme south of the North Island, well known for its seasonal gales as "Windy Wellington".

The Air Force Administration was located on Stout Street in one of those characterless gray cement buildings that the British Commonwealth has reproduced endlessly for bureaucratic purposes, at apparently the lowest possible cost connected with safety! Wellington, after all, sits squarely on an earthquake fault!

I'm uncertain whose attitude was worse, mine or theirs, or perhaps it was all mine? Here I was, a mere twenty four years old, a "Brit" that New Zealanders often called "poms," the abbreviated version of the Australia "POME," an acronym for "Prisoner of Mother England." The term Pom could be used with affection, as in "he's a good old Pom," or mostly with real disdain, "he's a real Pome bastard." I was also the former General Manager of the Royal Ascot Hotel and came complete with a "toffee-nosed Public School accent." Collectively, I was unlikely to meet with anything other than disdain.

I looked Brit and sounded Brit, and began to understand why I had been sent on ahead to become "acclimated." In so many ways I was actually isolated. I lived, once again, in an Army Officer's Mess at Fort Dorset and would eat and sleep there for six months. I was also ex-Army, almost a fate worse than death amongst the so-called "Gentleman of the Air Force."

Worst of all was the *distance*. It became more than miles and was the first shade of gray that entered our married life. In Wales, before we married, I wrote daily to Treena, finding all manner of words to try to find a way to communicate how deeply and desperately I loved her. Now, in New Zealand, once again in the Army Officer's quarters, I was not so urgent.

I had much to learn in what seemed to me to be a moderately hostile environment, one that was continually saying, "Prove it...let's see why they chose you to lead us!"

Within two weeks of my arrival I had my first test.

One of my old customers at the Royal Ascot had been appointed Governor General to New Zealand. He heard that I had arrived and suggested that there be a dinner at Shelly Bay, the non-resident Officer's Club/Mess a few miles outside Wellington.

The menu was left entirely to me. I recall two items...Trout Woolpack, which I had invented while in Tenterden at the Woolpack Hotel. This was a small brook trout stuffed with shrimp and mushrooms and grilled under a radiant overhead gas "salamander." This was to be followed by a simple butter braised "Aylesbury Duckling" with a French-style Bigarade Sauce made with a deglazing of the braise pan with orange and lemon juice.

I was told that trout could only be authorized through the Department of Fish and Game, and that they were not permitted, for some obscure reason, to be sold.

I ordered forty, since there were thirty eight for dinner. It took a small truck to deliver the forty fish that weighed in at just over eight pounds each. I had expected them to be more like eight to ten ounces! I set aside three for the dinner and found good homes for the other thirty six by using them as a "calling card" with several Senior Officers and their wives.

The ducks, I was told, were Muscovy, with which I was unfamiliar. They appeared to be, well, ducks! I mean if it looks like one, it's...right? This is where my eventually triumphant relationship with the very Senior Flight Sergeant "Phil Eyton" began.

It was not a good start!

"Sergeant Eyton," I addressed the senior non-commissioned officer, who was also a Chef Instructor and who was in charge of the kitchens on that fateful night.

"Sergeant," I continued, "I want you to roast these duckling breast down in a little clarified butter at 375 degrees for 30 minutes per pound."

"Sir," and then followed a long pause.

"If I were you—Sir —I'd boil the buggers first!"

Quite shocked at the idea and the way it was suggested, I found myself insisting, as I had done on Shrove Tuesday back in England.

That evening, with many medals reflecting candlelight on a beautifully set long Heart Kauri table, I sat in the kitchen awaiting a call from Viscount Lord Cobham to attend for a glass of port and the appreciation of those gathered.

The Salmon Trout was a success...but could have looked better had they been small!

The duckling looked great and cut entirely into four pieces glistening with the reduced citrus and butter.

There was silence—quite obvious, even in the kitchen.

"There," I smiled at Sergeant Eyton.

"When there is silence, it means that they are enjoying the food." I explained, as one who had such long experience in the "old" country.

The Mess Sergeant backed through the swinging door to the dining room, holding two plates of duck, his face drawn and white.

"They're bendin' their bleeding forks in it—Sir!"

Sergeant Eyton turned to face me directly and muttered quietly..."I told you to boil the buggers!" He left off the *"Sir!"* Every one of those ducks was inedible. They might as well have been alive and quacking during the Maori Wars (1845–1872). It was later that I came to appreciate the difference between an Aylesbury Duckling and a Muscovy Duck.

I was not invited to take port and did not receive a single word of appreciation. The story went viral on the bush telegraph of the day. The Pom had struck out on his very first event.

The naysayers were smiling.

In an attempt to regain some status, I joined the newly formed Wellington Wine and Food Society. It had been established to somehow promote the idea of more *international* eating, as well as to promote a small but exceptional private dining club called Monsieur Robert, pronounced "Rob-air", in the very French manner.

Monsieur Robert was, in fact, Robert Beasley, a fellow Brit who had excelled as a student at the then famous Westminster Tech's Culinary Program in London. He had been a student under the fearsome tutelage of Monsieur (French this time) Vincent, pronounced "Vansant!" He did so well that his grades remain, to this day, a target for perfection.

It should also be noted that there was only that one restaurant with a wine license, the Gourmet in Auckland. The only opportunity to drink wine with meals was in a hotel and that was mostly a meat-and-potatoes experience. The Wine and Food Society set out to suggest that wine with food was a *civilized* experience, to be greatly enjoyed by good friends in each other's homes.

There was one small bistro where a Mary Seddon created one-dish casseroles/stews, and permitted patrons to bring their own wines in brown paper bags that were then decanted into large white coffee mugs.

It was a perfect launching for the phrase "nudge, nudge...wink, wink...say no more!"

To my knowledge, she was never busted!

For the most part, I lived and ate "in the mess" (officers club) and gained a respectable thirty pounds doing so. That's not so easy in just six months but judging by the food and my miserable life apart from my beloved it was not entirely unreasonable!

I also allowed myself one Coca-Cola (8 ounces) per week, one movie complete with one ice cream, out of nostalgia? I spent nothing else, except to stamp my occasional letters.

During this first six months I did little else but try to understand how the Air Force catered for itself and how I might...with more understanding than I had at my first dinner, help to *improve* matters. Had I not been so borderline obsessive compulsive I might have been a better husband and written more often about how much I missed them both...but I didn't. It went back to the loss of our second child and the counsel to say nothing, "Just get on with life as though it never happened."

This awful advice had inserted an editing device into our conversations and letters. It remained unaddressed, and yet as present as a seed waiting for its time to germinate.

This it would do when we were to be reunited as a family, a day I longed for that turned from utter joy to despair in a few short hours.

Please join us in the Reflective Readers Club
www.grahamkerr.com/rrc

Rite of Passage Fourteen: "A Journey Resumed" (1959)

I admit that this life without borders is amazing. I swim in the company of others just like me, and judging by their behavior and size...I, too, must look pretty good.

I must be longer, stronger and faster than ever...brilliant silver that catches the light as it filters through the uneven waters above.

The water appears to be increasingly alive with other great schools of glinting silver fish that cross our route. What they are I don't know, but while some are nearly as large as me, others are just small enough to single out from the passing school...and swallow. It only takes a few successful chase-downs to fill me for the entire day...and yet my hunger increases daily...I am driven by my appetite.

Recently I felt a strange pull to one side as though the vast waters were themselves turning and moving.

The other great schools of fish also seem to move, or concentrate, within this movement of waters...particularly where there is a confusion of currents that collide and come together.

Quite early, when the light came in sideways, I caught a glimpse of a hen that reminded me of my companion that I had left behind some time ago.

I quickened my speed and sped alongside. She was in the company of others. She was smaller in size but just as silver and just as nicely rounded as I had fixed in my mind.

She noticed me and in a moment swam to my side...our fins touched.

It was my hen; I knew we would meet up again. Suddenly she swam away and stopped, simply buoyant, but still with her eyes upon me, they seemed to question.

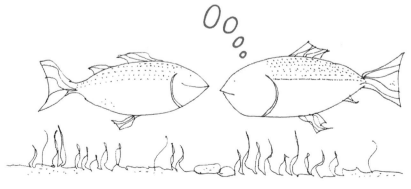

An Understanding

Our Chinook was feeding on the smaller members of the great passing schools of baitfish —sand lance, herring, and sardines —that depend on the zooplankton that tend to form dense clouds of life in colder waters of the oceans. This is especially true along the continental shelf in the best years when these waters are particularly cold. In the case of the Columbia River yearling spring Chinook, they tend to migrate rapidly (due to their larger size) on entry to the ocean travelling at 10–40 kilometers a day.

Willamette River origin spring Chinook disperse in their first months of ocean entry from along the southern Oregon Coast to Southeast Alaska by June, with particular concentrations along the West Coast of Vancouver Island and the Washington Coast. By August they are rarely south of Vancouver Island with migration that is progressively northward. By fall they move off the continental shelf.

Microscopic life forms are eaten by very large whales, and also by juvenile fish of many species; this can include Chinook at smaller sizes. But our salmon has now grown beyond what the plankton of itself can provide him, and in his marathon travel he needs the most with the least effort. Chinook are one of those that specialize in eating other fish.

But it is the plankton that supports the baitfish and all move together, predator and prey, with the ocean currents and water temperature in a timeless dance of life and death. Our salmon travels a well-established route to find feeding opportunity to sustain rapid growth…the route is passed through hundreds of preceding generations of salmon ancestors. What guides him? Part is an inner magnetic gyro, part may include phases of the moon, part may include the scent of currents, but much remains unknown.

In this case, our salmon tracked the plankton and baitfish schools staying close to the Alaskan coastline. He made fairly swift travel and by fall of that year had moved well off the continental shelf into deeper waters. It is here in offshore Alaskan and Northern Canadian waters where he will spend most of the rest of his life…often diving down 50 to 100 meters or more as is characteristic of Chinook.

It was here that he, with considerable poetic license, reunites with his childhood friend, the one he remembers with as much clarity as the scent of his natal river birthplace.

He is much larger now, over a foot long. She is smaller and more vulnerable. With each new inch of growth the likelihood of becoming prey to something larger diminishes.

1959
I am twenty five years old

I was at the Wellington docks at least two hours before she docked. The Athenic was part of the old White Star Lines that merged with the Cunard in the year we were born (1934).

The Athenic had a remarkable history. She was built in 1902 for the express purpose of connecting the UK to New Zealand with both passengers and trade. She served as a troop transport in World War I and was again converted as a whaling ship by a Norwegian company who renamed her "Pelagos."

She was captured by a German raider in Antarctica. The German converted her once again into an oil tanker for their U boats.

In 1942 a British submarine sank her.

In 1945 the Norwegians salvaged her and refitted her once again for the UK to New Zealand trade. She was then, in 1958, a mature fifty seven years old, which considering her variety of occupations (and sinking!) speaks well of her builders!

She was, by the way, retired in 1962, just three years after she had come alongside the Wellington docks to deposit my loved ones in the new home I had gone ahead to prepare for this very moment.

I decided against turning up in my Air Force Officer's uniform...and opted for my old Harris Tweed jacket and cavalry twill trousers, a new shirt with a larger neck size to fit my thicker neck, and I think I wore a dark brown tie to somehow match one of the tweed colors.

My extra 30 pounds had taken me from 187 pounds, which was my official weight on my Air Force Medical exam, to 210 pounds. Every button I owned strained at its threads, and the cloth met in folds at each fastening.

Even though I had gone through a New Zealand summer (my first experience with a 90 degrees Fahrenheit Christmas), I had remained, for the most part, indoors in the big gray building on Stout Street, which, come to think of it, was aptly named for both my condition and complexion.

The passenger stepladder was lowered. My heart rate increased.

Had I sat down and reviewed the last six months I would have been apprehensive. How should the love of one's life respond to a man who penned, at most, half a dozen letters in over 180 days?

How should she respond to a husband who had, at very little expense, sent her a black and white photograph of a decorated Boars head he had made for a Christmas buffet in the Officer's Mess...it was stuck onto a card and had become her Christmas present!

It is well said that thrift carried to the extreme is *meanness*, but this wasn't just about money; it was a complete failure to communicate my love.

How much does a stamp cost…nothing, yet how unwisely I had spent my time preparing a home, and ignoring her heart.

I should have known…but I didn't.

Then, I caught sight of her with not-so-tiny Tessa by her side. She made her way down the gangway like the beauty queen she had been…but so much more. Her naturally curly black hair fell down to her shoulders and glistened as she moved.

Unlike me, she had found the sun on the over four week journey. She was perfectly bronzed with only a trace of lipstick, her skin shone, and her eyes reflected the colors of the sea with such clarity and light. She was slim, yet wonderfully rounded, wearing a black dress smothered in tiny colorful flowers. She stood there with a beautiful blonde, curly haired Tessa grabbing at one leg and just stopped, her eyes upon me. She seemed to question…

There was, in that moment of hesitation, so much pent up emotion.

This was, to me, our new life, so full of promise, so far away from our painful past; or was it?

I had found a two bedroom apartment that I could afford at 168 Oriental Parade on the western waterfront, overlooking the harbor. I had also managed to furnish it, in a spartan fashion, with the £600 I had saved. You may recall that, as hotel management who lived on the job, we actually owned no household goods of any kind.

Okay, well, there was the silver flambé lamp, the copper pan and the silver tray, all pillaged from the Royal Ascot, partially in lieu of severance and wages!

I had enough left over for our first couple of nights at a bed and breakfast run by a charming Lebanese couple just a few doors up from the new, pristine…well, at least it was clean, dwelling place. They had kindly offered to watch Tessa for a while to allow us to have time to ourselves in their sun-filled front room with the lace curtains.

They even gave us both a sherry.

Again, Treena was still and questioning, very much aware and not at all hesitant.

"I need you to know that I had an affair of the heart on the ship on the way here." She looked carefully at me as she gradually provided me with news I did not want to hear.

"He is a ship's officer. He was kind and attentive to us both, Tess and I," she added.

My mind raced ahead of her…I watched as she spoke, my imagination unable to picture this lovely woman in someone else's arms. I briefly saw two hands touching at a cinema in East Grinstead; it was what I had dreaded when I heard about Colin when we were eleven.

"I'm going to give you six months to prove to me that you should be my husband and Tessa's father." She'd had a good deal of time to consider this requirement, and she was perfectly poised and confident.

I was a mess. I had no time at all to consider what was being asked. I felt betrayed, I felt angry...I felt a sadness that I had never believed possible.

My hand holding the sherry shook. I swallowed it and set the glass down, unable to look up, knowing she would look right into my eyes and see my confusion.

I never gave the six letters and the Christmas Card Boars Head a moment's thought...all I heard was "affair of the heart" and "six months to prove your love."

Please join us in the Reflective Readers Club
www.grahamkerr.com/rrc

I'm almost off my food...almost, but not entirely. It is, after all, my nature to eat.

The distraction is my hen. We are reunited, which at first was amazing. I was moved to leap out of the water with joy...but that behavior is unseemly at this stage in my life.

She withdrew to a distance and another shadowy buck seemed to lurk way beyond.

I twisted and turned so that the sun flashed off my flanks...all to no avail. She held her distance and she occupied almost all of my mind...leaving room for the odd snack.

An Understanding

Poetic license is a fine thing, as is imagination. Combine the two and some would call it fiction? Yet in this case the marine partnership truly mirrors another reality. Do other created beings suffer from rejection and earnestly desire acceptance? It would seem so...at least it does to me as I, too, suffer and earnestly desire.

1959
I am twenty five years old
Proof

"Prove my love?" My deep inside sense of loss was proof enough, at least for me, that my heart was close to breaking, my chest full of tears.

Wasn't this love?

We were together, yet apart. I was torn down the middle. Jealousy blazed on one side, a desperate desire on the other. Somewhere in between I had a new and challenging job to do, and a new life to build for my family. Yet the foundations had almost given way. Everything I had known as secure had been shaken.

It is at times like this that we need friends and, fortunately, I had made friends during my early solitary days. Kay Fernie, Peter Rodenberg, Robin and Beryl Rowe. I knew them well enough to spill out my confusion and to question how I might achieve some kind of reconciliation.

They met Treena and loved her on sight. Treena is like that...if the entire world is a stage, then Treena is one of the stars.

Their best counsel was, "stop feeling sorry for yourself."

"She has asked for proof, so prove it; first to yourself, and then it should become clear to her".

It meant reordering my priorities. Treena would come first, and our daughter second, the new "house" third, then my job for the Air Force, and lastly my need to be recognized with rather more status than a Catering Advisor usually warrants!

My appearance would have to be last, a kind of temporary death to self.

How does one prove love...short of tearful groveling? Self-pity, fortunately, was short lived, its place taken by *doing*. There was, after all, a nest to build, with furniture from a second hand store and everything we needed to equip a small apartment.

Our savings quickly ran out and my Air Force salary only barely met our basic living expenses. We owned no car, or even a stroller for Tessa. I could no longer afford a movie, or roses, or a night out. I walked about three miles back and forth to work each day, often in the now driving winter gales.

I couldn't *buy* her love!

I had to let the jealousy pass, and it did, with the understanding of how deeply I had wounded her with my apparent indifference, first with the loss of our second child and, second, by my perceived preoccupation with my new job so far away; so much so that I had let our love languish without tenderness for six months.

By coming to understand what I had sown, I came to understand what I had reaped.

I was, once again, able to declare my love...not by doing anything, but by simply being.

Treena's ultimatum had been delivered in February 1959. Our son Andrew was born in early January 1960. Counting back nine months suggests that by April we had decided that our marriage would survive and that we might, together, prove its worth...with another love child.

Nothing in those early New Zealand days was easy. We learned to be content with very little and to greatly value what we did have.

Treena took a part time job at the "Milk Bar," as it was called, just down the road. She made their sandwiches and was rewarded at the princely rate of 50 cents per hour. Among those traditional delights were "chip sandwiches", the filling of which was well-salted, malt vinegar seasoned French fries...cold, soft, sodden, and *popular!*

Fortunately, this did not go on for too long. Help came from New Zealand Broadcasting who heard of her earlier stage life and wanted her to audition for their Radio Drama Department in Wellington.

She was accepted and began her second life on stage as a radio actress. Her ability to mimic others, from babies to 90-year-old Russian nobility, kept her constantly in demand.

We now had two very small incomes. One month I would use mine to pay the bills and Treena would set out to save hers for our future. I wouldn't quite meet the needs, and she would bail me out.

Most months we would switch, and were simply making no progress. Our friend Peter Rosenberg presented us with a gemstone (New Zealand jade) egg and suggested we create a budget and "stick to it."

"If you do," he suggested, "I'll give you a second egg as a prize."

We still have that solitary egg!

Very gradually we began to acquire things, a stroller for Tessa came first. I still walked to work, and so did Treena.

I began to supplement my income by renting a small trunk and attending Turners and Growers Fresh Produce Market in the early hours of Friday morning. I would then "set up shop" in the inner courtyard of the Air Department Building and sell fruit and vegetables to my fellow officers. I would mark them up just enough to afford to take the remainders home at no cost to ourselves.

I had become the Vice President of the Wellington Wine and Food Society and created "One Dish, One Wine" suppers for the members. I would demonstrate the dish, and one of my Air Force cooks would serve the members buffet style and would pair that to a good table wine.

I got to "sing for my supper" and didn't have to pay.

During my first six months, I had been invited to a dinner party by members of the Wine and Food Society and met Shirley Maddox, a popular broadcaster/journalist.

"Have you ever thought of doing a radio program?" She asked casually.

"No," I laughed. "That's way beyond me," I replied.

"Well…let's see. I'll introduce you to Elsie Lloyd, the head of Women's Broadcasting."

She did.

I recall drafting my initial episodes at least six or seven times, only to be told that it "simply is not what we need," or, "it's not the way we speak."

It took almost exactly nine months to be accepted.

It was in late 1959 that I recorded episode #1, "A Cook's Tour," for NZBC Radio, Women's Hour. This was roughly ten minutes of verbal torture, for me, for the audience and especially for Elsie Lloyd.

I was seated at a large round, green-beige covered table above which hung a huge microphone…not unlike a Mortadella sausage. Elsie herself was the producer and we were recording my finally accepted script.

"When the red light goes on…you start." She used a speaker system in the control room and her strident voice boomed…

The light went on.

"I first discovered that cooking was an art when I visited Prince…"

The control room burst open and Elsie stormed into the studio.

"For God's sake," she yelled, "put some bloody oomph into it!"

"I don't care if you can cook beans…what I need is some passion and enthusiasm, as if you actually LIKE what you do!" She slammed the door.

The light went back on.

And off…

And on…again and again.

I left the studio soaked to the skin with sweat, my throat burning and dry, and my knees shaking.

I made a vow that day to never-ever return…broadcasting was definitely not my thing!

Much to everyone's amazement, the solitary episode was a success. The switchboard wasn't exactly jammed, but there was rather more mail than usual.

Reluctantly, Elsie Lloyd commissioned another dozen episodes at, as I recall, £NZ 10 each, and the £NZ 120 contract swiftly overcame my reluctance to "perform." (Their one pound NZ equaled one US dollar at this time).

There was, however, one major drawback.

I wondered if I had had enough experiences to fill so many programs because the format was to describe a visit and wax enthusiastic about the food I had eaten. At episode six I did, in fact, run out of places! Fortunately, there was the "Esquire International Cookbook," 1955.

The book contained detailed accounts of various author visits to some of the world's most exotic culinary destinations.

It was just what I needed.

I explained my situation to Elsie and its apparent solution.

"Sure, use it, by all means," she suggested; "only avoid the first person. You can't say that you visited...it's enough to say "let me tell you about Pappagallo's in Bologna, Italy!"

"Add your imagination to the research, don't ever use the same written sentences...and you are home and hosed." Whatever that meant, it worked...for a while. What I said was accurate; the impression it left was certainly not true.

I had garnished my limited experience with the excitement and adventure of international travel...and had become known as a "man of the world," which I certainly was not! What I was becoming, however, was an increasingly large frog in a relatively small pond.

Our second love child, Andy, was born on January 7, 1960.

We were now a family of four with a strangely improving quality of life. The foundations were now well mended and we were quite busy; busy enough to be blessed by an Irish "grandmother" who adopted us en masse to replace her family back home in Ireland.

We all called her "nana." She was a devout Roman Catholic and had a wonderfully easy way of expressing her love for us and for God without seeming to take a breath in between. We were eager for her love but not so keen on her "God."

I should explain that we were loosely connected to a spiritual search that might better explain, to us, the apparent inconsistencies between a loving God and a ruined world. Our way of thinking placed us somewhere between esoteric Buddhism and reincarnation. In short, we would need several lifetimes to help us to eventually make the right choices.

Nana's view of there being just one life and then the judgment was too immediate and uncomfortable because it meant making a decision right now, and we really didn't have the time.

Strangely, we had another close encounter with religion when a local Church of England vicar visited us and suggested that we swap information on our respective beliefs.

I loved our chats...and the man. He was so easy to talk to; he simply sat and listened as I warmed to my subject.

When it came to his turn, he appeared to have much less to say. Everything, for him, revolved around the possibility of having a personal relationship with Jesus Christ.

"It would be like having a one-on-one supper with God," he tried to explain without much success.

Having supper with God was more than my fertile mind could manage. At our last meeting, on leaving, he admitted that his wife was not able to grasp the idea either. I felt sad for him. I wished him well and shut the door.

My evenings with the Wine and Food Society coupled with the national radio program had earned for me a degree of public attention. This resulted in an invitation to speak at a Parent Teachers Association meeting in the small town of Taihape; nearly a three hundred mile round trip on Route One North. We had just purchased our first car, an old Riley that used almost as much engine oil as gasoline! Would it make the trip? I doubted it but went anyway. I mean, live people actually wanted me to speak, and cook!

I packed up my silver flambé lamp and copper pan and promised to repeat the Crepes Suzettes I had cooked for my first customers back in the Roebuck Hotel days when I was sixteen.

I arrived to find an embarrassed PTA president and three parents. Three hundred miles and perhaps a gallon of engine oil...for four people!

I tried, unsuccessfully, to swallow my pride and cooked the crepes, "just for you lot".

As it happened, one of those parents was also a contributor to the very small local newspaper, the Central District Times that was published every Tuesday and distributed free in that somewhat remote area. This eager young lady wanted a "scoop" for her readers and needed an interview.

I had read the Esquire International Cookbook as research for my radio program, so it seemed reasonable to live out my public persona as a "man of the world" and let the local readers regret missing such an important speaker and his delicious crepes. Everyone who attended got one...including me. The recipe made eight!

I entered a kind of Walter Mitty experience. Do you remember the Danny Kaye movie, "The Secret Lives Of Walter Mitty" made in 1947? (It is worth seeing if Netflix has it!)

Well, for the evening, Walter Mitty was me; with my imagination in full flood, I simply slipped into the Savoy Hotel in London and began my career there, instead of at my parent's hotel. My reference book helped me with the name of the chef, Maître Chef des Cuisine Silvano Trompetto, and so...he became my...mentor.

It was all over pretty soon, and I cleaned my copper pan, jumped into the old car and drove the hundred and forty miles, with stops for oil, without giving my invention a second thought.

I never saw the article, but that was not to be the end of the story, by far. This would wait its proper time, which would stretch over many, many years.

Within a month or two I had another request to appear, this time on behalf of the Air Force.

The Battle of Britain is celebrated through the Commonwealth on the third Sunday of September; which, back in 1960, was the 17th. The Air Force was asked to "do something" on that day, or close to it, to celebrate.

On June 1, 1960, the very first TV signal was broadcast in Auckland. It was in this brand new media that the Air Force was to appear.

A jolly fellow who was our Senior Physical Training Instructor had been suggested and approved, but now at the last moment, he had sprained his ankle. And so it fell to me, "he is on radio, so why not," my senior officers thought. I refused. I couldn't imagine anything more impossible. Radio was bad enough, but this was terrifying, and unpaid!

"You are a serving officer in the Air Force and you will do as you are bloody well told." My immediate Senior Officer left me in no doubt. I was it.

On the 14th of September, I packed my silver flambé lamp and a small omelet pan and boarded the Limited Express train for Auckland.

I had all night in which to imagine the worst!

Please join us in the Reflective Readers Club
www.grahamkerr.com/rrc

Rite of Passage Sixteen:
"A Little Larger Than Life" (1960)

With my hen at my side...closer now than at the troubled period of our reuniting, I began to devour everything in sight. I had by now developed a big enough mouth and the speed to chase after "bigger fish to fry."

Occasionally I would pull the tightest turn I could manage and catch a glimpse of my long silvery side. I do believe that I must look pretty impressive as my hen seems to think so, and small fish tend to scatter when I turn up.

So, I guess I am on the way to being of some note in our ever-changing shoal.

An Understanding

Our Chinook is now into his third year, with over a year in the food rich North Pacific Ocean. He is now up to about 4 pounds and over 20 inches in length. He still swims in the company of other salmon and will eat juvenile fish such as northern anchovy, rockfish (when small), Pacific herring and sand lance.

He may occasionally chase and catch a young salmon, though most will be quite a mouthful by the time they may encounter our more than two-year-old with an appetite attitude as he circles the deep waters offshore from Alaska and British Columbia!

1960
I am twenty six years old

Since I was to represent the Air Force, it was decided that I should appear in uniform. I was made up by a young lady who explained that the "real makeup gal is in Aussie gettin' trained."

She then proceeded to encase me in a muddy mask of pancake that glowed orange and appeared to me to flake off in a fine dust every time I smiled which, at first, was not often.

"You'll need this because of the black n' white camera." She then sprayed my hair as stiff as cardboard with a faint sheen.

It was an early talk show format called "On Your Doorstep." The host was a veteran radio man, Ian Watkins, who had taken a blue rinse to help his wonderful head of white hair to escape the same black n' white camera reaction as my apparently dead white face!

The format called for the guest's arrival at yes, you've guessed it, a door...hence the name "On Your Doorstep," which it nearly was. I had to carry all my *stuff* on a tray...silver flambé lamp (alight to save time), copper pan, eggs, cream, etc., etc.

I then had to knock, which meant balancing the lot on one hand.

The door opened and I nearly dropped the lot; this was my first sight of his blue hair. He looked like a Dowager Duchess cross-dressed in a smart tweed suit!

"Come in...COME IN!" He was urging me to break my *deer in the headlights* response.

I set the tray down on a side table that was itself surrounded by daffodils growing out of the studio floor. They were plastic...but here and there they had been "garnished" by two frightened baby lambs (September is spring in New Zealand). A vast mock cherry tree with pink crepe paper blossoms obscured the back drapes—it and the lambs, plus compost, were all props for the next act who would sing "Springtime" into each other's faces while standing very close together. There were only two of these "black n' white" cameras, after all.

I remember NOTHING about that show. I somehow recalled my early tableside behavior at the Roebuck Hotel and felt that I was serving someone, somewhere. I had a story to tell and Ian and I finished off eating the omelet. There it was…serve, tell a story, and eat the food…the basic thrust of all that was to follow.

The next day there was a splendid write up by the newly appointed TV critic John Berry…

"The appearance of Flight Lieutenant Graham Kerr proved to be perhaps the best live show to date. The Air Force should release him to do more television…he is a natural."

The Air Force apparently felt that they had achieved some kind of public relations breakthrough, as they actually encouraged me doing a series on local Wellington television when it began in June 1961. It was actually billed in the TV guide of that era (called the "Listener") as *Eggs with Flight Lieutenant Kerr.*

I performed these episodes at the end of the newsreader's desk, roughly where the sports or weather folk stand or sit nowadays.

My sole source of heat was the flambé lamp again, and I had roughly five min-

Photograph Credit © John J. Grey
of New Zealand Listener, September 1, 1961

utes to show the variety of dishes that the simple egg can provide.

UNBELIEVABLY, I was a success...it actually worked out, and I was asked to do twelve half-hour shows on national television. I would drop the Air Force rank and appear in civilian clothes. So, how should I dress became the big question.

Exactly what I must have been thinking I now have no idea, except that perhaps here was that old issue raising its weary head once again...outward appearance.

The traditional white jacket of the Chef was impossible due to the image orthicon camera that "blossomed" when confronted with white.

My whites would have to be rinsed and dyed a pale blue (like Ian Watkins hair) to make the grade. This could have happened, but then I would have to *pretend* to be a Chef. Having been raised in the company of chefs I knew the difference and I respected that difference. A Chef has an extraordinary daily task of serving and pleasing many people who hopefully return, and by doing so helps the owners to make enough profit to keep a business open. He or she does this in the company of others in a highly pressured environment day in and day out.

Certainly, I too was *involved* with food, but not in such an immediate and essentially commercial way —so I was not, and never have been, entitled to the title of *Chef.*

It was a combination of my past in the hotel business and my present association with the Wine and Food Society that helped me to grasp the idea that having meals with friends at home would be a great way to introduce slightly more adventurous dishes to a nation that had such extraordinarily high quality food of all kinds; livestock, produce and fisheries. Their natural enjoyment came in relatively simple "meat and potato" packages.

Only when it came to baking was there much evidence of culinary innovation.

The experience was described as "Home Entertaining" and so I named this new national TV show...

"Entertaining with Kerr"

I should explain the play on words here. I'm a Scot, and in Scotland the name Kerr is pronounced, "care"...so if you said it out loud it sounded like..."Entertaining with Care." This was all well and good had it not been for the New Zealanders (and many other nations) who pronounce Kerr as "cur." This sounded like either a canine circus act, or an amazing way of serving pet food to friends!

Notwithstanding this title, we hoped that the content would be literally "entertaining" because it was placed between "Peyton Place" and "The Avengers" at 8 p.m. on a Tuesday night. I hasten to add that there was no daytime television. The TV set came to life at about 5 or 6 p.m. and went dead at 10 p.m.

Largely because of my earlier attempt at radio for Woman's Hour and its international culinary flavor, I had gained a reputation for being aware of *good food and wine* and of having the credentials of a "gourmet." This again I found uncomfortable. Surely at 27 years of age, regardless of my hotel background, I didn't have anything like the experience needed to be so highly described.

I did my homework before considering the word as suited to the task ahead. *Gourmet* is essentially a commercial definition that began as a lesser official of the French court. He would taste a vintage wine and give his opinion to the Palace Chef on the kind of food that would go well with that wine.

A London-based wine importer used to place an advertisement in newspapers in which this type of advice was brought up to date and repeated for the British public. It was signed, "The Gourmet."

The advertisement became a popular column and the use of the word "gourmet" began to widen out to encompass all manner of upgrades from fine dining to wooden handles on cookware. Essentially, it had become a marketing gimmick rather than a serious definition of a food "authority." More accurate would have been the word "gourmande," describing an expert in the study and enjoyment of gastronomy. I went along with the word gourmet in lower case because of this understanding.

SO...how does a gourmet (lower case) dress to do a TV show on entertaining?

He dresses as he would when cooking at home for friends.

New Zealanders may have been laid back and warmly hospitable...but they still dressed up in collar and tie and colorful dresses to go to someone else's home for dinner.

I chose a charcoal gray three-piece suit with a double-breasted waistcoat (vest). I did this because when the camera came in for a frontal close up...a regular button-down-the-front vest would be distracting. At least, that was my excuse for having a *different* appearance. Remember how I had wanted to wear a morning coat with a silver-gray tie?

I was paid £25 per episode for the full rights to be played nationally in, as I have said, prime time (not that there was any other time). I did all my own shopping and preparation, and washed up my dishes in the studio men's room.

I was given a producer, Roy Melford, who, like everyone else, was new to this media and decidedly theatrical.

We all agreed that I should be *entertaining*, but what exactly did that mean?

I remember vividly watching several black and white (no color yet) programs made by the BBC (British Broadcasting Corporation). Two stood out and greatly influenced my entire career.

General Sir Brian Horrocks covered the "Great Battles" on a large sand table model with tiny toy soldiers.

John Betjeman, the British Poet Laureate (1972) was famous for his treatise on such matters as Manchester Marsh Gas and its influence on architecture.

He began his lifelong creative pursuit with a book published in the year I was born (1934) called "Ghastly Good Taste."

We had so much in common!

The one thing that the good General and the Poet had in common was... *ENTHUSIASM*...by the bucket full! They were able to make pretty dull stuff come alive.

They became my model...only at that time, for me, it didn't work!

Please join us in the Reflective Readers Club
www.grahamkerr.com/rrc

By now you may have noticed that I have a good appetite and have kept on growing both in size and speed.

This increase has allowed me to go after larger and more active fish that often give me quite a run for my money (whatever that is?)

My hen doesn't even try to keep up, and sometimes it takes awhile for me to retrace my fins to find her.

Recently she swam in front of me just as I was taking off after another very agile feast, and we simply stopped and floated mouth to mouth.

I could see she wasn't pleased and for once I decided to match my speed and agility to her...more graceful style. It felt good, for now at least, until perhaps an especially tempting meal should come within reach?

1961–1962
I am twenty eight years old
The Making of a Name

I made these early episodes entirely on my own with the advice from an extremely theatrical yet inexperienced TV producer. Watching them back with Treena on our small black and white TV set was not much fun.

"My God man," Treena huffed during one especially slow moving episode.

"You have to be the most unutterably boring man in the entire world."

I had turned twenty eight and we had been married for just under seven years...was this the famous "seven year itch?"

I responded to her apparent slight with, "Well, if you are so clever, why don't you produce the show!"

She remained silent until the following Tuesday when I would attempt to break out of my gastronomic shell and be less "boring." The boredom issue arose out of what is often called the "imposter syndrome," a term that was coined in 1978 by Pauline Clance and Suzanne Imes. It occurs among some successful women and men who somehow feel that their achievements have been more due to "luck" than to ability. This may even spill over to the notion that they have been less than truthful; even fraudulent, and that somewhere, at some time, they would be *found out*.

I was feeling this way in 1961, sixteen years before the term "imposter syndrome" was introduced. It was this emerging syndrome that was at the root of my boring performance that flew in the face of the title "*Entertaining* with Kerr."

I discussed Treena's criticism with Roy Melford at our next weekly recording session, and we agreed to see what we could do to *lighten things up a bit*.

During the rehearsal I had shown how to keep peeled potatoes from discoloring by immersing them in a bowl of water with a piece of well-washed coal (it does work!) I lifted the coal out of the glass bowl and commented..."I suppose you could call it coal storage (sounds like cold storage?)"

Roy burst into the studio from the control room flushed with excitement.

"That's it...so this is what we will do!" He rushed on, grabbing the coal from my hand and holding it up between his face and the camera.

"I want you to lift it out of the bowl and say...*you could call this*...and then pause for two heartbeats—raise your left eyebrow—look past the coal at the camera and say *coal storage*. Let's try that!" He was then off to the control room to rehearse me.

I did exactly as I was told and with some degree of trepidation awaited the Tuesday night debut of my less boring personality.

It was AWFUL...truly awful...and Treena actually screamed, something you simply do not do in New Zealand!

"You stupid, stupid man," she stormed. "What on earth possessed you...I'm speechless," which of course she was not. I could not disagree or try to shift the blame...it was AWFUL.

"Well," I said weakly, "like I said last week...why don't you produce the show then!"

"Alright, I will," she replied firmly, and that was that until the next morning when she sailed into the broadcasting house off Lampton Quay in Wellington and announced in no uncertain terms...

"You are ruining my husband. He has a natural sense of humor and your production is... is...pathetic!"

"Alright, Mrs. Kerr...so why don't you produce him," they replied, with disarming logic.

"Okay, I will," she replied. She joined up with me in my as yet undiagnosed "imposter syndrome."

There were now two more of us in the same inexperienced boatful of quasi professionals, all sailing by the seat of our pants into uncharted prime time waters. Imagine how it felt sandwiched between Peyton Place and The Avengers!

My early "Entertaining with Kerr" TV series was limited to twelve episodes a year. The reason for such a brief run was to avoid "personality overexposure". Since there were only about five hours a day of television and only one channel, I could see their point!

Treena's earliest involvement as producer was to arrange for me to rehearse each show before a panel of her theater friends from the Drama Department of the world famous New Zealand (Radio) Broadcasting Corporation (NZBC). They, much like the British Broadcasting Corporation (BBC), had a great many brilliant plays that were distributed worldwide. Many of her friends were expats from England; the rest were very talented locals.

My TV performances were also becoming more polished, thanks to Treena's pals and her insistence that TV was a means of entertainment *first,* and only after having achieved its primary goal could it be allowed to inform. This tension between us never lessened. Even to this day, I remain convinced that everything I say or do must be factually correct and as practically achievable as possible.

Treena, on the other hand, wanted the viewer to find it amusing...even fun!

I took some solace in the fact that both General Sir Brian Horrocks and John Betjeman were both *amusing* in their manner of presentation that was over-the-top enthusiastic.

It was about this time that Robert Beasley, the great young British chef, with the famed private dining club; Monsieur Robert (pronounced Rob-air) came into our lives...big time!

Robert was a genius in the kitchen and a disaster in business!

I was called one chilly mid June morning by a member of the Wine and Food Society, who was also a member of Monsieur Robert's private dining club.

"Graham, I have a favor to ask of you." He was an impressive fellow who just happened to be a Senior Judge.

"I'd like you to come to my court at 10 a.m. tomorrow. I'm hearing a case and I'd like you there."

"Why me?" I inquired, since I had nothing that I knew of that could have remotely been of use in a Court of law.

"Just wait until tomorrow and you'll see for yourself."

I turned up well ahead of time and saw to my surprise that the case involved no less than "Monsieur Robert" himself, Robert Beasley.

Apparently, Robert's fixation with perfect food had gotten him into trouble with the law.

He had a habit of putting his shoes and tins of truffles in the small safe (he valued both highly), and kept the money open in piles on a kitchen bench. Invoices were kept in a kitchen drawer in which they were jammed. Invoices offended Robert because they were not a standard size or color, so they were not given priority in his overall scheme of things gastronomic.

Eventually his suppliers rebelled and insisted on cash. Robert, at this time, was sleeping on the floor in a backroom of this converted house. All he wished to do was cook for his patrons. He had to have cash to get the food he needed.

One day he was clearing his post office box when he noticed that another box was slightly ajar.

He peeked inside to see a number of envelopes addressed to a large department store.

He opened one, still simply curious! It held a check, so did several others.

Robert saw this as purely providential...why not, he needed cash and here it was! Well, almost.

He took the checks and bought small things throughout the store, receiving his change and the cash he had to have to get that day's menu before his members.

The police found him the very next day, and so he now had to account for this apparent (though he didn't really see it that way) transgression.

The Judge was now addressing his courtroom before the trial was to take place.

"I need you all to know that I am a member of the accused's private dining club. I consider him to be a genius at his trade. However, he has much to learn about its administration. Accordingly, I have decided, with the agreement of all parties concerned, to place Mr. Beasley in an unusual form of house arrest for four months." He paused for a moment, spotted me, and gestured with his hand for me to rise.

"This is Flight Lieutenant Graham Kerr, the Chief Catering Advisor to the Royal New Zealand Air Force. Before coming to New Zealand, he was the General Manager of the Royal Ascot Hotel. He is now also the Vice President of the Wine and Food Society." He paused again and looked up.

"Now, Flight Lieutenant Kerr, I have a favor to ask of you."

"Yes, Your Honor," I replied, feeling very visible.

"I would like you to have Mr. Beasley stay in your home for this four-month period and during this time do your best to help him understand how he might better administer his undoubted talent." He paused again with a questioning look.

I really had no alternative. With every eye upon me, including Robert's cool gaze.

"Why...er...well," I stumbled. The truth was that our small flat on Oriental Parade was only barely enough for my family let alone a ward-of-the-court...who might cook...in my... tiny kitchen!

"Well, will you or won't you?" The Judge was becoming impatient.

"Very well, we will, Your Honor," I replied softly and sat down.

"Excellent...so ordered!" The Judge slammed his gavel down and the deal was done.

It was not an easy time for any of us.

That evening I cooked a simple supper. At the table, Robert asked, "Is this the best you can do?"

"No," I replied, "but it is as good as it is likely to get."

"Then I had better cook," he replied disdainfully.

And cook he did, mostly alone in our small back kitchen on a gas stove that leaned alarmingly to one side. This allowed for relatively fat-free frying, as the pan tilted to the left, draining fat from meat.

He had asked to be alone, so we left him to it.

The food was wonderful. I hesitated for a day or two from saying so, but in the end I could see that this might be a great two-way street.

"Tell you what," I started.

"I will trade you for my advice on administration if you will let me into my kitchen to see you at work."

He agreed, reluctantly. It was, after all, a very small space.

Eventually he began to explain what he was doing, and as he warmed more to his subject than to me, he literally became the food being cooked.

He described the feeling of hot oil on a slice of onion as its volatile oil sacs ruptured at above 300° F.

He visibly swelled as he absorbed a great stock and, as a single grain of rice, became a pilaf.

As a steak, he took on the "Maillard-effect" aromas of seared animal protein.

As butter, he melted gradually to a froth surface and sediment base in order to become clarified.

Up to this time the culinary world that I had observed and participated in since I was a child was a good-natured professional trade practice. What I was now seeing was a deeply felt and understood art form that embraced both science and creativity.

Robert Beasley, over his brief confinement, changed my life.

I, unfortunately, did not do so well for his. We lost track of him when we heard that he was painting lines down rural country roads.

I should love to hear that he was able to return to his art.

You see...I'm simply grateful and would like to tell him so.

We had, following this time, moved from Oriental Parade to Clifton Terrace. We needed more space and could *just* afford the ground floor apartment of a duplex fashioned out of former Prime Minister Seddon's old family home. Seddon, sometimes called "King Dick," was the 15th Prime Minister of New Zealand from 1893 to 1906.

His home, on Clifton Terrace, up the hillside on the west side of the harbor, wasn't exactly awe inspiring and was, after our time, entirely removed to make way for the Wellington Urban Motorway.

We turned the large front living room, with its wide windows overlooking the docks and the harbor beyond, into a kitchen/dining room in which I could test, develop and later photograph dishes for what would become an international bestselling cookbook.

The back of the kitchen was planked in yellow-knotted pine that was stained to a walnut shade and then polished with Kiwi dark brown boot polish! We used dozens and dozens of cans, and we did it plank by plank with our own hands...it took hours!

Please join us in the Reflective Readers Club
www.grahamkerr.com/rrc

Rite of Passage Eighteen:
"More of the Same, But More So" (1962)

Okay, I admit it...I'm a big eater. There is so much food swimming about, and so many new tastes and textures.

It doesn't seem to be doing me any harm. I feel stronger and I can swim longer and faster, either to catch a meal or escape becoming one.

From the admiring glances of our shoal it also seems that I'm bigger than they are, certainly longer than my hen...but not as comfortably rounded. I've always admired that about her.

I can see the bright surface above, but being a Chinook we spend much of our time deeper down in the waters than the other salmon, sometimes encountering species such as squid or prawns to eat but still largely preferring the chase of schooled baitfish. For the moment I am simply glad there are no more black and white monsters and that's a relief...but will they return...and where...and when?

An Understanding

A great deal of research and data collection has taken place on the migration routes taken by each type of salmon that even differs by their river of origin. It would seem from the charts that our individuals remain most of their adult lives in the Gulf of Alaska, eastward paralleling the extent of the Aleutian Chain, south to northern Vancouver Island, and west to the edge of the continental shelf off Southeast Alaska and northern British Columbia.

Our salmon happens to be in a period of good ocean conditions and abundant food but it can also mean that predators are numerous as well, and none more deadly than the Orca (black and white monsters) whose ranging schools often intercept the lines of salmon migrating throughout this region making for a pretty dangerous existence when they are also looking for a snack.

1962
I am still twenty eight years old

Our time in New Zealand was a rich a la carte of unusual opportunities that would never have happened elsewhere, especially in "Old Europe" or the "Brave New World" of the Americas. For each of these fresh experiences we shall be forever grateful.

On my second day, back in September 1958, I had dropped by the Officer's Mess Kitchen at Shelly Bay, a few miles out of town near the end of Wellington International Airport.

Sitting on the floor was a forty pound case of cauliflower. I immediately asked why there was so much when there were only ten officers at the time. Four pounds per head was unlikely, even with savage trimming!

"It's easier to send a whole case than divide it up and weigh it at both ends," I was told by the Corporal Storekeeper.

"But surely that's a waste?" I observed.

"Oh well, we've got plenty of food out here," he replied cheerfully. He didn't need to add that he felt certain that, as a very new arrival, I was accustomed to being half-starved.

As I toured all the airbases and quietly observed the way all this "abundant" food was handled, it was clear to me that there was enormous waste, very little creativity, and almost no pride in doing a job well. Most of all, I wanted an improvement in *status* for those under my leadership. I wanted them to be regarded as true professionals and admired by other service personnel. It took a while because change in the Armed Forces doesn't happen overnight anywhere (unless there is a coup!)

I introduced the ICA (Incentive Catering Allowance); *incentive* because there was no way in which to reward the amount of extra work and attention to detail that was needed in order to reduce the habitual waste.

The Air Force catering system was based on a "standard price list." A fairly limited number of foods were each given one price; say tomatoes were 89p for a pound, and flour was 20p per pound. These prices were averaged out over all the bases so that each kitchen had the same food range at the same price...regardless of local or seasonal conditions.

From memory, we had, say, 50 pennies (we were still in New Zealand currency at this time) for each person for one day. I reasoned that if they spent less, say, down to 40 pennies per day, that they could use half of what was left...10 divided by 2 equals 5 pennies, on anything they could get their hands on *locally* which had to be purchased at the very best price.

It worked wonderfully...everyone tried really hard in order to get their hands on duck, rock lobster, red wine, mushrooms; the list of truly wonderful local foods was amazing.

The food standards went through the roof, not just the variety. I saw cooks use stop watches to time potatoes through a potato peeler in order to cut down bruising that dissolved during boiling and flushed otherwise good food down the drains. Meat thermometers were used to get the exact degree at which meat was cooked...thus avoiding overcooking and shrinkage through evaporation. So even "meat and potatoes" were cooked much better and enjoyed more, and my cooks were being more highly regarded as *professionals* who were good at their job.

Add in the occasional *luxury*, the red wine added to roast gravy; duck and shrimp rice dishes and fresh fruit with local cheese...amazing!

This sort of thing, however, couldn't go on for long.

We were saving several thousand pounds on our budget and this worried my Senior Officers for two reasons.

The first was..."why did we spend so much in the past (relatively speaking) when we were in charge?"

The second was..."if we don't spend it on food this year the budget will be trimmed by that amount next year."

Remember, all I wanted was *status* for my cooks and, I suspect, for myself as well. The money really wasn't the motive.

On top of these concerns came the clincher; the Army and the Navy complained that we obviously ate at a far higher standard than their systems allowed.

"What do we have to do to stop you doing this?" My Group Captain inquired as he gave me the news that my ICA system would have to stop. I was only a few heartbeats away from threatening to become a whistle blower and going to the press with my self-righteous savings to prove my rebellion.

"We can't pay you to stop it, so what do you WANT?" He was clearly frustrated with my reluctance to agree.

What an opportunity...could it have happened anywhere else in the world?

"Well Sir," I replied (a completely new idea was flooding into my mind as I spoke), you could provide me with a test and development kitchen, a Senior Warrant officer and two cooks and I will create a cookbook for the entire Armed Forces in New Zealand."

They agreed—amazingly—they agreed!

The ICA stopped but many of the earlier cost savers remained and a few more foods were added to the standard price list...and my cooks retained their professionalism.

I got my team of three, complete in a well-equipped kitchen.

Over the years that remained in my service, I conducted tests that compared seventy three basic methods of cooking such as boiling, braising, roasting, shallow and deep frying, etc., etc.

The idea was to find the "best of the basics" that had ever been described and taught by anyone…worldwide.

As the Armed Forces book went forward, so did mine, at home. I would get up early at 4 a.m. and work on my book until 6 a.m.

My first book was "Entertaining with Kerr," and I set out to record the recipes I had used in both radio and television over the earlier years up until 1963.

The second book, one very much in the making at our test and development kitchen in the Air Force, would become known as *The Graham Kerr Cookbook* in New Zealand and Australia where it won a gold medal at the International Culinary Olympics in Frankfurt in 1968.

This basic work would eventually be called *The Graham Kerr Cookbook*, by the Galloping Gourmet, and was republished by Doubleday in the U.S. and worldwide in 1969.

In the introduction to the worldwide edition I wrote a simple, yet essentially accurate, introduction that summed up much of my life at that time.

"Traditions are useful as armor against professional attack—they are also a form of self-induced contentment created by stamping up and down on one spot— getting nowhere, risking little, and achieving an immortal zero.

I regard my move to New Zealand as the most important step in my life. New Zealand, unlike any other "Western" nation, did not have culinary tradition to return to—that is, apart from her rich farming heritage. There was no establishment to carp, criticize, or snigger. There was a desire to learn and, above all, a love for the practical. New Zealanders are essentially a great practical people who are not in the least concerned with status.

I lived and worked in this refreshing climate of opinion for seven years, and it was during that time that this book was written. It was born from a desire to question, to compare, to experiment, and to decide—an equation of great importance to all cooks.

It had occurred to me that all cookery could be broken down into three simple stages.

The ingredients

Their preparation before cookery

Their assembly by using a method of cookery

It was the last stage that interested me the most—after all, the ingredients are a matter of taste, cutting a matter of skill, but a method of cookery should be a practical matter and not necessarily subject to international culinary traditions.

I set to work to examine every possible "method" by which food is cooked and attempted to reduce the variety to a few basic, often used "methods."

I then undertook a study of comparative tests in which I literally conducted my own bake-off. Eventually, after some four years, I discovered those methods that suited me best.

Over the years that have followed, these "methods" have been constantly revised in an attempt to keep them practical.

At the date of publication of this book I know of no easier, no more satisfactory method of achieving a well-cooked dish. But I am equally certain that, in the years to come, our advances in food technology and kitchen appliances will require revision being made.

So, until that day comes along, I present to you my experience and enthusiasm—for it is all I have to offer."

"All I have to offer." That's the way it has always been, a mix of enthusiasm and a growing experience...testing, tasting...testing, tasting...driven on out of a tricky combination of a fascination with pleasure and achievement, and fear of failure.

The more I studied and compared results, the less concerned I became with being an imposter. Life was gradually becoming better. I was growing in both understanding and stature.

Then suddenly three bombshells landed in quick succession, which were to change everything that appeared to be so orderly.

The Air Force dropped the first bomb, which seems to be perfectly natural behavior!

I was summoned by my Group Captain who didn't ask me to sit.

"It has been reported at the Air Board that you recently used foul language whilst in a drunken state in front of members of the opposite sex."

He didn't add...how plead you? ...but that's what it looked like as he looked at me over his glasses, a look I recalled vividly as like the one used by my House Master when I was "late for God."

I flushed, and my skin felt as though it had become radiant. I began to sweat, unable to respond.

"Where...?" I managed to gasp.

"For diplomatic reasons that must not be revealed," he answered.

"However," he added, "the Air Board has unanimously agreed that my request for extension of your service will, as a result, be denied."

I had been found guilty as charged and my accusers left hidden for "diplomatic reasons." My shock dissolved into disbelief...*where...how*...were my inner questions but ones that were beyond answer, at least right then.

I left his office abruptly without closing the door and immediately sought out my closest friends and fellow officers. Not one had ever seen me evenly remotely drunk or even intoxicated. I had occasionally used a "swear" word, but *never* in front of women.

They all seemed as shocked as I was.

My shock gradually became anger, my anger to an overwhelming sense of injustice.

I returned to the Group Captain.

"Sir," I began in as measured a tone as I could manage.

"I should like to apply for a *redress of wrongs* allowed for in military justice."

"I need to have a formal written apology from the Air Board and all reference to my supposed behavior stricken from my record.

Again, that over-the-glasses look, "Sit down Kerr." He gestured to the chair in front of his desk.

"If you pursue this course, you will forever be known for your (he hunted for an appropriate word) for your *supposed behavior* rather than a possible apology."

"But Sir!" I now felt anger toward him too. "This is so damn unfair. I'm accused, yet I can't confront my accuser!"

"Exactly, and you never will," he added abruptly.

I left his office that day with less than two years left to serve and at that moment all sense of loyalty to anyone else but my friends and my cooks lay in shreds.

Any even remote possibility of extending my service contract was at an end. I now began to plan deliberately for the way I would provide for my family from 1964 onward.

Much, much later (as I shall report to you) I was told that a Junior Catering Officer had gotten drunk at a party in the French Embassy, had used awful language and had pretended to be "The Chief Catering Advisor." The French Ambassador complained to a Senior Air Force Officer and asked that it not become public, and so I was judged and found guilty as charged without recourse.

At that time, and really ever since, my respect for "their" system evaporated. I simply dismissed the Service and began to see the whole issue in really positive ways...without that event, I reasoned, I might have remained where I was comfortable?

The second bombshell was from a genuine press misquote that also proved to be hugely upsetting and eventually a blessing!

I was quoted from a speech at the Wine and Food Society as saying, "Unfortunately, most hotel staff in New Zealand are criminals, drifters and misfits."

The hotel/restaurant workers union went ballistic and threatened to sue me, the Society, even the Air Force; who were certainly unprepared at that time to rush to my defense.

I called the union chief in Auckland. After silently enduring his considerable wrath, I was able to speak...

"The Press missed two words and the context," I ventured.

"So, what were they?" He asked suspiciously.

"*Regarded as,* and my point was that they needed a nationally organized training system."

Silence...

"You said *regarded as criminals,* etc." He was more measured.

"Yes, Sir, I did...and (I added with enthusiasm) that they need a hotel school to help train them as...professionals."

That led surprisingly to my being appointed as a "Special Advisor to the Ministry of Education for Hotel Training." I served alongside the Union Leader and we became reasonably good friends.

Once again, it was a question of status for a generally poorly regarded class of worker... the cook and those who stand and serve so many others every day of their lives. This had become a major concern for me and unlike anywhere else on earth; I was actually getting the opportunity to make a real difference. Of course, a good deal of this was happening because of my presence on television.

The term *Celebrity Chef* had not yet been coined and in New Zealand there were very few TV personalities...just a shoal of newts on their own journey to be small frogs in a medium puddle.

I had just been awarded one of the first of the "Penguins," an award given in New Zealand that recognized local productions, a little like a tadpole-sized Emmy.

As the news rippled out, it was hardly *breaking.* There was a new TV reporter for the New Zealand Herald...the major national newspaper. I thought her name sounded familiar...she was the self-same amateur journalist who covered my earlier Crepes Suzette demonstration lecture in Taihape. She had kept her old notes from that interview and used them to cover my Penguin Award as "Personality of the Year".

There it was in plain type for the nation to scan into its collective memory. The new-found *Celebrity Cook* had been trained at the Savoy in London under no less a celebrity as Maitre Chef des Cuisines Silvano Trompetto.

An idle, self-serving "conceit" in a small country town in a remote nation was now a matter of record, one that would be repeated again and again as well-meaning journalists searched my public record without ever checking at the reported source.

Talk about status?

Please join us in the Reflective Readers Club
www.grahamkerr.com/rrc

Rite of Passage Nineteen:
"Keeping to the Cold Waters" (1963–1964)

Our more depleted shoal began a slow turn several dark surfaces ago. I felt it myself. The water had become slightly warm and the schools of baitfish began to diminish. As if of one mind, we all turned back north toward the colder currents of abundance that guided us to a continuous supply of food.

A good fat fish is quite tasty but messy, and I always like to finish what I start. It seems such a waste to take a good bite and leave the rest to the scavengers.

My hen eats less compulsively than I, and while she continues to grow (I think she gets easier to look at), I must now be twice her size. (Males tend to exaggerate!)

An Understanding

The Chinook's ocean migration may take as long as four to five years and may involve several rotations of the North Pacific, although no one knows this for sure, before the pull of sexual maturation sends them back homeward to their river and specific spawning area of origin.

Their senses would suggest time by the arrival and departure of surface light. Their ability to feel the water temperatures could also cause them to adjust their direction, as would the absence or abundance of prey.

Our Chinooks are now in their fifth year when really robust eaters may be over 40 pounds and more than 40 inches in length.

No wonder he is pleased with himself...on the other hand, his very size and appetite is beginning to attract those who hunt for just such a trophy as this.

1963 to 1964
I am thirty years old

I remained deeply upset by the injustice served me by the Air Force. It simply wouldn't go away. I continued with my research on the cookbooks, for the Armed Forces and for myself, but in all other respects I began to plan ahead.

During my W.O.S.B. (War Office Selection Board) as an officer in the British Army, we had to solve an obstacle as a team (men only in those days), and see who could overcome a practical problem and then who might emerge as a leader who could make the solution happen.

In those bygone years the obstacle was a ten-foot wide "bottomless chasm" (actually four feet deep). The task was an "atomic bomb" (actually a 40-gallon oil drum half filled with water). All we had were two nine-foot long heavy planks and a twenty-foot coil of rope.

The answer was to bind up the planks, allowing one foot on each bank and an eight-foot overlap. We got it done!

Now I faced another "bottomless chasm" with a team of four...myself, Treena, Tessa and Andy; that was it!

We had to go from a secure government post where I had the freedom to do limited outside work in the media, to a media-only life which appeared to be seriously limited to the twelve episodes a year that brought in £25 each episode out of which I had to pay for the food! Clearly, this did not appear to be a tempting career opportunity. I began to piece together what "planks" I would add and see where they might overlap in the last of my five years of Air Force service.

Any television program, even those of today, can rely upon one simple and often obvious fact...it's called *placement.* Food is needed and so is equipment. The folks who produce food are interested when one uses their product, and so are those who make saucepans, knives, and several gadgets, the more visually unique the better. While trade names and labels may well be either unmentioned or taped over, their sheer use in a demonstration tends to prompt consumer awareness and even a purchase.

In these early days it was like the Wild West. There were very few rules, and so connections were made between myself and producers and manufacturers. It was all above board, yet not often mentioned. There wasn't any money that changed hands, as with formal advertising, but what took place was a series of consultations during which I sold my advice on marketing in general. This grew at such a pace during my last year in the Air Force that I formed a small private company to validate the "placement" issue and convert it into consultation. I called myself...New Zealand Food Consultants (Pty) Ltd.

Within several months I had paid opportunities to serve many of the New Zealand Primary Produce Boards and an additional eight major companies. Buoyed by this success, I negotiated a space in the New Zealand Display Center. I laid out a New Zealand Food and Wine Center that had a television demonstration set that looked the same as my front room in Clifton Terrace with the same "boot-polished" planks. Clustered about the studio were twenty six booths shaped like gothic arches that displayed my clients' produce and equipment. Public demonstrations were given, both on television and to those who dropped by, to be "informed and entertained". A young wine man, John Buck, joined me and with matching enthusiasm to my food, he became the wine authority.

The Display Center was the perfect *overlapping of planks*. The combined income from consultancy and display rental was sufficient to carry our family across the *bottomless pit* of the immediate future.

I followed this early success with the first ever New Zealand National Food and Wine Fair in Christchurch. It was this exhibition that caught the attention of New Zealand-born impresario, Harry M. Miller, a hugely successful agent based in Sydney, Australia.

By this time, I had very quietly and with great relief, left the Air Force.

Harry M. Miller was, to the best of my knowledge, a nonreligious Jewish promoter of all matters theatrical that included the great world-class concert artists of the day and nationally known *Tonight Show*-styled personality hosts such as Australia's Graham Kennedy.

Harry saw in me what Treena had seen and was nurturing behind the scenes with her theatrical friends, all of whom pitched in with great advice on how I might use my gifts to serve, tell a story and provide a tasty outcome.

It was Harry who would take us to another level altogether and charm us along the bumpy road with an amazing mix of humor, enthusiasm, exploitation and eventually, theater.

It all began with a phone call from Australia.

"Is that Mr. Graham Kerr?" The operator pronounced my name "care," not "cur." "Would you please hold for Mr. Harry M. Miller?" Yes, she used his entire name as she had correctly pronounced mine.

"Graham?" The voice was warm and brisk. "This is Harry." He didn't use his full name.

"I've been watching your shows in New Zealand and wondered if you'd like to give Australia a go?" His accent was not as soft as New Zealand nor as hard as the Australian accent can sometimes be.

I was literally stunned...Australia was HUGE and I was already pretty *stretched* in New Zealand.

He continued with what was, for him, a completed plan.

"You would need to do a pilot series of thirteen episodes, and if they went well, you would then move over here and do thirty nine a year."

I found my voice.

"Mr. Miller"...I started.

"Oh, do call me Harry...*please.*" There was that easy warmth again.

"Er...Harry...um...really, I'm very busy here these days and I could never leave New Zealand, and..."

"Graham, of course, I completely understand...so you just do thirteen episodes..." and then he used the tactic that was to rule my entire life for the next thirty six years.

"What's the most money you can think of for one episode?" He asked, quite softly. I thought about my £25 with New Zealand television and blurted out..."£400" (The Australian and New Zealand pound were then equal to the US dollar)

"Umm, that's a bit steep but I'll see what I can do." He promised to call me back.

This meant over five thousand pounds for perhaps two weeks' work using recipes I already had!

Within a day Harry came back.

"Okay, I did it...you get £400 an episode and I've booked you on Qantas. You'll stay at the Hilton at Kings Cross in Sydney." He paused for my reaction.

My mind was racing ahead and it felt completely unreal; uncharted waters...not only uncharted but dangerous?

"When?" was all I could manage.

"Soon as possible...how does it look for you?"

"How long will it take?" I asked, playing for time.

"Ten days. I'll need what you want for a kitchen set layout, and my designer will put it together...allow two weeks for that...say, this time next month? Come over on Friday to chat with my director."

I looked at my diary. It was possible with a few minor changes.

"Okay, so Friday it is. I'll need to be back in two weeks," I added as my only contribution.

"Good-O, that's fine. Get me your set layout as soon as possible and we'll do the pilot series."

Click...I was left looking at the phone as though it was about to strike!

Treena was encouraging. No, she didn't need to come. She had already been involved with the New Zealand production and this would be the same content.

I sent off the plans, identical to the front room and the Display Center kitchen, and gathered up my notes and recipes for thirteen episodes...wondering what Australia would make of my decidedly British, or "Pome" personality.

Harry made several calls in the weeks before filming. His designer had added a dining room with a French door looking out over a nighttime scene of Sydney Harbor. The kitchen was upgraded with a Westinghouse range and refrigerator.

"You'll love it!" He exclaimed. "The dining room is so that you can serve your food to a celebrity guest...I'll fix that for you."

This was to prove to be Harry's main strength. He was always on the lookout for an upgrade where he might somehow benefit. By adding the dining room he could get free public relations for his visiting artists who would join me at the table and promote their appearance.

Now I had to become a host/interviewer as well as an entertaining cook!

I simply went along for the ride. After all, it was only thirteen episodes and then I'd be home. In two weeks I would be able to buy our very first new car...ever!

The filming went well enough. I never worried that it might possibly fail...I *knew* that I would!

Australia was a huge culture shock after New Zealand. It was fast-paced, glittering, even brash in its energetic creativity. I did what I'd come to do, and clutching my cheque I flew home to be embraced by the familiar.

"So, how did it go?" Treena was bubbling over with the good news that she too had had an interesting offer during my absence...but wanted to hear from me first.

"I think it went well. I met all kinds of artists and they enjoyed the food. I don't think I'm really suited for that kind of life. So, tell me your news." I asked, smiling. I reached forward to hold her hand.

Both of her hands flew up in the air. She stood and twirled around. "I've been offered a part at Downstage Theater...back on stage, live!" She was so excited.

I sat still and remembered the small backyard garden at the Woolpack Hotel in Tenterden, Kent, in England, where I had proposed to Treena when I was just twenty. I had reasoned at that time, that I didn't have what it took to be the husband of a star, which I was quite sure that she could become. I knew I'd find it hard to find a place in her theatrical world.

Now it was a switch. She had agreed to give up that life to simply be my wife and, as a result, had greatly helped to get me into a somewhat theatrical spotlight. Now it was her turn again. Since I was a more "substantial" being; how did I now feel about her return to the boards?

It felt the same...

I saw the life in her, the vitality, the joy, and I knew that I could never compete because my competitor this time wasn't flesh and blood...it was grease paint and applause.

I was, on the other hand, only one stage beyond being "the most unutterably boring man in the entire world."

In Australia I had thought of my television future as a possible failure. Now I faced the same future for my marriage. Of course I couldn't let her know this...she was way too thrilled at the prospect.

"Great, good for you!" I gave her a hug to hide my face and its sense of loss.

The Australian television version of "Entertaining with Kerr" went to air early in 1964 when I was just thirty years old. It was put on at 9:30 p.m. on SAS 10, a new network that had only recently been added to the other three. The switchboard was jammed that night as hundreds of people reacted to the program. "Take that fruitcake off the air" was pretty much the overall opinion.

I had replaced professional soccer and this infuriated the legions of soccer fans that had come to live in Sydney. The program manager looked at the extraordinary response and made a most unusual decision.

"This much emotion is going to get the show talked about...the more talk the more free publicity...let's stoke the fire and see."

So stoke they did, both SAS 10 and Harry M. Miller, and behold the blaze began, albeit artificially, to burn ever brighter. The soccer fans were given a new night and I stayed put... gathering viewers that further fanned the flames.

Harry called.

"Quick, pack your bags...I've sold a series of twenty six episodes at five times your original fee. The ratings are great...it's a winner!" He was genuinely delighted, almost as amazed as I was.

Five times £400 was £2000 an episode, or £52,000. That was much, much more money than I had ever thought might be possible for...anything!

"I'll have to consider it, Harry. I told you, I really don't think..."

"Stop *thinking*," he shouted. "Get moving! Take my word for it, you are on your way...big time!" He was now almost pleading.

"I'll call you back." I was quite quiet.

"Soon!" He replied.

Click.

Please join us in the Reflective Readers Club
www.grahamkerr.com/rrc

Rite of Passage Twenty: "The Storm" (1965–1966)

I feel like I've been here before.

It reminds me of my early days when I swam with the waters and could see the bottom and sides of my world. I welcomed times of sudden cool when the brightness above me became a shadow. If I turned on one side to look up for a reason, I would see a tall green thing that seemed to move gently.

I'm moving in their midst but they are now with me. They go all the way to the rocky bottom and great clouds of tiny treats...all kinds of dwellers, appear, for the most part, to have found a place of peace.

Little brown furry creatures with round heads and big eyes use strange fins to carry off sharp pointed balls of spikes...why, I can't imagine.

It's so thick with the great green towers that I've lost sight of my hen. We got separated in a sudden up-and-down with the surface all broken and gray and white. We swam to this place to hide until it stopped.

It seems more peaceful here?

Like before, I'm sure we will see each other again. It's a big space, and yet such a special feeling must keep us looking out for one another...surely?

An Understanding

Our salmon has reached one of the National Marine Sanctuaries of the Northwest coast.

What he saw in his early days were the trees on the riverbanks that provided welcome shade on warm, sunny days. What he sees now are giant bull kelp (macrocystis pyrifera and nereocystis luetkeana) that grow in literal underwater forests close to the coastline in depths of six to ninety feet.

The little furry things are sea otters and their favorite food is the sea urchin (strongylocentrotus). By carrying them off from the rocks they clear space for the kelp to begin their sometimes giant size.

Our faithful pair got separated in a Pacific storm and even like huge whales, found a relatively peaceful place amongst this true sanctuary.

1965
I am thirty one years old

I was about to enter the greatest, most damaging, painful storm of my life...one where it would take almost nine years to find a sanctuary. There are natural storms and there are storms of consequence caused by human choice. Both cause devastating ruin, both physical and emotional. One such physical storm was to take place nineteen years later on September 18, 2004. I take this leap forward to help me try to understand why I made the human choices that resulted in so much ruin.

Let me tell you what was to happen...how I wish that I had then had the understanding that this tragedy eventually provided.

The place is Gonaives in Haiti. People had gathered in this quiet valley, sheltered by a tree-covered series of large hills for about four hundred years. During this time they harvested the trees to make charcoal, which they used for fuel to cook their simple meals. As their numbers grew so did their need for fuel and so they uprooted the nearby trees from even the steeper slopes, even higher, until much of one large hill was almost bare.

Tropical storm Jeanne drenched the Northwest coast of the island. It continued to rain for many hours. The steep hillside that overshadowed the township gradually absorbed the water until it could absorb no more...in minutes it sagged and gave way, becoming a huge river of viscous mud. More than one thousand men, women and children lost their lives on that dreadful day. It had taken hundreds of years to uproot that sheltering forest, and only minutes to cause such a catastrophe.

The force of the natural storm combined with generations of human choices was the actual cause. It took both to result in so much pain and loss.

I was about to uproot the *trees of virtue* that had, to this date, sheltered me from the occasional temptation/storm that life and its hormones provide. Certainly there had been pain caused to others and by others, but there was, to my knowledge, no ruin.

This was about to change...

I had to scramble to film another twenty six episodes. Remember, I only did twelve a year and this would clean me out...still at £52000 and all expenses paid!

John Buck was of two minds about my doing another trip so soon.

"What about the Display Center? We've got a lot of clients now, mostly food companies, and I'm a wine-only guy."

"John, it took just ten days last time and that included the new set, so this time I can do two a day in just over two weeks...no problem!"

I called most of our clients to see what they might think and all of them were actually *impressed.* Some even suggested that this could be used to help promote primary produce exports to Australia, and even beyond.

My only deep concern was Treena. She had no reservation at all. After all, her theater work was going very well and she had landed a lead role in *"Oh, What a Lovely War"* which had started as a radio play by Charles Chilton and had been taken to the stage in 1963. It was later to become a major movie in 1969. Treena got to sing the music hall song that gave the show its name...and she *loved* it!

So...there was my concern. She loved the role and the opportunity, the greasepaint and the applause. Both of us had starring roles, an audience for Treena and £52000 for me. It troubled me, but I had to make the choice, regardless.

The uprooting of virtue had begun.

VIRTUE (Latin: virtus – Ancient Greek: "arête," is moral excellence. A virtue is a positive trait or quality deemed to be morally good and thus is valued as a foundation of principle and good moral being. Personal virtues are characteristics valued as promoting collective and individual greatness.

The opposite of virtue is vice. (Source: Wikipedia)

I had not, at this time, considered the word *virtue* and its possible meanings, and it would take many years before I did. My primary goal in life was simple...try as best as possible to avoid failure.

My understanding of failure was also very sparse. All I needed to do was record twenty six television episodes, take my money and get back home. I hoped, of course, that the programs I made would continue to be measurably watched, especially by those that represented the ratings. If I could also avoid being adversely criticized by my fellow cooks...so much the better!

My first virtue was uprooted before I left New Zealand when I picked up my air ticket at the Qantas desk. I had been "upgraded" to first class. I was at first surprised, then delighted! There was a small VIP lounge set aside for, well, *very important people*. I was invited to await the flight with a complementary glass of champagne.

I now understand that "humility" is being known for whom one is, and that as a direct opposite, "pride" is wanting to be known for whom one is not! I most willingly became a very important person, at least in my own eyes, in this privileged space to which I was completely unaccustomed.

My upgrade was my first uproot...I had begun to lose sight of who I was.

On arrival at Kingsford Smith Airport in Sydney, Australia, I had my second virtue uproot.

I stood in line to pass through Customs.

A quite large Senior Customs Officer with several rings up his uniformed sleeve called me out of the line.

"Mr. Kerr." He spoke firmly and took my arm, leading me to a quiet space.

"Yes...er...what's the matter?" I'm always nervous when confronted with uniformed authority.

"Oh, nothing at all," he replied with a big smile. "I just wanted the privilege of marking your bag myself."

He drew a chalk mark on my suitcase with a flourish and stood back to admire his handiwork. I too was looking, not at his chalking, but at my suitcase. It was old, made of some green fiber and held together by a much-used leather strap.

I felt ashamed of it...*immediately!*

"I'm a huge fan of yours," the Senior Customs Officer continued. "It's a great show, just wanted to pass you through myself."

He then gave me a wink and told me, "your Rolls Royce limousine is waiting just outside the door." He gestured just beyond our quiet space to a special VIP exit. I reached for my green fiber case, only to have it taken up by my new fan who handed it over to the chauffeur who seemed (to me) unable to accept that it belonged to me...or that it should be put in his limousine.

We purred off into the traffic and silently made our way to Kings Cross. It is said of a Rolls Royce that the loudest sound you hear is the dash-mounted clock. A Rolls Royce has a way of attracting attention on arrival at an important hotel. It is a merger of status symbols and doormen tend to almost leap in a gliding style to open the door, welcome the VIP to the hotel and then beckon a bellman to take the luggage from the trunk.

I was unknown by the doorman and my suitcase was equally unknown by the bellman.

"Is this...*yours* Sir?" he inquired.

It was now increasingly hard to admit but it held important program notes, so...

"Yes." I tried to appear important. "It is mine."

I was told that I had been checked in and would be taken directly to the Penthouse suite. The bellman, my bewildered self, and my old green fiber suitcase with leather strap and chalk mark made it in one mighty swoosh from bottom to top. I went up physically, but not with any inner understanding. Was all this really happening...*to me?*

The Penthouse had ceiling-to-floor plate glass windows overlooking Darling Point, where the iconic Sydney Opera House is located, and referred to by locals as "a clutch of nuns." The suite was carpeted in deep ivory shag, as was the designer custom back in the early '70s. It was deep enough for snowshoes.

"Where shall I put...*this?*" He held my suitcase between fingers that seemed unwilling to actually surround the handle. I gestured to the bed, and gave him an apparently insufficient tip. I sat down on the bed next to my suitcase and looked out over the dazzling array of lights with the harbor beyond.

It was all too much, too soon.

I sat there and cried...what was I doing here?

Harry M. Miller understood how to treat his "artists." He had arranged the entire transfer from New Zealand to the Penthouse so that I would be somehow transformed into an emerging important person who might be given enough taste of the privileged life to become hungry for it to continue. Such people begin, as I did that night, to imagine that I actually might become an important person...even perhaps a *very* important person who travels first class. But to do this, my old green fiber suitcase

would have to be replaced...uprooted, cast off, never to reappear. Who I was when I left home and what I thought I knew about virtue was being torn out of the ground, roots and all.

The very next morning I walked up to fashionable Kings Cross and purchased an extremely expensive leather "portmanteau," a large (enough) suitcase to have two equal sections, one for clothing, the other for traveling necessities, whatever they were?

It suited my new persona as an international traveler; a guest at famed hotels who was never to arrive in a...taxi!

I made it to the studios that afternoon, along with Harry, to meet the show's new sponsors.

Harry had explained that, unlike New Zealand's noncommercial network, Australia had three highly competitive commercial television networks and one that was publicly owned.

I would be paid considerably more than New Zealand because of the "commercial content." For this to work for everyone's benefit, I was to do commercials for the sponsors. In return for this extraordinary opportunity, Harry told me that he intended for me to receive the "lion's share" of all remuneration. "You deserve your 60 percent." He patted me on the back like a good and trusted fellow worker.

The next virtue was now loosened and about to be torn from the hillside of my understanding.

"Every man has his price." This is not true, but for every man there exists a bait which he cannot resist swallowing. To win over certain people to something, it is only necessary to give it a gloss of humanity, nobility, gentleness, self-sacrifice...and there is nothing you cannot get them to swallow. To their souls, this is the icing, the tidbit...other kind of souls have others.

(Source: Friedrich Nietzsche, *"Poor Man's College"*)

I was highly resistant to media advertising. My entire exposure to broadcasting media had been free of commercial announcements, which, as a result, I considered both crass and demeaning. Now here I was being told that there really was no other way to proceed. You either speak up or shut up, and what you speak was somebody else's message with which one may not necessarily agree!

There was an already agreed price. I was to get my £52000 *because* of the time advertisers would buy on the show. They would each own 30 seconds of me and in return I would have 24 minutes to be "free" to say and do whatever I wished, within reason! That was how Harry attempted to explain the, to him, profoundly logical exchange which he said was "slanted heavily in your favor by a five-to-one time ratio."

Again, that friendly pat on the shoulder.

I was not to meet my sponsors face to face on that day or any day following. They were comfortably settled in a sponsor's lounge complete with an open bar, coffee, and a television monitor that allowed them both visual and audio access to the studio floor, and direct voice communication with the Director in his control room.

My first encounter was with the "100 Wringer Mop," a colorful rod with a highly absorbent "head" that could be rung out with a remote hand control. There was no script...I was to "wing it," which I found amusing, "don't you mean...*wring* it?"

I smiled into the camera at the unseen sponsor. No response...he could not talk to me directly.

"So, why do you call it the one-hundred wring-a-mop?" I asked in an effort to please.

Somehow the sponsor had managed to get an open mike and literally bawled out in a very harsh Australian accent...

"Cos there's 100 ways you can bloody well use it!"

I responded without much thought, but with the full weight of distaste that I felt for the entire process... "Well, why don't you step down onto the floor and I'll show you the 101st!"

The "mop" was to be my second sponsor. The show went to air with only one, and that was Nestles...yes, *the Nestles!* One of the products they wanted me to promote was an instant onion soup that came in a foil packet. Once again, I could say what I liked. I was intrigued and made it up according to the package instructions. It was extremely salty, quite dark and unlike any onion soup I had ever tasted. "Surely", I asked, "you have something you would like me to say about it?" I was now borderline desperate to please since my £52000 appeared now to be in jeopardy.

"All we really need is for you to hold the packet and say its name...the rest is up to you."

In the end I added Dijon mustard, sherry, and parsley...using it as a sauce. It actually tasted quite good, even though their original formula could no longer be tasted.

That one sponsor was to lead the way into commercial television and beyond for the next forty years. I found that I did, indeed, have a price, and once I had begun to count up my 60 percent of all the opportunities that quickly followed...the price looked pretty good!

The virtue of never being "bought" had been removed.

The virtue of never telling lies about my acceptance of a sponsor's product...quickly followed.

I was afloat on a sea of compromise and the tide was coming in rapidly.

I didn't understand that I needed *somehow* to get to higher ground and avoid being drowned.

I stood on shifting sand...unable to move.

Please join us in the Reflective Readers Club
www.grahamkerr.com/rrc

Rite of Passage Twenty-One: "Hook, Line and Sinker" (1965–1966)

The tall green towers came to an end and I swam clear of them into relatively clear waters. I can see, but not for a great distance. I keep turning to look for my hen. She must still be in the tall place.

I slowed down and looked around. It is much the same, and gets warmer as I swim up towards the brightness. I prefer the cooler deep, but the best snacks are usually above me.

I can hear a possible meal approaching. I can feel it down my side, on my head and back. It tingles a little like when my hen's fins first touched mine, but this is a deeper, more intense and driving...desire.

It feels like it's in some distress...an easy prey?

The waters are cloudy. I can't see anything yet or catch its smell. I need to be right behind it.

There it is...catching the bright it flashes...it's wounded somehow...it's MINE!

I swim into the warmer waters and pick up speed. It's closer now, all the hairs on my neck are heaving, my eyes are seeing, and now I can smell...this is a splendid meal.

It's going very straight...I lunge forward. It's whirling so fast I miss it.

I turn back...again...missed. This is serious. I've got the scent; all my senses are in hunter mode...it's MINE, MINE, MINE!

Got it, my jaws close on its soft flesh. I turn away to enjoy the reward of the chase.

I feel a biting pain in my jaw. It can't be a bone; a meal this size doesn't have bones like this!

I turn again and my head jerks the other way...something is pulling. I jerk back and begin to run away from the pulling.

I'm free and it stops. It still hurts but now I can eat.

Jerk, pull, pulling harder. I'm turning back toward the moment I closed my jaws. I don't want to return, it's hurting more.

I need to drop the meal...I can't.

I roll right over and back. I swim fast for the brightness. I leap beyond it and back in with a splash.

The pull is constant and the pain is now biting me. There is blood in the water...it's mine!

I must go deep. With all my strength I dive down into the darkness until I see the rocks and spiny things. I swim close. The pull comes again, but much stronger this time.

I have enough strength to pass between two large encrusted rocks, and then with all my strength I'm going almost vertical toward the brightness. I'm through and beyond the waters...I'm going higher. I twist and turn and fall back...

The pull tries harder and then...it's gone. The pull has gone. I don't know which way to turn, my whole world has changed.

I lay still, just floating; a pale pink rose to one side as my jaw slowly releases blood. The pain was there, bright and insistent, but without the pull.

Where was I...and where was my hen?

An Understanding

Our Chinook has left the kelp forest and began to swim north.

The water here is clouded from the rivers and pollution.

It's a popular fishing ground. The season has begun and skilled deep-sea anglers are out on the hunt.

> *The most important fundamental, if you want to catch salmon, is the action of your bait or lure. If you have a good rolling and erratic action, you will have a much better chance. When a salmon hits your bait or lure he is looking for dinner.*
>
> *Salmon have three sensing mechanisms...they are sight, smell and lateral line response (sound).*
>
> *If you are trolling and your lure passes within a few feet of a salmon and he sees it, you will probably catch him. The problem is that the salmon can't see more than a few feet (in cloudy waters).*
>
> *Salmon have an extremely sharp sense of smell...but he will never smell the scent trail left by your bait unless he gets right behind it.*
>
> *Down a salmon's side, on his head and back, there are tiny hair-like projections called cupula. Each of these has a nerve cell at the end. These cells pick up vibrations in the water.*
>
> *(Source: LeeRoy Wisner of www.pugetsoundanglers.org)*

Our salmon first felt the sound waves, a little like the woofer base speaker of a good Hi-Fi set.

He moved in on that vibration until he saw the source of the "noise," a twisting, turning bait that suggested a wounded fish.

The moment he got close he was able to smell the fish. Now all three senses were engaged.

The pain came from the hook catching in the jaw, the jerking and pulling from the angler playing him.

He leaps, twists and turns to no avail. Finally, he passes the line around rocks and in one great leap he breaks free.

Now totally bewildered, he has lost his sense of direction. His only thought is for the familiar, to regain his natural senses for life that lay ahead and to return to that which was...normal!

1965 to 1966
I am thirty one to thirty two years old

Harry had arranged for my visit to the VIP lounge in Wellington. He had booked me first class. He hadn't arranged for the Customs Officer, but the Rolls Royce and the Penthouse suite definitely had his stamp upon them. He had negotiated this deal with the station and the sponsors. I was doing my thing, with Harry's help, and for that I was grateful.

The early ratings were good enough, but how does one keep a relatively good thing going and, if possible, keep the audience growing?

Harry began the image building business.

I was introduced to the Gourmet World of Sydney and to the image-makers in the media. I was reasonably young at thirty one, and apparently *unattached* with Treena back in New Zealand on stage in her own right.

I was different, and so was the show; it was becoming the talk of the town.

My early research for the "Woman's Hour Radio" in New Zealand had equipped me with stories to tell that suggested that I was a well-traveled man of the gourmet world, and my decidedly English accent and humor allowed me to be well received even amongst the kind of Australians for whom I was, after all, a POME (Prisoners of Mother England).

I thoroughly enjoyed this new fast-paced "community." I discovered that a combination of beautifully ripened French Brie, Bavarian dill pickles and excellent Verona Salamis served with a Riesling-styled white wine from South Australia's Barossa Valley was enormously enjoyable, especially in the company of such bright, and somewhat less experienced world travelers.

My next virtue was about to be uprooted.

To get a good grasp of this virtue, I need to explore with you the word "hedonism."

Hedonism: noun \ he-da-ni-zam\
The doctrine that pleasure or happiness is the sole or chief goal in life.

Example

An ancient Egyptian song with harp accompaniment:

> "Let *your* desire flourish
> in order to let *your* heart forget the beatifications for *you*
> Follow *your* desire as long as *you* shall live.
> Put myrrh upon the head and clothing of fine linen upon *you*
> Being anointed with genuine marvels of God's property.

Set an increase to *your* good things;
Let not *your* heart flag.
Follow *your* desire and *your* good.
Fulfill *your* needs upon earth after the command of *your* heart
Until there come for *you* that day of mourning." (Italics are mine)
(Source) XII Dynasty Pharaohs 1878 –1991 B.C. Wikipedia)

Later on in my life, I was to be referred to in the press, as the "High Priest of Hedonism" which I thought at that time was a nice alliteration. Right now, I was pulling at the virtue of *restraint*. Treena and I had become well adjusted to trying to live within our very limited resources and restraint *in all things* had become our way of life.

All of this careful living was now suddenly uncapped...not unlike the manner in which champagne is treated when the bottle is "riddled" to help the first fermentation to settle at the declined cork and then when uncorked, the debris swooshes out with the foaming wine. It's called "degorgement." Fresh wine is then added and the bottle recorked and sealed for the eventual buyer.

I quite simply *degorged* without restraint since I no longer appeared to be in need.

I suppose that this could be called "freedom," and it certainly felt that way. I had subconsciously uprooted several *virtues*. I no longer knew who I was. I wasn't able to say "no" to being bought. I was prepared to lie if it suited me, and now I had shrugged off restraint in pursuit of pleasure. My well-forested hillside had been harvested for purely economic purposes, its bare slopes exposed to the relentless rain of opportunity. It was beginning to shift and threaten all those whom it had previously sheltered.

I had been invited to an engagement party held in a disco at Kings Cross. A very "with it" young executive had been accepted by another in this yuppie world...many of us in the inner circle were invited. I went that night feeling very much on my own. I was missing Treena and at the same time deeply concerned about her new stage life. You may recall that I had asked if she would be prepared to give up her acting career to marry me. I had not thought that I had what it took to be married to a star. Now here she was in a starring role, and regardless of my apparent ego increase, it didn't help to reduce my fear that what she was getting from the public was a whole lot more than I would ever be able to give her as her husband.

I was jealous of an occupation rather than a person.

The music was loud, the people louder, and I was feeling left out. I met briefly and congratulated the radiant couple and then retired to graze on Brie and salami. The newly minted fiancé appeared to me to seem less radiant after each introduction. As the evening wore on, she had become almost glum. She looked my way, as though aware that her situation had caught my attention. She didn't avert her gaze...just kept on looking.

I was not hunting for a meal; neither, I think, was she. If anything we were both wounded bait without much cause for complaint. Our lives, for whatever reason, had failed to connect with pleasure and happiness. It had been expected, yet was beyond reach. So eager to swoop in on the promise of pleasure...only to once again miss out on joy.

My rain-sodden character subsided as suddenly as the hill had in Gonaives, Haiti. Without warning it had swept forward, converted into a wall of viscous mud that enveloped and suffocated all in its path.

A time of deep and lasting regret...

Please join us in the Reflective Readers Club
www.grahamkerr.com/rrc

The pain remained, now more a dull persistent ache that I couldn't get out of my mind.

Then there was the fine weed that I also couldn't shift; it seemed somehow stuck to me... following wherever I went, fast or slow. I even tried to leave it behind by leaping above the brightness, but it wouldn't detach.

I guess it is part of the new pain, and sometime it, too, will pass?

I swam slowly to the rocks and turned along the shoreline until I reached the tall greens where I had last been with my hen. I couldn't go on without her.

A quick aside from a trusted source about salmon taking the bait:

The Scotty Pro Team worked eight years filming salmon hitting baits and lures in the ocean.

They learned that the salmon come after your bait time and time again. The average salmon misses, or just grazes, the bait at least twice before he hits solid enough to get hooked.

They observed one salmon hitting a bait twenty two times before he got hooked on the twenty third try.

(Source: LeeRoy Wisner of www.pugetsoundanglers.org)

An Understanding

Our salmon had been hooked. The pain and bewilderment accompanied this first time encounter with man and his carefully arranged bait. The hook had buried itself through the lower jaw and a long length of the filament nylon remained attached and would stay so for a long time.

This brush with the unnatural was shocking and disorientating. He seeks to recover by returning to what he knows. The rocks, the kelp forest and his...hen...

1965
I am thirty one years old

I completed the twenty six episodes of *Entertaining with Kerr* and in a bewildered state, packed my leather portmanteau and took a taxi to the airport to return to what was real... and now deeply missed.

My flight was still first class but without the VIP trappings. I sat there, ate my upgraded in-flight meal, sipped a fine Australian Cabernet Sauvignon from the Hunter Valley, and toyed with a little fruit and Brie.

I had succeeded...and failed...all in the space of twenty days.

It hurt somewhere deep within me, a dull, nagging pain, as though some vital organ had been replaced by something artificial that would keep me alive for the time being. The failure itself trailed behind me as a memory that I wished strongly to forget...and yet, there it was, it had happened. To me it was so obvious but must never be noticed by others...ever!

We landed in a typical rainstorm at Wellington with the waves breaking out to sea off the end of the ocean-approach runway.

I took a cab to Clifton Terrace, carried my portmanteau to the door, set it down and used the old brass knocker to announce my arrival…I didn't have a key.

I heard Treena's swift steps, the door opened and there she was.

The pain *almost* disappeared.

She was radiant, so lovely, and so delighted to see me.

How could I?

I smiled, laughed a little and cried inside.

"Come see what I've done!" She pulled me excitedly by the hand and took me on a tour of our apartment.

Everything shone! There were new drapes. I saw it all through eyes that had spent twenty days observing all things that were first class and now here was reality. It was small, almost tacky.

With unbelievable error, I actually said so.

"Oh my, but isn't all this shabby!"

Tears welled up in her lovely eyes.

She later wrote of that pain…

"My darling was coming home. I scrubbed and polished and vacuumed up and down the stairs. In fact, I had spent the whole of the previous day getting ready. I had even made curtains for a large walk-in wardrobe and quilted the ceiling with material and brass studs.

This was actually a very small room where one person could now stay for the night. I was so thrilled. The house looked lovely.

I welcomed Graham home with such joy, waiting for him to praise our spic-and-span paradise.

I couldn't even believe his remarks. Perhaps he was joking, but he wasn't. I was devastated.

What was wrong, what had I done? I had worked so hard! I felt as though I had been stabbed in my heart."

We stood looking at each other…I apologized and tried to explain. Treena simply looked into my eyes and didn't move. She saw that something else had changed.

I turned away to get my leather portmanteau. It was outside in the rain.

Life's pressures quickly rebuilt. Treena's stage success continued, as well as my consulting work with the National Display Center and our clients.

We decided to hold the first NZ International Food and Wine Show. It was planned for Christchurch in 1964.

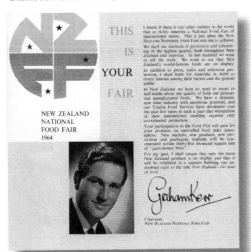

I used my very newly found celebrity in Australia to try to attract buyers from overseas to visit New Zealand and see what fabulous foods and wines my clients (and others) had to offer. I named myself Chairman of the Organizing Board and filled all the other roles of space salesman and publicist, etc., etc. It was an amazing experience that has now morphed into an annual event in each of New Zealand's main cities.

New Zealand will, forever, remain for me the land of first time opportunities...for which I shall always be thankful.

In 1966, the Queen Mother visited New Zealand and in the midst of a great many civic events, she visited our NZ Food and Wine Center in Wellington. I had prepared an original dish that I had created for her visit that I called Kare Poaka #1...a pork curry made with green peppers and coconut milk, root ginger and garlic. It had quite an aroma and Her Majesty, unable because of security to actually taste odd foods at random, did remark on its "heavenly aromas", as I held up a spare ladle-full for her to sniff.

These were brief highlights. Behind the scenes I was busily assembling a completely new series of television shows for Australia and photographing the major book that was to follow *Entertaining with Kerr*!

It was during this pressured time that I set up a TV program development system, one that I kept to for the rest of my career which was to cover an additional one thousand seven hundred and twenty two individual programs and separate *segments*.

Since I had done the research for every one of my early (12 episodes a year) programs on my own, I could see that I was going to have to have some help if I was to do 39!

In the early years, it took almost six hours for the entire process, including the recording. At $25 an hour, that was a rate of just over $4 an hour. (At that time the NZ dollar was equal to the US dollar) Without book sales it would have been a pointless occupation, but at least it was *something* and hugely better than Treena's 50 cents an hour at the local milk bar making sandwiches with unmentionable fillings!

The Australian series at $2000 an episode was then $333 an hour, although most of that was payment by the sponsors for me to hold their product and call it by name.

My research system was relatively simple. I planned for only one recipe for each program. That recipe had to have enough interesting teachable content to fill the half hour show which, discounting commercial time, was about 26 minutes, including the titles.

I had to have a story to tell about the dish, to put it in some geographical or historic context.

In Australia, I had added the need to serve it to a guest to consume it, and spend a few precious minutes helping the guest to promote themselves. Recipe cooking time was now down to about sixteen minutes and would remain there.

Elizabeth Angela Marguerite Bowes-Lyon…the Queen's mother

Since there was only one recipe it meant that I could plan the television method so that it showed every step and mentioned every ingredient by its weight and every process by the time it took to complete.

I reasoned that, if I did this clearly enough, someone could jot down the essentials and be able to make the dish without further reference. Judging from mail I received, many thousands actually did just that.

I really don't know who started the multiple recipe content programs on television, and it doesn't matter. It just became *loaded with content* yet did not show all steps or quantities. As a result, you had to *buy the book* if you liked the briefly described dish.

For me, that meant a need for a *completed* service, a permanent record. Which of course was a book. In my case that was never the purpose for the show.

Where a recipe called for several stages…like, for example, baking a loaf of rustic Italian bread within which was folded some *roasted* vegetables I would show the yeast starter; mix in the flour, cut and sauté the vegetables

—NEXT STAGE, show "proved" dough, fold in the "cooled" vegetables, remold showing a few kneading turns

—NEXT STAGE, show second proving ready for the oven, which I would put in the top of a stacked double oven and open the lower oven to take out the final loaf (cooled enough to handle).

I would slice it and serve it.

Four steps...everything shown!

Recipes always start somewhere...either tasted when dining out and carried as an idea to be tested, or received from a Chef in his broad notes, usually without measurement. There were also some classics, so well known that to fiddle with them would have lacked integrity. These were always referred to their original source, if it was known.

Then there were those that I *imagined*. To achieve this, I would take the fresh, edible seasonal produce of a given geographic area and see what was available at any one time. This was the way in which all the great classic regional dishes of the world came about. They began before refrigeration and speedy transport; it was always what was seasonally local.

The "classic" would thereafter be called by its location name.

I followed this early idea by finding place names in both New Zealand and Australia that were well known for an essential ingredient in the recipe.

Lambs Kidneys Manawatu used a tomato wine sauce.

Roast Leg of Lamb Nelson used an apple-orange sauce.

Wairakei described long, slow cooking of cheaper cuts (it was a thermal energy region).

Long White Cloud (a translation of the original Maori name for New Zealand) was a midsummer Christmas pudding served with ice cream and Apricot Brandy sauce.

I even called Chinese gooseberries (Actinidia), which grew in profusion in the Hawkes Bay region of the North Island...*New Zealand Goodberries.* That didn't last and we wound up with Kiwi fruit!

I now found myself researching the rich agricultural and wine regions of Australia to see what might become a fundamental style for my new audience. As a result, the foods of both nations began to merge, at least in my mind.

It was in the midst of all this activity that I prepared all the food for the book that had begun its days back in the Air Force in 1959; the one that would take basic methods and slowly build upon them with three recipes from extremely simple to quite complex. I hoped, as a result, to have the reader understand a good basic method and then easily use it to gradually increase their creative enjoyment of cooking because, at last, they had the method and could then add their own ingredients to meet their own preferences.

This, above all, was my early and continual goal, to encourage individual creativity that I later called "*indivity*", yet another of my words that went nowhere!

I was greatly helped during this time by knowing Hubert Sieben, the great German photographer who had immigrated to New Zealand. Our combined efforts resulted in the *Graham Kerr Cookbook*, first published in 1966 in New Zealand and Australia, which went on to win a gold medal at the 1968 International Culinary Olympics in Frankfurt, Germany.

I was now completely overwhelmed, and left once again for Sydney to finish another series of thirty-nine episodes for an increased price, due to competing sponsors. I have no memory or record of what I was paid, since deadlines had now become my focus, and whatever I was paid was a great deal more than we had the time to spend.

I flew, once again, into the first class world where my secrets lay alongside the nagging pain.

Please join us in the Reflective Readers Club
www.grahamkerr.com/rrc

Rite of Passage Twenty-Three: "You Always Hurt the One You Love" (1965–1966)

Some of the giant green towers had been wrenched free from the rocks below by the storm and lay in crumpled heaps or floated in dense layers that blocked the brightness above.

I swam about for several "darkness's" until I found my hen. It was as though she had waited for me to return and her eyes showed her delight.

I was careful to keep the pain side of my head away from her. She seemed to notice but showed no interest in why I kept turning as I did.

The sudden tugs and pain, and the long weed had had a profound effect on my willingness to explore and to hunt. In the green towers there were plenty of well known snacks but I shied away from anything that looked wounded and moved in a straight line.

More brightness and darkness went by, and the need to move again prevailed. My hen would stay behind and await my return, I would go out to see if it was safe for us to go together.

143

An Understanding

The West Coast kelp forest can be badly damaged by very high seas if driven by gale force conditions. The air sacks in the pods can cause most of the kelp to float free, leaving heavier growth ends to sink back to the rocks below.

Our pair of salmon reengage with poetic license, and I imagine his concern for his hen and his reluctance to speak about the pain from the hook and the memories of the unrelenting line that had tugged him in directions he had not wanted to go.

1965 to 1966
I am thirty one to thirty two years old

"You Always Hurt The One You Love"
Words by Allen Roberts. Music by Doris Fisher.

Recorded by the Mills Brothers on Decca in 1944, briefly #1 on best-seller charts. Included here because it represents an interesting example of a commonly experienced *"rite of passage"* for a great many of us humans.

"You always hurt the one you love,
The one you shouldn't hurt at all
You always take the sweetest rose
And crush it until petals fall.
You always brea-eak the kindest hear-eart
With a hasty word you can't recall, so
If I broke your heart la-ast night
It's because I love you most of all

You always hurt the one you lo-ove
The one you shouldn't hurt at all
You always take the sweetest ro-ose
And crush it till the petals fa-all.

(The words then repeat.)

That song was written and recorded when Treena and I had first met and love had arrived in our very young lives. Her one time date with Colin had broken my heart, as had her "affair of the heart" with the Ship's Officer on her way to New Zealand.

Now it was my time with both a hasty word, "isn't all this shabby," and a hasty action that was now a sharp, painful memory with obvious strings attached.

I was going back through the VIP lounge onto a first class flight, an "ordinary limousine" and arriving in a very upscale apartment rented for my exclusive use during this next recording session.

All in all, the trip was about four hours door-to-door.

As each hour went by, my spirits sunk lower.

My worst fears about Treena's return to the stage had not come to pass. She loved the part, and the audience loved her show-stopping number but she loved me more, not less. How was it that I could retain such a love from a beautiful, talented woman? That had been the reason for my "wound." I couldn't see why I should be the one amongst so many who would be so much more deserving of her delight.

And now, of course, there it was...the secret that was shrouding the brightness of our days in the darkness of uprooted virtue; the result of a major storm stirred up by self-inflicted imaginary wounds.

There was much to do the next day when I met up with Barbie Small for the first time. Barbie was a delightful young "foodie" before that term was ever coined, but it could have been created just for her. Barbie was almost my age and had recently returned from the Cordon Bleu in Paris. The original school was founded in 1885 and has now spread worldwide.

She was delightful then and remains so today...we are still in touch.

Barbie became *an essential* part of our inner team. Her role was to run the back kitchen and to be an essential part of all the research and development. Her fine palate and good-humored common sense blended perfectly with boundless energy and a true enjoyment of good food and wine. I could not have had a more talented and wonderfully patient collaborator.

Throughout my career I have always rehearsed every program fully on the day of recording.

That meant that every action and every ingredient was timed and weighed and learned by heart by me, and faithfully put in place by Barbie with, at most, one competent assistant.

I have always recorded in real time, making the actual time for commercials the only real breaks we would have. This meant that there could be no mistakes. We almost never went back to cover up a missed step. If it happened, which it did often, then it was left in place for all to see. In that way, the viewer sensed that all this was very much "live television. "

Treena had earlier decided that I should *never* see a program played back, in the studio nor on television. She reasoned that I would see things I liked and repeat them, or things I did not like and try not to do them again. "If you do," she insisted, "you will become a self-editing person attempting to be better at what you *appear* to be."

This worked especially well on this, my last recording session without her presence on the floor during rehearsal and in the control room during recording.

It was essential, because I was not what I appeared to be.

I had been bought, hook, line and sinker, and was being pulled painfully in directions I did not want to go. I struggled...ran free for a while...only to be aware, once again, that I was being "played."

My self-serving rationale of having a star as a wife who chose to be adored by her audience more than me had evaporated.

It just wasn't true!

I was left to confront what was true, and it wasn't pretty.

The song "You Always Hurt The One You Love" had reached #1 during our earliest days together. Over twenty years had now elapsed since then and the song had become a top 20 hit again in 1961 during our time in New Zealand.

I had done precisely that...I had hurt the one you shouldn't hurt at all, and had crushed the sweetest rose!

In a brief weekend recording gap, I went through a stumbling explanation to the self-same other man's fiancé...that I had made an awful mistake and misread my situation. My wife had not preferred the applause of many, but had warmly reminded me that it was I that she loved.

"I must therefore ask you to understand why our meetings must end...now!

She appeared to be as relieved as I, and left silently, not to be seen again.

I was indeed relieved. I felt the tug and pain drop away, leaving me with the trailing memory of my deceit.

I completed the second series as the weather gave way to the humid heat of summer. It was almost Christmas, a time when so many greeting cards were characteristically covered in a mantle of Northern Hemisphere snow.

We "abnormals" were on the beach.

It only took another four hours and I was home again. This time we were packed and ready to venture upcountry to Masterton, about 62 miles on Northeast Route 2.

We had made good friends with the then owners of Hansells, a company that made (and still does) great flavorings for food products and home cooks.

The company had been founded when we were born, back in 1934, so we felt an extra affinity for these dear people.

I had the opportunity to host my early mentor, Andre Simon, the founder of the Wine and Food Society. He had agreed to visit us and tour the emerging wine and food industries, many of whom, including Hansells, were exhibitors in my corner of the New Zealand Display Center.

Andre had been fascinated by Charles Maunsell's gas chromatography equipment that they used to analyze volatile flavor compounds with great accuracy.

It was during our brief visit that Charles offered us his home during the Christmas break, since they were off for a nostalgic business/vacation in snowy Europe.

The Maunsell residence was, for us, flat-out gorgeous. One story, it sprawled outward into a fine garden surrounding a large swimming pool with a substantial brick barbecue.

What a special gift and I loved it...nothing shabby here!

We settled in, the four of us, to enjoy this great Christmas together.

The television programs were in the can, more were ordered, and money was in the bank. I had come to my senses and was trying to replant one of the torn-out virtues. I was beginning to forget the memories that had trailed behind me from my darkened days in Australia.

It was Christmas Day 1966. I was almost thirty two years old and happily taking an extra hour in that very comfortable bed.

I became aware of Treena standing in the doorway that opened onto the covered patio and the garden beyond.

The light was bright behind her; in contrast, her face was shaded.

I leaned up on one elbow and shaded my eyes to try to see her face clearly.

She was completely still...and yet stiffened. Her hand clutched a sheet of paper tightly so that it splayed outward.

It shook very slightly.

"Hi," I smiled. "Happy Christmas."

"You utter bastard." Her voice was low, measured and cold.

My breathing stopped; my heart beat against my ears.

"What...what's that?" I pointed to her hand with its fiercely held paper.

"It's your bloody woman...that's what." Her voice had now risen considerably.

She threw the crumpled letter on the bed, turned abruptly and walked out into the brightly lit garden...leaving me and the paper in darkness.

I scrambled for the simply written one page...it was from *her*. It had come in with a bunch of fan mail that I had brought home to answer.

It predated my decision to separate, and was explicit enough to allow no further deceit. There was no longer any secret between us.

The shadows were gone; only a stark white light remained.

How could I possibly explain? Treena hadn't been there to see the Rolls Royce, the Penthouse, the leather portmanteau, the Brie...all the stuff that had gone on and on.

I was marshaling every possible excuse, every unreasonable reason.

I hadn't known why it happened at the time, how could I explain or excuse it now?

I tore up the letter, but that wouldn't change the words that were already deeply in both our minds.

I dressed quickly and followed Treena out to the garden where she sat beside the pool.

"It's over," I reached for her hand, but she moved hers away.

I explained that it was all a mistake. "I had imagined that the theater would take you from me...but it hadn't...so...it is finished." I hesitated to reach out my hand again.

"You broke truth," she accused. "You broke that word...you lied...why, why did you do that to us...all of us?

I could find no words. My chest was full of tears and I ached deeply; every joint became a complaint.

This had to be resolved. This was Christmas Day. The kids would be up soon and find us...like...*this?*

The 25th of December 1966 became the deepest, darkest day of my life. I was without defense, and now I was unloved by the only one I had ever loved.

My love had been crushed; her petals fell at my selfish feet.

"Happy Christmas, Happy Christmas!" Andy and Tessa came dashing across the lawn, full of joy and anticipation.

They hugged us both and didn't notice our tears.

Please join us in the Reflective Readers Club
www.grahamkerr.com/rrc

Rite of Passage Twenty-Four: "We Depart...Again" (1966–1967)

I couldn't hide it any longer. I must have been sleeping. My hen had swam around to the "other" side, the one I had tried to keep hidden, the one with the pain and the trailing weed.

I was alarmed by her reaction. I couldn't see the source of my discomfort, but she could and she shied away from what she saw.

It held her back, and our fins no longer gently touched as we swam away from the green towers into the troubling waters where the pain and tugging had been.

My hen stayed behind, just within sight. I would turn often...to see that she was still there.

She seemed somehow listless, without her quicksilver energy, her eyes averted and downcast.

I continued to eat and to grow...ever larger...every time the brightness came.

An Understanding

The hen has now seen the hook embedded in the buck's jaw and the fishing line attached to it.

This was completely unknown, and somehow it shocked and terrified her...as though it threatened by its very presence her buck, and if he was pierced...then so could she?

In her deep concern, she falls back...putting distance between herself and the unknown that was now a part of her buck.

1966 to 1967
I am thirty two to thirty three years old

Treena proved her great acting ability that fateful Christmas, her audience was simply our children, Tessa and Andy. Their joy at having a swimming pool, the garden, the barbecue and...presents, was literally over the moon.

They may have never noticed the pain we both felt because Treena joined them in their abundant joy until it became time for them to go to bed.

It was then that our newly discovered hell resumed.

I begged to be forgiven. Treena really didn't know how and really didn't see why she should.

She had trusted; I had lied. She had believed that the word *truth* was the absolute that secured our lives, helping us to feel safe. Now that was all gone. She was hurt, bewildered, and completely insecure. Surely, that I had done this meant that I didn't love her as I said I did.

And so our discussion...often heated from her and defensive from me...continued throughout our "great" vacation.

I had to fix this somehow...and soon.

There were more episodes to research and develop, and nearly thirty exhibitors at the New Zealand Food and Wine Society to satisfy, along with new demands for profitable endorsements from Australia. Harry Miller was hard at work building my image and pocketing his forty percent, which was now becoming a problem, since it had now become unreasonably large.

My life was full on the outside, but empty on the inside. The tension was almost at the breaking point.

"I can't go back to Australia without you." We were trying to plan our new year.

"I don't want to go anywhere where you were with her." Treena was adamant.

"I've signed contracts, I'm committed." I explained.

"You signed one with me too...it's called marriage," she shot back, "and you broke that one!"

And so it went in endless circles...we were now both bleeding but couldn't let go.

Neither of us expected the Australian opportunity to be long lasting, and we finally agreed that we should strike while the iron appeared hot and do our best to somehow get on with our respective lives.

Harry found us a most unlikely apartment just up from the famous Bondi Beach on Penkivil Street; unlikely because it closely resembled a rather low budget Hollywood set!

Imagine a huge circular bed flanked by marble-like Grecian pillars from which dangled yards of white tulle. You entered this area over a large indoor shallow pool, bedecked by numerous artificial Lotus blossoms and the inevitable plaster cast statue of a young cherubic boy endlessly emptying his bladder amid the plastic leaves.

I believe the intent was to provide tranquility, a singular failure which was easily cured by twisting a small tap between his pudgy feet.

The kitchen was far too small for the R&D needs, but we made do.

There were some memorable moments. We wanted to show how eels could be cooked and since they needed to be living...they were so ordered by Barbie. Unfortunately, before they could be swiftly dispatched, they escaped under the clothes washing machine, where they hid their slimy bodies from us nervous hunters. The often-used recipe heading "first catch your eels" was more easily directed than done since they had sensed the presence of the wading pool and clearly loved the plastic lotus.

An eel resembles, of course, a snake, and moves with somewhat greater speed and is very hard to grasp.

It was nothing short of mayhem in the midst of designer tranquility.

Oh, and did I mention the full-sized standing up Bengal Tiger who simply stood in his regally stuffed state watching several humans behaving as though they might not be the ruling species of planet earth?

Our children, at this planned interlude, were at boarding school, Tessa in Masterton in New Zealand, and Andy at Knox, a well-known private school in Sydney.

This we did not like at all. I had hated to be "shoved off" to such schools as a very young boy, and here I was doing exactly the same to them.

Treena was now suffering deeply. Her audience of two was gone and there was only me, Barbie, and those...eels etc., etc. that demanded my time and attention.

"I need to go away," she explained. "I've got to find a way to be happy again, and I can't do that in this...this...place!"

We found a small private hospital run by the Seventh Day Adventists who offered a kind of retreat, a place apart for people suffering as Treena was.

We could not afford to miss out on such an opportunity.

Treena went into the retreat to seek silence and, hopefully, some peace.

I went on "chasing the eels" that now represented my illusive quest for the sweet smell of success.

What I really wanted was to be loved again by Treena, but she was in no mood to comply.

I was now suffering from self-inflicted wounds and tumbling through time on a straight line between sleep and the bank, and it added up to *nothing*.

The once "funny" apartment had become a pathetic parody, as had my life.

I went searching for a home –my income, albeit sixty percent of the total, allowed me to look at waterfront in the middle harbor in Cremorne.

I found an older home right next door to another extraordinary architectural conceit...a castle, no less! Its owner was a lover of fine classical music, and he had invited a famous violinist to play in his smallish basement at a soiree.

The violinist had become transported during a spirited rendering of the Shostakovich Violin Concerto No. 1 in A minor. In a wild stroke, his elbow collided with the wall.

Mortified, our neighbor proceeded to excavate the entire acre of land to such an extent that he could now house a small orchestra and a reasonable audience.

He kept on building and wound up with a musical castle and a tennis court.

Our house, by comparison, was...well...*ordinary*, but what a location!

I took Treena on a short drive out from the hospital to see what I had found.

I was desperate. I needed her to say yes, to recover our family, to escape this loveless world of work and unrewarding celebrity.

Treena liked it. It helped to get her reengaged with life...at least on the fringes.

Harry did another deal with a department store. For a credit on the show, we could furnish our house.

Another deal was made with an appliance company, and our kitchen was equipped.

Yet another deal, and we built a boatshed test kitchen right over the water, complete with a sauna, bath and pool.

The Boatshed

If we no longer enjoyed each other, we at least had the "trappings" that might somehow ease the pain.

We moved in and began to settle; so to speak!

Treena's success in New Zealand Radio led to her being offered the lead role in the Australian Broadcasting version of *The Life of George Sands*, the novelist, dramatist and campaigner for all kinds of political reform in the mid 1800s in France. She was apparently the great love of Chopin's life.

Treena *became* George Sands...a highly emotional part to play during an equally emotional time in her own life.

It was in the midst of all this that Qantas Airlines offered to fly my newfound wine associate, Len Evans, and I around the world, first class again and all expenses paid. All they wanted was for us to write a book of the experience as a way to promote their brand new worldwide service.

I had not the slightest idea where this would lead. The writing, had I but known, was not on the wall but on the book's front cover...

"The Galloping Gourmets"
by Graham Kerr and Len Evans

An idea was about to be born.

Please join us in the Reflective Readers Club
www.grahamkerr.com/rrc

Rite of Passage Twenty-Five: "Once Is Enough?" (1967–1968)

Having had one disturbing experience in these waters, I was on the lookout for anything unusual...any troubled fish going in a straight line, sometimes closer to the rocks than we were swimming. Of course we had to eat, and this we did with caution.

One time, just after the brightness above us began, we were being passed by several wounded fish, at different levels, all at the same speed in the same direction. I swiftly turned and as fast as I could swim returned to my hen. I swam about her so that the trailing weed brushed her nose and then lay, just ahead pointing at the lines of disturbed water on our every side.

She came close, and our fins touched. We watched as they went by...until it felt safe to continue.

An Understanding

Each year from April to October there is a west coast season for Chinook salmon.

Chinook are highly sought after by sports fishermen, both for food and their fighting qualities... and this had been our salmon's recent encounter. During their sea travels it is the commercial fisheries that predominate in the catch of salmon, but this initial sport fishing encounter has resulted in a change in our Chinook.

A commercial trawler with many lures working from the long poles off the vessel has just passed over our salmon. The lures are intended to both attract attention and to resemble wounded baitfish. As a result of their many hours of sea experience and technological fishing advances, commercial fishers have a good idea at what depth these fish can be found, since there is a preference for water temperatures, ocean currents, and where and when local snack supplies that salmon feed on might be.

It is uncertain as to whether a once hooked but freed salmon might profit from the experience and become less tempted...but I have chosen to imagine that this might be so.

1967 to 1968
I am now thirty three to thirty four years old

Exactly why Treena and Trish (Len's wife) agreed to our taking up this extraordinary offer to fly around the world I have no idea. They were releasing their husbands, the fathers of their children, into the first class world of fine dining. We were to visit sixty-eight restaurants in thirty-five days, and with never more than seventy two hours in one city.

In a series of Qantas Boeing 707s we visited Honolulu, San Francisco, Los Angeles, New Orleans, New York, London, Copenhagen, Cully (Switzerland), Vienna, Paris, Rome and Hong Kong.

Around the world in 35 days: We decided not to count the amount of wine consumed, even though Len easily outdid my samplings, largely because I had to find the space for over two full meals of many dishes every day!

I had agreed to the trip, in part because it would allow me to visit my parents in England after almost eight years. They had been recruited from the Gravetye Manor to run the Forest Mere Health Hydro in Liphook, Hampshire (UK). This British version of the Golden Door Spa in California was owned by Ken Wood, the same company that made the electric mixer that I used on television for several years (Kenwood).

Ken eventually sold Forest Mere to the Savoy Hotel in London.

My parents had aged, especially my father who had had a cerebral hemorrhage and took a regular dose of "Warfarin," (which he called rat poison) to help keep his blood thin because of several thrombosis –a kind of medical catch-22? It seemed obvious to me that we should ask them to join us in Australia where we could, with our newfound income, provide them with, at the least, a long ocean voyage to recuperate and visit their grandchildren for the first time.

On my return I had hoped that *absence* might make the heart grow fonder for the two of us. It hadn't. If anything, we had begun to live in the midst of the volatile fumes of mistrust.

Treena's success with George Sands had led, much to Harry's concern, to a major part in the Australian made-for-TV series "Hunter," that was shown on the Nine Network from July 1967 to 1969. Treena played a beautiful spy being tracked down by the very handsome lead actor, Tony Ward. It was shot on location and so she had now left home to pursue the very career about which I had been so fearful.

The Galloping Gourmets
by Graham Kerr & Len Evans

Note: The book is occasionally listed on Amazon.com. Be careful to note that it is Galloping Gourmets in the plural, published by A.H. and A.W. Reed in 1967.

We had also been set apart without any meaningful reconciliation. I had ruptured her trust and so she had a valid reason for distrust. I had to go back several years to justify mine; back to her 1959 voyage to New Zealand and her affair of the heart with the ship's officer.

These were the fumes that we both inhaled that fueled our occasional outbursts of jealousy.

It didn't help that our Cremorne pharmacy owners were ecstatic at Treena's debut on "Hunter." "Graham, she's flat-out gorgeous and such a talented actress." Up until then, it had been my celebrity that they enjoyed…Treena now eclipsed me.

This rite of passage appears pretty normal for show business celebrities if one is to believe the lurid stories at supermarket checkout counters. In many cases the results are often a public divorce; in ours, it was a form of shared PTSD (posttraumatic stress disorder) in which *anyone* might be a potential adversary on the prowl for the other's love and affection. Harry was also unhappy because traditionally couples that were both in the limelight seldom succeeded, especially in those days in Australia. As a result he did his best to dissuade his fellow media types from hiring Treena Doorne. She had now taken her maiden name to help us offset the relationship issue.

Our lives were coming apart at the seams. My parents had arrived for their visit and it wasn't hard for them to see that there were deep problems.

Harry could also see the writing on the wall and hastened to milk me as a property for every available dollar from which he was extracting his 40 cents.

I was extremely unhappy at this exploitation and sat down in his very show business office, surrounded by all his posters for his past classical triumphs, to explain my concerns.

Harry somehow signaled his accountant, Anthony Hollows, who was himself a concert violinist, to enter quietly and begin playing softly several well-known violin pieces for sad people. There are many such pieces. I refused to let him dissuade me from my own laments. Harry took on the appearance of one who shared my sadness. He even mopped at his very dry eyes at one stage. Eventually, we all collapsed in laughter and once again Harry won.

During this time I did commercials for Polaroid by snapping buxom bathing beauties on Bondi Beach. At least it was a good alliteration!

I almost *appeared* to sing on the Graham Kennedy Show in Melbourne as I stumbled through "Autumn Leaves". None of this was my day job and surely resulted in the dreaded "overexposure" that often came with a limited number of television channel choices.

My ratings were beginning to suffer and I finally decided that I had had enough; at about the same time Harry had seen that I was on my way out of favor with the viewing public. I returned to his office but this time there was no violin and no laughter. Harry wanted $240,000 in return for ending our contract. It had to be repaid at $10,000 a month and would immediately earn interest if I missed a due date. This was not easy and meant that I had to replace Harry with someone else who knew the marketplace.

Enter Arthur Pettit, an advertising executive with whom we had shared a pleasant and profitable relationship. Arthur would be happy with a 20 percent share and believed that we could easily outdo Harry and salvage my career. Since Harry had constantly tried to derail Treena's acting opportunities, she was fully in favor of this major change.

We signed the papers late in 1967 and once again we were on our own.

This disruption allowed us to become distracted from our mutual distrust. We had agreed about Harry and were now back in the same boat trying to stay afloat.

We decided to make an Italian television series, and set out with the help of a restaurateur I had met on my Qantas adventures in Rome. Signor Antonio Prantera was at that time the President of the Italian Restaurant Association and the owner of the Helio Cabala and the Hostaria dell'Orso in Rome, both of them expensive, elegant and over-the-top delicious.

Antonio set up our tour, which began in Naples and finished in Campione d'Italia on Lake Lugano, a distance of 528 miles on the autostrada Del Sole. We were provided with an

Alfa Romeo convertible and once again all our expenses were covered in the name of "public relations." We had no crew, so I filmed the entire journey with a small Canon Scoopic 16mm camera, tripod and very ordinary battery operated lights.

It was a tremendous adventure with a real challenge to reinvent my flagging career and it was so good for the two of us to leave all our distrust behind, at least for a while. The food and the people were extraordinary, and I was certain of our eventual success with the series.

On our return we engaged the Australian film director, Ron Way. Together we set up a splendid al fresco styled set and filmed the series at SAS 10 Adelaide.

It took every dollar we had plus a loan on our home, and with the payment due to Harry, it was all...or *nothing*!

I made and kept ten appointments to see the program manager of channel 7 in Sydney in order to place the series. He broke, changed or escaped from each of these dates, and with each failure my enthusiasm was dampened and then eventually extinguished. We had failed. A giant step out of what seemed like a form of slavery had resulted in a professional catastrophe.

My parents were now dependent upon us; our children were at boarding schools. There was a huge loan due on our house and the monthly payments to Harry.

Two almost funny events allowed us to go down laughing.

I did a commercial for the Dairy Board with milk pails and a wooden yolk, which was hugely (awfully) funny, and then the appliance people came and removed all our kitchen appliances since we were no longer "on air."

There is some dark humor in a gourmet kitchen without a range and refrigerator.

The last laugh was yet to come, and it came very soon from a totally unexpected source in the midst of chaos. The last laugh was to be ours!

Please join us in the Reflective Readers Club
www.grahamkerr.com/rrc

We moved carefully, trying hard to not leap at the next meal that seemed so tempting. But caution was a problem...both my hen and I were now quite large; in fact, larger than a great many fish like us that were all heading our way.

As we emerged from the protection of our kelp sanctuary there was something familiar in the water...it went way back in my memory. A time when the waters were—different—when I was very young.

It was a pleasant thought, and we were momentarily attracted to follow that memory, until we both sensed that we were off track—that this was an important way to go, but not yet.

We turned and headed back into the big waters.

An Understanding

Our reunited pair, still very conscious of the lures in the water, were more selective in their eating. They were attracted by the distant smell of their natal river to the south...a collection of aromas that provide the unique homing device that can guide most, but not all, salmon back to the river in which they were hatched.

This time had not come. The essential maturing of the hen's eggs and the male's matching milt was not yet at the level that would provide the essential drive to reach the gravel beds in the stream's headwaters.

Without that urgency, the call of the ocean of opportunity proved stronger, and together they left the kelp forest off the Queen Charlotte Islands and began, once more, to head north toward Southeast Alaska to resume eating the baitfish their growth and continuing maturation depended on...with greater care to avoid the dangers of embedded hooks and lines.

1967
I am thirty three years old

We were desperate. Every cent I made doing ever-cheaper commercials went to pay off Harry.

I bought a small under-counter refrigerator and a two-burner propane camping stove to replace our repossessed kitchen appliances. The vast holes left behind were a stark reminder of our plight.

The phone was still on, fortunately!

"Can I speak to Mr. Kerr?" It was a man with a soft-spoken American accent.

"Speaking," I replied.

"My name is Paul Talbot. I'm the President of Fremantle International. We make TV programs."

"I see...er...how can I help you?"

"I'm in Sydney on a local production. I'd like to meet with you to discuss a program opportunity."

"Sure, when and where?" I responded eagerly. It didn't matter where he was from or who he was. If it meant a few more dollars I would be the first to say yes.

We agreed to meet at the American Club in Sydney later that week.

I had not the slightest idea where this might lead, so I went searching for some understanding of who Fremantle was.

It turned out that they produced a most unusual "franchised" local television show that had begun in Baltimore, Maryland in 1953. It was called "Romper Room" and was aimed at preschoolers' –a kind of commercial forerunner to Sesame Street. It typically offered during a show its cast of youngsters a glass of milk and cookies before which they would pray what was to become a famous prayer.

"God is great, God is good. Let us thank Him for our food. Amen."

My heart sank. This could be the bottom of the cookie jar for me, a walk-on appearance on a program for preschoolers. Would I have to bake cookies?

I didn't notice how widespread and popular this show was, which eventually ran its course by 1994; a 41-year run in many international markets is no small pickings, even when compared to the singular achievement of "Mr. Rogers Neighborhood" (1968 to 2001), a total of 33 years.

Romper Room had local hostesses for each show in a great many cities. In Australia, it was made at Channel 7 in Sydney and its hostess was Miss Susan.

"Miss" as each hostess was politely addressed, went on to marry no less a person than Paul Talbot—the big boss from New York who had called me.

Paul had red hair, bushy eyebrows and wore a Parisian style black beret—quite stylish back in the mid 1960s.

Myself and Paul Talbot on the set of
This Is Your Life

He had very precise, almost courtly manners that seemed to keep him on a permanent edge of self-concern, even when he would lean in to listen with great care to what someone might say to him.

He did have a proposal and it went way beyond cookies for Romper Room.

He wanted to make a series of 650 shows for the United States and world market!

He put it in such an unemotional, matter of fact way that it almost failed to register. All that stuck was the *six hundred and fifty shows!*

"That's impossible!" I exclaimed, as indeed it was. I had gone from twelve a year in New Zealand to over thirty nine in Australia and that was difficult enough!

"That will take over sixteen years to complete," I explained.

"No, only three years and a bit," he replied.

"But that's over 190 a year." I was incredulous.

"195 to be precise," he replied with practiced precision.

"It can't be done." No matter how great was our immediate need; there was no point in assuming for a moment that such a schedule was possible.

"It might work for a kids show with cookies and milk, but this has a great deal of research, testing and rehearsal."

He nodded as though he clearly understood, and then in his edgy, precise manner made a simple suggestion.

"Do you have scripts for sixty five shows that you have done here?"

Quickly I added all the New Zealand shows and the Australian...

"Yes...just." I replied.

"Okay. So, let's do those again for the first sixty five shows and see how it goes...then we can decide if we should go on?"

His proposal met all our immediate financial needs. We could pay off Harry, the house loan, and be back in the black with just sixty five episodes.

I buried the impossibility of the rest of the episodes and signed a contract for $2 million that would cover the 650 shows IF it seemed to be possible.

On the day we finally signed, Treena hit the jackpot using his club's small "one-armed bandit" and went home happily loaded with quarters.

The local press quickly found out about the signing, and we purchased a suite of Westinghouse appliances to replace those that had been repossessed. The great gaps in our lives were being filled back in as the day of reckoning came near.

We flew to Ottawa, Canada, roughly 11,000 miles, and made a pilot show.

Treena had decided that we should have an audience. This was to be our first major break with the "tradition" of TV cooking that began in 1937 (when I was 3) when Marcel Boulestin, as I had done, made an omelet for the early experimental days of BBC Television.

It is both pointless and boorish to suggest that we were the "first" to do, *anything*. It is, perhaps, enough of a conceit to suggest that we were amongst the first to create the oxymoron of "culinary entertainment."

Treena had never been a "foodie." She had a very simple childhood with few, if any, culinary adventures.

On the other hand, her experience on the stage was to be invaluable, as had already proven to be the case in Australia.

It was now time for these disparate gifts to collide...on screen.

Back in Wellington I had rehearsed all of our early shows in front of a live audience of Treena's actor friends. Such a wonderful audience! I discovered, in their very warm company, an ability to tell jokes which, when fed by their appreciative reception, became greatly garnished. These were mostly in the style of the so-called "shaggy dog" which is described by Wikipedia as "an extremely long-winded anecdote characterized by extensive narration of typically irrelevant incidents terminated by an anticlimax or a pointless punch line –which can last as long as five minutes."

This was to be her great gift. Treena was ultimately responsible for the first of six minutes of the show, a time in which I would shake hands with the audience, jump over a dining chair, introduce film shot on location, and deliver an often "irrelevant incident," concluding with a "pointless punch line."

It is a curious experience, a little like being Bambi-on-ice, expecting at any moment for the ice to crack.

Recipes were relatively easy to find; jokes were something else again, especially those that could be stretched to fill an entire four to five minutes on every single show—no reprieve for either me or the audience.

That 22,000-mile trip to Ottawa for one simple program without a kitchen set, and only a few willing people sitting on folding chairs, was really quite risky.

We took with us an elaborate set design, should the budget cover it; larger, I suspect, than any other kitchen set had ever been (there I go again with odious comparisons!) It had a bar and dining room, and a completely separate, yet connected, kitchen, with a total frontage of over 70 feet.

We didn't know it at the time, but we would need this entire frontage to be able to fit the 280 that would pack the rest of the studio wall to wall.

Apparently, the test run went well enough to confirm the first series of 65 shows to be made late in 1968 for a release in 1969.

Paul Talbot had lots of experience working with Romper Room internationally, and while that show had very local hosts, city-by-city, nation-by-nation, this program would be resting exclusively upon our shoulders. My British Public School accent, tempered by pan washing in the Army and by nine years in New Zealand and Australia, was an odd enough mix to prevent being pinned down to any one location. I was, if you will, an international person of no *fixed* abode!

The recipes were, in and of themselves, multicultural, and would be increasingly so as we spent more and more time filming in every continent.

Finally, there was Paul's brilliant idea of recording in Canada. Back in the 1960s there were tariffs that prevented some nations from the overuse of American-made television programs. The BBC, for example, was allowed 40 percent of its content to be *American.* By recording in the United States, we would have to compete with all manner of great productions, which was hardly possible! There were no tariffs against Canadian content, largely because of the Commonwealth ties and their small number of programs suited for world play.

The book that birthed the idea was the one written at Qantas' request, *The Galloping Gourmets.* We wanted to strike off the "s" and let it go singular.

Very few people agreed. Galloping Gourmet was, in itself, almost an oxymoron. It even suggested "unseemly behavior."

It was here, once again, that Treena prevailed, in part because of her condition.

Treena was pregnant.

We counted back over the days, looking for a date when this could have happened. It proved to be Venice and the Hotel Luna Baglioni, a lovely old place that was once a monastery.

Treena was now six months pregnant and quite large. She was also determined to survive amid an avalanche of "suits," all male, who were experienced in the North American media. They were, however, all influenced by Treena's obvious condition and were loath to get into

Our first, small but willing, audience.

a fight and risk the production with unwanted consequences. They all, eventually, agreed on the title and even the first six minutes of "shaggy dog entertainment."

These men included senior executives of what was then the largest advertising agency in the world, J. Walter Thompson. One of these gentlemen in a gray flannel suit was Colgan Schlank. It was Colgan who was charged with the task of inventing or applying the concept of "barter," that had yet to be used in such a major way.

The idea was to offer the program to individual stations, normally called *distribution* rather than network, and to do so in return for several commercial breaks for J. Walter Thompson's client companies who would then be the sponsors. There was enough money to be made by all parties for this to become a new business model in the industry. I'm certain it didn't begin with our show, but we helped to make it an interesting alternative method of placing independent programs.

The first series was recorded in the winter of 1968 and took just over eight weeks away from our Australian home. We recorded two episodes a day, five days a week, for six and a half weeks. At the end of the seventh week we made commercials for our sponsors and immediately jumped on a plane to return via Asia to pick up new recipes, and on location film for the next series.

It was a brutal, punishing schedule, especially hard on Treena's pregnancy. We missed our children, but we had grabbed a tiger by its tail and were too scared to let go.

The first episode went to air in January 1969 on the flagship station NBC (4) in New York City, sandwiched (appropriately) between "As the World Turns" and "Secret Storm".

I mean...how could a guy fail?

Please join us in the Reflective Readers Club
www.grahamkerr.com/rrc

Rite of Passage Twenty-Seven: "How Doth the Gourmet Gallop?"

After emerging from the security of the kelp forests there was the slightest hint of familiar waters from below us. The vague memory of our early lives had its attractions, but we turned once more toward those without limits.

On the one hand, there was such a strong drawing from within...yet a hollow response, as though this had to be done, but not right now.

Almost immediately it seemed that we had made the right choice because the waters became colder and the snacks that we had left behind when we had swam down towards slightly warmer waters had reappeared; delicious, easy snacking.

The only downside from going were the much larger ones who saw us as a snack, although by now either of us would have been quite a mouthful.

My sides are really long and sleek, and when need be I can swim really fast. I've used this to draw the big black and whites, and the larger hairy ones, away from my hen who is shorter and more delightfully rounded than I.

We swim on. We gain size and strength. We avoid being eaten. This seems to be the way it should be...for now!

An Understanding

Our Chinook are back at sea and heading north (which, for them, seems to be up). The northern waters, off Southeast Alaska, can range from 50 F to 58 F in August. This can be compared to Newport Beach in California that is from 69 F to 70 F in August.

It is in these colder waters that krill and other small marine life feed upon the abundant phytoplankton with a little zooplankton as a garnish!

> *Note: The study of both of these very small organisms (in most cases, but not all for the zooplankton) is hugely interesting but distracting to our story. This is the stuff of both life in the oceans and the very air we breathe...do look it up!*

Of course, wherever the most basic elements in the food chain are abundant then so will be the great gray whales, black and white Killer whales, and the "furry ones," sea lions.

All of these are present and ravenous in the North Pacific. While the grey whale, enormous as they are, feed directly on the plankton and krill, our Chinook will continue to feed on the abundant schools of baitfish like Pacific herring, and sometimes prawns when available. The furry ones will likewise be chasing the baitfish schools along with the salmon and occasionally will snag a "salmon" as a "chaser". The black and white ones (orca) can be both migratory populations and resident populations. The migratory populations consume other marine mammals that include the furry ones and even the juvenile gray whales, while the more localized resident populations target salmon.

Such is life in the ocean of opportunity...for us all?

1968 to 1969
I am thirty four to thirty five years old

Clearly, there had been some improvement in my relationship with Treena. Babies do not arrive when the parties no longer communicate! Yet there was now the proverbial skeleton in the cupboard!

Mine was a shameful secret that we had chosen to hide away from the public view, yet it was so well known by the two of us that it would swing ghoulishly into plain view if we somehow opened the doors of distrust.

Of course, we both did whatever we could to keep the doors closed, and to a major extent the life we were leading was a great help.

When we added up the time it took us to simply meet the one hundred and ninety five program schedule that played five days a week for thirty nine weeks of the year, it came to about nine hours for me and about six hours for Treena. Mine was more because of all the recipe testing and writing. Hers was in our shared location; work, hunting down jokes and editing all the film we took on our world travels, as well as overseeing the recording of each episode.

Just multiply 9 x 195 and you get 1756 hours. Assume a normal week of 40 hours and divide this into our work and it goes 43 times.

That meant that after our totally committed program time was done, we had just nine weeks for our family and ourselves.

On the face of it this seems reasonable until you assess the intensity of the work and the immense amount of detailed recipes to be written *that had to be as accurate as they could possibly be.* On top of all this was public relations and somehow keeping the sponsors happy.

And that came out of the remaining nine weeks!

Treena invented her very own rating system for each show. When it met with her absolute approval by being both hugely entertaining /funny, and where the food was well done and looked great, she would award me an "A+."

A very good balanced show would be an "A."

B+ was given for a reasonable performance, but either the joke or the food wasn't up to the best standard.

B's came when I failed to connect with the studio audience or simply had a bad day.

"C" meant looking seriously at doing the whole show again, which we never did, largely due to budgetary constraints.

I kept this score in my dressing room on a large white board. As each series of sixty-five flew past, I tried my best to improve my score, or was I trying somehow to please Treena and to keep the closet door closed? I suspect it was both, and added to that total was my ever-present fear of failure.

On the Wednesday of our first week on NBC Channel 4 in New York City, Kay Gardella, the TV critic for the New York "Daily News", declared after watching two episodes, that this was simply someone without culinary ability that was filling in the cracks with odd British humor. She declared that it wouldn't last. (She was to be officially named TV critic in 1975, but had her pen poised and ready for us in 1969.)

Photo credit ©Bob Peterson

On Friday of that same week she recanted and declared that it was a "sleeper" that should be watched to see what transpired over time.

Note: I have tried unsuccessfully to uncover the actual clippings and so these comments are now the best I can do from memory.

This played directly into my fear of failure that had dogged me from the beginning and now fueled my determination to do the best food possible within the unrelenting schedule. Here then was the essential tension that literally made the show the success it became. Treena wanted to entertain; I wanted to teach. I feared professional and personal failure and used every ounce of personality to avoid both. The pressure was endless. I would begin the process of a block of sixty five episodes by sketching out the nations we would cover; for example, in series four, recorded in late 1969. We chose to cover the UK and its Pub food, as well as the great food of London, Vienna, Moscow, Zurich, Athens, Kuala Lumpur, and Australia.

I would then set out to list the great popular dishes of each region, like the Tiddy Oggy (Cornish pastry) of England, and the Stroganoff of the then USSR, and the Kaiserschmarren (soufflé omelet) of Vienna. The dishes were then sorted into a kind of weekly menu that would have appetizers, seafoods, meats, poultry and desserts with a constantly changed order—never just fish on Friday.

I would then dash off a letter to the respective national tourist agency of each location asking for their help in pinning down a restaurant or hotel that did a splendid job serving the best example of the classic dish.

By series four, our audience had almost gone into orbit and covered many nations, so it was judged as an excellent means of promoting international tourism. We were never turned down and always brilliantly assisted by their own researchers who obviously wanted the best outcome.

Over the years, none of our trips was ever able to compete with our visit to Moscow, which we made in 1969, several months after Pan Am made its historic first flight 44 into Moscow in July 1968.

I had initiated the visit with a somewhat halfhearted attempt at creating cooperation with their Committee for Television and Radio; halfhearted because I really couldn't see why they would agree.

They did, and we arrived at Sheremetyevo Airport with very little idea as to what had been arranged or even why!

Our stay was to be almost one week at the one time cost of bed and breakfast, which had to be paid in advance without knowing the name of our hotel. Apparently, that would depend upon where a bed was available.

The arrival proved unusual. We had to sit in a cubicle with an official who had an old fashioned automatic rifle propped up against the wall. He wanted us to complete an inventory of all we had brought with us, including lipstick, ballpoint pens and "any Beatles records." He warned us that we would have these checked out when we departed and that we should not even think about giving them to anyone we should meet. We came to understand that these "Western Capitalist luxury goods" were in great demand and could be used to bribe their comrades, thereby tempting them to commit some "crime against the people."

We were taken directly to a meeting with the committee in a modern office building that had not yet received carpeting to cover its cement floor. There was a low long table that was completely bare except for several glass bottles of mineral water that remained untouched. Eight men interviewed us; all were moderate in height and less moderate in girth. All were gray, or going so, with their hair cut short. They wore dark gray or black suits and white shirts with completely nondescript ties.

We were introduced to our English-speaking "tourist guide," Valia, a delightful young woman who watched over us (literally) on behalf of—well—who knows who; we were never quite sure.

The Committee wanted to know what we wanted to film and why. I explained, as I had in my original letter, that we needed to meet Russian chefs and to know more about the foods of the USSR in general so that the rest of the world (well, the part that we were then reaching) would know them better—as people.

They nodded and conferred amongst themselves.

"Would you distribute these programs for us to play in the USSR," they asked.

"But of course," I replied.

"Payment in dollars not possible." A thickset, brush-cut leader-type announced.

"You choose payment in caviar or tractor or fur coat?" He gestured.

"Is the tractor red?" I replied.

"All our tractors are red." He replied brusquely.

Surely being paid with a red Russian tractor would be worth its weight in gold for public relations. We could mount it on a platform outside the studios of CJOH TV in Ottawa before we made the shows!

It seemed as though we had a deal, but then all was not as it seemed throughout our brief visit.

We stayed at the Hotel Metropole, large and quite bare. We were given a suite of two large rooms lit mostly by bright fluorescents; each room was about 20 feet square.

The curtains did not keep out the light. The mattresses were "biscuits," four to a bed, encased in off-white sheets that were not changed for the duration of our stay.

The towels had once been on a roller and had been cut to provide "bath-length."

The TV was huge, and quite the largest we had ever seen anywhere...but it didn't work. Treena, ever the producer, set to work with her "declared" nail file to take off the back. There was *nothing* inside, only the gray painted glass screen! It was, I guess, a status symbol? There was a phone, but no phone book. "If you wish to talk to someone, you will know their number," we were told.

Treena decided in a rash moment to have her hair done at the hotel. Standing against one wall of the "beauty shop" was a small BBQ unit with an overhead vent that let out through the wall. It contained curling rods resting on hot coals!

We had requested a local TV crew of two; one camera, one lighting. This we got on our first day. By the end of the workweek we had twenty. It was beginning to look like a remake of "Ben Hur!"

Where full employment is mandatory for socialist success, there were curious examples of organization. Not only was our crew huge, but in each State kitchen there were at least four cooks for each job to be performed.

The grill cook would make one dish and then step aside for the next in line to cook the next order, and so on in a cycle of four or five.

In spite of such excess, the food was really quite cheap...between $4 and $5 a dish with good wines at less than $9 a bottle.

Our big moment came when we ate at the Restaurant Slaviansky Bazar, a truly excellent mostly seafood spot, with taped Glen Miller music. We had a grand time with our now large crew. Treena had a large red scarf and her new silver fox coat with a black pantsuit.

She attracted the attention of two Russian Generals who sent over a bunch of more than wilted flowers and raised their glasses in a salute. This was our swan song event. We sat down for a farewell dinner with the entire crew, feasting on scampi and lots of vodka. Somewhat emboldened by the vodka, I stood to offer a toast that Valia translated for me.

"May our children grow up to play together," I proposed, and raised my glass.

There was silence as the toast was translated into Russian, then there were tears on several faces followed by the drawing back of chairs as the crew stood unsteadily and sung some clearly patriotic party songs.

We hugged and promised to return...which we have yet to do.

When we returned home to process the film we had taken of street scenes and the hotel room, including the empty TV, all our 16 mm was "fogged," a uniform pinkish haze caused when film is exposed to the light.

All was not to be as it seemed.

Please join us in the Reflective Readers Club
www.grahamkerr.com/rrc

Rite of Passage Twenty-Eight: "Serious Eating"

It really feels like we've been here before and done that (French salmon might call this déjà vu, or "seen before.")

The snacks are welcome; so many...although they seem a little less clustered than the last time?

Now that I'm much larger and quicker off the mark I can run down even the largest and fastest of the fleeing baitfish. My jaw is becoming more pronounced which helps me to tear into large prey and then share it with my hen who hasn't developed the same set of teeth, or attitude, for that matter.

We keep on moving; it seems that there is no quiet place where we can let our guard down and just hangout. As always, we have to keep an eye out for the Black and Whites, the furry ones and those wounded bright fish that swim in a straight line.

For all the down sides, I must say that eating here is such a pleasure and it seems to suit me.

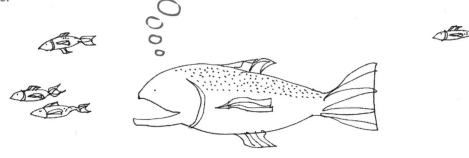

An Understanding

Our couple has now reached the northern point of their journey...just south of Kodiak Island of the Aleutian Island chain.

Just north of the Aleutian Islands, but beyond the extent of the migration of our two salmon is the proposed Pebble Copper Mine in the headwaters of a river running into Bristol Bay, Alaska.

Bristol Bay is an incredibly rich marine area, alive; at this time with huge amounts of seafood… all threatened by human desire for the inedible material with which to make inedible things that cause inedible cash flow with which, eventually, we can buy something edible that might have been modified?

Our Chinook know nothing about this other than noticing that the quantity and density of plankton and resulting krill and baitfish were more sparse in much of their southern migration travels, and along with its gradual shift it has less oxygen-releasing properties…just another distant early warning sign of what, in the past, has been called the "unintended consequences of climate change," but which now must surely be called intentional consequences.

The buck Chinook has begun to develop the pronounced jawline that so clearly marks the difference from the female as their more visible sexual differences as they become increasingly mature.

This is their time for moving and eating, and it occupies every waking moment.

1969 to 1970
I am thirty five to thirty six years old

When I had begun my media life on New Zealand Radio with Elsie Lloyd and Shirley Maddox on "Woman's Hour" back in 1959, I had rapidly run out of personal experiences with food. Living in New Zealand, while it had a great many advantages in climate, natural resources and wonderful hospitable people, there were few "new food" experiences and almost no status providing history…other than their unrivaled "baked goods" and farm fare.

My answer had come from the "Esquire International Cookbook" and the in-depth articles of famous restaurants around the world complete with recipes.

It *seemed* as though I had visited these places. I never claimed I had done so, but a listener could easily put two and two together and come up with their own conclusion that I was clearly "well traveled."

Now, it was a different day and the world was my oyster. All I had to do was to find the time to open it, cut it free and swallow.

A small team of professionals now made the films we shot on location and Treena and I were always there, right in the midst of the greatest culinary experiences that the world of the late 1960s to early 1970s had to offer. I would never have dreamed of ever meeting these culinary superstars, let alone having them sit down and explain both how and why they chose to do what they did to delight so many.

Our small team of professionals

This was both an adventure and a long overdue exercise in credibility that I had felt I always lacked... and had fueled my fears of failure in the past.

Of course, it took a great deal of time and energy both to travel and eventually to put all my notes into tested recipes that would work with ingredients that were globally available.

It was the knowledge that my audience was international that made the recipe creation such a complicated business.

In my early major book that I rewrote for Doubleday in the U.S., I had given every recipe in three measurements, U.S., Imperial (UK) and Metric. While that was helpful for some, it had the appearance of added complexity.

We decided to opt for the "old" U.S. measurements since this was our immediate audience. Where translations were made, the recipes were adjusted to each market.

In some cases, words such as "basil" would be pronounced in British Commonwealth nations as "B-A-S-I-L" with a short a. In the U.S. and some other U.S.-influenced nations, it became "bay-zill."

To use "bay-zill" on BBC would have generated hoots of derision from their viewing audience.

"Look at 'im, who does 'e think 'e is..."bayzill"...I suppose 'e calls sage "saarge!"

The answer was to use both in one breath, and so it went on with meat cuts, most seafood (fish types/names), even some produce such as the mixup between chicory and Belgium endive and root chicory. We did our best to be clear enough to everyone who might be listening!

In Japan, the Galloping Gourmet has been repeated many times right up until 2012... and then, well, who knows? The interpretation and lip sync was done brilliantly by a Japanese Christian comedian who was deeply offended by my "double entendres" (double meanings used deliberately with intent to *amuse*...such as "throw your breasts into the pan")

He was able to change these weak attempts at humor in the same way that the measurements had gone from cups to metric. He even, so I am told, changed my sign off, "Just for you, God bless." I have yet to know what I wound up saying!

We had built an elaborate boathouse at the bottom of our garden on Shellbank Avenue in Mosman, which borders the inner harbor of Sydney, not far from the famous Sydney Harbor Bridge.

It was two stories high and cantilevered out over the water. The first floor was my office with a shower and sauna that opened out onto a saltwater tidal swimming pool. The top floor was all business; a large round dining table and chairs for six to eight, a simple enough kitchen for demonstrations, tests and rehearsals, and back offices for Barbie Small and our secretary.

It was here that I worked at the next series, as Treena grew heavier while editing the location films.

The great day arrived on October 21 1968 when our youngest daughter Kareena was born. The travel and production stress had taken their toll and Treena was suffering from a liver toxicity caused, in part, by fluctuating high blood pressure. Because there was some danger to both mother and child, she needed to have the birth induced.

The hospital had strapped her arm onto an ordinary piece of yellow pine plank to keep the intravenous tubes firmly in place. It all seemed so...*rural?* I was invited to wait to be a part of the birth, but apparently was at the point of passing out and was firmly told to "go home and wait." No sooner was I home than the phone rang and I was off to the hospital again to greet our very new daughter and my tired but triumphant Treena. Our family was now five; much had changed with our new addition, but not the pressures to produce the exact number of episodes on the contract.

I had always thought that sixty-five episodes would have been enough. When the second series was ordered, I was convinced that I would then be "personality overexposed."

Then came "Time" and "Newsweek" both in the same week, followed by a four-page spread in "Life."

I was in the midst of my fifteen minutes of fame, except mine was going way beyond – normal?

Paul Talbot came to the pretty obvious conclusion that we should find a home in Ottawa and take up residence with all our children; at least until the six hundred and fifty shows were completed. Then, if we chose, we could return to Sydney.

There really was no argument. We simply went along for the ride, much as a family is forced to do when once you've paid the price and settled into a roller coaster. It starts, and there is no way you can get off!

Our very young Kareena obviously needed a mother's attention, but then so did the program so we found a Karitane nurse, a justifiably famous New Zealand nurse-come-nanny movement that started in New Zealand. Gillian Cullinane now joined the family and was more or less "in charge "of our little ones, as we left home each weekday at 10 a.m. and returned, usually, by 10:30 p.m. On the weekends, we crashed. After six weeks we jumped a plane and flew off to collect the next series. A month later we were home to cook, cut and edit for eight to ten hours a day until we were ready, almost to the day, to reenter the studio.

We left messages for the children on the refrigerator door. We knew each other by name, but that's about as far as it went.

Our major sponsor, Westinghouse, paid for the basement of our four-story high "rental" on Acacia Avenue in Ottawa, to be converted to the test and develop-

ment kitchen, and we dug up the back yard to install a swimming pool. These are apparently the essential fringe benefits that keep people going round and round the oceans of opportunity, getting larger and larger, while consuming anything that seemed worth swallowing.

Some "wannabe" Hollywood celebrities go to the extent of placing a mirror on their bedroom ceiling, never to lose sight of themselves? We chose to put up the plans for a 71-foot ocean-racing ketch, modeled on the hull designed for the famous South African yacht "Stormvogel."

I needed something more than a former diplomatic residence and a swimming pool. I needed a huge yacht (well, not *huge* by world standards), much bigger than the last one I had sailed, a 14-foot Redwing dingy in Torquay, Devon, UK, when I was seventeen!

I set up a series of squares to cover the large formal plans to represent the remaining number of episodes that we had yet to record. They accounted for four hundred and fifty five programs.

Dividing the length of the yacht, 71 feet = 852 inches, by these programs provided me with what I came to call the "1-1/2 inch incentive."

When we returned home I would stand on the bed and mark off another two or three squares. (On Tuesday and Thursday we recorded three episodes back-to-back, the rest of the week were just two.)

By each week's end we were 10-1/2 inches closer to reaching our goal to "own" such a vessel!

A celebrity has been described as "someone who is well known for being well known." This was becoming true in our lives, largely because we were continually being trotted out on the much larger stages of public awareness and seen by people who had never seen the program itself. "Galloping Gourmet" was becoming a *brand*.

I had two wonderful evenings with Johnny Carson, one of which has a permanent place on You Tube, in which we used the old wine skin "container" and drank directly from it. Johnny went everywhere you could imagine and was, as always, hilarious!

I had, on another occasion, found an electric spaghetti fork in a store in Southern France. A small battery twirled the fork in circles, thus gathering the pasta in the traditional manner, yet without the apparent effort!

This ridiculous item just begged for a "Tonight Show" outing. I had it fitted with a two-stage emergency dental drill motor so that it would gently loop at lower speed and go into wild gyrations if pushed to the second mark.

I made an especially goopy tomato-sauced spaghetti and, sitting at a table center stage, demonstrated how it worked on stage one. The audience found it amusing but hardly funny.

Johnny had been briefed. He asked to try it and dug the fork into the mound of pasta. He then pushed the switch all the way and the motor took off; laboring at first to wind up the mass, it suddenly broke loose and long strands of dripping spaghetti whipped across Johnny's suit and spun off to cover Doc Severinsen and members of the band.

Johnny did his classic slow double take as the spaghetti continued to wildly lash him into what looked like a weekend with the Marquis de' Sade!

It was following that event that I was asked if I would consider being a "guest host" for a week when Johnny was due for a break. It was Treena that reminded me, "you already have a day *and* night job."

It might have been fun –for a celebrity?

"Is that Graham?" The caller had a firm American accent.

"Yes, it is." I answered, wondering who had my very private number.

"It's Danny Kaye." He answered.

"Sure it is," I laughed, wondering which of our friends was on the line.

"Where are you?" He continued.

"Ottawa, as always."

"No, you're not, you're here in LA," he ploughed on.

"Get your ass round here...we need to cook."

"I assure you that I am not in LA and who is this?"

"I told you, this is Danny Kaye." He now sounded a little impatient.

And so it turned out that a real celebrity, who also loved to cook, had got my number and wanted me to visit him...SOON!

I explained that my schedule couldn't possibly allow for such a trip.

"I'll send my plane for you." He insisted.

We met eventually when he conducted the Boston Philharmonic Orchestra.

Danny did such concerts many times as a way to raise funds for retiring musicians and their pension funds.

He was great! Our evening in 1970 was not recorded, but you can see him in action on YouTube at a Lincoln Center event in 1981.

Joyce Chen, Danny Kaye and myself.
Photo Credit © Stephen Chen

We actually had a good deal in common between his love of music and our mutual love of food, coupled with a sense of humor.

Danny couldn't read a note of music. What he did was to memorize every note for most every instrument in over a two hour long concert.

In the midst of such detailed understanding, he found opportunities to be outrageously funny. His audience expected it of him and he went along with their need, while all the time relishing the opportunity to conduct such famous orchestras playing music he deeply loved and respected.

He saw some of his life reflected in my own intensity interwoven with the lightheartedness that Treena had so skillfully injected into our culinary classics from around the world. We remained friends. He got each of my books as soon as they came off the press.

Danny died in 1987 and bequeathed his vast culinary library to the Culinary Institute of America (CIA) in Hyde Park, New York, where he had also donated the Danny Kaye Culinary Theater.

I was also to teach in the "Great Chefs Series" in that CIA Theater and found all my autographed books, side-by-side in their library

There were some good celebrity moments in the midst of so much trial and error.

There were, however, very few family moments and those nearest and dearest to us began to feel the strain.

Please join us in the Reflective Readers Club
www.grahamkerr.com/rrc

Rite of Passage Twenty-Nine: "Kicking the Furniture Helps"

When I first encountered the new "taste" of the great waters in which I lived, with my hen, in the midst of many others; quite a few were of my own kind. We looked alike, and were all feeling a sense of urgency, coupled with apprehension, because it seemed like the open waters were beckoning.

It wasn't just the idea of new things to eat, it was the challenge of the —new itself!

I felt this in the close company of the others who gathered about me, making up a shoal, or family, instinct.

Now here I am, well traveled in the great waters, beyond the boundaries of rocks to the side or even rocks below. Above us, it changes from bright to dark, below it's darker and darker...with no apparent end.

It is comforting in all this space to have some of our early family still with us. Like us, they have grown, and by doing so allow us some idea how we must look.

We are never alone. There are those like us who are going our way into the almost unknown.

An Understanding

The Chinook had taken their time in the fresh waters of their birth stream and its estuary, when the salty seawater began to mix with the river. Life, in this early stage, was lived in often-dense gill-to-gill shoals where similarity attracts.

It may be that the conversion to salt water has a kind of odd response, a mix of expectation and the fear of the unknown. With increasing confidence that comes from size, there comes a community "agreement" that the time has come to brave the big waters. The fact that our fish tend to move in shoals suggests that the familial is important, and that when there is a common instinct, movement is not only possible but actually desired.

1970
I am thirty six years old

At least we were now all in one place, if not of one *mind*.

The days of boarding schools were over; Tessa and Andy were able to walk a short distance to good local private schools. These schools had, amongst the student body, a good number of children from diplomatic families and a few senior executives who needed to be close to the National Government of Canada in Ottawa.

Tessa was now fourteen and Andy had just turned ten. Kareena was still in her first year.

Our Karitane Nurse, Gillian, was a constant part of our family and had begun to bond deeply with Kareena who suffered early on with profound bouts of colic and other general upsets.

We supposed that our life, outside the studio walls, was pretty normal. We were neighbors to fairly affluent people who accepted us for who we felt we were.

There were no press photographers as in Los Angeles and other media centers. We seldom ever ate out since there was an endless stream of recipes in the basement kitchen pipeline. What we missed, however, was actually *living* together. We were almost *out of sight and out of mind*.

Our large rental home had a spacious separate dining room. It was of sufficient size to need a pretty big table to avoid looking ridiculous. As it happened, the Swedish Embassy was selling an oak dining table nearly twenty feet long, complete with twelve vast red and gold brocaded chairs. It was heavy, relatively old and quite impressive.

We bought it for a song...well perhaps it was an aria!

There remained then the table settings.

During our international adventures, we had asked famous restaurants and hotels if they would share a complete place setting of their china and silverware with us. Many did and we had a full twelve sets that represented several of the most highly regarded culinary meccas of our days.

One of our positional sponsors (PS), Waterford Crystal, came up with a full matching set of their least "cut" glasses (now termed "clear light").

We invested in two silver candelabras and some silver cruet sets and BINGO, we had ourselves a Downton Abbey styled table at which to entertain...well...anybody!

We never had a single dinner party – everything was left unused by royalty, celebrity, politicians or even family.

It remained –all packed up –but no time to be used!

It was during these months of endless productions that I received our bank statement from Peat, Marwick and Mitchell, the international accounting firm that managed our money. For the first time our account had just over seven numbers. *We were millionaires!*

I ran into the lobby and called up

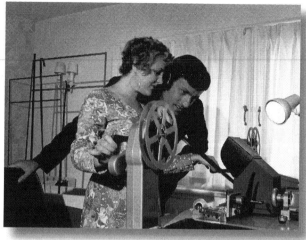

Treena in her editing room

to the minstrel's galley that ran around the third floor rooms where Treena did her editing.

"Darling," I shouted... "Darling!"

Treena came to the railing and looked down.

"Yes...what is it?" She obviously was in the midst of a complicated edit.

"We are millionaires!" I waved the statement excitedly.

"Don't forget the script conference at noon." She replied and turned back to the editing room, closing the door with a firm thud! I was left holding the statement that now hung motionless and a little limp in my outstretched hand. The joy of that achievement evaporated immediately and in its place came a wave of frustration, and even anger. I went around the ground floor kicking our rented furniture in our rented house. "What's the point...what's the damned point?" I shouted at the walls, the artwork and the huge empty dining table and its twelve empty chairs. In the space of a few minutes I had come to understand that life was not about a string of zero's, but at the same time, what upset me most was that I had nothing to fill that space...only the next apparent achievement, whatever that may be.

It came almost immediately.

It was Paul Talbot on the phone.

"Treena has been nominated as daytime TV producer of the year for the Galloping Gourmet!"

He was obviously thrilled and so was I.

An Emmy award, at least a nomination, meant being recognized for all our work. It wasn't just the money or the endless schedule anymore; it was being accepted by our peers! We attended the awards ceremony in New York and waited breathlessly for our time to come...

"and the award goes to –The Today Show!"

Exhale slowly. Our table partners squeezed our shoulders and melted away.

We left on our own and chose to walk back to our hotel, holding hands. "At least we were nominated," we agreed quite happily. Then came the rapid tapping of high heels on hard pavement. A well-dressed woman dashed up brandishing a program of the awards evening.

"Oh please, please...do sign my program...I'm such a fan," she chattered, excitedly.

We both signed it.

She looked closely at our scrawl and then back to our faces.

"Oh!" She exclaimed. "I thought you were David Frost."

Back in Ottawa and very much back in our place, I found time to take Tessa into the studio one day to experience what "mommy and daddy do all day."

She was fourteen and quite forthcoming.

We were driving to the C.J.O.H studio in our vast boat-sized Oldsmobile 88 convertible, 1969, painted gold; yet another attempt at outward appearance benefits that worked, for a while.

The top was down, the weather warm and humid. I smoked my other positional sponsor's cigarette, direct from its maroon and gold metal package.

"Why do you and mummy work so hard?" she asked.

"Well, we've got a contract for six hundred and fifty shows," I explained, "and we have to finish what we started."

"What do we do when it's over?"

"I'd like to get us all on that big boat that's on the ceiling over our bed and sail around the world...so that we could get to know each other...again," I added lamely, well aware of the distance there was between us.

"I guess we'd all have to have a medical checkup before we leave?" She was making a point, so I simply murmured in agreement.

"Wouldn't it be awful," she rushed on, "if you had an x-ray and they found out you had lung cancer because you smoke so much," she paused briefly before a final thrust...

"and you died and never fulfilled your dream."

These were her exact words, and they remain with me to this day, because it was at that moment, on that drive, that I dropped my Benson and Hedges cigarettes out onto the roadside (I do *not* litter, but this time it was different). I also threw away the matching gold lighter and I have never touched another cigarette since.

Tessa had been primed for this encounter at school and it had given her a way to let me know that she cared for me...but did my response prove that I cared for her and the needs she had that she had no easy way to express to her "distant dad."

At that time, I had no idea that our busy lives were of such concern to our beloved daughter. It seemed enough to me that my explanation for why we "worked so much" was understood and that the end was in sight and it was a time of "being together...*again.*" I just didn't get it...that it was *now* that she needed the *knowing each other* to begin without delay.

We shall, as a direct result, never forget the movie "Lawrence of Arabia," starring Peter O'Toole. We had a Saturday night free so Treena and I went out on a rare "date" to dinner and a movie. Roughly halfway through, an attendant with a hooded flashlight found us in the darkened theater.

"Mr. Graham Kerr?" She asked in a whisper.

"The police have called; your daughter is in the emergency room at the hospital."

We took off at a run and were informed that our little one had taken an overdose in an apparent suicide attempt. It was iced water time; not just in the stomach somewhere...it was total immersion!

We didn't really have to ask why; it was obvious that she needed us...NOW, not in two hundred episodes time! But, now wasn't entirely possible; it became partially so because we were now acutely aware of our entire family's need for us to be parents and not just "busy" for their sake at some future date. And so we added to our impossible daily task, the need for family time.

Our neighbors had children of roughly the same age as ours, but unfortunately they also shared our lack of time or availability because they, too, were affluent and therefore, busy!

We discovered that some of these children had resorted to using illegal substances including marijuana, which they smoked around our pool while we were at the studio. I called a meeting of all Tessa's friends and explained our position.

"I am talking to you, rather than your parents, and I need you to know that I am really serious." I was trying hard to be stern and measured, but above all, not angry.

"This house and the pool are now strictly off limits for all kinds of drug use. If I catch one of you just one time, then I will take you directly to the RCMP (Royal Canadian Mounted Police) along with the evidence."

"This kind of behavior is now OVER." They appeared sheepish and one or two mumbled an apology with a promise not to do it again. I found out much, much later that they had resorted to taking small sample "shots" from our bar since apparently I hadn't banned these substances from *my* life.

Andy was just too young to be an active participant in the process, but not too young to be threatened at the "good" neighborhood school.

He had shared his concern about being beaten up by a small group of bullies.

I handed him a baseball bat, complete with instructions.

"Take this to school; show it to those who are threatening you and tell them that if they attack you, you will choose the right time to break their legs with it."

He did exactly that...and the threat went away.

Is this, I wonder, why we in the U.S. have approximately 5,113 nuclear warheads that cost about $60 billion a year to maintain and safeguard?

Then there was Kareena, who by now had stopped her colic attacks and had settled down as an amazing fashion model. Our Karitane "nanny" was engaged in a full on "dress up baby" routine. With unchecked funds at her disposal, she set out to achieve her possibly frustrated maternal urge by entering the, as yet, undeclared contest for "Best Dressed Baby." Clothes led the way, swiftly followed by the love and care of a nanny; followed by a kind of possessiveness that was beginning to concern us.

Our way of life, at the pace we were living it, which I had considered to be impossible, was now proving to be exactly that. With one hundred and ninety five shows to record, we left our children behind once again and set off to scoop up the next sixty-five classic

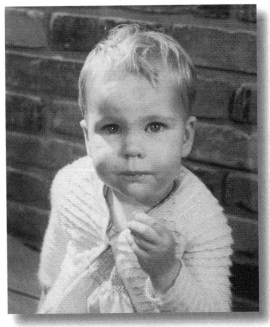

"Best Dressed Baby"

international dishes. We arrived at London's Heathrow Airport to be met by a BBC TV film crew and a happy, good-natured producer in a cable stitch pullover and corduroys who announced cheerfully...

"Welcome, welcome...got some great news. We've got permission from the Savoy Hotel to film you in the kitchen where you began."

He rushed on as my heart sank. I knew that one day I might have to confront my early self-serving conceit. It had never been a deliberate intention to deceive.

My "conceit" back in 1959 was an attempt to patch up my damaged pride at having such a small audience. Somehow, to say that I had received my early training in the Savoy Hotel kitchens was to have someone out there regret having missed the opportunity to see me in action. But oh, how those few words had followed me everywhere we had gone. Even Treena had been deceived. "So..." he continued, "the really good news is that Chef Silvano Trompetto is still the Chef des Cuisines, the same as when you were there."

That was it...there was no retreat.

We were driven directly to the Savoy where we were staying and ushered into the kitchen where the crew had now established their camera and lights. Over the years I had made it my business to know as much as I could about Chef Trompetto and his kitchens just in case anyone had ever asked. I was never challenged by anyone...until now! I spotted the Chef in his high white Toque Chef's hat. I knew that his personal friends and close associates called him "Tromps."

The cameras were rolling. I had been given a radio microphone, so I called out.

"Hello Tromps!" *Might as well be hung for a sheep as a lamb!*

Maitre Chefs des Cuisines Silvano Trompetto turned and raised his elegant hand in an open greeting.

"Hello Graham." He called back across the open kitchen. "Welcome back" he added with a wide smile. He hadn't remembered me, I knew that, but he also didn't doubt that I, like hundreds of other spotty-faced youngsters, had had an early start in his kitchens.

I was home free! The dreaded confrontation had happened and the long-ago lie could remain forever buried.

Yet another source of my fear of failure had been removed...or so I thought!

Please join us in the Reflective Readers Club
www.grahamkerr.com/rrc

Rite of Passage Thirty:
"The Broken Wooden Spoon Award"

Our shoal, when we first left our quiet estuary and birth river, was numerous. I remember those of my family flashing about me on every side.

We had swum together through many light and dark surfaces and had grown in size and strength, and yet...

There were times, when we finished feeding and gathered together to rest, that we sensed that there were less of us than those with whom we began our journey.

Some we saw leaving; they swam away on an early felt current. There were those who vanished in the midst of the black and whites and the larger furry ones. Others seemed unwilling or unable to keep up. Still more were tugged away through the bright surface in struggling numbers hard to comprehend.

These are the ones we left behind. In season, we were emboldened by their presence, feeling some safety in numbers. Now, when we rest, we remember and have a sense of loss mixed with gratitude.

Were it not for them, we might have been the ones who vanished or were "tugged away." Yes, we are grateful indeed.

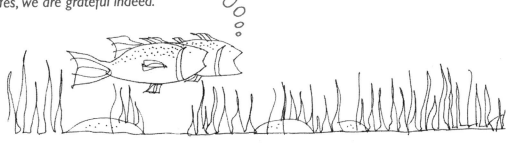

An Understanding

There is just so far that Marine Science can go in understanding exactly why salmon live as they do. By tagging juvenile fish in their natal river and relying upon later fishermen to make notes of their vast "catch" in the varied ocean commercial fisheries that occur in their long migration it is possible to know where they travel in a natural sequence.

The inner motives and emotions that might guide the salmon in a unique way is still beyond science, and for the most part it continues to be as difficult to make definite conclusions as it is in our own human behavior!

This is where we are forced to imagine, or simply give up for lack of proof.

I like to think, as one who has become submerged in the life of my subject male Chinook "King" salmon, that he really is aware of the relationships with both his hen and with others in his "family" shoal (or school).

Why else would they swim together, why else would the fully matured male be equipped with both the strength and the teeth to chase away competitors when the time has come for the laying and fertilizing of the eggs?

And so, we imagine both sorrow at leaving and gratitude for relationships along the way!

1970
I am now thirty six years old

There isn't one of us who "made it" who hasn't had considerable help from others, some of whom we rewarded directly as a result; others were thanked profusely, at times but nonetheless, were left behind without benefit.

Some we simply left behind without understanding quite what happened and, as a result, they felt poorly treated and became understandably upset.

All of this was true in our case and was perhaps all the more evident when the rate of change is so fast that the "advance" swiftly leaves behind most sources of supply.

We had gone too far, too fast, for anyone's good.

My own distant dad, whose upbringing had conditioned him to be quite impersonal, had nonetheless been there for me whenever I had needed wise counsel. I would come to know in time that he had not abandoned me to a violent boarding school, but that would come much later...when it was too late to remedy with him one-on-one.

I chose to distance myself from both my mother and father because we needed to get away from our roots in order to be a new family in a far distant land. I failed to communicate, and even at the very end (with my dad), I more or less left him to his own desires as he slowly smoked and drank himself to death; drowning in disappointment.

For his occasional help, I'm grateful; for my thoughtlessness, I'm *sorry...*

Major Andy Silk and Brigadier Horsfall were my British Army supporters. Without their help I would never have become "Maître d' to the Army" at only just twenty three years of age with a peacetime Captain's rank.

I never reconnected with either of these men. I simply left without saying how grateful I had been for their early encouragement.

For this I am now *sorry*.

It's hard to see our time with Alex Taylor at the Royal Ascot Hotel in a positive light, but truly the disciplines and the struggles of being completely *out of my depth* were, and continue to be, important lessons. I would have liked, *eventually*, to have said thank you for their thoughtfulness, but by the time I began to understand, it was too late.

Flight Sergeant Phil Eyton of the RNZAF was my right-hand man during my time as Chief Catering Advisor in the Air Force. It was he that repeatedly suggested ways to achieve my goals that were better suited to the local culture than my initially pompous POME attitude. "I'd boil the buggers first," had been his advice on roasted Muscovy ducks...and he had been right. He continued to offer good advice to me over our five years of service together. I'm grateful to Phil, and I'm *sorry* that I never followed up as I was swept away.

John Buck, my very well qualified business wine partner at the New Zealand Display Center, had every reason to believe that our venture would endure and expand over time. My sudden departure to Australia was, I promised him, just a brief interlude and would be good for our business as food and wine (in his case) consultants. In the short term, it was... but in the long-term I had to leave him, and while I explained, it was clear that I was not understood. I left him in the lurch. He had helped me, and I had failed him...I'm grateful and I'm *sorry*.

Harry M. Miller yanked us out of New Zealand to Australia and used his considerable skills to position me on multiple rungs up the ladder of celebrity. As it turned out, it was far too high and too fast for anyone's good. I am grateful for his efforts and saddened that I am unable, due to his physical condition, to thank him for his *early* work.

Arthur Pettitt was an enormous help as we left Harry M. Miller's management. He felt that he could help us; he loved us, and he worked really hard on our behalf. In the midst of this survival exercise, we were suddenly rescued by Paul Talbot and literally plucked out of the Sydney marketplace and whisked off to Canada for our very full time "Galloping Gourmet" exploits. Arthur was devastated, as I completely understood. I should have explained our needs with greater care...I didn't and for many years he felt that we had just left him out-to-dry. I am grateful for his friendship and help in those very difficult days when I needed a good friend...I'm so *sorry* that it took so many years before I was able to say so, face-to-face.

Len Evans, the famous Australian wine expert, was a close yet always bristling companion. He used me to help him showcase the vineyards he reviewed and represented. I used him to gain access to the then influential leaders in the wine and food world in the Southern

Hemisphere. I remain grateful, and yet so *sorry* that we lost touch, and then one day he passed and now it's too late.

Robert Beasley, the Chef and owner at "Monsieur Robert Dining Club," was enormously influential in opening my eyes to another level of what *cooking* can mean.

I'm truly grateful, and yet so *sorry* that we have lost touch...perhaps he will read or hear this and get in touch?

> Note: In case you might think that we had very few helpful people in our lives, let me explain that there were many that we were able to reward and thank. These are those whom we somehow left behind and now deeply regret having done so.

In a classic athletic track event a relay race usually involves four participants; while each runner does their very best, only one of them crosses the line to be declared the winner. Later, at the awards ceremony, all four are given their matching medals; all four are winners.

As we looked back during this moment of maximum success, we should have wanted everyone who had passed on so much, both good and often difficult, to have been rewarded by at least a visit, phone call or letter to say "Thank You." This is therefore the reason why the ones with whom we did not communicate are added here. We won the race, but then, so did they!

It was at this time during 1970 that we received an unusual award.

"The Broken Wooden Spoon"

This is quietly but firmly awarded to the individual that they described as...

"Public Enemy #1 International to those wishing to lose weight and regain health."

The award was given by Weight Watchers International who sent me a real wooden spoon, snapped in half lengthways; not an easy feat!

I remember writing back to the then President.

"Madam, thank you for your award; I shall frame it and treasure it. My concern for you, however, is that in your personal pursuit of the perfect diet you may one day be run over by a bus and that in your last lucid moment you might wonder what a classic Fettuccine Alfredo really tastes like!"

This recognition of my success was by no means the only correction or criticism that I received, but since the overall viewership of the program kept growing, all the way to a reported 200 million worldwide (a number touted by the agency but never able to be confirmed), I felt that if nothing else I should continue to give them what they apparently preferred.

In the midst of several critics came an especially strong letter from The Temperance League in, as I recall, Halifax, Nova Scotia. They were especially concerned about my obvious enjoyment and liberal consumption of wine throughout the show.

Again, this was Treena's genius at work.

Because the show went to non-commercial networks such as the BBC in the United Kingdom, we had to include opportunities for commercial breaks that were apparently seamless.

"Let's have you raise a glass and say *time for a short slurp*, and then drink and put the glass down on a set spot. We can then cut in the midst of that movement."

This we did, and thus the need to drink on camera throughout the show. The not entirely unexpected result was being called...

"The Dean Martin of the Kitchen"

"The High Priest of Hedonism"

and

"The Hedonist in a Hurry"

I made no attempt at restraint. Every time I poured cream, fried in clarified butter or set something ablaze in cognac, the studio audience laughed and even cheered me on! I was in the midst of a feeding frenzy of luscious treats that I chummed over the stern of our TV show into the ocean of opportunity.

We had, during this time, several major sponsors whose name and products I enthusiastically endorsed. At one stage, I sat in an old-fashioned bathtub set up in the studio dining room. I was dressed above the surface in dinner jacket, black tie and white shirt, and busily floated Dixie cups on the surface, saying how useful they were for so many things!

For Uncle Ben's Long Grain Converted Rice I wore a suit of armor to underscore their special treatment.

All in all, it was more than a little odd, and all *ad lib*. We were, perhaps, the only endorsees that ever insisted in saying only what we wanted to say about their products. The client, through the Agency, gave us their USPs (Unique Selling Propositions), usually two or three essentials. Treena and I then made up to twenty takes before we liked one or two that we felt were truthful, on target, inclusive of the USPs and, if possible, funny.

The Agency had to sit through each session in silence and even not object when we wiped the ones they preferred to the one we selected. I'm amazed that this was done, and can only see that we got away with it because the advertisements were restricted to our show alone. We were back in the days of "just hold the packet and say the name."

These were the *obvious* sponsors. There were also the positional

Uncle Ben's commercial

sponsors that we called "P.S." These were the folks who made saucepans, knives, sold wine, kitchenware; the list goes on and on. Mostly they provided the equipment needed and received a credit, but now and again this went further and I began to select and in some cases, invent, products that we sold under my name.

As our celebrity increased, so the competition for association of any kind increased. I had unwittingly become a "style leader" for moderately excessive conspicuous consumption –the good life indeed! I hadn't realized that I was being used to stimulate marketing. It should have been obvious, but at the time everything was so immediate, and the thought never occurred to me. There appeared to be no downside; nothing I used or endorsed did anyone any harm and someone always paid for the so-called privilege...so why not?

We had a young scriptwriter from Los Angeles who tried to find acceptable "shaggy dog" stories to fill four to five minutes at the head of the show.

He handed me a slip of paper with the words...

**"Golden Rule: Everyone, no matter how affable he is,
wants his pound of flesh. It's your flesh, mate."**

I have this framed in my study to this day. There really is no such thing as a free lunch; no matter who is doing the cooking!

A reputation can easily become eroded when tiny bites lead to the loss of a major limb. I was being rapidly eaten away without even noticing. It took a great many years to once again fully occupy my own space and resist the marketer's need for bait.

Now awash in cash flow, but still suffering a relational deficit at home, both personally and with our children, we were trying to find a less exhausting schedule for the remaining one hundred ninety five shows.

We decided that since we had girdled the entire world so many times, that it was now time for Canada and the United States.

We set out to do a complete circumnavigation of the United States and Canada by road in a small caravan of motor homes built and provided by Winnebago. We chose their 1970 "Brave" D series, with single berths on either side and an aft bathroom.

The idea was to track down one hundred ninety five recipes that had arrived on the continent along with immigrants who also brought their own seeds and culinary techniques. We wanted to see how these had "taken root" and been modified by the new American environment.

Spaghetti Carbonara is a good example. In Rome, it is simply spaghetti tossed in Prosciutto (air dried, thinly sliced ham), Parmesan cheese and beaten eggs, with perhaps a little olive oil. In the United States, this has been "Alfredo'd" with a rich, thick cream, butter and cheese sauce that easily doubled the calories found in the original.

I wanted to find out why the changes had taken place and see if there had been an "improvement."

I still think this was, and still is, a great idea for a major book!

We went on the Dinah Shore show to promote the idea, complete with the motorhome, and everything was arranged coast-to-coast. What a terrific way of saying farewell to such a wonderfully rewarding pair of nations. It would be our way of saying "Thank you, from sea to shining sea and nobody left behind."

We described it in playful British terms as a "smashing idea."

How right we were!

Please join us in the Reflective Readers Club
www.grahamkerr.com/rrc

Rite of Passage Thirty-One: "The Way of Escape"

My hen was the first to turn. She had begun to be much less active. Even while resting near the bottom of sandy banks she would always come alive to chase after the silvery slim launce fish; but she had recently remained still as though no longer hungry.

She still looks fine, beautifully rounded and so much larger and stronger...but quieter and more pensive?

I, too, sensed something stirring deep within. When I feel like this, I know that a good belly full of fresh food always does the trick. Not this time, this deep-down feeling wasn't going away that easily.

In the midst of these emotions, the waters seemed to be curving around and moving downward again. We hesitated for a moment and then, in a quick flash of our broad tails, we gave way to the movement about us and began our trip back to what, this time, felt like —home?

Always aware of the dangers about us, but never timid or put off in our journey, we were now practiced at escaping the large black and whites, and the large furry ones.

The bright wounded fish that swim in straight lines were now pretty obvious even though occasionally tempting.

What happened next was a terrifying moment for which we had no understanding.

There is a disturbance on the bright surface with many dark and vivid white patches that fold the waters.

We go up together to marvel at the foaming white waters and thrust forward to let the pressure try to push us back but we are stronger and make our way ahead. I leap out of the water and land on my side with a huge splash in a deep green-grey fold in the waters.

My hen, admiring my leap, tries one of her own, not bad! She really is quite beautiful and graceful and yes...well rounded.

And then, in the midst of so much pure joy, I am caught in a coarse floating "thing" that forms regular squares attached to each other that float.

I turn down sharply to swim down deep and fast, and run head on into the same coarseness that seems to be everywhere and moving slowly against the waters.

My hen swims to my side. We rise again, close together and swim in the midst of the white foam and folds to find the edges of the thing. I turn in the direction in which it is slowly moving. I see a small space, an opening to the waters.

I point the way with my nose and my hen rushes forward; I follow and break out into the great waters.

We found a way to escape the coarse moving thing that had no end.

We were frightened...but free!

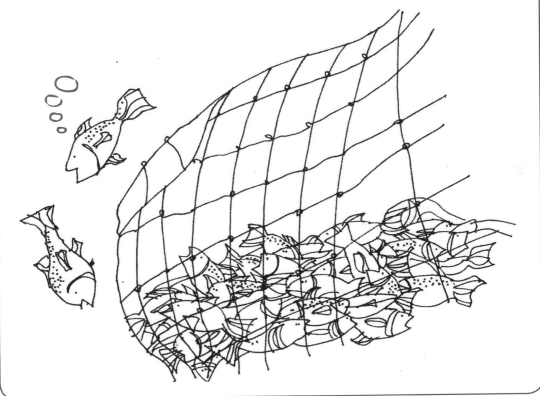

An Understanding

Our fish have begun to experience the elements of new life beginning to grow within them. They are now fully matured. The buck is nearly four feet long and approaching 50 pounds. The hen is a full six inches shorter and just under forty pounds.

They are both fine Chinooks, with eggs forming in the hen and milt in the buck.

This internal treasure has begun to fill their inside cavities and make them less anxious to fill their bellies.

The water currents, driven by winter storms, have begun to move southward, and our pair quietly submit to go along for the ride.

Their time to frolic in the small storm brings them into a large dragnet from which there appears to be no escape, but in their maturity they go looking for a way of escape.

They find the net opening just before it is winched aboard; just wide enough to allow their passage.

1971
I am thirty seven years old

We set out from Los Angeles on the day after our appearance on the Dinah Shore Show in the spring of 1971. I was then just thirty seven years old and beginning to feel the approach of middle age.

Both Treena and I took a deep breath as we turned onto the US-101 going North with Charlie, our professional driver, who would do the driving from city to city as we slept. The Winnebago was a brand new 1970 in the D Series. It had twin beds and a rear bathroom. The length overall was just twenty four feet; quite small by present day motor home standards but it provided everything we thought we needed.

Our small film crew was following in a matching rig that pulled a sixteen foot trailer jammed with film equipment and promotional literature.

By visiting just sixty nine towns and cities and finding two recipes per location, we would be able to complete the contract of six hundred and fifty and have honored the deal that we had thought was impossible.

We planned to do this in two bites (if you will permit the use of that term!). Each would entail just over thirty locations that were an average one hundred miles apart, or three thousand miles each in five weeks.

We made Avila Beach in just over three hours drive and had a splendid lunch. We filmed at the Avila Beach breakwater in the Olde Port Inn that still has an exceptional reputation for the seafood we enjoyed.

Our next stop was to be Pebble Beach, and we would achieve this overnight as we tried to sleep on-the-move.

We were late in leaving because the film trailer had a light connection problem with the second rig, so rather than hold up the process we swapped the sixteen-footer to our twenty four footer and set off on Highway 101 for Carmel and its famous beach.

The weather was calm and quite misty with an ocean fog forecast. We slept fitfully as we made our way at a measured pace, consistent, we hoped, with a few hours of decent sleep.

I awoke with a start and with one explosive movement swung out of bed onto my knees, grasped Treena and pulled her onto the floor.

Immediately came the crumpling, screeching crash, and we were punched forward briefly, sliding off to the right. Metal sparking on metal.

"JESUS," cried Charlie as he wrestled with the wheel.

We were now close to the driver's seat by the dinette, holding onto each other, my shoulder crushed up against the galley cabinets. The violent rocking slowed and the metallic scream abruptly stopped in a sudden slushy hush. Steam rose around us from the crushed ice plants in the meridian, our lights still on, crazily slanting up and over to fields beyond.

Charlie moved fast to turn off the propane furnace heater and prevent a fire. We found out later that the sudden up-rush of ice plant had done that for us.

We laid where we were, frozen in the stillness, steam and light.

We heard a conversation between Charlie and whoever had apparently hit us from behind. We moved slowly, checking to see if anything was broken; my shoulder perhaps, but otherwise I was far too concerned about Treena, who seemed to be awake but unresponsive. An ambulance came and we were x-rayed and checked over.

All I wanted was a cup of tea. All the nurses wanted was an autograph.

An empty sixteen-wheeler returning to the San Fernando Valley at about 1 a.m. had come round the bend doing 70-plus miles per hour in light to moderate fog and had run right into our white painted film trailer pulled behind our RV. Its front wheels ran up the curved back of the trailer and literally blew it apart as it came into the rear of the RV where the bathroom took the brunt of the collision.

Had it not been for that novel configuration and the trailer, we would almost certainly have died in that crash —which was exactly how the media covered the story.

Our children heard on the news in Ottawa that we had died in California.

One glance at the wreckage would have left no one in doubt that there were fatalities. Treena remained silent, yet mobile, until the nurses wanted an autograph. In an instant she reacted, and it wasn't hard to see that something had snapped.

At the beginning in Australia, I had told everyone that what we were attempting was impossible and yet we had done it, keeping to the schedule, not letting anyone down; including our faithful, enthusiastic viewers.

Well, we had let our children down, and I had let Treena down, and my parents, and my past business associates...our dear friends also!

We had climbed up a large tree and then moved out on a long sturdy branch until it began to taper off gradually...*it had just broken!*

"I can't possibly go on, that's it. I'm finished." Treena leaned up against me, tears flowing, her whole body shaking.

I rubbed her back gently. "That's okay, you don't have to, I agree, it's over."

From memory, that was it...twenty two words and we had found complete agreement.

It was the end, for Treena yet also perhaps it was the starting point of an emerging darkness that would terrify us both in the years to come.

I sat in the hospital, complete with a poorly made cup of tea, and waited for Paul Talbot to arrive.

During that wait, I sat reviewing how we had arrived at this point in our lives. Having narrowly escaped death; what had it been that kept us going?

In the beginning it was the need to pay the bills, food and rent, then a simple car. The big leap was to exchange my old fiber suitcase for the leather Portmanteau, the Rolls Royce limo, the Penthouse suite, first class airfare, The Tonight Show, big houses, swimming pools, Alfa Romeo, Oldsmobile 88, cooking with celebrities, awards, book sales, and on and on... stepping stones of acquisition across an angry torrent of time forever rushing past.

There were only a few more stones and we would be over and able to go on our way.

Could we do it?

Treena was now asleep, having been given a mild sedative to lessen her upset over the autograph request. Even in her sleep she was clearly troubled, her fine forehead rumpled in a frown, her mouth turned down tightly. For her sake, which was also mine, we could not go on.

Paul knew enough not to argue the point when we did get to meet.

I wanted to go directly to the Forest Mere Health Hydro in Liphook, Hampshire, in England. This was the "spa" that my parents had run that was now owned by the Savoy Hotel in London. The Director, Norman Sanderson, was still the "expert" in charge of their medical services. He was the only person that I knew I could trust.

My left side had become partly paralyzed; I was able to stand briefly but could never again leap over a dining chair. Treena suffered a deep post-accident trauma that included an absolute fear of large green trucks and moved onward into multiple issues, not unlike those suffering from PTSD (posttraumatic stress disorder).

The Galloping Gourmet series stopped abruptly and began reruns as we entered into a gentle debate about the one hundred ninety five shows remaining.

Unlike many others, Paul did not insist. He only wanted to see if there was *anything* that could be done.

I was now flying solo, and unable to stand for long or jump a chair.

I decided, without Treena's input since she was still in a guarded position, to reinvent the idea of reruns by replacing the front six minutes of film and jokes with celebrity guests who would be invited to watch a previously recorded show and comment with me about the food.

We called it "Critics Choice."

Liberace came. So did Tiny Tim, Stiller and Meara, and my now old friend, Maître Chef des Cuisines Silvano Trompetto.

We tried; my goodness, how we tried, but it couldn't replace the original...and so the curtain drew slowly and quietly and we all made a measured retreat.

Well...almost!

There were still those positional sponsors (PS) with whom we had made things that sold, including books. If I would just *do* something to keep my celebrity alive, then perhaps there might be an after-market?

When all the failed expectations had been settled, insurance paid and contracts renegotiated, we had enough to afford the seventy one foot ocean racing yacht that we had over our bed in Rockcliffe Park.

We would go to sea; we would film the adventures, we would call it "The Wet Set."

Perhaps that would kill two birds with one stone?

It almost did...

Please join us in the Reflective Readers Club
www.grahamkerr.com/rrc

Rite of Passage Thirty-Two: "The Big One"

We left the colder waters and made the long sweep home, just waiting for the ocean's increasing warmth to guide us.

In the past in our deep-water time we had gradually moved to the left, which I knew more as the side that had the pain and the long weed.

I knew that if I followed the warmth boundary that it would lead to the fresh smell that had beckoned us before, and that it was those aromas caught up in the waters that were now calling us...again.

An Understanding

Our faithful pair, having escaped from the Alaskan dragnet were now heading south and will follow that line skirting the western edge of the Queen Charlottes and Vancouver Island and then along the Continental Shelf off the West coast of the U.S.

It is to be their longest journey and one in which they are eating less because of the ever growing element of life, both eggs and milt, taking up more space within their large, sleek, powerful bodies, weighing in at over 50 pounds for the buck and nearly 40 pounds for the hen...truly huge prize fish!

1971 to 1972
I am thirty seven to thirty eight years old

In time my partial paralysis began to improve, but taking its place had come what I can only describe as pre-vertigo; a sudden onset of dizziness that didn't lead to a wild swinging sensation, that was to come much later.

These events seemed to come after a good meal, especially one that our entire family (now very much moving en masse) enjoyed in Edinburgh, Scotland.

I had actually collapsed on Princes Street and, supported by the family, wound up with a Scottish specialist in matters of balance.

After careful testing, he provided the final push to make the really big decision.

"What you need to do," he suggested with his strong Scottish brogue, "is to buy a sailboat, put your family on board and go for a long sail; catch your balance and pull some lines," he paused, "and then I think you will be fine."

This was all I needed. We traveled due south to Poole in Dorset to Southern Ocean Shipyards where the early Ocean 71's had been built. It was the summer of 1971, a pretty neat year to commission an Ocean 71 to be put together according to our own plans for the below decks space.

We agreed upon the price of £100,000 and with $2.41 as the exchange rate at that time, we were at the quarter million dollar mark, which, in today's dollar, would be about $560,000. We took another of our deep breaths and agreed together that we should bite the bullet while we had the chance...

We also added into the decision mix the prescription given by the Scottish specialist, the insurance settlement from the accident, our children's ages and the need we had to "be together"...*at last!*

It also met the need to be doing *something* to keep my celebrity alive for marketing purposes.

Then there was the *flash of silver* example provided by the famed British yachtsman, Sir Robin Knox Johnston, the first man to make a nonstop circumnavigation of the world under sail.

Robin had bought the first of the Ocean 71's named "Ocean Spirit" with which he won the round Britain Race in 1969 with Les Williams, a race restricted to two "hands" only, which they won with a lead of two days!

That was all enough for me.

"Let the building begin!"

We found a rental house on Banks Road, a spit that provides a massive breakwater that protects the splendid Poole Harbor.

I rented a mobile office and converted it into a study. We parked it in the shipyard within yards of the construction shed. During this time, I worked on an assembly of all the recipes recorded in the Galloping Gourmet days called "The Complete Galloping Gourmet Cookbook," published in 1972 by Grossett and Dunlap; a huge, almost four pound doorstop of a book.

Every hour I would take a break and walk across the often cold and rainy boatyard to the giant hanger in which "Treena," our 71-footer, was taking shape.

I was immediately fascinated by Naval architecture, where function had to fit form and every inch of space could be, and really had to be, useful.

I come from a long line of architects on my father's side going back to my great grandfather, Robert Kerr, the first President of the Architectural Association in London in 1847, and a Fellow of the Royal Institute of British Architects in 1857. His son, my grandfather Henry Kerr, was at one time District Surveyor of St. James Westminster, and later a prominent London architect with my uncle in Lincoln Inn, London.

All this wound up in my blood, and I've always loved drawing plans, mostly for kitchens which I also did during this time with John Prizeman, the famous British designer/architect with whom I had a great time. John's influence was felt in my design of the galley and main saloon, both of which broke with traditional design in both form and function while permitting fixed camera angles while underway for the planned filming of the Wet Set.

We were also helped at this time by Stefan Sargent; the talented filmmaker who was an old friend from Sydney and was now part of London's avant-garde. It was Stefan and his wife Tricia who had helped me handle the Canon Scoopic 16 mm camera for our Italian adventures and were now coming full circle to help us plan for the Wet Set that might help to keep our *celebrity* intact; or at least ongoing.

While we were immersed in building and planning for our projected circumnavigation, our old Galloping Gourmet team in New York were anxious to get some big city promotion.

We were invited to speak at the Savoy Hotel at a luncheon where Maitre Chef des Cuisines Silvano Trompetto was still in charge. He would present a luncheon of dishes that I had created over the years. The food and service were both wonderful; the after luncheon speech was something else again.

A columnist for the London Daily Mail provided a perfectly reasonable and very succinct critique of my performance.

"Without doubt Mr. Kerr's speech has to go down as the most boring that London has heard this year." At least it wasn't, "has *ever* heard"!

There was a somewhat silver lining in this escapade; our own marketing people decided that perhaps it would be better to keep me away from the spotlight until I *recovered my senses."*

As a family, we were reading books by experienced yachtsman and getting used to possibly providing first aid. We practiced giving hypodermic injections in oranges; nobody wanted their skin in the game.

It was then time to get the medical checkup that had occupied Tessa's imagination back in Ottawa when she helped me to stop smoking with her famous words...

"You could have a checkup and x-ray, and they could find lung cancer because you smoke so much, and then you could die and never get to fulfill your dream."

We had now reached that very time; we all went through a kind of medical sheep dip and confidently awaited the obviously positive answer.

We all passed with flying colors…except for Treena.

There was a suspicious shadow in her left lower lung.

Multiple x-rays followed as our entire family held its breath.

The shadow turned out to be an almost completely circular growth measuring 5 mm, about 1 inch. We were immediately referred to an extremely well known surgeon who had determined that there was a strong likelihood that the growth was malignant and should be removed as soon as possible. Treena was moved to a Southampton Hospital and scheduled for a "posterolateral thoracotomy" that would allow a "pneumonectomy," or the "removal of tumorous tissue from the lung."

I sat there as these procedures were explained by an unsmiling gray-haired man in terms entirely unsuited to the English language, especially if there was a need to be understood! He did not add what Wikipedia now describes as "thoracotomies are thought to be one of the most difficult surgical incisions to deal with postoperatively because they are extremely painful."

I left our family in our Karitane Nurse Gillian's hands and moved to the Southampton Hotel to be close by. Our friends Stefan and Tricia Sargent visited me during the actual operation. It was during their visit and some hours following the extensive surgery that the phone rang.

"Hello, Mr. Kerr, this is your wife's surgeon."

"I'm pleased to tell you, actually I'm *very* pleased to tell you (I could hear a smile lift his previously static facial tone) that the growth appears to be a TB focus and not cancer. We have it all and she is doing well. I expect a full recovery."

I thanked him, put the receiver gently back in its cradle, let my head fall forward and then came the tears; first tears of relief and then came joy and laughter, so much so that I found it hard to breathe.

My friends Stefan and Tricia put their arms about me as my whole body shook deeply with an enormous desire to say something, to someone, about how grateful I was. The "thank you, doctor," to the surgeon wasn't enough. Nothing I knew was enough, so I cried, and laughed, and cried until I was finally done. My friends quietly left me to sleep face down and fully clothed on the hotel bed.

The BIG hurdle was cleared and the family rejoiced, but a long line of hurdles swiftly appeared as our loved one began the tortuous period of rehabilitation.

We moved from our Banks Road rental to a hotel in Bournemouth where the Menzies Hotel is located today. We took a suite of rooms overlooking the English Channel and began the long, slow watch of our living Treena's recovery and the final outfitting of her namesake in its giant hanger.

Treena began to be mobile again with the help of some pretty serious opiates to manage the pain, others to help her sleep, and still others to somehow balance the two!

The yacht "Treena" was to be launched in early February 1972 and we set out to do her proud.

We invited friends who bordered all the oceans of the world to send us one-pint samples of seawater. We drained these into a "yard of ale glass," a singular piece of glasswork with a bulbous end and a fluted mouth that holds about 2 1/2 pints usually of beer, but in our case the salty seawaters of the world into which our "Treena" was to be launched and through which she would eventually sail.

Treena smashes the "yard of oceans" against the bow

To add to the fun, we had our "rehab" Treena lifted in a boson's chair by crane to bring her alongside the hull so that she could smash the "yard of oceans" against the bow and thus signal its crane driver to lower both Treena's, one to the pier and the other to the chill waters of Poole Harbor.

A brass band played and we all rejoiced greatly as we saw our future home begin to float into her element.

And so the work on both Treena's continued as our start date in April arrived.

The sea trials almost matched the launching for spectacle. The shipyard had invited the British press to come out on the very first "trial"...a risky business but one that gave an adventurous edge to a story.

To add to its newsworthiness was our winning the runner up position in the Lloyds of London "Yacht of the Year" award, and the presence onboard of the Sailing Master of the Royal Yacht Squadron; and oh, the most boring speech of the year award winner...me.

Several of England's newspapers came aboard and were rewarded for doing so with champagne and smoked salmon sandwiches.

The Yacht Master preferred a "large gin with angostura bitters."

A thoroughly imposing man, over 6 feet and some 250 pounds, wrapped in a double-breasted dark navy blue blazer with submarine non-reflective Royal Navy buttons. He never sat; he simply stood, never seeking any means of support in spite of consuming several large pink gins.

I, as befitting my role as *owner*, am nervously on the wheel. I had previously sailed a 14-foot Uffa Fox Redwing, which had a tiller! The "ship" under me was 66 tons and five times its length and it had (of course) a compass!

"Can you make Balcome Pier," bellows the Yachts Master.

"Er...I think so," I mutter in response.

"What's your heading then," he cries out for all to hear.

I glanced down at the brand new compass and wildly tried to count the numbers on the gimbaled card...

"Three seventy five," I eventually announce with some confidence.

Silence...other than the sea and the wind against the hull and sails.

Silence...as my words fill the air between the yachting "experts" who turn, as if one person, to look at...me!

There are, of course, only three hundred sixty degrees on a compass and I had simply added 15 degrees north to round out my mathematically correct answer.

Silence...each person's unspoken words were clearly obvious to all, especially to me!

"What is a man like you doing with a yacht like this?"

Please join us in the Reflective Readers Club
www.grahamkerr.com/rrc

Rite of Passage Thirty-Three: "The Long Road Home"

Author's Note:

This rite of passage has provided me with a good deal of concern. How does one cover two years of life and 24,000 miles under sail; in just one episode of our story?

It's not possible to provide an understanding of the sheer adventure and pure pleasure of such an incredible opportunity while, at the same time, continuing to live in the deepening shadows of the past.

This "rite of passage" needs another book all of its own to be clearly understood.

I shall leave this up to you, dear reader (or listener), who has been with us for thirty-three "rites" so far. Should we set out to add to this collection another book in the series, another seventeen rites of passage that focus on a family that goes to sea in search of itself?

Now let's at least touch on the highpoints in this, the end of Book Two, leading to our whole new life *upstream* in Book Three.

It's a long, long journey over the darkness below and many brightness's above.

We have learned to eat less...life is building within us.

There is a desire to see the rocks below and the green towers and that strange fresh scent in the waters that beckoned to us before.

My hen is now sleek and so much larger; I feel even more so, even in my own eyes?

The gash down her side where we escaped from the "roughness" has now healed...yet she moves as though it had never done so...

We seldom swim close enough for our fins to touch...I mostly go ahead in what seems to me to be shafts of brightness; she follows in the shadows that lie between.

An Understanding

This is their longest migration and the last of their ocean circuits as they curve down south by southeast as they head toward the Pacific Northwest coastline.

The wound cut by the exposed end of the split ring that secured the shackle on the fish net has been drawn together, washed clean by the salt waters constant flushing as she moved.

The bright shafts and shadows are the increasing cloud cover of changing weather systems as they follow the natural jet stream from west to east, both lightening and darkening their shared passage and even their perception of the burgeoning life within.

1972 to 1974
I am thirty eight to forty years old

Treena's wound healed, on the outside. The inner severances took much longer, and then there were those that no surgeon could address.

The physical met the emotional pain and became one.

Treatment on the surface was effective. The opiates quieted the rehab pain and even spilled over to shade the, as yet, unreached inner pains of rejection and an inability to even think about forgiveness. As the time came to withdraw from the opiates, the inner pains came raging back; released to dig in deep and steal away the adventure that surrounded her family. She followed, in her own shadow, and moving within her wounds as best she could.

Treena had nearly drowned twice as a child and had a deeply centered fear of the sea. Add to that the exhilarating behavior of a sailboat when it leans with the wind and plunges headlong into a steep sea. The fear joins with the unresolved inner pain and storm clouds cover, almost without end.

Our son, Andy, went aboard for the first blue water passage as I stayed behind to accompany Treena, Tessa and Kareena to Antibes in the south of France to await his arrival with our professional Skipper (boy, did I need one!) Dudley. We called him "Duddles" and he came complete with his Jane who would replace Gillian, our Karitane Nanny, who had returned to New Zealand.

I flew to Palma de Majorca to go out into the Mediterranean to rendezvous with the "TREENA" as she completed her stormy voyage through the Bay of Biscay and the Straits of Gibraltar.

I found a willing fisherman who offered to take me out to meet and board my "ship" as she was half a day's sail from Palma.

I saw her masthead on the horizon, and then her vividly colored running sails, finally the gleaming white hull crested the waves.

What a glorious sight...and she was all mine!

The mainmast was 92 feet, the hull 71 feet, and the sails totaled 3,800 square feet when running before the wind.

I boarded and was embraced and actually honored by all, as the owner come aboard at last. I was given the wheel and completed the day by bringing her alongside safely in the Palma Marina. We celebrated that night; what a celebration, with shades of another that was to follow soon. We gorged on roast suckling pig and cheap Spanish champagne.

Our plan was to bring the two Treena's together as soon as possible. We set out the next morning somewhat the worse for wear, on the more or less straight shot from Palma to Antibes across the Gulf of Lion.

Our only forecast had been in Spanish and our own senses. It was a brilliantly clear, sparkling spring day with a scattering of clouds in the north and a brisk yet pleasant Nor'wester that "TREENA" loved. Andy and our crew, which included several from the shipyard, rode the pitching decks with the ease of their practiced sea legs. I staggered about in search of mine, mostly hanging onto the wheel for support, gazing at a better-understood compass for direction!

The northern clouds thickened and darkened and gathered overhead, *goodbye sun...hello wind.*

As night came, the wind rose and my enthusiasm waned.

"Wake me for the morning watch," I cried to one and all, and fought my way below to the owner's aft cabin and the lee canvas that would keep me from being pitched from my berth by an increasingly angry sea.

In the pale gray morning, after a fitful sleep I was called.

"Your watch, dad." It was Andy, as perky as ever.

I struggled into my foul weather gear with increasing nausea and made it to the saloon steps. These I mounted to the cockpit, which was whipped with spray, the wind noise like a NASCAR meeting a mile away.

The spray stung my exposed face as I lurched over to take the wheel.

Turning to the bow, I saw the waves for the first time; huge angry, gray beasts streaked in white foam that were flung away from the crests. An enormous tree trunk was out to the portside wallowing with menace, as though saying, "try hitting me and survive!"

It didn't last long.

Suckling pig, champagne, poor night and no sea legs combined with what the Spanish weather forecast had been warning; had we had ears to hear!

"Force 9 gale for the Gulf of Lions!"

A Force 9 gale is 47 to 54 miles per hour and raises 23 to 32 feet high seas. It's *ugly* weather!

Within the half hour of my watch, I was defeated. So much for my satisfaction at owning this magnificent sixty six ton "ship" that was now being tossed about like a cork. I called it quits and returned below on my first full day at sea, ever!

I lay in my now fouled weather gear, in the drumbeat of a major storm, wretchedly sick and encountering another basic means of evacuating the excesses I had consumed. In doing so, I managed to wrench the top of the "owner's" head following my tenth (or so) visit. Andy rescued me that lurching day with Lomotil, which stopped the *rite of passage* in its tracks!

Close to midnight on that frightful day "Duddles" came below to my unseemly cabin and asked if I would like them to put into sheltered waters offered by the Porquerolles Islands on the east side of the gulf.

"We don't have detailed charts, but I think we can make it." He added, gazing at me through red-rimmed salt encrusted eyes.

"By all means," I muttered; now almost delirious.

I will never forget the almost instant change as we made the lee of those islands...how amazingly calm it was. I seemed to dream of throwing myself off the wild bucking boat onto the island which was entirely covered with very flat, very cool, red quarry tiles. Within minutes of anchoring I was up and in the galley, feeding the exhausted crew as though nothing had happened.

How quickly we humans can put the bad stuff behind us!

They all had their sea legs. I had failed utterly but at least I could still cook and they were all very hungry so all was not lost!

I learned, with the help of one other celebration, to avoid the excesses of my past. It was as though I was a laboratory experiment; shaken about in a test tube instead of just, well, suffering with morning-after feelings.

I came to the conclusion that I had been sub-clinically sickened by my splendid gourmet adventures; all I needed was a good "shake up" to see what needed to be changed. This was to be my wakeup call. I needed one other similar meal to convince me that sailing and the rich foods that had been my whole life were *incompatible*. Would I have changed my daily food intake (I hate the word "diet") without such an ever-present reminder? I simply do not know!

A good friend, who provides recovery services for people who have severe addictions, told me that changing a "well-entrenched food habit is roughly forty percent harder than breaking a heroin addiction."

We sailed on, as a family in search of its identity as an intimate gathering. As we began to bond, we also relearned a way to eat wholesome foods and avoid excess.

At the same time, I worked hard at mastering a large sailing vessel and eventually, after several thousand miles, achieved the reward of being both owner and Skipper. The joy of keeping my family safe in such an extraordinary vessel was one of my greatest personal achievements.

We sailed the Mediterranean as far east as Sardinia. We crossed the Atlantic from the Canary Islands to Antigua with Andy on board to represent the family.

As a complete family we went north across the Devil's Triangle from the U.S. Virgin Islands to the Chesapeake Bay and then north all way up the east coast. We went up the St. Lawrence River to the Great Lakes and with masts out, came down the Erie Canal system to New York City where we crossed over Manhattan from the Hudson to the East River via the Harlem River; which was an amazing experience, conducted close to midnight in the fall of 1973.

With our masts replaced, we sailed out into the Atlantic going south to Clearwater Florida and then head for the Panama Canal in our voyage to reach Sydney Harbor in Australia where, in a most ungentlemanly manner, I intended to lift less than a whole handful of fingers as a salute to those we had left behind who had insisted that we would "never make it out of the English Channel."

En route, we stopped in at the Chesapeake Bay once again and on the advice of some locals, we went in search of Peach Blossom Creek on the Tred Avon River.

We found the charming village of Oxford way up on the eastern shore and motored into the Tred Avon, following its starboard bank until it ran off into the famed Peach Blossom Creek; famed because it had been used many times as a rendezvous by several prestigious cruising yacht clubs because of its fully protected beauty.

It was beautiful, indeed, on that very quiet fall day. The huge trees on every bank had turned gold and reflected off the still river at low tide, only disturbed by our wake as we passed slowly by. Then suddenly our world came to a slow stop; not with hitting a rock as we had done in Montreal. This was a short, yet oozing, stop, like arriving in a muddy bank, which indeed we had.

The tidal range in that part of the eastern shore is not at all extreme. At most, it is maybe just two feet and we went aground at its lowest; with a possible wait of five to six hours to begin the embarrassing business of getting clear. It is said of the Chesapeake that the only folk who haven't gone aground are those who are liars or have never been there!

No problem, perfectly secure, calm winds and no schedule to meet. We just sat in the sun and waited for the tide to raise all boats; especially ours.

We lay exactly abeam a lovely three story high white colonial mansion with six lofty Grecian pillars supporting a slate gray roof. Its many large windows looked out at the river over large tidy lawns, huge trees and…swans.

There was a long, almost new dock, stretching out like a finger toward our now *fixed* location.

"Isn't that a beautiful house?" Treena said somewhat wistfully; after all she had been at sea now for two years and houses were beginning to register as a deep longing.

"Sure," I replied. "Cost a fortune, just look at that water frontage; it must be over seven hundred feet, it's ten times our length."

Later she mentioned the house, and then again. Treena is one of the least acquisitive people I know. She had never, ever, become attached to a place or building. I always took this to be a genetic throwback to her Romani Gypsy roots.

"Tell you what," I said with a grin. "Since we are stuck here for at least another three or four hours, I'll row ashore and make them an offer for it –just for fun," I added quickly.

"You wouldn't, why would you do that?"

"Just to while away the time…you know…have some fun, but don't be surprised if the owner chases me down that dock with a gun when he hears my offer."

I set out for the shore in our dinghy and made my way to the back door. It was opened by a smaller man in his mid 50's, a little stout but not overly so. He wore jeans and a cream fishnet pullover.

"Yes?" He enquired.

"Oh, hello. I'm from the yacht over there." I gestured over my shoulder, "and we've been admiring your house," I added with a smile.

"Really? I've been admiring your boat."

"Do you have a large gun?" I asked, getting to the point quickly.

"Sure, a duck gun...but why do you ask?"

I explained to him my mission and his more than likely response to my offer.

He seemed amused at the idea.

"I'll get it," and then he paused.

"But...just make your offer." Now he was smiling.

"Do I really have to do that? I'd prefer to just have you chase me."

"No," he replied firmly. "Let's do it right, then we can both play the game!"

I made my perfectly ridiculous offer, feeling quite absurd.

"You're right," he said, "I'll get my gun."

He returned with a huge double-barreled shotgun, just what we needed to make the point from a distance.

"I was thinking," he stopped and cradled the gun in his arms.

"If you could get that in cash, how long would it take?"

"I really don't know, does it matter?"

"It might...but let's keep playing the game, okay. Call your broker and find out."

I made the call, cupped the telephone receiver in my hand and said "next Tuesday, for sure."

He reached across the desk and shook my hand. "It's yours."

I don't have the exact log of that date or day, but I know it was in October 1973. It just so happened that it coincided with the start of the OPEC oil embargo that was one of the root causes of the 1973 to 1975 recession when the Dow Jones average fell 45 percent to a low of 577.60 on December 4, 1974, *just* after we had removed our money!

At the very time we ran aground, the U.S. went off the Gold Standard, printed more money and caused rapid inflation; all of which contributed to that recession in 1974.

This was to mark the end of the golden years of economic growth that began at the end of World War II in 1945. The entire world was changing because of these pressures. Perhaps this is why the owner accepted only $250,000 ($1,316.875 in 2013 dollars) for 9 acres of lawns, 650 feet of waterfront and a 10,800 square foot colonial mansion.

We shall never know what prompted him to sell but it completed our time at sea. We had arrived in our new home, in our new country, and were shortly to enter into a whole new life experience.

**The journey "upstream" continues in Book Three
"Upstream on Purpose"**

Please join us in the Reflective Readers Club
www.grahamkerr.com/rrc

FLASH OF SILVER

3

...the leap that changed my world.

BOOK THREE:
UPSTREAM ON PURPOSE

Author's Note:

We have now arrived at the third book in our journey together, one that will contain Rites of Passage 34 through 64.

Books 1 and 2 have described, in part, the way in which we lived our lives as fully as we knew how. There were times of exceptional success and others of abject failure. The sum of it all was external value, yet an inner sense of growing fullness; much as our salmon are experiencing with the growth of eggs and milt within their sleek, large powerful bodies.

The salmon's voracious appetite for their own sake had now lessened and been replaced by a truly remarkable transition from the desire for self to the passion to set aside consumption and to fight their way back upstream in their natal river so that they can provide the full opportunity for new life.

So it is with our story. We are about to transition from celebrity to servant and experience life that is truly life.

Graham and Treena

Rite of Passage Thirty-Four: "A Rising Tide"

Suddenly, out of the waters below, the rocks appeared once more.

As each brightness passed, they became a welcome foundation for our future.

We swam through all the familiar treats. It wasn't that we had lost our appetite so much as being replete and fully energized for the way that seemed to be ahead.

As before, we turned in with the surface rocks and felt a lifting of the waters that seemed to gently carry us further and further until we caught the first strong scent that stirred the memory. This time we were ready and felt no need to return to the big waters.

We were on our way back home; at last!

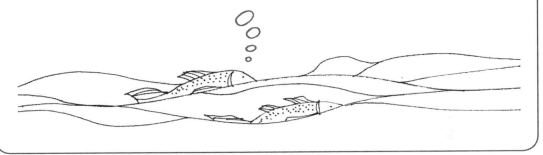

An Understanding

In their sixth year, our two impressive-sized Chinook salmon have reached the Pacific Northwest coastline. An estuary has opened up before them and they are being lifted, almost carried, by an incoming tide.

They can scent the rainwater that carries the signature of their birthplaces mixed with the salty waters that had surrounded them for several years.

*Their natural world was slowly changing and with it a deeply felt need to **keep on going** with every ounce of stored energy they had.*

1973 to 1974
I am thirty nine to forty years old

Our life at sea stopped in Peachblossom Creek. We arrived within days of the start of the OPEC oil embargo that, along with other important issues, was to mark the end of the "golden years" of economic growth in the United States.

The world changed in mid October 1973, and that change began to ripple through the way we have come to look at our world and its declining finite resources.

At that date, however, we were completely immersed in what was happening to our small family in its large house, with a really big yacht at the bottom of the garden.

During our first visit to the Chesapeake Bay seven months earlier, we had spent some time with another Ocean 71 owner whom we had met and thoroughly enjoyed.

Jim was a Mormon Bishop who was doing very well in real estate development as well as designing new, energy conserving modular family homes.

As a Mormon, he felt that he had been *called* to use his talents to better enjoy a more healthful family-centered life. We were deeply touched by both his commitment and design ideas.

Jim took us for an aerial survey over a peninsular just north of Annapolis, an area bordered by Route 301(the Revell Highway) and west of Sandy Point State Park. He offered this parcel as security if we chose to invest in his future-looking plans.

We decided to put most of our remaining savings into the project and left the details in the hands of our very expert accountants at Peat, Marwick and Mitchell. The Senior Partner from long experience, was a little less certain about the proposed deal and had preferred that we create a loan at a "beneficial rate of interest" with a "demand note" in lieu of the proposed real estate; all perfectly fine on every side.

Unfortunately, the papers remained in his drawer during the time that he was suddenly diagnosed with throat cancer and his life and our investment was on hold.

In October, when the cost of gasoline spiraled and the market collapsed, our demand note lay unattended, until it was too late. Jim's entire housing enterprise became a house of cards and in an effort to avert its complete collapse, our very good friend tried all that he knew to save both himself and all of his investors, including us! I have no idea what he attempted to do; only that it didn't work and his other investors, who appeared to be members of his church, sued him and accused him of fraud. Jim went to jail and we, now without our retirement cushion, had to go back on television in order to restore our losses.

Jail and television might seem to be worlds apart until you compare the levels of resistance. Jim certainly did not want to be locked up and neither did we want to return to the restrictive life of endless hurdles to be jumped on strict schedules.

For Treena especially this was a horrendous idea. "I can't, I simply can't do that AGAIN," she wept.

"I can barely get through the day, let alone produce programs again." She seemed to collapse in upon herself and become deeply depressed.

I really had no alternative!

We now owned a huge house in an extremely poor housing market. Our grand yacht had been for sale for several months and not even one buyer!

Now all our savings had evaporated and there were school fees, living expenses, and everywhere the recession was getting worse. In the midst of this sudden downturn, I read a small paperback book by Susan George called "How the Other Half Die" and one other book; the famous "Future Shock" by Alvin Toffler, first published in 1970.

The turmoil that surrounded everyone at that time began to mesh, in my mind, with the catastrophic effect that our "moderate" economic decline was having upon the most vulnerable, the poor, in every nation. Until this time, I had never given poor people a second thought. They were, in my opinion, either poorly educated, lazy or somehow disadvantaged by climate. I could see nothing that I could possibly do to help even one of them. So I did nothing, except to read and to quote the authors and carry about their passion in a kind of backpack that I had to shrug off in order to sit down, which I did, most of the time.

I was not, however, without a spark of my own passion!

I had learned, at sea, a whole new way of eating and living an active, outdoor life. Our entire family was living proof of how much our physical lives had improved. Surely, I reasoned, as I must return to some form of *business*, I could try to explain how others might also find the abundant health that we now enjoyed?

Treena listened, yet without much creative interest; the very idea still terrified her.

"I could do a kind of magazine insert..." I explained.

"It wouldn't have an international travel component or a joke, or a chair to leap." I smiled at the idea!

"What I would do would be straight to camera, no audience, in a very modern set." I had some ideas for that already.

"I could show people how to lessen their risk and at the same time improve their delight in eating." I was now beginning to listen to my own emerging enthusiasm and was actually enjoying the closed-circuit feedback!

Our business partners at Fremantle International, with whom we had produced all of the "Galloping Gourmet," shows were delighted to hear that there was even a possibility of my celebrity being revived.

They went back to the sponsors and rapidly a new quite short program was born. We called it "Take Kerr" (pronounced "care"); a familiar phrase that would forever be mispronounced as "Take Cur" that could easily have met the interests of dog owners? The program lacked Treena's input, but since it was only four minutes long it allowed no room for "fun," only for some solid, enthusiastic information with a smile!

It worked!

The episodes were placed "hither and yon" in a great many magazine-styled shows run by local stations, and eventually wound up on the earliest days of CNN in 1980. I was back on the media treadmill and our depleted finances were gradually being restored.

I rapidly discovered an important truth. Apparently, I was more attractive to advertisers when I cooked with *absolute abandon*. The more butter, cream and brandy poured over large cuts of expensive meats, the more the sponsors paid for each commercial spot. As I began to actively describe how best to retain flavor and reduce risk by using less saturated fats and refined starches there were fewer sponsors and those that did turn up paid less.

I suppose that this isn't exactly *news*. Here I was, at one time called "The High Priest of Hedonism," now showing ways to consume less of the apparently *good* stuff that everyone seemed to enjoy! What audience I did attract in those very early days of dietary change came out to quite a large gathering in the spring of 1974 that was held in Fort Lauderdale, Florida.

I spoke about excess and compared it to human need. I used the image of a father, sitting on an earthen floor in a mud and grass hut looking at his youngest stick-thin daughter, sitting and watching him with huge, glistening dark brown eyes.

He held in his hand a small mound of sticky cereal. He knew his daughter was dying from starvation, yet for the sake of his family he had to eat in order to find the strength for another day in the field. He had to live so that at least some of his family would survive.

A week later my agent in New York called...

"Graham, I've had a call from the Episcopalian Bishop of Southern Florida." My agent was a very unorthodox Jew and there was some surprise in his voice, even suppressed amusement.

"He wants to know if you would consider a multi-church speaking engagement covering your speech last week about childhood nutrition."

"The Church wants *me* to teach them!" I wasn't amused; in fact, I felt angry that the Bishop had thought it even likely. Surely the Church, whatever flavor, was practiced at *doing* what I was only *saying*. I used the idea of the child to gain attention for my programs and to somehow offset the less enthusiastic response that my "lesser foods" had received.

I turned down the offer because I felt completely unqualified and that whatever they might do was clearly not of any real practical value. People would always be poor and even die and nothing was going to change that. Besides, I had to get my family resources rebuilt. That was my priority.

I did, however, respond to an invitation to teach at Cornell University, also in 1974, at the Hotel School that was then, as it is now, a world leader in the field. I was given the title of Adjunct Professor, and the Dean arranged for his twin-engine Cessna to fly me from our county airport at Easton to the strip at Ithaca in New York State at regular intervals.

I loved those days and found, amongst the students, an eager and very intelligent bundle of future industry leaders. We enjoyed one another, hugely!

It was there that I attempted to introduce my theories about how to rethink portion sizes and actual classic recipe content and thus better serve the dining-away-from-home public.

"Chefs are style leaders," I challenged them.

"Will you profit on the back of excessive consumption, or will you gain customers who choose to be well and are becoming informed?"

My classes grew until they were close to the brilliant Dean's gatherings.

The Cornell School of Human Ecology also asked me to lecture; again on an ad hoc occasional basis and were very supportive.

During this time, I had converted an old garage/shed in the Easton township as a test kitchen in which to research and develop the ideas to be used on the "Take Kerr" series. I employed a young dietitian to assist me. Ann Collier was a perfect choice; she was skilled, well educated and lived amid the farming community on the Eastern Shore.

Together with The School of Human Ecology at Cornell and the Hotel School, I was in my element.

The work went forward and the program spread in spite of its being "damned by faint praise" from culinary critics who found my newfound enthusiasm for less consumption to be a direct personal challenge to their status quo.

To help in this image problem, I chose to put a credit on the show that drew attention to my connection with academia.

GRAHAM KERR WISHES TO ACKNOWLEDGE WITH
GRATITUDE THE ASSISTANCE GIVEN TO THIS PROGRAM
BY CORNELL UNIVERSITY.

The credit was up for about one second; yet, at least for me, it made all the difference.

I was no longer Graham doing my own independent thing; I was part of a truly prestigious university, world leaders in the academic and business community.

How, with such a background, could I fail to make an impact?

While all was going splendidly at work, our home life was coming apart at the seams.

Treena had become a medical "addict". What had begun as a series of postoperative drugs to ease the pain had now become an increasing problem for her, and from time to time for the whole family. At sea, her needs were somewhat obscured because we were a family facing the elements and this largely preoccupied our thinking.

On shore, with my almost total immersion in teaching both on and off the tube, she had become isolated and by choice uninvolved in the TV production that had once been her responsibility. She spiraled downward and at each twist the prescribed medications gradually took over. There were several frightening outbursts when all the smothered emotions broke free from their medicated crust and poured out in violence. She would scream and then scream again without apparently taking a breath. Saliva gathered as spittle around her lips and her wide beautiful eyes would become bloodshot. In these rages she would miss the doorways and rush into the walls.

Our physician drew me aside late in 1974 and cautioned me strongly.

"Mr. Kerr, your wife is very sick. I cannot; actually, I *will not* keep on increasing her medications. The mix of Darvon, Mogadon, Valium and Benzedrine are really self-defeating. What she must have is a gradual program of withdrawal and for that she needs to go away for an undetermined period of time to an institution that specializes in such rehabilitation."

He had held my eyes with his during this long explanation, and I felt both a sense of loss and responsibility. I had failed her; broken her special word, "truth". She had tried to simply live on with the unresolved inner pain and had found some measure of surface relief in the medications, but they only went so deep...and then?

If she became drug free, would that then leave only me and could she take that exposure without any respite? Those were my thoughts as he held my gaze.

Gradually, the waters were changing. The time between each brightness also changed in the way the waters moved about us.

We felt both carried and then...pushed back almost in a rhythm.

Large dark shadows passed in straight lines above, both coming and going and the waters grumbled as they went their way, leaving a churning whiteness behind.

My hen kept up when we were lifted but fell behind when everything seemed to be against us. I swam ahead, turning to keep her in sight.

The waters were thinner and had an increasing long-remembered scent.

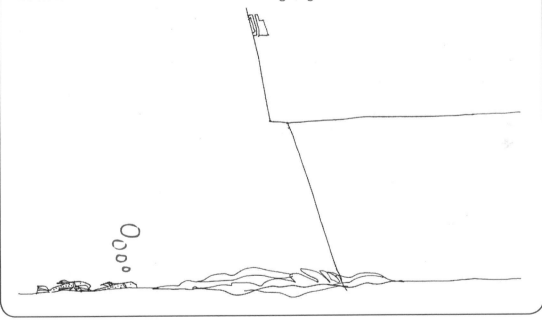

An Understanding

Our Chinook are now in the tidal estuary and day-by-day (measured by them as "brightness") they are swept inward by the incoming flood of the tide and held back by the ebb.

The long shadows are ships passing overhead to ports beyond.

The hen is still hindered by the healing wound along her side.

The waters are gradually responding to the fresh water coming downstream that carry the faint aromatic signature of their birth river.

This is their beacon and their incentive as they turn their backs upon the oceans of opportunity.

1974
I am forty years old

The Cornell Hotel School, The School of Human Ecology at Cornell, and now the Culinary Institute of America at Hyde Park, New York, had been added to my teaching opportunities.

Every visit to these extraordinary institutions increased my confidence in the way I was beginning to see the culinary world of the future. I felt the rush of a flood tide when eager, innovative chef instructors and students debated my proposals that included reshaping the way menus were written so that they carried discreet nutritional guidance for those like Treena and I, who definitely needed it!

There were also those deeply entrenched in the status quo of the great classics; Master Chefs justifiably proud of their long service and training in the authentic cuisines of the world, especially those from Europe. These men and a few women provided the ebb tide that is a perfectly natural response to innovation. I felt that ebb quite keenly because it confirmed my impression about my ability and how little I *actually* knew; regardless of the new world-wide research I had done.

I no longer suffered from the "imposter" syndrome in which, in the past, I had worried about being found out as being too inexperienced; what concerned me now was the *mixing of the waters.*

My experience had been in the "salty oceans of opportunity." What was now foremost in my mind was the new (for me) knowledge about both the nutrition and behavioral and agricultural sciences. I had to deal with this "salt and fresh" combination and, at this time, there were few who had found a happy balance between the two. So, while the ebb attitudes were challenging, they also gave me added reason to go deeper and deeper into how I might find a "sweet spot" that others might think of as reasonable and perhaps even moderate?

At both the CIA (Culinary Institute of America) and Cornell, I managed to straddle the gap between the "classics" and the emergence of "human ecology." The CIA had a restaurant named St. Andrews Cafe, that served lighter food to the visiting public than was available at its more consumer oriented "American Bounty" where the food was a better reflection of the mid to late 1970's.

I was delighted to have the opportunity to teach at the CIA in the Danny Kaye Theater, a beautifully designed demonstration kitchen. They had what was called "The Great Chefs" series that had already gone through at least twenty of the world's best known professionals; who were masters more than celebrities. I was added to that list and was greatly honored, but was rather soon to be forgotten because I went too far too fast!

Pictured on the set of The Great Chefs series with Chef Ron deSantis (who is now the director of food services at Yale)

In the midst of so much apparent "approval" I had ventured to propose what we called Menu 2, to be tested in the American Bounty Restaurant.

I had had the idea at Cornell where we tested its forerunner at the Statler Hotel, which was an on-campus teaching facility with real live "guinea pig" clients. That experiment was jointly undertaken by HumEc (Human Ecology) and the Hotel School.

Each and every dish on the menu had a simple reference number: 1 through 84 at the time. At the back of the menu was an enormous page of numbers. You found that the prime rib, for example, was #24, located that number on the left, and then scanned the "numbers" for fats, sodium, carbohydrates, fiber and major micronutrients.

It was far too complicated and also well before its time.

The nutrition facts labels instituted by the FDA (Food and Drug Administration) first showed up in 1994 with revisions in 2008 and 2009...so back in 1973 there were few folks who even knew what these numbers meant.

The CIA experiment was greatly helped by the expert help I received from *Catherine Powers, R.D.,* who headed up the institute's nutrition education program.

We offered two menus. The first was the standard and handed to guests with the server saying...

"We also have Menu 2 if you would like to see it."

Often the guests would ask...

"What's Menu 2?" The server would reply, "it's the exact same as you have now...and it includes brief nutritional information if any of your party would like to see it."

More than fifty percent asked for Menu 2.

Each dish had, below its ingredient description, what looked like a telephone number. 360–24(15)–20. At the foot of the menu was the code…360 was calories, 24 was total fat, (15) was saturated fat, and 20 was carbohydrates.

The experiment lasted only one night!

The reason it was removed was the extraordinary effect it had on the choices made.

The very popular steak dish had shown over 1,000 calories, and a less popular Blue Fin Tuna at about 350 calories. On that one night, the average orders switched to a preference for the tuna to such an extent that the instructors feared that the Menu 2 would represent a business model that was not the one for which students were being trained *at that time*.

I understood but nonetheless argued that, in that one evening, the customers were given the tools by which to choose…

"Are we not here to serve, and to meet real needs with great food?"

And so it goes when fresh water mixes with salt. You simply move on, as I did, until the waters freshen and the river reduces in size!

My life had gone from a small at-home stream to a widespread delta of public activity! It had begun simply enough; our financial tide had gone out and needed to come back in! All I had to do was return to the media to fix it and so it was!

Funds flooded in because I moved back into the oceans of opportunity for one primary purpose; cash flow!

However, life is never that simple; to be a public person again I had to go beyond the immediate and respond to invitations that often come only to public people.

Why else would Cornell and the CIA invite *me* to teach?

My time away from Treena and our family increased; back to Ottawa in Canada for the "Take Kerr" series (now up to 195 new shows a year). Up to Ithaca and Hyde Park, both in New York State; in between, over to the test kitchen in Easton.

My absences did not make Treena's heart grow fonder. While she had chosen not to become involved in the production and, indeed, had asked that the research be removed from the house, she had now found her own self-imposed task of making huge complex curtains for the over thirty windows in order to find creative satisfaction.

"Nothing I do makes any sense," she complained.

"Here you are running about all over the place, and I'm stuck in a large dark cloud of me!"

"I hate it here, I'm lonely, the doctor won't get me the pills I need…*I just want to go away!*"

These were the exact words she had used back in Sydney when my unfaithfulness was still a raw and immediate wound. Back then, in those very dark days, she had found some respite at a small Seventh Day Adventist Hospital. Could this be an answer for her again? I now faced two spoken "requests"; our doctor's insistence that she be admitted to an institution, and Treena's plea to "go away".

Perhaps the two could be combined?

In the midst of my travels and deadlines I found the time to think this through.

As I did, I realized just how much I had always loved her, right from our school days. She was my first experience with love and yet I had managed to hurt her so deeply that NOTHING we had done for over eight years had apparently helped.

When the wound had cut into her life she had begun to bleed out. We had clung to each other believing the hemorrhage of a broken heart would heal, in time.

It hadn't.

Even if she were to go away and get free from the drugs, that still left me.

Was it me that she needed to leave; would that staunch the wound?

The idea stole into my mind like a thief and took up residence.

Did I love her enough to...let her go?

It was late autumn in 1974. The leaves had mostly blown away and gathered limp and discarded on the large lawns. Some still clung to the trees in a brisk breeze.

Dark clouds skidded by overhead; it was a chilling wind.

We sat by one of the huge picture windows overlooking the creek, its waters steeply rippled and just beginning to curl.

"I've been thinking a lot about us," I started.

"I can see that life isn't good for you right now," I added.

"That's true." She looked down at her hands folded in her lap.

"You said, the other day, that you just wanted to go away; do you still feel that?"

"Yes." Again, she didn't look up and remained still.

"I think you need to be free; of me." I had almost stopped breathing as I spoke. My chest seemed to be crying; yet my eyes remained dry.

She looked up her eyes questioning.

"Leave...you...how?" She added.

"You could return to the theater. You have always loved it there. Resume what you've always given up for me."

No reply, only that steady gaze.

"I will help you to do that...anything at all so that..." *Heaven help me not to cry, the tears were gathering behind my eyes.* "so...you could be happy again!"

That was all I could get out; I had said the impossible. My life, as I understood it, had come to a stop...

Treena stood slowly, came over and brushed her hand on my shoulder.

"I'm going upstairs," she said quietly, "to think about what you have said." With that, she left the room, closing the door behind her.

I sat where I was. It began to rain in scattering drifts across the water and even the more stubborn leaves began to fall. One had spiraled from a bough and was held to the outside of the window amid the raindrops.

It grew darker. I remained where I sat.

What on earth had possessed me? I loved this woman more than...life itself? Was there actually such an emotion as the one I now felt?

I continued to sit. Whatever hope I might have had for my sake began to fade; yet now I began to see that perhaps this really was the best for her. At that thought, I finally began to think about smiling.

The door to the living room opened. It was her. She held one small sheet of paper in her hand. Unlike that dreadful letter that had been clenched and splayed out in 1965...this one was held loosely, even gently as she handed it to me.

"I wrote this poem," she explained. "It's for you."

Throughout our lives together Treena has often sorted out her feelings by writing them down as poems; it was a gift she had, very private, almost never shared, until now. It was titled:

"To Love As One."
to be aware
and love in faith
is all one should desire
to try,
and learn,
and rectify,
some seeming wrong,
this should be done.
yet, do not be alone,
for when two love
one is half
if left,
or leaves
the arms of one
whose life is stressed.
I prefer, to be complete
and walk with you,
along the street
toward the other half of self.
to learn with you,
to help,
to understand,
the way we lost ourselves.
we have the right,
to right the wrongs
to each we've made.
no one, alone is wrong,
no one, alone is right;
in marriage, we are one,
and love is ours—not flight!

As I read it through for the second or third time, I began to cry in earnest. This time I couldn't stop. She wouldn't leave me, she would stay, regardless.

Somehow we would find the way to love again.

"No one alone is wrong, no one alone is right; in marriage, we are one. And love is ours – not flight!"

The leaf on the window let go and fell to the cold ground outside in the rain but it was warmer inside.

Please join us in the Reflective Readers Club
www.grahamkerr.com/rrc

Rite of Passage Thirty-Six: "Into the Gloom"

Suddenly we swam into waters we had never encountered before. It was strangely dark and I had to swim back out to find my hen and stay close. I can still just sense the aroma that had so motivated us, but now it was indistinct and I couldn't be sure that I knew the way.

I circled about and stayed behind the acrid sour stream of waters ahead.

A large shoal of smaller ones; a little like us, came up from behind. They, too, slowed down and circled but one by one they kept disappearing into the gloom. One of them appeared to offer us some encouragement and swam about with us on the very edge of this barrier. Since none of the other small ones had turned back, we swallowed what we understood and ploughed through into the unknown.

It was all we knew how to do to somehow keep moving!

An Understanding

They had struck a thick band of runoff pollution, the waters became turgid, sour smelling and even toxic; so powerfully polluted that it had masked the scent of their natal river. They had lost their sense of direction but not their inner drive to keep moving.

The smaller fish are Steelhead, typically 4–20 pounds in weight. They were formerly listed separate from the other Pacific salmon species as a sea-run trout. But they are now considered to be of the same larger Pacific Ocean heritage of salmon/trout species that are distinct from the Atlantic salmon and Atlantic trout.

In February and March, as our two salmon make entry toward the Columbia, their spawning is still 6–7 months distant in early September. In contrast, the Steelhead are in a hurry for more immediate spawning from February through June.

Our bewildered Chinook were simply encouraged to follow their example and their flash of silver as they disappeared into the gloom.

1974
I am forty years old

I had correctly understood that I was Treena's most serious stumbling block and by offering her freedom from me, I had addressed the root cause.

Her poem had done nothing to address the need to deal with that deep pain but it had moved both of us into a sense of hope. If we could just keep moving, we believed it could get better.

It immediately got worse...much, much worse!

Our son, Andy, was happily at a great Quaker boarding school, Westtown in Westchester, Pennsylvania. He had previously risen to be Head Boy at Hurstpierpoint in England and was both bright and a great young leader.

Our youngest, Kareena, now six years old, who had been born in the midst of the Galloping Gourmet production days, lived with us as we lurched from day to day in these troubled times.

Our oldest child Tessa was now passing through hormone alley and feeling her oats. She was attending a local community college in Easton, Maryland, and had found a ready supply of illegal drugs.

Exactly what happened to Tessa is now lost in our collective minds, but we do recall the impact of those dreadful days. There had been an *encounter* and Treena's medicated crust had broken and white-hot anger had erupted. It was with such a frightening intensity that, in an effort to intervene, I ordered Tessa to leave our home. I actually commanded our 17-year-old child to leave home so that we might avoid such awful confrontations. She left and I was able to provide her with support as she stumbled into her apparent freedom.

It was then that I got the call from Andy's housemaster. He had been caught sharing a bottle of whiskey with his dorm friends; remember this is a Quaker school!

Both he and I had been warned, *this* time!

Another call from our doctor and again he insisted that we decide soon to transfer Treena to a drug detox center he had found in Virginia.

My answer was still to plead for a delay.

"Very well, but January must be the absolute limit, both for her sake and for your entire family." He was clearly frustrated with my procrastination.

Then came the knock on our very large, white painted front door. The old-fashioned brass knocker was being repeatedly and annoyingly clapped against its shiny base.

"Yes, yes," I shouted, "I'm coming!"

As I opened the door the knocking stopped, and a very small young black woman, dressed entirely in white, stood with her right hand still up in the air.

"Yes?" I inquired, somewhat brusquely.

"Good mornin' sir!" She smiled hesitantly.

"Are you wantin' a maid for your big house?" She let her eyes go back and forth to encompass the entire frontage.

We were still cutting costs so I didn't think so.

"No, thanks, we're fine." I returned her smile with mine; also somewhat halfheartedly.

"I am not exactly a maid," she explained, and then rushed on to deliver her pitch.

"I'm actually a missionary and I want to go to my brothers and sisters in Haiti who are sufferin' so much." She kept going, this time with a good deal of passion.

"My Pastor says our church is too poor to send me an' told me to find some rich folks who lived in a big house by the water." Again, she glanced about her and opened her arms wide.

"Like yours," she added, "and then to serve them and put the money away in a savin' account until I had enough to go." She stopped suddenly.

"Can you speak their French patois?" I asked, in an attempt to provide a rational basis for my rejecting her proposal.

"No Sir," she replied with a shrug.

"But I've got a strong back an' willin' hands and I've got Jesus in my heart."

I had, over the years, had several encounters with people who had claimed some kind of "relationship" with this well-known religious prophet. There had been our school chaplain who had beaten me for being late to chapel. *You will not (thwack) be late for God (thwack)!"*

There were others, all better intentioned but somehow flawed, and certainly without this young woman's sincerity. She, at least, wanted to do something to help people not unlike herself. My intended refusal melted and I invited her in to meet Treena. Perhaps we could use some help in such a large house, especially since our daughter and her chores had now evaporated.

We agreed that day on a quite generous hourly rate that might, in time, help her on her way. It felt good to be a small part of any kind of a solution and it became the first donation that I had ever given to anything; albeit substantially self-serving!

Ruthie entered our home and began to apply her "strong back, willin' hands" and her heart filled with her faith in Jesus.

Ruthie made an immediate difference. The house sparkled; she was always helpful and seemed to anticipate our needs.

She said very little. She mostly hummed as she worked. It sounded like an old hymn I used to sing (reluctantly) at school, though she never sang the words.

Each Friday, she left on a long bus trip to Wilmington, Delaware, where she attended her small inner city Pentecostal Holiness Church of about seventy members who met and worshipped in an old store that had been simply converted into a church. She returned on Mondays and appeared refreshed in spite of the journey. She was enormously helpful, and it lifted quite a load, especially with Tessa gone.

However, her main contribution was her eyes; deep, dark brown, they literally danced with an inner beauty. Her eyes alone would have drawn us to her, let alone her diligence about the house.

My life continued at its now *normal* pace, and regardless of adverse weather conditions I was airborne once again in the Dean's twin-engine Cessna en route for Ithaca, New York State.

We took off into clear blue skies and flew over thin, and then thicker, cloud cover. I was the only passenger along with the Captain and co-pilot who flew out of Ithaca as their home base.

"It's going to get a bit nasty on arrival," the Captain had advised before we left Easton, "but it will only be for the last 10 to 15 minutes of flight. So, sit back and enjoy the ride."

I hate it when pilots say this. "A bit nasty" is always an understatement and certainly provides little to encourage either sitting back or enjoyment!

About twenty minutes out of Ithaca he throttled back and began a somewhat steep approach.

He shouted over his shoulder, "cinch your seatbelt up tight, here we go, on the ground in ten minutes...or so!"

With that, he gripped the steering column and drove the relatively tiny plane into the pure white surface of the clouds. Immediately it darkened to pale and then a darker gray. The engine pitch increased as he pushed the throttles forward to meet the first soft bounce.

The Dean didn't smoke, so the ashtrays on either seat arm had been removed, leaving a neat three-inch round hole, just big enough for my gloved fingers to enter and grip. I was now tethered at three points, both hands and the extremely tight strap across my lap.

LURCH...BANG...THUD. We were suddenly in a sharp downdraft caught with a loud, almost cracking, sound and then squealing upward and over some air-filled obstacle to plummet downward again. I could see nothing but the deepening gloom and the pilots fighting the controls as the plane became a living frenzied thing trying desperately to be free of any mechanic restraint.

RUSH...WHOOSH...SCREECH...we yawed from side to side.

Suddenly a wall of white hit us along with a deafening sound, as though we were caught in the crossfire of a hundred machine guns. It was a dense drift of hail; it drowned out the screaming engines with its high-pitched rattling impact. The dense clouds parted as we seemed to skim some two or three hundred feet over mountainous forests of dark pine trees.

In mounting terror, holding on for dear life, I recalled the Lord's Prayer and began it through clenched teeth meaning every word.

"Our Father which...LURCH...art in heaven...BANG...hallowed be Thy name... SCREECH...WHOOSH...Thy will be done..."

I had enough time to complete it before we broke free of the clouds and hail and could see the Ithaca Airport dead ahead.

The wind was blowing hard *across* the North-South runway, which itself seemed to be solid ice. The plane continued to swing wildly up and down, side to side.

We approached more or less into the wind at an impossible angle to the runway, at the last moment...gear down and we snapped into line. We slid onto the ice like a feather, followed by reverse-pitched propellers slowing us down enough to lightly touch the brakes. Both pilots attempted to look cool, as though this was normal, and for them it may well have been, but for me to be on the ground was a direct answer to prayer, one I hadn't used since school.

For those brief moments...I truly believed!

It took perhaps thirty minutes to return to the very solid, predictable world about me. I had three classes to teach, dinner with the Dean and some VIP donors, and then to bed before a big speech to the entire school the next morning. I spoke my heart out that day. My brush with almost certain death, in my eyes, had given me an edge and I used it to cut my way into my student's consciousness. I needed them to hear me! I pleaded with them to understand... *to meet their customers needs!*

I kept insisting on my vision for the future over dinner with the donors, gulping down the food between rushed and passionate sentences. Close to 11 p.m. I turned out the light and drifted off into a much-needed sleep.

Suddenly, I felt my lips go numb; my breathing raced with my heart...now my fingers were clumsy thick and also losing feeling. I found the light and the bedside phone and fumbled for the operator.

"Please let there be someone there," I managed to mumble...my words slurred as I spoke.

"Good evening, how may I help you?" A bright young student was on duty.

"I am...er...sick, having difficult speak," I stammered, getting more and more disoriented.

"Ambulance...please." I dropped the receiver on the bed where it said something and then began to purr.

Quite soon, or so it seemed, there was an ambulance stretcher and first responders in my room and I was lifted onto the gurney, blood pressure cuffed and wheeled out into the freight elevator used to take garbage and used laundry down to the road level.

So much for my celebrity, I thought, this could be it for me, and my exit is with the garbage!

The ambulance wound through the sleepy town to the hospital as I began to be less certain that I might die.

Following swiftly done tests, a very kindly older doctor told me that I was "fine."

"Have you been talking a lot recently?"

"Sure, all day it seems," I replied.

"Well, you need to exhale more completely in between your words," he explained.

"You should get some help to show you how to breathe using your diaphragm."

"You've had a hyperventilation event and that possibly triggered a panic attack."

I had actually depleted my carbon dioxide level in the blood by gulping down lungs full of air without properly allowing the lungs to deflate. The kindly doctor advised and taught me there and then to blow into a used brown paper bag and then inhale the trapped air. It felt better!

I need to add here that while this worked for me; it is no longer recommended because with certain conditions it has proved fatal.

Since I found it difficult not to speak, *with enthusiasm,* I traveled from then on with my humble, well-crumpled brown paper bag.

At the first sign of lightheadedness I would excuse myself, head for the nearest washroom and blow into my little brown bag.

Such is the life I lived in those busy years!

My good friend, the Dean, came to get me that next morning and we shared a hearty eggs and bacon breakfast in the hospital.

"Okay...ready now for the big speech," he smiled.

"It's like falling off a horse...best thing is to get right back on and keep moving."

I now had a perfect explanation that gave meaning to the title Galloping Gourmet...

Please join us in the Reflective Readers Club
www.grahamkerr.com/rrc

Rite of Passage Thirty-Seven: "A Broad Highway"

As quickly as we had entered the gloomy waters, we left them behind and could once again see with clarity what lay ahead.

It was confusing!

The smaller ones traveling with us were darting off in all directions. We could still sense the aroma but there were so many small channels created by sandbanks and merging waters, which one to take?

My hen, who had been content to follow my lead, had now become quite active, even getting ahead of me and following some of the small ones up a promising looking, but nonaromatic, entry.

I waited at the opening for her to hopefully return, where I could still catch the scent of our destination.

An Understanding

Our salmon have made it through a stream of pollution and are once again in the clear waters.

The "steelhead" (smaller species of salmon) are also in upstream migration, they are winter-run steelhead with spawning close at hand that return to all the streams, large and small, of the Lower Columbia from December through May.

Each is following its own scented river.

The hen Chinook decides to continue to follow several up their river as the buck keeps station where the unique aromas are still more obvious.

1974
I am forty years old

In Rite of Passage Two, in my eighth year just before I was sent off to boarding school, I had begun to wake up after just one hour of sleep and begun to scream, sitting bolt upright and still fast asleep. My parents would calm me down gently, tuck me in and then I'd sleep the rest of the night through. This became a nightly pattern and my parents could get no understanding from our family physician other than *"he should grow out of it."*

Obviously, since I appeared to be terrified about *something,* my parents decided to consult with one of the leaders in what was called "The White Brotherhood"...a quasi-religious group that met in the Aeolian Hall on New Bond Street in London.

Mr. Wyeth was one of their frequent lecturers and knew my father well enough that he offered to come down and sit at my bedside to assess what might be happening. This he did and was rewarded by one of my episodes.

He informed my anxious parents that he had "seen" what was happening, had dealt with it, and "it will not happen again."

Much later, my parents explained to me that Mr. Wyeth had told them our apartment on Cromwell Road in Hove, Sussex had been built over an ancient burial ground where humans had been sacrificed. Some of these "spirits" were still trapped and were in torment. I had been able to "see" these *beings* on the "astral plane." The fact that I had stopped my nocturnal sit-ups immediately following his visit was evidence enough to confirm my parent's interest in these teachings; ones that revolved around reincarnation and to some extent racism, with a handy smattering of politically correct Christianity to ease its acceptance amongst mostly upper middle class white intellectuals.

My father was especially impressed with these ideas and remained convinced that he (and us) were somewhere in the middle of a series of incarnations as we learned, from each of our lifetimes, to gradually evolve out of having to be human.

Eventually, we ourselves would become "keepers of the lodge" and help others to choose the multiple life experiences they needed in order to make right choices and finally ascend, as we had done, as spiritual mentors.

Over time and without any obvious pressure, what they believed had been loosely passed on within the family and seemed rational enough to make sense out of circumstances that appeared to be so...odd!

Like two vast world wars with multiple millions killed in less than half a century?

When asked what we believed, in religious terms, I would often reply, "A sort of esoteric Buddhism mixed with reincarnation."

I had, regardless of my early encounter with the "wrath of God" expressed during a beating by an ordained Anglican Priest, been confirmed in my eleventh year as a "Christian" and from then on used the abbreviation C/E on all the British forms I completed (C/E = Church of England).

In Rite of Passage Seven, when I was eighteen (1952), I had entered the Army to serve my compulsory two years of "National Service." I had filled in the form with the accepted C/E and found that my name was listed, with most of the other new recruits, for the Sunday Church Parade, where we had to "spit and polish" our best uniforms and be inspected by a duty officer as "suitably turned out for God."

Since we were inspected every single day, it occurred to me that I might get a day off by changing the C/E to E/B for Esoteric Buddhist.

I doubted that there would be a special service for *that!*

I was wrong.

The Sergeant waved my change of religion form under my nose.

"I see 'ow you have 'ad a change of 'eart about God," he inquired softly, almost with a degree of personal understanding.

"So, I want you to take this." He handed me a tin of Kiwi brown boot polish and a yellow cloth. "Follow me."

He led the way to the latrines, and lifted one of the scuffed wooden seats.

"Whilst you engage in your meditations I want you to highly polish this seat UNTIL YOU CAN SEE YOUR BLOODY FACE IN IT," he roared and left me to my religious experience.

I quickly applied to be restored to the Church of England with, of course, my own unique spin on how my life should be lived.

It was therefore not too hard to accept Treena's wish to go to a retreat at Goshen in upper New York State that offered yoga, TM (transcendental meditation), vegan diet and other recent Far Eastern religious practices made popular by the Beatles and other luminaries of that time. She was away for a month during which she was encouraged not to correspond with the outside world. I continued leaping over all my "scheduled" appearances and hoping that the poem would mesh with the meditations and the macrobiotic menu and help her to avoid going to the institution to detox.

It didn't!

What it had done was to convince her that she should donate, in addition to the monthly fees, $10,000 to the "retreat" to help them to help others to "find peace!" That would have been fine had it not been for the red light outside our bedroom door.

Treena would turn on the light during her yoga/meditation times when "I shall be seeking deep inner peace and healing."

If ANYTHING disturbed the *peace* when the light was ablaze, there was an immediate explosion! We had exchanged relative peace for open warfare.

It was obvious that NOTHING helped. The bottom of the barrel had been reached. We were now only one month away from the new date of commitment and the attempt to be drug free! I was living in domestic chaos in spite of a handful of drugs each day, what on earth would it be like without any "medication?"

I returned to Ottawa to make yet another sixty five episodes of "Take Kerr" just before Christmas of 1974. The unbearable was bearable when I was away. It was long, tough hours but it was without the tensions of home. At least there was a reward for effort!

I made it back home on December 20th that year. I parked the Volvo under the western trees and crunched over the gravel drive with my old leather portmanteau to the large white door, where I stood for a moment to brace myself for the reentry to disorder.

Kareena had heard me arrive and flung open the front door.

"Mummy, mummy, it's daddy...daddy's home and now it's Christmas!" She raised her arms wide for me to scoop her up and ruffle her blonde curls.

"Yes, I do believe it's Christmas!" I agreed, gave her a kiss and set her down to run off and get Tessa.

Tessa had returned home to await a decision on going off to a similar detox center to the one Treena was scheduled to attend, one that specialized in teenagers since she was now eighteen.

I had serious misgivings about that Christmas with both Treena and Tessa awaiting treatment, even though as yet Treena was completely unaware of my agreement with our doctor to place her in professional hands early in January.

It was then that I saw her at the end of the entry hall that stretched the entire width of the house.

She had come out of the drawing room, where I had sat awaiting her decision and poem, the room that overlooked Peachblossom Creek where we had run aground.

She simply stood there, a little like I remembered when she had entered her parent's front room on our first date after their return to England. Twenty years had now passed since that treasured memory and now here she was again, strangely different, almost as shy as she had been so long ago, shy and vulnerable, almost hesitant?

She just stood there.

I had dropped my old bag in order to pick up Kareena and left it there by the still open door as I walked slowly to where she waited. We stood quite close, a foot or so apart and searched each other's eyes for some understanding.

Her eyes glistened, reflecting the light, as deep and as beautiful as they had been before our troubles and the medications had glazed them over. I reached out to take her hands in mine but hers had already been raised, like Kareena's had been, they gently encircled my neck as we moved close enough to almost feel our hearts beating together.

There was little to say, just the usual…"did the shows go well?" …and my brief remarks that they seemed to…"but who knows…I miss you being there…you are the only one whose judgment I truly trust."

We had tea with the children. Andy was home from Westtown, Tessa was awaiting a decision about her treatment, and Kareena could scarcely wait for the "presents" that were now heaped under a spectacular tree that almost touched our twelve foot ceiling. It seemed that we might have a better Christmas than I had thought. I put the sense of peace and joy down to something to do with the Christmas spirit.

It felt good…at least for now.

Christmas was good, the best I ever remember having. We spent the entire period without a single upset.

I began to relax and put the finishing touches to our "Great Gatsby" New Year's Eve party, where we would try to stage a rather "lowercase" shindig with plenty of 1920 cocktails and a reasonable cold buffet.

Our guests were encouraged to come in costumes of the prohibition era and we would have big band music playing so that we could dance in the Great Room.

I drove into Easton with Andy to find some good hams and was busily checking the labels at the Safeway deli, when I heard a woman's voice behind me.

"Hallelujah! Isn't it wonderful?"

I turned to be confronted by a tall, thin woman in her late forties with a pile of braided hair on top of a dead white cosmetic-free face.

"Hallelujah!" She repeated, her eyes dancing with excitement. Breathlessly she announced...

"I was baptized in the same way your wife was," she was clearly delighted to be the one to pass on this hugely funny piece of misinformation, so much so that I humored her, agreed quickly and hurriedly left the store. I was struck by Andy's silence as I chortled all the way home at this remarkable piece of misunderstanding.

"If mum had got close to a baptism, she would have made it boil." Andy smiled at my amusement, but said nothing.

We had four carpenters and painters in the house putting the finishing touches to the party rooms. I gathered them all into the Great Room where a painter stood atop a ladder with brush in hand.

Everyone waited expectantly...

"Boy, have I got something funny to tell you all...it's hilarious!" I laughed and actually slapped my thigh with the pure pleasure of knowing I had a great punch line for the joke of the year.

"I was buying a ham when this strange lady, no makeup and a beehive hairdo, comes up behind me and says..."

"Hallelujah!" I'm almost collapsing in laughter as I go on..."and then she says"...more laughter..."that she was"...pause for effect..."baptized just like your wife was!" Now I hooted at this amazing ending.

My audience remained unmoved, pretty well silent.

I turned to Treena who was sitting on a small swiveling organ stool. She wasn't even smiling.

Very quietly she said...

"I was."

Please join us in the Reflective Readers Club
www.grahamkerr.com/rrc

Rite of Passage Thirty-Eight: "The Ultimate Shrink"

I didn't have to wait long. My hen returned from the coastal waterway and we continued to follow the aroma into fresher and fresher water. She swam so close alongside that our fins just touched...briefly. No mistaking it now this was our birth river, this was the way home!

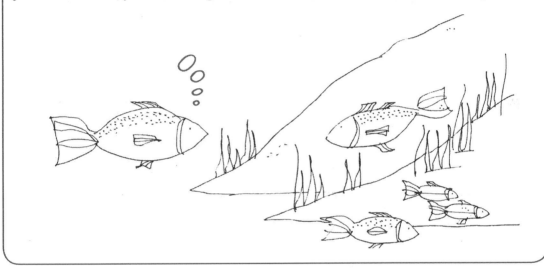

An Understanding

Salmon can occasionally take rivers other than their own and by doing so they help to diversify the gene pool, which can sometimes become weakened through close family inbreeding if the population size in any one stream becomes too small. Of even greater importance, if a stream is adversely affected by an ice age for hundreds to thousands of years, or briefly impacted by a volcanic eruption with loss of all salmon, straying from other streams provides the important mechanism for recolonization in waters that have become vacated.

Our Chinook hen had followed a friendly steelhead because of the relationship that had helped them take the plunge through the heavy pollution...but it wasn't her stream.

1974 to 1975
I am forty one years old

I, too, stopped laughing when I heard that Treena had indeed been baptized. I went, in one crashing moment, from being the center of audience expectations; waiting for their laughter and applause to, in my own eyes, an object of almost ridicule.

I recall the painter on the ladder; he turned his face upward to the ceiling and dabbed at it with a kind of knowing smile, or was that a smirk?

Hastily...I responded to Treena's admission.

"Can we discuss this privately?"

I suggested we move into my spacious, very sparsely equipped study with its ultra modern furniture and a huge white drafting board. As we left the Great Room, I could have easily, again in my own mind, walked fully erect under an unopened door −so utterly diminished had I become.

We sat on the floor. "So..." I began, trying to recover some kind of self.

"So, do you want me to become a Christian too?"

I admit I really didn't like the idea because Sunday was the only day completely devoid of a scheduled performance. It would be ruined by having to go to church. I also wondered if there was room for a...*Jesus* in our home. It seemed to me that he might take up a lot of *space* although precisely what that meant I didn't even try to grasp.

"No," Treena replied softly. "I need Jesus, I really don't know about you." She reached out and took my hand in hers.

"What about belief in reincarnation?" I asked.

"Again darling," she replied, "this is all so new to me that we shall just have to see" (no insistence, just quiet and peaceful).

Within days I had to make the detox commitment decision, and now wondered if I might delay it once again because of this "Christian experience." I didn't have to call the doctor −he called me. He wanted to pay me a visit, at home.

He arrived and we sat over a coffee in the same chairs that overlooked the creek, where so much had happened just a few weeks ago.

"Mr. Kerr...er...could I call you Graham? You see, this is rather personal." He was a little hesitant so I warmly encouraged.

"Sure, can I call you Jack?" I responded.

"I'd like that. Well, you might not know this but I'm Roman Catholic. I believe in miracles, but I'm also a scientist and mostly I have been able to explain so called 'miracle cures' as more physical than somehow supernatural." He paused to sip at the coffee and set it down carefully.

He leaned forward and looked at me directly, clasping his hands together tightly.

"But, I can't find a physical answer for what has happened to Treena." He looked down and took a deep breath; when he looked up his eyes had filled with tears.

"Graham...Treena is a miracle, God has sovereignly decided to have himself a miracle. He has reached into your family and made himself evident, and you need to know that."

He paused, not for effect, but because apparently there really was nothing more he needed to say.

Of course, it wasn't enough for me! I needed to know why and how, all kinds of questions. This was completely new territory for me; I had nowhere to put my feelings. It was quite similar to when the surgeon had called to say that Treena's lung growth was benign and I had nobody to adequately thank, apart from the obvious.

I was then provided with a careful, somewhat detailed understanding of the science involved in the intervention required to detoxify a medically addicted patient and the long, slow withdrawal period needed; especially for Treena's list of prescription medications and her length of time taking them.

"Treena had very clear symptoms that showed me that she was suffering from medication addiction. She was anxious, agitated, even at times aggressive and off in a rage. She had numerous hallucinations and difficulty sleeping without Mogadon.

"Her apparent consumption of Valium per day may have been as high as 60 mg, and 40 mg is about as much as is normally prescribed. I was trying to ease her down but it wasn't working. Sometimes that can take six to twelve months."

Now it was my time to be shocked, I had *no idea* how serious it was and yet...the doctor continued.

"She is now more sane, lucid and at peace than I am, although that doesn't mean much." He managed a brief chuckle.

"Treena told me she has thrown all her medications down the drain *all of them*," he emphasized.

"You can't just do that! The normal result would be severe withdrawal symptoms, even coma and death!"

"But, she had a good night's sleep and absolutely no adverse symptoms, now *that's* the miracle!"

Amid all the words, all the explanations, all the religious thinking, it was the tears that convinced me. Doctors, it seemed to me, do not often cry. If they did, it was either a primetime doctor movie or perhaps...*a miracle?* I thanked him. We agreed to keep a careful watch over her and he left me in my, at that time of day, empty house.

I walked outside into the nine acres of gardens and approached a large tree.

There was nobody I knew that I could go to with this amazing information. Treena had received a miracle healing —no other explanation was possible.

"Okay..." I faced the tree and began a request, "I believe that you are a living organism, so am I, so is Treena." (It really didn't feel foolish at this time, or even now as I recall it vividly, to speak to that aged tree).

"Neither you nor I have a personal relationship with God but Treena apparently does." I paused.

"So...I want a miracle too." Now, that felt pretty lame. It was almost as though Treena had a Platinum Credit Card and I had Sears revolving credit.

"I want a miracle too" was personal, relational, even selfish, but that's what had been stirred up in me and so that's what I asked for, or rather in a sense, demanded of the tree!

Nothing moved. Dead leaves rustled underfoot but there was no breeze or even sounds.

I couldn't see anything or hear anything, so I turned from the tree to return to the house and my schedule, my survival business.

Everything changed. My selfish request had actually been heard and immediately granted; yet it remained unseen and misunderstood for many months to come.

My chief concern became this "watching brief" over Treena.

We had numerous periods of peace in the past when the old skeleton had remained in its cupboard. This could be another and I feared that, this time, everything seemed to be both new and completely independent of human intervention.

We were, quite literally, *on our own* with God?

The light had come on in the bathroom after midnight. I turned over and slept. Awakening at 3 a.m. it was still on. I went back to sleep again and first thing in the morning asked Treena "is everything alright? I saw the light on for a long time last night."

Treena actually blushed (she didn't do so often).

"No, I'm fine." She replied quickly.

"So, why was the light on?" I persisted.

"I was reading."

"Reading what...and why in the bathroom?"

She was now really hesitant...

"It's the Bible," she spoke in a near whisper.

"Do you have to read it in the bathroom?" I smiled.

"No, but I didn't want to read it in front of you...in bed," she explained.

"Why ever not? Tell you what...I'm reading about Chinese philosophy, I'll bring my books up and we'll compare notes; I'll tell you what my guys were up to when your Jesus was doing his stuff." We agreed and began to share from our respective authors, a kind of miniature book club in a king-sized bed.

On my side was Confucius, born about 550 years before Jesus; I was very interested in what was described as his precursor to the Golden Rule..."what you do not wish for yourself, do not do to others."

As far as I could judge, he appeared to be teaching about the same time as the Old Testament prophet Zechariah and so I read both and enjoyed this plunge into relatively ancient history. During this season of reading, I was discovering one of Confucius' basic ethics, that he described as *reciprocity*, that is often translated as righteousness by its application to personal decision making, you might end up "doing the right thing for the right reason." All of this seemed to work in well with Zechariah. "Administer true justice, show mercy and compassion to one another." (Zechariah 7:9)

Most of what I read seemed rational and to some extent even pragmatic. Both men obviously wanted what was best. Treena's guy was taking a great deal of time to nut-it-out and behave as best he could. He kept on getting great advice from God that his listeners found hard to accept.

"But they refused to pay attention. Stubbornly they turned their backs and stopped up their ears. They made their hearts as hard as flint and would not listen to the law or to the words that the Lord Almighty had sent by his spirit through the earlier prophets, so the Lord Almighty was very angry." (Zechariah 7:11–12)

These comparisons kept Treena out of the bathroom and fully satisfied my ongoing search for somehow seeking the "common good."

The more we shared over the weeks that followed, the more relaxed I became. Far from reverting to her earlier turmoil, Treena was now showing a contagious joyfulness. She had a butterfly style that seemed to flutter in a lovely display and everywhere she chose to alight she seemed to bring a kind of celebration of life, one that she had just discovered, or had discovered her?

Life was good again...life was fresh and new.

One other hugely important issue for me, who was still busy at Cornell, Hyde Park and Ottawa, was that Sundays had not been taken over by church.

Apart from our fifth century before-Christ comparisons, there were very few, if any, religious words spoken. Ruthie and Treena did spend time together; this seemed mostly about the house and whether I was in earshot. They did meet fairly often in the rather spacious closet under the main staircase, where we kept the brooms but that seemed private, so I left them to it.

All of this would have been fine had it not been for a considerable downside.

As my private life radically improved, my public life and its deadlines had become an increasing burden. It was now unnecessary to escape from domestic disorder and find some reward through my efforts, both financial and the old ego issues of being *well regarded* by many of my peer group. There was plenty of reward simply being at home with the woman I loved, who was now loving me back.

I also began to be less impressed by the outward appearance of all the "stuff" that surrounded me. Nothing provided the feedback benefit of ownership that it had previously done.

"That's my new car, my big house, my big yacht. my! my! my...*everything!*"

The trouble with things, it seemed to me, is that they had to be maintained and often upgraded and they gradually seemed to mean less and less a matter of me owning them, and more a matter of them owning me. I had begun to think of myself as some kind of slave to my stuff...my acquisitions appeared to have mastered me! That's how it felt when I left home in early March for another recording visit to Ottawa.

The house needed painting; the boat needed to be sold, the car's color was wrong, the grass needed...*whatever grass needed.*

It all took time and money and that was the reason I had to keep on performing.

The *lights* that had attracted me to this abundant materialistic life had dimmed. The only bright light that I now knew was to be found in Treena's lovely, clear, sparkling eyes.

I had asked for a miracle that I could now begin to see but still not understand.

God was turning down the lights that had guided me for many years.

By the time I returned, two weeks later, they were to be extinguished.

Please join us in the Reflective Readers Club
www.grahamkerr.com/rrc

Rite of Passage Thirty-Nine: "The Flash Ahead"

There was a considerable difference in the way my hen moved. She remained just ahead and seemed to know exactly which way to go. We had swum into a complex pattern of shallow muddy banks without shade from the tall green things.

There was less brightness and lots of dapples on the surface. All around us there were much smaller fish a little like us and the steelhead were not as schooled together as we larger salmon and seemed to be waiting around for something.

It was the strangest feeling; like having been here before but going the other way?

An Understanding

In Rite of Passage Eleven our salmon had reached the tidal estuary where the river had delta'd and formed the nursery for the small new salmon where they could adjust to the increasing saltiness of the incoming tides.

It was there that they had seen the mature Chinook returning, it was this faint memory and the reduced saltiness that had helped them to feel the connection to the river that lay ahead, one in which countless others had returned over many hundreds of years.

1975
I am forty one years old

As usual, I travelled first class, was met at the airport, picked up by limousine and dropped off at what is now called "ARC The Hotel" in downtown Ottawa.

All was designed to comfort me as I once again taped a new series for widespread distribution. This time, all the "extras" were not quite so comforting. Everything was just as soft and squishy, but I didn't bask in the *upgrade,* as it is usually called. It was pleasing but no longer *rewarding.* The only reward I had, at that time, was being home with my now thoroughly delightful Treena in the big house that needed painting, surrounded by the grass that needed...well...whatever scruffy lawns like ours needed!

Even the shows themselves did little to improve my mood. I did four a day and was told that all was going "well enough." My lower back wasn't at all "happy" and I dropped in at the chiropractor we had attended during our time when we were residents.

"Good to see you again, tell me, how is Treena?" He asked, as enthusiastic as ever.

"Oh, she's fine," I replied. "She is a Christian now and is much better."

"Hallelujah!" *There was that word again!*

He was obviously thrilled and seemed to be a fellow believer.

"What about you?" He asked, while cradling my head in his hands, moving it back and forth before the now old-fashioned "jerk." It's hard to completely relax at such a time, but I managed a cautious...

"I'm looking into it." I wanted to avoid any other description lest he excitedly tear my head from my shoulders!

When the deed was done and I shakily regained my feet, he made an invitation.

"Want to join my family at church this Sunday?"

"No thanks, I need all the rest time I can get...it's my one day off." I explained truthfully.

A couple of days later I got back in the early evening to the hotel after a long day and was greeted by the Assistant Manager who inquired after my health and comfort; was there *anything* at all he could do to make it more comfortable?

It was standard "patter" in most of the quality hotels of the world.

"No thanks, I'm fine." Again, a standard response.

And then I noted the stainless steel bird in his lapel.

"Are you a hunter?" I asked.

He laughed delightedly. "No, no, that's a dove," he explained.

"It's a symbol of the Holy Spirit of God!"

Oh my, another one...this is getting a little crowded!

"That's nice," I replied, for lack of anything else to say.

"Yes...I'm a Deacon at my church and I'm giving the sermon this Sunday." He didn't ask me to come to hear it, but I was intrigued.

I knew what hotel people did. I had had his very position before I had moved on to General Manager. I wondered what kind of sermon he could possibly give.

"I'd like to come and hear that." I couldn't believe my own ears. This was Sunday –*my only day off!*

He was clearly delighted and wrote the address down on the back of his business card.

"The service begins at 10:00; try to get there at 9:30, okay?"

I agreed.

The next day it began to snow heavily and it kept up for three days, including my only day off. I called for a taxi and asked if they thought they could get through the partly plowed streets.

"Sure, no problem for us. Hey, this is Ottawa man!"

Obviously, the dispatcher didn't know my driver, and my driver didn't have a clue where this small Anglican Church was located. I sat in the back of his overheated cab, dressed in my large fur coat that I'd picked up for a rather out-of-tune song in Palma de Majorca and a handsome, if huge, beaver hat that really was a great buy in Moscow.

My watch showed nine 9:45 and we were still crunching slowly through back streets whose road signs were encrusted in snow and ice. At 10 a.m. I was ready to turn back to the hotel when suddenly there it was. A geodesic dome, most unusual for an Anglican Church, better suited to a Mongolian Muslim? There was no defined entry, only two lines of footprints going in both sides.

I was now in quite a stew. I hate being late and was in painful recall of the beating I had received at school for being "late for God" at morning chapel. I could hear somewhat lusty singing and an organ. I opened the door and found myself in what looked like a boiler room, with a flight of stairs leading to another door, where the singing seemed to be. Yanking that door open, I appeared, in full snow-covered fur, like some startled yeti...behind the choir.

I was swiftly "captured" by an usher and led to the back row amid a sea of swiftly turning heads as the congregation made note of my unusual entrance. I removed my fur coverings and sat sweating heavily.

A kind couple in a pew directly in front of me handed me a hymn book and another book that explained the ups and downs that Anglican services use to provide at least some form of aerobic activity.

My "friend," the Assistant Manager, gave a sermon that made little sense to me...other than when he drew attention to my having joined the service.

The congregation turned around, almost as one, to observe for the second time, the "Galloping Gourmet" in the back pew.

I waved weakly and put on a brave smile over gritted teeth.

After the service I would have escaped if I'd had a car. Instead, the Vicar invited me to his Manse next door to "meet some of the flock." They were gathered in his living room, many were smoking and all were enjoying an especially stiff Bloody Mary (vodka and tomato juice).

My mind easily drew the comparison to the congregation of St. Mildred's in Tenterden, Kent, UK, when they would come to our hotel next door for "refreshments". Always good for business after a quiet Sunday morning.

During this extended time of being seriously out of my depth I was asked if I would like to return for dinner.

"We are having Boeuf Bourguignon and your friend from the hotel is bringing it," he added.

I had no doubt that it would be well made and this local dish of beef braised in red wine with a whole small onions and mushrooms had always been a favorite. I agreed, mostly because of the beef, to return that night and even purchased a reasonable bottle of French burgundy as a guest gift. The beef was better than I had expected, he had used blade beef with its mass of connective tissue that had melted out over a long slow braise, so much so that my lips held lightly together...*delicious*!

There were five others that surrounded the table that night, enough for one reasonable glass of my good burgundy, not enough to change one's mood.

Yet my mood changed that night at that table.

Their reason for gathering was to discuss how their small congregation could respond to a huge famine in Africa.

It was clear that they wanted to help, to provide something to alleviate the pain and suffering, but to whom? Where could such a small sum make the most difference? I listened to them and their passion. At first, I was amazed at how concerned they were about such a small donation. Several hundred dollars would go nowhere; it might even go unnoticed amongst all the Government aid being supplied.

"So...*why all the drama?*" I thought but sat, ate and drank my wine and began to listen with almost another set of senses?

One Deacon was especially moved by the urgent need and had recently returned from a brief visit. His description of the devastation was so intense that I could almost *see* and yes, even *smell,* the unfolding disaster.

There was a stirring in my chest. I'd felt it before during past hard relationship times at home with Treena when I had longed for our pain to be resolved; even if it meant that I should let her go!

I remained completely silent. I pushed back from the table into relative shadow, still holding the wine glass with a couple of sips remaining. As the sense of loss rose to tighten my throat, it was harder to swallow. It was then that tears began to form and then flow slowly down my face.

If people like this could also love like this, then there was still hope for people like that.

There was a solution and it was here, at this small table. It had nothing to do with how much was needed and how small the donation. It had more to do with seeing their powerful urgency as they faced and seemingly overcame, an enormous obstacle.

I slept well that night. I like to think that I slept with a smile!

My host had not asked me to contribute. I would cheerfully have done so. They didn't ask for my opinion, I could easily have done that too. It was a favorite pastime that I had practiced for years!

It was almost as though I hadn't been there...like a fly on the wall –unnoticed?

I was back in the studio for another two full days to complete the sixty five shows. I then had one final day before setting off back home via Las Vegas where I had been booked to "play" the Celebrity Room at the MGM Hotel; a far cry from my Sunday supper with a bunch of Anglicans!

This final day was packed. I had agreed with the faculty at Cornell's School of HumEc (Human Ecology) to make a series of short videos to be played to inner city youth in poverty stricken areas, such as Harlem. I believe I made twelve in that one day. It was the first time in my entire life that I had ever done anything like this for nothing. Neither had I ever made a donation, of any kind, to any charity.

Yet, here I was, with some new kind of passion that surprised me. I even sounded a little like my Sunday evening dinner host whose passion had moved me to tears. I spoke and cooked with an urgency that had very little to do with entertaining or gaining approval, I just wanted to connect, for *their* sake.

By the time I got back to the hotel I was spinning tired, I felt as I had at Cornell when I had hyperventilated. I thought of blowing into my well-used little brown bag but took a long shower instead.

Too wired to sleep, I leafed through the yachting magazines by my bed. Nothing caught my interest. I picked up the small bible I had been trying to read so that I might have something to share in my conversations with Treena when I got home. I flipped the tiny pages, much as I had with the far larger magazines, and wound up in the book of Mark, early on in Chapter 4...I later found out it was verse 21.

"He said to them, is a lamp brought in to be put under a basket or under a bed, and not on a stand?"

That was quite enough for me...of course not...that was a simple fire precaution. Perhaps that was why it was printed in red? I went to put it back down, only to sense a growing frustration. Treena, our chiropractor, the Assistant Hotel Manager, the Anglican Deacon...I was surrounded by people who used words like *hallelujah* and smiled a lot. They all seemed to share a common relationship, one that I did not have. If I had, then the small bible might become interesting, like it had for Treena.

I left the easy chair, walked out in the middle of my quite large room and knelt down.

We had to kneel at chapel and at Army church services and I had done so in my sweaty condition last Sunday, so I knelt to see if that might help.

It didn't.

I clenched my fist around the bible so that it folded in half.

I looked up at the ceiling in frustration and shouted.

"I want a personal relationship with you and I want it NOW!"

Nothing happened! I was tired and angry and didn't know what else to say.

I fixed my eyes on the three way connection between the ceiling and the corner of the room, right at the point that they met.

By this time I was almost too exhausted to speak...

"What do I have to say to you to know you like Treena does?" I almost pleaded for an answer.

The answer came when I opened my mouth and heard myself say...

Please join us in the Reflective Readers Club
www.grahamkerr.com/rrc

Rite of Passage Forty: "A Splash in the Face"

We had now come quite a way upstream and had left the silver clouds of tiny fish going the other way.

The tang had gone out of the water and we were no longer feeling the lifting of the counter pressure that seemed to be somehow regular.

The brightness above was less now and often dappled, sometimes even going white and churning. When it did, it tasted and smelled wonderful. The familiar aroma at these times was as strong as the waters that now flowed in only one direction, although it was against us, it was welcome because the faster it went, the better it felt.

We were born for such a time as this!

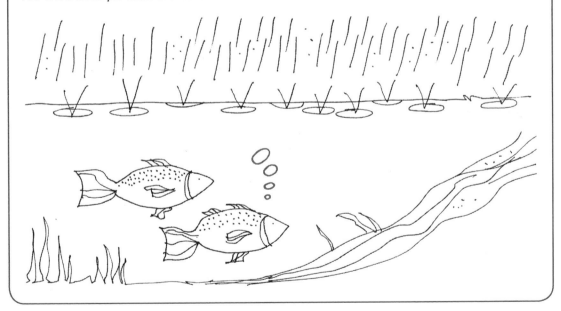

An Understanding

Our pair of Chinook had now left the tidal estuary where the earliest new smolts awaited their full readiness to strike out into the Pacific Ocean. It was raining heavily and the river was filled with waters that drained down the mountains and swept over the gravel beds where they had received life. It was this fresh aroma that now filled them with an urgency to literally fight their way upstream.

1975 – 18 March
I am forty one years old

At that very moment, self-consciously kneeling, close to midnight in a very upscale hotel room, I had a confused emptiness like being in a deep, dark unfamiliar place. Others appeared to know which end was up; I didn't even know how to ask why I felt so completely lost.

So I asked what it was that I needed to say. I didn't have a clue what needed to be done.

I opened my mouth as though somehow it might be filled with words.

I heard myself say...

"Jesus, I love you."

There was no conscious thought behind those four words, all I did was listen...with, at first, considerable surprise. It was not, in any measure what I had been feeling and yet, as I heard the words, I went from frustrated, angry and exhausted through a wave of emotion that brought freshness to the very air I was breathing.

I felt the heaviness lift and a lightness take its place.

I sat back on my heels; my gaze now fixed where the three lines met up in the corner of the ceiling by the heavily draped windows.

I began to speak, at first slowly, and then with increasing pace, my words poured out making not the least sense to me so I have no memory of them. It was just after 2 a.m. when I stopped and noticed the time on the bedside clock, glowing red.

Without thinking, I grabbed the phone and dialed our home number.

A sleepy Treena answered..."Hello, hello?"

"It's me." I answered her.

"Is there something wrong?" She was alarmed.

"No but something has just happened to me."

"What's that?" She was beginning to awaken.

"I really don't know but I feel different –all of a sudden." I explained.

"How are you feeling, can you tell?"

"Not really except that...er..." I was embarrassed to say what I had said to the ceiling, even to Treena. It's not easy to be a man sometimes and to use the word *love* beyond its normal boundaries.

"...er...mm...like I'm fresh and excited and I think I'm a Christian," I added hesitantly.

There was a long pause.

"When will you be home?" She asked, carefully.

"Two days now...about 11 o'clock at night."

"We'll talk about it then?"

"Of course...hey...sorry to have woken you up," I apologized.

"You can call me anytime with news like that." She was now fully awake.

The Vegas event had been orchestrated by my agent Wilbur, who was really eager to have his property on stage at the MGM; for him it easily transcended anything we had ever done on television. For me it was simply another hurdle to jump before I got home to talk about my Ottawa experience.

We flew to Salt Lake City to pick up a connection to Las Vegas. When we arrived we were greeted with the news that Vegas was blanketed by heavy local fog; that was unlikely to lift for two days! Wilbur, fearing that we wouldn't make the appearance, shopped around for a commuter or private plane that might boldly go where no commercial plane might venture.

He found a single-engine Beechcraft Bonanza with a single pilot. I could fly in the right seat, and there was room in the back for him and our bags, this included my leather portmanteau of Sydney fame!

We took off, having set up the radio direction finder (RDF) for the Las Vegas airport and quickly saw the fog begin to settle below us. It was now almost dark. I began to watch the RDF and listen to its increasing pitch as we neared our destination.

"Should be any moment now," the pilot announced through the earphones.

He switched to the Control Tower frequency, announced his flight number and asked for permission to land.

The Control Tower advised, "wind calm, 10 yard visibility, runway clear, lights on, if you can find them!"

We crossed over the invisible airport and began to descend in a long steady 360° turn. Now my eyes were on the altimeter as it unwound through one thousand, five hundred, three hundred.

This was going to be another opportunity for the Lord's prayer!

Suddenly, a stab of brightness lit up the fog ahead and we passed right over a large illuminated arrow. We were just below 200 feet. The pilot lowered full flaps, the landing gear was already down, and pushed the nose down into the fog.

There it was...right ahead...the first lights of the runway and the striped threshold. With a thud we were down, losing speed and feeling our way to the terminal. Whatever new faith

I thought I might have had remained unused. I could claim no answered prayer because I hadn't asked.

Once again, I was unaware that I should be grateful; so I simply remained relieved!

The stage folks at the MGM Celebrity Room had done a great job. A complete kitchen had been built for me and was revealed when the curtains and a thin veil were lifted. In front of the stage was a barstool with a crystal glass of red wine, lit by a single spot.

They played the signature tune from the old "Galloping Gourmet" show by Champ Champagne and on I walked, in dinner jacket, black tie and big smile. Deep bow to the applause. I did my *thing*. The people laughed, the dish was done and it was over.

Wilbur enjoyed himself thoroughly. It was, for him, a singular achievement to have booked me at such a venue.

My greatest concern was whether the fog would lift and allow us to leave for the long trip home.

It did!

As I had thought, it was close to midnight when my headlights lit up the white flank of our home at the bottom of the long drive through the big trees.

I quietly opened the front door, dropped my leather portmanteau in its usual place and climbed the stairs to the second floor. The light was on in our bedroom. Treena had fallen asleep while reading. I awakened her very gently with a light kiss on her forehead...

Her eyes opened and she sat up smiling.

"You're home." She blinked and smiled again.

"Yes, safe and sound," I replied.

I took off my jacket and sat down on a very small brocaded chair with a heart-shaped back. It was covered in rose chintz, a ridiculous chair for a man my size.

"I'm sorry to be so late, this is becoming a habit," I laughed self-consciously.

"No...no..." she responded. "I'm fine...do you want to tell me about –your –feelings now, or in the morning?" She was giving me some space.

"Now would be fine, if it's okay with you?"

"Sure." She plumped the pillows and sat upright, drawing her knees up and holding them loosely with her arms. She looked so lovely, with only the soft lighting by the bedside.

I told her the whole story; our chiropractor, the Anglican Church. She loved my furry entrance and was also moved by my tears at the evening dinner.

I detailed what I had done for the inner-city youth and then tried to explain my mix of exhaustion and frustration that had led to my one-sided conversation with the ceiling. It was now that I had to actually say the words that I had said, or been given to say, as an answer to my demand to, "know you like Treena knows you."

She was listening very carefully, her head inclined very slightly towards me.

I opened my mouth and heard myself say...

"Jesus, I love you." I stopped.

"So...what happened next?" She asked.

"I don't really know. I started to talk. I think it was about my life. It felt very personal but I can't remember a single word." I paused.

"It just felt *fresh,* I wasn't tired or frustrated anymore. I had real energy." I searched for some kind of explanation for the feeling.

"It was like I was a young child again in a bathtub and swishing up and down to build up a wave, and then suddenly stopping so that I met the wave head on and got water splashing out of the tub."

It sounded silly...and yet it was that water rushing toward me and cascading over me that was as close as I could get.

"I think I can understand." Treena was being cautious.

I hurried on.

"I now pray holding my small bible in my left hand, like it was when all this happened."

I got it out of my pocket and held it, folded in half so that my fingers just touched my palm.

"Can we pray together?" I asked, tentatively.

Treena was out of bed and on her knees in almost a cartoon character's flash. I crossed the room and knelt beside her, taking her hand in mine. Even her hand felt new, it was the same hand I had held when we were at school and yet it was warm and soft and so gently quiet and still.

We prayed that night. I can't recall about what, all I remember is that this, too, was utterly different, so incredibly intimate to listen to her words spoken so conversationally to God, with whom she had such a personal relationship. She then began to pray more urgently in Latin, at least that was how it sounded. The words tumbled over themselves and I supposed that she had learned them during her three months of solitary prayer. As I listened, I was overwhelmed with a complete sense of joy, so much so that real tears ran down my face.

And so we entered the *river of life* that is described in scripture. It seemed to flow toward us, splashing in our faces, encouraging us from that day on. There was a faint fragrance in our room that night. Gradually it filled the house and all of us who were in temporary residence.

Before too long that fragrance would increase as our long journey upstream began in earnest.

Please join us in the *Reflective Readers Club*
www.grahamkerr.com/rrc

For almost as long as I can remember, I have been swimming in tangy waters that had no boundaries from side to side or below.

Only the brightness above had a sense of limit. I could go through it but never very far before I was back in my element again, with a splash!

Now everything is different. I swim closer to the brightness because I can clearly see below and it is mud, branches and stones. Often I can see a long barrier on one side or the other, never two at the same time.

The tang is gone, replaced by an unceasing flow of water that carries the aroma that goes beyond my memory to an instinct that now summons all the energy I have stored for such a time as this.

My hen already seems to feel the way I do, in fact, she continues to swim ahead of me. I'm content to follow.

An Understanding

They have been at sea in the salty waters for about five years —most of that time in ocean depths without shorelines or estuaries.

Now they experience a river that is wide enough to let them see one bank at a time.

As they move onward they enter more restricted waters. The more they go upstream the less freedom they have to maneuver.

The only sense of freedom that drives them onward is the aromatic promise of what lies ahead, and that promise grows stronger every day.

1975
I am forty one years old

Treena had read in her first small bible, the one that Ruthie had urged her to buy, that she should apply a "golden zipper to her mouth" and to rely *completely* upon whatever God wanted to do with her husband.

The verse that motivated her was in Matthew 15:11 (NIV):

"What goes into someone's mouth does not defile them, but what comes out of their mouth, that is what defiles them."

There had been not a single *religious* word spoken in my hearing. Ruthie and Treena did set up a kind of closet under the stairs where they prayed for me, about which I was completely unaware.

This quiet zone prevailed because there was no Sunday church attendance and no religious books or tracts in the house other than Treena's small bible with the red writing that highlighted the words that Jesus spoke.

All of this had now changed with my "apparent" choice. I didn't understand exactly what had happened to me and the same could be said for Treena and Ruthie who were understandably cautious. Treena felt enough freedom to visit our local Christian bookstore, one of many that were an interdenominational "hub" in the early to mid '70s.

"Can you tell me which of the local pastors is reading books that help them deal with new believers?"

The owner was surprised by her question; it wasn't at all usual; in fact he had never heard it before.

"Why do you need to know," he replied.

"My husband has just...er...had an experience and so have I, very recently and we —well, we want to see if there is a church that can help us to try and understand our —feelings?" She hesitated, searching for words to explain our needs.

"Well now, could you tell me how you came to know Jesus?" It was a quiet day and he was trying to know how much Treena knew so that he could steer her to the "right" church. Treena told him the full story that I had yet to hear, largely because I hadn't asked. Months later we met a woman who was in that bookstore on that morning, who had listened in on Treena's explanation and told us that Treena's story convinced her to make an on-the-spot commitment in her own life. In the game of pool or snooker, that would be called an *off-the-cush* shot; one in which the ball is directed at a cushion in order to strike an otherwise obscured target ball!

The bookstore owner suggested the Pastor of the Church of the Brethren in Easton (Maryland) on Harrison Street.

"Their Pastor has been buying several books recently about the charismatic movement," he explained, obviously impressed by something that was happening that he felt would be good for us.

Treena and I went to church together for the first time on March 23, 1975. It was Palm Sunday, and the very simple whitewashed (inside and out) church was crammed to its eighty or so capacity. At the end of the service the Pastor invited people to come forward to the small rail for prayer. Two or three responded but we stayed in the pew because it wasn't clear to us what was taking place. At one part of that service we waved palm fronds that were handed out as we came in and we shouted "Hosanna" several times which appeared to mean something like the Hallelujah that everyone had used before I had begun my experience. It was all quite different from my school days, very simple and yet joyful. The Pastor smiled a lot and was obviously enjoying himself and his small congregation.

Pastor Ken and his wife Marion found time for us at their home, where we began our search over their lunch table and a salad that included mandarin oranges in a sweet lime Jell-O

with cottage cheese.

I was obviously going to have to adjust to this way of life!

"What's all this about a charismatic movement?" Treena asked.

Ken, with a big smile, responded, "well, it's not without a degree of controversy." He chuckled.

"It's when the Holy Spirit provides gifts to the church that members receive and use to build the spiritual nature of our lives together."

"What are those gifts?" I asked.

"One of them is healing and being healed." He then went on to explain what had happened to him only a couple of months before our arrival, just after the New Year.

"One of our leaders in the Church of the Brethren stopped by to preach a sermon; so I sat in the front row."

"He spoke about the Holy Spirit *gifting* and explained how he had discovered that he had the gift of a *word of knowledge*. He went on to define this as an awareness that someone in the congregation was suffering either emotionally, financially, or physically and he would then name that disorder!"

Ken's smile was radiant as he recalled the special moment that followed.

"He spoke out the understanding that someone had a severe digestive disorder and that God was healing him literally as he spoke."

"I felt a warm, almost hot flushing through my upper stomach; it came in waves. It didn't hurt, it left a cool easiness behind." Another big smile!

"I got healed in the front pew of my own church! Hallelujah!" There was that word again!

"So I, too, have prayed to receive whatever gift God may want for me; there are many." He added.

"So...what are they?" I was eager to know because I had wanted a relationship that had some membership benefits and rewards, and *gifts* sounded like it might be interesting. Ken looked at me over his black-rimmed glasses. The twinkle had left his eyes. He became quiet and serious.

"At this time Graham, you have a greater need to know the giver than his gifts." It was to be my first correction of many that followed almost daily.

"I can tell you this, there are seven gifts that are able to be absorbed into your life *over time*," he added as a caution.

"Then there are over twenty abilities, sometimes called spiritual gifts, which flow through the inner workings of the Holy Spirit. You can't learn them or even practice them. When they are genuine, they happen as God wills them and therefore will have nothing to do with you other than their acceptance with a healthy dose of awe."

He seemed satisfied with his explanation and then, after another pause, he removed his glasses and laid them carefully on the table.

"There is one last thing; for now." He paused again. "Now and again you will hear the words *fear of the Lord*. Since God is also all about love, you may be confused about using the word *fear* so often. It means...do anything you possibly can to avoid any action that may be counter to your best understanding of his will for both your life and those who will observe your actions and listen to or read your words."

With that, he was done; at least on that occasion.

Both Treena and I had been *born again* in the midst of a charismatic revival; one in which the spiritual gifts (charismata) were very much in evidence, especially in Pentecostal churches that had a long tradition of accepting such gifts as tongues and their interpretations, healings, and to some extent, prophecies.

The public utterances were, to some denominations, "an unseemly tumult," not considered proper, decent or in order.

Our church was one of those that understood that these gifts were recorded in the Bible but were, for the most part, meant for early believers when the church began to gather. The sense that such things had ceased was couched mainly in the idea that is found in 1 Corinthians 13:9-10

"For we know in part, and we prophecy in part; but when the perfect comes the partial will be done away. When I was a child I used to speak like a child, think like a child, reason like a child; when I became a man I did away with childish things." (NAS)

Our church thought of the word *perfect* as meaning the entire New Testament of the Bible. Others claim that *perfect* refers to the return, at the second coming, of Jesus.

We were trying hard in *the fear of the Lord* to understand how we might live in this brand new relationship that we had received.

It was during these very early formative days that we were faced with a critical choice. Was our relationship to be within a prescribed denomination or was it to be somehow *open?*

We didn't have to wait long for our answer.

We had chosen to accept that the New Testament was, indeed, *perfect.* Its words had been inspired and were the actual work of the Holy Spirit expressed through man who had faithfully written them down and collected all of what we needed to know about God's will.

At that time I thought that when people said they'd heard God speak, that what they really meant was that they had read a verse at some time and the Holy Spirit brought it back to their mind, when they needed it.

We were on our way to bed and I had gone to get Treena her glass of water.

As I poured the water into the glass I had a really strong, clear *idea.* On my way back along the foot of the bed I repeated the words to Treena who was sitting up in bed reading.

"The true face of Satan is the compromiser"...just the eight words that I had *thought* in the bathroom.

"Where did you read that?" Treena asked.

I was, at that time, less than two weeks into this new experience and so my reading of scripture was, to say the least, limited.

"I have no idea; do you think that it could be God speaking?" It felt as though the hair had risen on the back of my neck.

I just stood there, holding the glass; we had no answer. Treena broke the silence.

"Let's ask Pastor Ken what he thinks."

Pastor Ken confirmed that while its meaning in no way contradicted the scripture, it was not, in fact, a verse that could be found in any translation.

"You may have heard something through the Holy Spirit's gifting *directly* because a unique situation will face you in this new experience."

We went home and I began to doodle a kind of slogan that might help remind us of this *word* we might have received to help us to understand the way ahead in our shared relationship.

Eventually this spelled out a family commitment. We would live our lives for... "Jesus without compromise."

I had a kind of notary public embossed stamp made with the words in a circle surrounding a dove descending in the center...

The die was cast and our child-like life of faith had begun.

"Look! I stand at the door and knock. If anyone hears my voice and opens the door, I will come in and we will share a meal together as friends." Revelation 3:20

How's *that* for a relationship?

Rite of Passage Forty-Two: "A Face Half Shaved"

I am aware that the bottom is getting closer and along the edges there are looming forms above us and upright lines of logs. The water is different, a continuous opposing current... concerned about this change, I took up the lead and my hen followed closely behind.

We had also joined up with several more just like us, really quite big compared to our earlier companions.

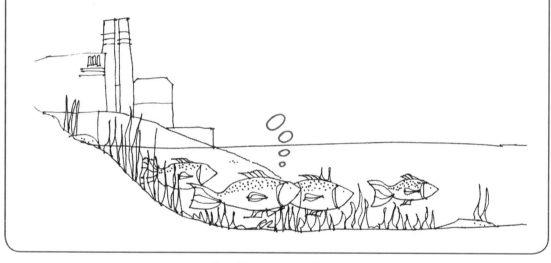

An Understanding

As the riverbed becomes shallower, the ceaseless flow of the Columbia River current toward the sea can't be avoided. They work upstream, sometimes following along the shoreline. In places there are docks and wharfs built out into the river and the forms of buildings and machinery jutting up above them.

It is quite a change from the almost limitless space that they had known for so many years in the ocean.

The narrowing of the stream had also brought them into closer contact with other Chinook on their own journey upstream.

1975
I am forty one years old

Treena's miraculous change had an almost immediate ripple effect throughout our family. Our youngest daughter Kareena had been the first to notice and in her childlike way had responded as I had done.

"Can I have Jesus in my heart as he is in yours?"

Our son Andy, who heard Treena's entire story, had felt the Lord enter his life during a telephone conversation in a phone booth (shades of Superman?).

Our troubled eldest daughter Tessa had sought help on exactly the same day as I had done (March 18th) but over a thousand miles apart and without a word of contact.

We had become an entire Christian family based almost exclusively upon our shared awareness that a miracle had taken place and that love had replaced chaos in the place we called home.

It took a day or two to get all of us to sign on to the new family "motto"...

"To live for Jesus without compromise."

In a way it was like the slogan used on our U.S. currency, "In God We Trust." This was formally accepted as the official motto of the United States on July 30, 1956, when it was added eventually to all paper money.

When we adopted a publicly displayed statement that we claimed to represent our full commitment it seemed reasonable to me that this might result in it being tested. To say one thing and live in a directly opposite manner, even to me with so little understanding, must be as offensive to God as it had been for me. For a great many years I had seen so many examples of so-called good, religious people behaving badly that it had been a major reason for staying away from church. I certainly did not want to fall into that category when I really didn't have a clue where the *religious* landmines had been buried in the road ahead.

My education began almost immediately and took well over a year to begin to understand. It began with a morning shave. For some unknown reason, I had the time to shave just half my well-lathered face —exactly!

My left side, as reflected in the shaving mirror, was completely white. A clear-cut line above and below my mouth continued under my chin and down to my neck.

I am a hairy man!

At the moment that the line was well defined I thought I heard (again inside my head).

"I want a credit on your TV show."

I pointed my razor at my reflection and laughed out loud.

"That's not God speaking, that's you!" I looked myself straight in the eye.

"God Almighty, maker of heaven and earth does not need, or want, a credit on a TV cooking show. The idea is laughable!"

And so I laughed and shaved off the rest of the lather.

I was *not* to have the last laugh!

We were making plans for our daughter Tessa's marriage to an Eastern Shore farmer's son and had agreed to have it performed on neutral ground at our home, with our Pastor and their Priest conducting the services. It was to take place after Easter in early April.

Shortly after our first church attendance, Tessa told us that her husband's parents had arranged for a quiet pre-marriage ceremony at their local church.

They were Roman Catholic's who were deeply committed to their day-by-day devotional life.

Their priest had let them know that our *neutral ground* idea for a *politically correct* service was impossible and that he could not participate. Eventually, for the sake of a peaceful *no compromise* solution, we accepted the fact that they would marry in their local church and we would take the money set aside and spend Easter in Florida. We never did see a positive outcome, as our families were unable to discover an overlapping faith. Our daughter Tessa's personal faith did survive but more of that comes later.

The Florida trip was an amazing time. We stayed at a simple hotel at Duck Key and ate at a small French restaurant that offered an ocean side view of the sunset.

I had become preoccupied by the whole idea of receiving the gift of tongues. This had been the "Latin" that I had heard during my first prayer time with Treena, the one that had moved me to tears, without understanding why.

Having now read about it in John Sherrill's book, *They Speak with Other Tongues*, which was published in 1964, I was convinced that it might help me to understand what might have happened to me back in Ottawa. I had decided that while Treena's prayer language had reminded me of my schoolboy Latin classes, I would somehow speak forth in Russian! I took long showers during which I would let the water flow over my face as I burbled "rimsky–bomski–chofski" in an attempt to become fluid (which I did) without any sense of spiritual breakthrough. While at Duck Key we met some Russian tourists and I asked the husband, an exceedingly tall and broad-shouldered man with an unkempt beard, if he would mind if I spoke to him in...Russian (?) or at least what I had hoped would be his native tongue. He agreed and I loosed off for a minute or two in shower-practiced words; mostly ending with "ski." He listened carefully, shrugged and gave me my answer in a thick Slavic accent.

"I'm so sorry to have to tell you, but zer iss not one zingle vord zat I understand."

I wasn't exactly devastated; I rather knew that I had pushed the envelope of self-interest a little too far.

I did, however, return to the shower and make another more humble request...

"I wish to be filled with the Holy Spirit and to receive in Your time whatever gifting you may choose for me."

It was perfectly clear to me that I was now a celebrity Christian in a charismatic movement, yet I knew almost nothing. It felt worse than it had when I had begun to cook on television in 1960. *I didn't know enough to be on prime time.*

Now it felt as if I was a VW bug firing on three cylinders coming on to the US-101 at Los Angeles and the freeway was filled with sixteen-wheeled trailers marked Billy Graham, Pat Boone and other publically recognized Christians.

I really had no business on such a highway and could never, ever see myself catching up. Yet inexplicably I was now attracting more attention than I had ever received as a gourmet. I needed some sort of gifting or I would have to "get me to a monastery."

We dined that night on a perfectly fresh-caught fish in a light Velouté sauce. I ordered a bottle of Pouilly Fuisse, a good white French burgundy. Treena didn't want to join me, so I drank half the bottle.

On day two I ordered a half bottle and drank one glass.

On day three I ordered a glass of Napa Valley white (a house wine) and didn't have more than a sip.

That was to mark the end of my life as a gourmet, since that term embodies the marriage of wine with food.

I had asked to be *filled* with the Holy Spirit and the immediate answer had been to be *emptied* of whatever had been uppermost in my public persona.

During our days in Florida our son Andy had stepped barefoot on a sharp rock hidden below some drifting sand. His instep was black and blue and painful.

Treena prayed for it, holding his wounded foot in her hands while I watched. It was good to see her motherly care. I didn't expect much from the prayer but it was a nice gesture. The next morning all trace of the bruise and pain was gone. Hmmmm! I made a note to join her in future prayers.

Andy and I went out fishing with a local guide and we hoped to catch a bonefish, which are prolific from March onward. This was early in the season so we were warned not to expect too much. We lost count of the fish we landed that day. I think we returned only because we ran out of room in the Boston Whaler.

Things were happening. We were happy; we were changing. This was our first white water experience.

I still didn't have a clue what was happening. I was just hungry and thirsting for more, and it had *almost* nothing to do with food!

Rite of Passage Forty-Three:
"Treena's Story"

> *The way ahead continues shallow with a relentless current against us. The tightly packed shoal of others like us has spread out, some to one side, some to the other. We appear to be on our own in the middle with a whole bunch ahead and behind.*
>
> *The bottom is mud and sticks and is more turbid than the expansive waters we had so long traveled. Still, it feels really good to be moving against the flow.*

An Understanding

The Lower Columbia River is deceptive, the current is not fast, but broad and powerful...and with rain in the spring and melting snow it does not have the clarity of the Pacific waters. As the river widens the salmon spread out and become left or right "bank huggers"...or simply stay midstream where the current runs faster with fewer back waters and obstructions.

Our pair find themselves in a true run of mature Chinook...quite an encouragement for each other as they spend their stored omega, their energy, swimming against the rain—flooded river.

1975 – April
I am forty one years old

So much happened in such a short time.

We returned from our Easter break to our small church where a Baptismal service had been arranged for our daughter Tessa, myself and several others. It was a reasonable crowd because the elder responsible for "House and Grounds" didn't want to "heat all that water for just two people."

I was happy to be less a center of attention and joined the line as we proceeded like sheep through the dip. Neither Tessa nor I had any special revelation from the experience. It was strongly recommended...so we obeyed.

Had I then known Treena's story I might have had a completely different attitude.

During that spring we began to have a few people come to our home on a Tuesday night. It was not so much a small group Bible study as a "gathering."

We asked Pastor Ken if he would lead it for us.

"I'd prefer to just turn up and see what the Lord has in mind for all of us," he replied.

We had now come to understand what he had meant about the charismatic movement being controversial.

Our small congregation appeared to be somewhat divided on what had become an obvious manifestation of some of the gifts and the joy that went with them.

It seemed to us that those who preferred a conservative, traditional continuity of the church's 300-year-old practices sat on the left side of the single aisle, and those who were willing to listen and explore sat on the right. Then there were those who, having listened, had gone forward at the now weekly invitation for all kinds of prayer reasons.

Treena and I were amongst this third group *every single Sunday*!

We sat up front on the right in order to get a place at the rail before the crush. As it happened, we were mostly the only ones there, often complete with tears. Pastor Ken seemed to address our immediate needs in every sermon and each word was so fresh and new and made so much sense!

One dear, older lady, quite small and frail, who wore the traditional lace head covering and sat on the left side, told us...

"You are so dear to us and we understand how amazing all this is to you. After awhile you will settle down and you will find rest for your souls."

She was so peaceful and so loving, and we seemed almost brash and agitated in comparison.

Should we not respond, the call seemed so very personal, we *had* to go forward didn't we?

Our church had an annual foot washing service followed by a love feast, at which it was this tiny woman of God who came to wash my feet. It is hard to find a more humbling moment in our modern world. I forget whose feet I washed, but I feel sure he sat on the left! It is far harder to be washed than to wash!

Tuesday night multiplied quickly and it was good that we had such a large house! Within a couple of months it was over one hundred. We had no leadership. We simply gathered and sang the current memorable, tuneful and meaningful praise songs. We prayed for each other and listened, as several felt moved to read from the Bible and occasionally prophecy, speak in tongues and interpret.

No doubt that back in the pews we were left and right of center but out here without liturgy or order, we simply experienced the Kingdom as it happened.

When the heat of summer arrived we met a little later after the sun had set and the day cooled. We had four Klieg lights left over from our filming days. We sat these up at each corner of the big white house and let them send narrow columns of light, cutting through the overhanging trees into the night sky.

The evening was also bug time on the Eastern Shore of the Chesapeake Bay. The bugs were attracted to these intense arc carbon lights and swiftly incinerated, sending defined columns of smoke into the heavens.

When the mood hit us we would gather outside on the lawns that ran to the still water's edge and shout "J–E–S–U–S...Jesus!" several times, sending combined voices skipping over the water to our wealthy neighbor's homes.

A witness? Somehow, with the benefit of hindsight, I doubt it, but at the time it was an exhilarating experience that we are unable to forget...or regret.

Author's Note: Were these to be our sand box days where we played with our Father God and made imaginary castles to represent His Kingdom? Was he laughing with us and not at us, as we delighted in the joy we felt in His close presence? Or...were these childish ways that we would be set aside when once we had become adults in our faith and conformed to that which would be proper, decent and orderly in the close presence of our fellow believers? We shall see.

Our church remained gently and respectfully divided on the charismatic issue and yet, standing back to get a bigger picture, there was much going on in the Church of the Brethren at this time.

We attended the 1975 Church of the Brethren Charismatic Conference where several hundred Brethren had gathered to better understand what was sweeping through many denominations, including the Roman Catholic Church at that time.

There was a significant atmosphere of revival in the air and as we walked around the conference campus complete strangers would cry out "Praise the Lord" and yes, that word again, "Hallelujah!" It truly felt as though we were all in one place and of one accord, we were free in the spirit!

In one of the plenary sessions, with well over a thousand in attendance, Treena and I were asked to give our testimony amongst others, before the main message.

This was to be the starting point of a great many such opportunities and it was the first time that I was to hear how Treena had received her miracle healing and salvation. I stood two paces behind her on the stage at a midpoint between the lectern and a large grand piano. It was a fully packed hall with folks several rows deep standing at the rear and sides. A Fire Marshall would have immediately told several hundred to leave.

Treena's early life on the stage allowed her to approach the microphone with relative ease. She stood still for a silent moment or two and then began to speak in her light, yet lovely, British accent.

My Story – (Treena)
I am forty years old

Before Ruthie came to help us I was going through a very tough time. I couldn't sleep unless I took a medication called Mogadon. I was so wound up that I would take Valium by "handfuls" (up to 60mg a day). I liked Darvon, as they made me feel better. I would get them from various doctors as we traveled around the world in our sailboat.

I was having awful hallucinations, seeing little boys' heads fall off. When driving back from Annapolis, I saw the cars in front of me falling off the bridge into the sea below. It was horrid and I didn't know what was happening. I was very angry at everything and everyone.

One day a darling black girl came to the door. She needed to work for some money so she could go and serve her "brothers and sisters in Haiti." She began to clean for us.

"Treena, have you ever thought of getting baptized?" She said, right out of the blue one day.

"All English people are baptized when young," I answered.

"What, drowned in water?"

"No, sprinkled with water."

Why is she asking me that, I questioned. Maybe it would help me to become well if I took the water. I had been feeling awful and very bad tempered for months. It could help and there was no harm in trying, so I called Ruthie.

"Yes, I'll take the water and maybe it will help me. When?"

"I'll phone up the Pastor and find out," she replied. "Can I use your phone?"

"Yep," I said, "of course."

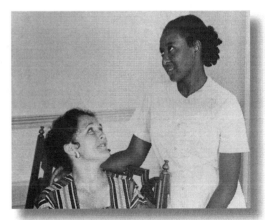

Treena and Ruthie

On December 17, 1974, Ruthie took me, our oldest daughter Tessa, and Graham's secretary Michelle, and we drove to Bethlehem in Maryland, just a few miles from where we lived in Easton. It was very cold that night and Michelle and Ruthie sang some pretty songs on the way until we arrived at a very small church.

The lights, such as they were, were on and Ruthie took me to meet a very large black man whose name was Pastor Friend! Ruthie introduced me, and the Pastor asked me if I was "ready for it," whatever IT was!

I replied in my best English voice, "Yes, I'm ready for it!"

Ruthie added, "Yes, she's ready for it."

I was then taken and dressed in Ruthie's white gown, the one in which she had been baptized. We went back into the church, where unbeknownst to me all Ruthie's congregation, who had prayed and fasted for me, came and filled the little church. Everyone was smiling and singing. They had taken me on as a commitment for a whole three months, and near the end they prayed for me in twenty four one-hour shifts. I didn't know this until weeks later.

I sat down on the front pew with Ruthie, close to where Tessa and Michelle were sitting, near a bath of water with peeling blue paint inside, and out.

The Pastor started by saying..."All the Angels in Heaven are singing for this new sister tonight. Let us pray."

Lots of other things were said which I didn't understand. I do remember thinking "if he doesn't shut up I'm going to jump in that water right now."

We all stood for prayer. I suddenly felt pushed on the floor, and as my knees touched the ground I heard myself saying...

"I'm sorry Jesus, forgive me Jesus."

The very name I had sworn just hours before! It was water, not tears, that poured from my eyes, and all I could hear was myself saying...

"I'm so sorry, Jesus! I'm sorry Jesus!"

I stood up and looked around to see who had pushed me. There was only a pale-looking Tessa.

I was asked to step into the freezing water and was dunked in the name of Jesus. I stood up, and the Pastor asked me if I would like to tarry.

"What's tarry?" I asked.

"That's waitin' for the Holy Ghost."

"Well, I might as well as I'm here. What do I do?"

"You just kneel down and thank Jesus for the gift He is going to give you."

I did!

"Thank you Jesus, thank you Jesus." I knew I was going out of my mind. "Thank you Jesus, thank you Jesus."

Suddenly a light shone on my face and I thought to myself... "now they have turned up the lights to make me think I am getting whatever I'm supposed to be getting."

I opened my eyes and there standing in front of me was the most beautiful man I had ever seen. He was smiling at me with all the love that I had never received as a child. I was filled with joy. He reached forward and touched my heart. He said something that I cannot remember and then he faded away.

"Have you received it yet," asked the Pastor.

"No, I don't think so, but I've just seen someone!" I smiled.

I looked around for Tessa. She was in the car and she wouldn't let me drive.

"No mummy...it was all evil." She swore.

"If that's evil, I love it," I said quietly.

Before I went to bed I poured every pill I was taking down the loo, even my aspirin. It was a rainbow of colors. I grabbed the bible Ruthie had told me to buy, "with red writing because this is what Jesus said," she had emphasized.

I read Psalms 141:3 *Set a watch, O LORD, before my mouth; keep the door of my lips.*

I took this to mean that I should not tell Graham right away.

The next thing I knew, the bible had fallen on the floor, I was awake and it was morning. I jumped out of bed and ran to the mirror to see if I looked like Ruthie looked; not black, you understand, but if I had the shine that was in her eyes. Then I heard a word in my head..."You've got it!"

I ran up the stairs to Tessa and told her. "I've got it!"

"What have you got?"

"I don't know, but I've got it!"

I rushed downstairs to my bible and there I read from Psalm 81:6 *"I removed his shoulder from the burden: his hands were delivered from the pots."* (KJV)

Now, if that wasn't for Graham, I don't know what was. Yes, God wanted him too!

Treena concluded; there was silence. I don't know if I was meant to speak or even if I did. There remains no memory or record of anything else but the story of one lost and deeply unhappy woman finding complete healing and joy with just one touch.

Now I was aware of what had happened. I already knew that she had changed, that much was abundantly clear and had completely changed my own life, not because of the *how* but because of the consistent measurable evidence borne out in her love, joy, peace, patience, goodness, kindness, gentleness, faithfulness and self-control.

Now I knew just how *uniquely* that had happened.

Shortly after we returned home from this extraordinary experience we received a call from Guidepost Magazine who wanted to send a reporter to write our story for a future edition! The reporter came to Locust Grove and we told her our respective stories. She made careful notes and promised to let us see her draft before it was published.

It was substantially different from what happened. We later understood that an editor, who had not been present at the interview, had provided an *amplified version* that was sincerely meant to help their conservative/traditional Christian readers to somehow grasp what had taken place.

We appreciated the effort but explained that it wasn't what actually happened.

A second interview was arranged with a more experienced reporter. Once again our story was very gently steered to fit on better-understood, well-travelled tracks. Once again we had to explain that it wasn't how it happened.

It was then that we met Jamie Buckingham, a very well known author of that era with whom Guidepost had a long lasting relationship. Jamie listened without taking a single note. When we had finished he suggested...

"You need to write your own account in your own words. I'll speak to Editorial and explain." He paused to give us both an encouraging smile.

"I believe that what you have said is the true account. The problem is that it just doesn't fit the usual pathways that lead to salvation for so many of our readers. Its very uniqueness is a little like falling off a horse and going blind. It is meant for you and your loved ones, and not as a template for many."

We did as he had said. It was printed word for word and as a result there began what we have described as our "Baskin Robbins 38 Flavors Tour."

We were invited to give our *unique testimony* to a great many *outreach oriented* larger churches. This included many different denominations; so many, in fact, that we exceeded our private joke about the ice cream company's multiple flavor options. We became aware that the way in which the congregations were told how they might wish to respond differed as much as one flavor does to the next!

Once again, those who heard our story were being helped to fit it into their denominational puzzle.

It was following an especially alarming "spin" that we went home to pray.

"Father, this is getting increasingly difficult. Could you please help us to understand why there are so many ways in which people are instructed to behave? Isn't there just one that is plain vanilla?"

Our answer, as best we could discern it at the time, was "you will try to understand the differences, but I will never allow you to reach or remember any conclusion."

And so it has been, to this very day, we have read and read and read, and can remember *nothing of any substance* that distracts us from our ongoing hunger and thirst for the plain vanilla of Jesus, just as he said he was and his invitations to follow...Him.

His life, death and resurrection remain, for us, the *Flash of Silver* that encourages us to keep on keeping on in our upriver pursuit of truth.

It's not so much "how" as "who."

Please join us in the Reflective Readers Club
www.grahamkerr.com/rrc

Rite of Passage Forty-Four: "Forgiven"

I've been aware of a change taking place where the pain had been and from which the weed had trailed.

I've seen other larger bucks almost my size recently, and they have a curiously altering nose and jaw. It's becoming Roman (whatever that means) and looks a bit like pincers (whatever those are).

There is a kind of menace about the mouth and an appearance of teeth that are prepared to bite.

I've also noticed, within myself, a certain willingness to fight off the younger ones who have decided to go upstream after having but a short time at sea.

My space has become an issue; one that I'm willing to defend if need be.

An Understanding

The wild Chinook salmon's head had gradually begun to develop jaws and snout with the characteristic early curvature that signifies a maturing male...possibly designed to send a warning signal to young buck salmon, often called "jacks," who swim upstream after only a few months to a year at sea. In some manner they sense the hens gradual "ripening" of her eggs and are drawn to that promise.

When they are, the older mature bucks increasingly curved jaw and teeth will come into play.

There is warfare...upriver!

1975
I am still forty one years of age

Our "small group" (of nearly 200) that met on Tuesday nights was beginning to go beyond merely skipping our voices across our otherwise silent river.

We saw things we didn't like and wanted to see them changed.

We had been courted by one of the older-flavored denominations that had a very service-oriented agenda, one that extolled in its magazine, the numerous virtues of Buddha, Gandhi and Martin Luther King, but somehow in its forty pages managed to avoid a single mention of Jesus.

Such, we supposed, is the consequence of seeking donations from those who might find Jesus' teachings less "humanitarian?"

We did organize an in-depth reception of the Hmong people who had sought asylum in the United States and two families had arrived in our area and needed help.

And then there was the issue of...pornography!

I had, as a youth and in my early service days, a form of addiction to this form of media fantasy, one that has existed since man began scratching images on cave walls.

I had gone to a *"fuggamuffie"* meeting (that's how it sounds if you run F.G.B.M.F.I together...well almost). The group was the Full Gospel Businessmen Fellowship International. We met at a local hotel and experienced a normal, rotary-styled chicken lunch. Following this, our Deputy Sheriff stood to his feet and with tears spilling down his starched uniform with its razor-like creases told us of his addiction to pornography and his powerful desire to be free of its influence. We clustered about him, laid hands on his uniformed shaking shoulders and prayed more earnestly for his (and our own) deliverance. This total and vociferous agreement with much charismatic evidence, led us to believe that we should do something to rid the township of Easton, Maryland of all forms of this *scurge*.

And so we began...

I found myself in some kind of default leadership. I could see that my earlier exposure could well have helped to lead me into the pain-filled decisions I had made in my own life.

"We can do this." I urged my new band of brothers as we planned our outreach. Our approach was really quite simple and based upon...

"If anyone causes one of these little ones, those who believe in me, to stumble, it would be better for them if a large millstone were hung around their neck and they were thrown into the sea." Mark 9:42 (NIV)

We were not angry or combative. I was, if anything, deeply concerned for those who were selling the magazines.

"Do you ever think of what might be happening, especially to the youngsters who buy this?"

I followed this up with the verse about the millstone and expressed my personal concern for them. The scripture was tough enough in itself that it didn't need me to deliver it in some kind of *rant!* One owner of one of the outlets was quite shaken at the potential consequences and agreed on the spot to stop ordering and selling Playboy, Hustler, etc. We were greatly encouraged and able to see this more as a "move of the spirit" than our own influence or efforts.

When we gathered at another lunch and compared notes, there were only three places that had held out. One major-flavored denominational member explained that he would remove his pornography if a popular General Store owner who attended a different-flavored congregation (that I will now call Rocky Road) would take it off his shelves. Then there was the pool hall where the manager at that time was reported as saying...

"If those S.O.B.s come near me I'll break a cue and ram it where it hurts!" (A not entirely promising encounter!)

I set out to get the job done with a visit to the convenience store. The owner met with me and wasn't the least impressed by my quiet concern for his well-being.

"You can get out of my store, right now, I have modesty panels that cover all but the magazine names, and I don't sell it to minors, so git!" He opened the door vigorously enough to make the bells ring more than once.

I had read in scripture...

"But if they will not listen, take one or two others along, so that every matter may be established by the testimony of two or three witnesses." Matthew 18:16 (NIV)

I returned that day with two other "fuggamuffies" and a tape recorder. We were not welcomed. The owner, now furious, had begun to threaten us with the police.

I almost suggested that he call the Deputy Sheriff for whom we had prayed.

The earlier scripture goes on to say...

"If they still refuse to listen, tell it to the church; and if they refuse to listen even to the church, treat them as you would a pagan or a tax collector." Matthew 18:17 (NIV)

Later that day I turned up at the "Rocky Road" denominational church and asked to speak with the Pastor about how I might *tell it to the church.*

"The owner is a pillar of our church and in all ways a fine Christian. You need to leave this to the Lord and get on your way."

He didn't have bells on his door but it was still flung open with something of the same vigor.

"May I ask when you have your annual convention?" I asked as gently as I knew how.

"Why?"

"So that I can attend and present our case to your "Rocky Road" denomination." I responded as I left.

That same day (no standing around on this issue) our Pastor Ken called me.

"Graham, the Pastor from "Rocky Road" church has been round to see me and demanded that I get you to stop upsetting his flock."

I explained what we had done and especially our use of "gentleness and respect."

"Sure...yes...I'm sure you did but this has really gone far enough. I'd like you to call it quits please, you have had your say. It's time to leave it up to the Lord." Then he added, "by all means, your band of brothers could avoid his store as you would a tax collector?"

Of course, this left the old established flavor church member who kept his copies, and was soon joined, once again, by most of the other outlets who, seeing such *pillars of the faith* engaged with the trade of sexual fantasy, must have been able to discount the millstone consequences of their actions.

That left the wall-to-wall display in the front entrance of the pool hall.

Given the warning of the "broken cue" I asked the largest fuggamuffie we had, a giant-sized lumberjack with an enormous red beard, to join me. We stood outside in the pouring rain, held hands and prayed that the Lord would go before us. Once again, the bell rang as we opened the door.

"Ding-a-ling!" It rang out.

We glanced ahead to the pool tables shrouded in cigarette smoke, dark above and brilliant green below the shaded lights. There was a moment or two of silence as men in plaid shirts and jeans looked our way.

We turned to the left, where the wall of fantasy was located...and there was not one single copy on display, only *Field and Stream, Hot Rods,* and *Gun Enthusiasts.*

The manager bustled towards us and reopened the door, the bells rang out again.

"I had a dream last night," he almost shouted the words, "and that's all you need to know."

The door closed behind us and we stood in the rain.

We had poured a cup of cold water into a sewer; did that make any difference? Perhaps it became a little less prurient!

I had been fully aware of the problem I faced as a brand new, yet forty-one-year-old Christian, and how my past celebrity was exposing me to opportunities that would never have been considered for someone so *young* in the faith.

We now had a large gathering at our home —at which we were, once again, default leaders.

Our brush with social morality through the Full Gospel Businessmen Fellowship International was another example.

Then there were the dozens of large churches who had us stand up and testify and even allowed us to venture beyond into opinions about spiritual disciplines.

None of these things would have taken place had I not been a celebrity with a current popular on-air program! It is hard to stay *humble* in such circumstances. Humility is often defined as "being known for who you are, not for who you were...or who you would like to be known as."

I was beginning to lose my understanding of who I was at that precise time.

Something had to change...and soon!

During our time at the Church of the Brethren Charismatic Conference there had been a workshop called "Pigs in the Parlor." The presenters were the authors of a popular book at that time by the same name.

The subject was spiritual warfare and specifically the way in which believers could engage demonic *beings* in a form of deliverance-styled prayer.

We did not attend the workshop because I was firmly of the opinion that these so-called *beings* had been rendered powerless by Jesus Christ who had defeated *them* once and for all at the cross and especially at the resurrection. Anyone who thought otherwise was being unduly influenced by a rash of exorcism movies that began with *The Exorcist* in 1973. I was not in the least impressed and regarded the whole issue as "fringe charismatic." *Something had to happen, and soon.*

Our son Andy was having some trouble keeping up with our worship freedom...on Tuesday nights. When everyone stood, he would often remain seated. Andy had always been his own man, some would say *stubborn*, but mostly he had to be convinced that something was true before he would move —not a bad characteristic in such a rapidly changing world.

I proposed that we gather to pray, as a family, for Andy and "oh, by the way...for all of us," that we would better understand all that was going on about us.

We sat in a circle in the "Great Room" where I had first heard of Treena's baptism. In the preparation prayer time I used the "Pigs in the Parlor" suggestions, which I had briefly scanned, to set up a kind of barrier around us that would keep out *evil spirits*. I then, without much real faith, called upon the "blood of Jesus to be upon us all...as we come in search of understanding." We then settled down to listen and hopefully, for Andy, to have a better attitude toward worship.

I confidently, in my default leadership awareness, closed my eyes to listen. Who knows, perhaps there was something for me also.

There was.

Guidepost Magazine had attempted to describe our story and then had gotten it wrong, twice. In the end, we wrote it ourselves.

Their editor had inserted words that described our full awareness of sin and how desperate that feeling had been, how aware of the need we had to be forgiven and how Jesus had set us free.

While this was partly true for Treena, it had not been true for me. I had been greatly influenced by Treena's "flash of silver" miracle and especially by her immediate and permanent freedom from drugs and despair. I had been deeply touched by the church supper in Ottawa and the hope that had been stirred up within me for a better world.

When, in my utter frustration, I had cried out "what do I have to say to you to know you like Treena does?"

I had opened my mouth and heard myself say...

"Jesus, I love you."

My immediate emotional reaction had convinced me that I had received the most desired relationship; an immediate sense of his presence...surely that was my moment of salvation!

Apparently, it was not.

As I sat, with my self-satisfied eyes closed, the space about me began to darken as though I had made a deep dive into a forest lake. I was drifting down under my own weight, letting a stream of bubbles rise to the surface as my buoyancy lessened. My feet were now moving into a tangle of weeds that seemed to wrap around my calves and cling. I began to see, as a drowning man might see. My life began to unfold in brilliant scenes, only what I was seeing had been edited to focus upon moments that my choices had caused others pain. I saw my actions and was shown each consequence. As I understood the sequence, the frames increased in speed. Dozens of acts followed at a breathtaking pace. I became dizzy. My life began to spin about me as a spool of film might do when shaken from its reel. More acts, more pain...I couldn't breathe. The weeds clutched at my legs and reached my hips. My heart broke at the suffocating sight of so much pain, so much deceit, so many lies...I descended deeper. There was a pressure now that squeezed inward...all the way inward to my very soul and spirit itself. I cried out in the darkness; I cried. I called out what I saw. I began to shudder at the enormity of my condition and in my despair I took stock of who I was and saw no virtue or relief.

How could I possibly be forgiven? I hung there, wrapped in the weeds of my actions in the darkness of my despair, sobbing deeply, gasping for breath. Our family had quietly left the room. Only Treena remained at my side. My head was well down, near my knees. The tears had stopped; at least I could breathe again.

How could I possibly be forgiven for all that I had done; what would this mean now to Treena's faith?

I turned towards her and looked up into her eyes.

"Please forgive me." I whispered, expecting nothing.

"Oh, I forgive you and I love you." Her eyes were filled with tears that had run down her cheeks in tiny streams.

As I watched I saw something else in her eyes, a faint reflection of a man dressed in white, who smiled...at me!

"The Lord is close to the brokenhearted and saves those who are crushed in spirit." Psalm 34:18 (NIV)

Please join us in the Reflective Readers Club
www.grahamkerr.com/rrc

Rite of Passage Forty-Five:
"A Credit on a TV Show"

It happened suddenly...

The scent of home was strongly centered to our right bank along with a feeling of a new flow that drew us toward it. I was swimming along quite happily, my hen close behind in this merging of river currents.

The entry current of the new waters was darker with the recent rain. I was focused on guiding us into our home current. The shadow came first. Before my tail fin could react there was a large brown furry one we thought we left behind in the endless waters.

I felt a quick pain near my tail, and some instinct thrust me out of my element into the clear air.

I had leapt before, with the joy of it but this was sheer panic.

Not good!

As I rose higher, I thrashed my entire body back and forth wildly.

The pressure tore, clutched and tore away as the shadow disappeared and I fell back into the stream. Shaken and now bruised and cut by a brown furry one I gasped for water. It was not such a...pleasant time!

An Understanding

Our Chinook had concentrated on diverting from the Lower Columbia River into the lowermost entry of the Willamette River, near Portland, Oregon, when a California sea lion waiting for such an opportunity, attacked.

Sea lions and seals have a long history in the Columbia River, as far as the Falls 200 miles above the mouth.

As salmon numbers have slightly increased in the Columbia River in recent years, so have the "brown furry" ones —one of the few remaining natural predators besides man.

As the sea lion tried to clamp its jaws onto the salmon's vulnerably narrow "handle" near the tail our large male salmon used its strength and weight to thrash itself free. The sea lion had chosen too large a portion and it must surely have returned to its brethren with an amazing fish story, which turned out to be true!

1975 to 1976
I am forty one to forty two years old

Grace is sometimes described as the "unmerited favor of God."

Following my prayer time in the "Great Room" I had a strong sense that I had encountered this...*grace* and was continuing to do so with a sharp awareness.

I had been set free.

"Then the waters had overwhelmed us, the stream had gone over our soul:

Then the proud waters had gone over our soul.

Blessed be the Lord, who hath not given us as a prey to their teeth.

Our soul is escaped as a bird out of the snare of the fowlers: the snare is broken, and we are escaped.

Our help is in the name of the Lord, who made heaven and earth." Psalm 124:4-8 (KJV)

I was now free from the pain-filled shadows of my past and a clear pathway lay ahead. It would not be without its severe challenges but I knew that there was within me a sense of *gratitude*. My foremost concern was to have a life that overcame obstacles and to do so in a manner that might reflect the source of my freedom.

The celebrity had been knocked out of me; it had been replaced by a much earlier joy that I had received when I cooked tableside at the Roebuck Hotel in England when I was sixteen.

I had a story to tell; a dish to cook that was enjoyed by the guests. Here I was again back as a servant with a story to tell and a life to be lived that could be measurably well received?

Such can be the reward from serving, a reward that is lost when demanding the attention of the listeners to ones self alone, for such was my compulsion as a celebrity. Even as a celebrity Christian where the attention was the same, only the music differed!

It was time for another teaching session at the Hotel School at Cornell University in Ithaca. My class had been broadly titled "Moral Management" and dealt with ethical boundaries within the hotel business. Specifically, it focused on the menu and its use by some guests to guide their choices should they have several dietary needs. This was a forerunner to the later attempt at the CIA (Culinary Institute of America) and Johnson and Whales University, Rhode Island, and the Spokane Trials that followed.

I had discovered, in quite small research studies, that chefs with some understanding were almost completely unable to assess a recipe's basic nutritional content. All they could do was guess at the calorie, fat or carbohydrate content, *please remember that this was back in 1974/75*, and they would usually give up entirely on the sodium (salt).

If a guest wanted less of anything, their response was either poached fish with spinach, an egg white omelet or the diet corner (as it was then called in family-styled restaurants) which comprised a 4-ounce burger with a canned peach half and cottage cheese.

No wonder it didn't sell!

Chefs would complain to me "I tried that and I didn't sell a single portion."

So how could we creatively assemble the great flavors of perfectly fresh, locally sourced foods, use less of the higher risk animal fats and refined carbohydrates, and then *compare* the results with just a few well placed numbers that would be offered to the diner without detracting from the joy of eating out.

That was my teaching task back in 1976 at Cornell.

Author's Note: To see where this early initiative has gone, please go to www.grahamkerr.com/menu2. It isn't dead yet!

On the second to last night of my teaching series I invited students to come to an evening session where I wanted to share "some thoughts on a more personal issue in my life." Over 400 turned up and I began by explaining that this was in neutral time, beyond the normal day for which they or their parents had paid.

I talked for over an hour about my past and the experiences I was having as a new Christian. There were some good questions that I did my best to answer, explaining often that I could not vouch for or really provide any theological background...it was just what I knew had happened to my family.

The next morning the Dean sent for me and cautioned...

"What you did last night is not allowed, you spoke about religion with a strong personal bias that would be construed as *proselytizing.*" He was trying his best to be reasonable.

"I wasn't trying to covert anyone." I explained in an attempt to avoid the term *proselytize* which I understood as a deliberate attempt to have someone switch to another religious belief.

"I was just telling them what had happened to us."

"Well, that doesn't work either, if you get specific," he paused. "As you did...when you mentioned Jesus." He was now getting a little stern.

"We are a State-run institution and as such, there is a clear separation of Church and State which must not be crossed. Look here, Graham, I'm a Christian too. (He mentioned his denomination's flavor) and many of the faculty are of the same faith but we have had to make that *compromise* in order to teach here!"

There was that word...*compromise,* the one we had used back in our earlier days as a family slogan.

"We will live for Jesus without *compromise.*"

Was this now being tested?

"Dean, you know how much I respect you personally and the University. I don't want to be seen as religious or to convert anyone—I love it here. However, I can't agree to compromise my faith in Jesus. As I see it, I'm a kind of living witness to something that I personally know to be true. If I compromise by going silent when asked, then am I not being a false witness?" I asked.

"If you want to teach here you will have to compromise –that's all there is to say." Now he was stern.

I paused and considered all that had taken place in our family life since March, all the forgiveness and freedom and yes...joy and excitement all of it so new and refreshingly different.

"I'm sorry then Dean, but I guess I'll have to resign."

I really didn't want to give up this incredible opportunity.

"Good God man, do you know what you are doing?" He shouted.

"You are genius...such potential to shape a better future..."

He ran out of words in his frustration.

At that moment, I admit to being pleased at being called a genius; strange how, in the heat of the moment, one's ego is ready to make note of any form of approval..."*good little boy, see how he has folded his clothes.*" (Rite of Passage One)

"...you are throwing away your future for...for...some religious experience that can easily fade away."

He was an extremely persuasive man; who was living his life with great integrity and could see absolutely no point to my on-the-spot decision. I stood up...and extended my hand to him. He took it in his and we shook hands.

"Thank you, Dean, for your trust in me and for the opportunity to serve the students. It has been an honor sir, and I wish you well."

I wish it had ended there, but it didn't, not by a long shot.

I packed my bags and flew home with a real sense of loss. There was so much that I had wanted to do and I also treasured being known as Professor at Cornell, especially having left school at age fourteen! But then again, I was, after all, only an adjunct professor, an occasional visitor, not really part of their esteemed faculty. Had I remained, I would have been contained and held, as it were, fully alive yet unable to fly.

Two days later an astounding thing happened. The Dean had immediately called both my publishers and our production company to demand that on all future books (or reprints) and television programs that any reference to Cornell be removed.

For my "Take Kerr" series, I had put a credit at the end of the show that read...

This is what they wanted to be removed.

I could see why and had it not been for my vivid memory of my half-shaved face I would have left it at that. It was months ago when I'd half-shaved and heard the words "I want a credit on your TV show."

I had laughed at the very idea...now I was not so sure.

Could this be God wanting our *personal* relationship to be known in public?
I tried briefly to see what such a credit would look like...

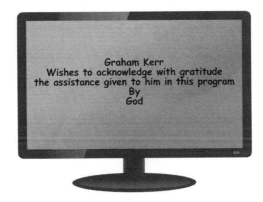

OUCH! Nothing about the declaration seemed right. Obviously, I must have misheard and had been right when I had laughed at my half-shaved reflection!

But, it didn't end there. We had met a Pastor Ron Hembree in our travels and were impressed by his ability to connect ancient scripture to the world needs of the present day. We went to see him at his church in Canada.

"Ron, what do you think about this TV credit issue?" We had carefully explained the whole lead up, including the very recent conflict at Cornell.

"I wouldn't discount it." He replied carefully.

"I see what you mean by simply removing Cornell and inserting God –that really doesn't work." He laughed at the apparent absurdity of it.

"On the other hand, I can see the wisdom of recognizing divine help in any one of our lives otherwise, it's too easy for pride to creep back in." He paused for a while as we sat waiting for any kind of help.

"Ah ha, I have an idea!" He reached over and grabbed his Bible and lifted it up.

"We agree, I assume, that we all see this as God's revealed word to us, as his people, that he caused it to be here for our good and the good of mankind?"

We readily agreed as he went on...

"...so, why don't you prayerfully select a different scripture to go with each episode of the show and insert it in the closing credits to take the place of the Cornell credit. You are simply recognizing Him and His wisdom, wouldn't that give Him credit?"

It seemed so right and so discreet—gentle and respectful. We agreed wholeheartedly and set to work to make the changes immediately. We used both Old and New Testament verses and kept them to only one verse reference number at a time. We did pray and tried not to manipulate the viewer who, after all, would have only one second's exposure to such a brief reference. We made these changes, along with several others that we hoped were also respectful of our viewers. The signature tune was changed to music that sounded like the popular "Hot Buttered Popcorn" (1972) version. It was actually the tune from "This is the Day that the Lord has Made," an equally popular worship song of the charismatic movement.

I also converted my wine cellar that was stage left on the set into a dovecote with stuffed white doves peacefully sitting on sturdy branches; it was nicely lit! Then there were the almost subliminal additions of the descending dove lapel pin and my bible opened on the counter where my recipe books had been.

All in all, as much as I could decently do to say "hello" to my fellow Christians who might then believe that I had, in fact, become a believer? This was important to me because there was a perfectly reasonable suspicion that jailhouse and celebrity conversions were somewhat suspect, largely due to the use of religion to gain some kind of obvious benefit. I was acutely aware of this and worked hard to overcome it any way that I could. It became an *appearance* issue.

Our conversion had become quite a hot-button issue in the popular media. Before an on-air TV or radio interview there was, at that time, a pre-interview Q&A with a producer.

I always started out with a stock statement, just for their ears...

"We will not bend a single question to suit our own purposes; we will answer each question directly as asked and never try to get our personal faith mentioned."

What happened, almost always, was that the interview began with...

"Something has happened recently concerning your thoughts on God; what is it about?"

We were then free to share our very personal story and move on from there.

During a second visit to the hugely popular Phil Donahue Show, an audience member asked a tough question of us, Treena and I, as Phil's guests.

"I am a Jewess and I love God but I do not know Jesus as the Messiah –therefore, am I going to hell?"

I recalled in that awkward moment what Treena had said to me just after I learned of her baptism. I repeated it almost word for word.

"I really don't know the answer to your question; why don't you ask him yourself?"

Treena met the lady after the show who told her...

"I've been asking that question for years and this is the first time I've been given such an answer."

She was very careful with her words...

"I shall do as you suggest," and then added "thank you."

We, of course, were pleased, at least until the following week when we began to be buried in mail.

None of it, that we ever saw, was positive.

The mood of the mail could be added up to say...

"You have consigned millions of Jews to hell. The truth is that that's exactly where non-believers of all kinds go. You should have quoted John 14:6 and left it at that."

In an effort to regain some semblance (for the third time) of acceptance we went back on the Donahue Show and I deliberately *bent* the conversation so that I could quote John 14:6 in full.

"I am the way, the truth, and the life. No one comes to the father except through me."

I did, on that day, tell the truth, the whole truth and nothing but the truth, as I knew it and understood it and believed it.

HOWEVER, I had spoken it out of a spirit of self-defense and without a shred of the unconditional love that its author had used when it had been first delivered.

It was a lesson that I had yet to learn...that the letter can sometimes kill if it is not accompanied, and indeed prompted, by the Holy Spirit.

Please join us in the Reflective Readers Club
www.grahamkerr.com/rrc

Rite of Passage Forty-Six: "Proof Positive"

There was considerable agitation in the water. It was a thrashing turbulence from some huge thing rising above us deep in and above the water at once. And from this thing there was a savage stream of brown water that had yellow-tinted clumps of foam floating on down.

We edged our way forward past the turbulence and onward for some distance until coming to a great change. Our river became swift and narrow and with tall forms close to each side. And then suddenly there came a great confusion of currents, turbulence and a sheer vertical wall of water before us.

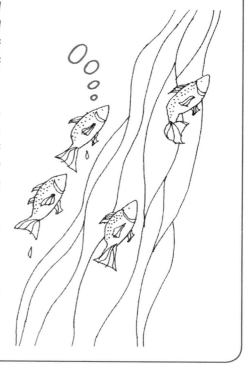

In the midst of a burst of spray I saw a large one, just like me, rise up out of the foam and in a flash of silver it disappeared into the white wall of rushing waters...then another, over to the left and another to the right...more and more attempted the giant leap. But all fell back with great splashes of defeat. Some were stunned, others badly bruised, but all kept on trying.

I doubted that I and my hen could do any better at getting beyond those falling waters. It seemed there had to be another way that we had somehow missed. Together we turned downstream.

An Understanding

Our two salmon have reached the merchant ship destination of Portland on the Willamette River. One of these massive vessels from a foreign port far across the Pacific has its huge twin propellers turning as it helps the smaller tug boats maneuver it into its docking. As it does so it leaks accumulated waters from inside the bottom of the ship into the Willamette —a foul brew of petroleum products and debris accumulated in its recent Pacific travels from port to port.

The two salmon continue upstream to the vicinity of Oregon City where the Willamette River constricts to the eventual plunge of the mighty Willamette Falls. It is a seemingly impassable barrier to salmon. Nevertheless, it is passable for the strongest fish when water height and temperature are optimal. Lining the sides of the former narrow natural canyon leading to the falls are manufacturing plants built to the very edges of the rock walls.

Our salmon have arrived too early for passage conditions by leaping the falls, and they have not discovered the narrow fish ladder that can provide easier passage in the turbulent flow after the rain.

Other salmon persist in trying the impossible. Their example dissuades our two from potentially injuring themselves in the present futility. Instead they turn downstream and try to find another option for success.

1976
I am now forty two years old

I was experiencing what I knew to be true; I was too young in spiritual years to be out there in a triumphal procession —especially up front with the musicians. It is well said of recent *converts* that they should either be *locked up or deep frozen for their first year.*

Of course, others would say, with equal conviction, that these *newly minted disciples* were wonderfully expressive in this period of their *first love.*

After my conflict at Cornell and the defiance on Donahue I had begun to see how much I needed wisdom, all the more as the public exposure kept on happening. Our previous production company with whom we had made "The Galloping Gourmet" had been busily keeping me alive and relatively well in the media marketplace.

In addition to television and daily radio programs on NBC's Emphasis and Monitor, I had a line of food ingredients sold under "The Galloping Gourmet" brand and another set of kitchen equipment, also with the same "brand."

In addition, I had a two-book publishing contract with Simon & Schuster and Revell.

I was busy and the royalties were rolling in, all this coupled with an increasing interest from the evangelical Christian community. There was an almost immediate clash of intent. Positive cash flow was, of course, in everybody's interest. The greater the exposure, the more volume in the cash flow *river.* The more the better!

Or was that true? It was, if you were going along for the ride. It can be a grand experience, a truly "triumphal procession." But what happens to the strong impulse to go *upstream* where it's not so deep and not so wide and where there are many obstacles. Would my form of going counter-culture be regarded as almost idiotic, ungrateful...well, even stupid? What, for us, was a *pleasing fragrance* had begun to be seen by others as the *stench of death!*

The only possible way to manage this perception was to apply the *deodorant of compromise* and effectively mask all forms of odor and go *neutral.*

We were about to be given that opportunity.

It had begun innocently enough with our family slogan to "live for Jesus without compromise" coupled, at the time humorously, with my half-shaved face and the words...

"I want a credit on your TV show."

This had now been achieved and I reckoned that was it, the deed was done! The first inkling that this was not to be so happened early in 1976.

I received a call from Paul Talbot, the President of our production company.

"Graham, we've received a complaint through our distributors from a very important TV station in Chicago." My heart sank —I have always hated receiving complaints, especially when aimed directly at some kind of personal failure.

"They objected to the scripture used in the credits." He paused.

"They called it a cheap plug for God."

A little background here is needed to understand why they were complaining.

Until 1960 most religious programs were provided free airtime. These were the Catholic, Protestant, and Jewish main line associations. The FCC ruled, in 1960, to allow stations to *sell* airtime to other religious entities, to include, for the first time, Christian Evangelicals. Before this ruling, 53 percent of all religious broadcasting was paid for; by 1977, this had risen to 92 percent. It was the age of the televangelist.

Of course this meant that millions of dollars were being poured through otherwise secular TV stations to buy *time* during which an Evangelical Christian message would be telecast and they were allowed to ask for contributions to keep the "show on the road."

What do you do if your business is to sell...*time*?

You might consider it an encroachment upon your turf, because you can charge people who want to walk on it. In other words, "a cheap (unpaid) plug for God" in much the same sense as if I had put up the words (1969 Oldsmobile 88). Jesus had, unwittingly, become a marketable commodity and we had tried to get a free advertisement or plug!

All of this could, to some extent, be understood had it not been so apparently petty. Surely a one-second exposure to a simple Bible verse reference could never be seen as getting free advertising time?

Yet, it was seen as perhaps the hole in the dyke by some?

What, then, were we to think about this?

During the months that followed our conversions as Christians, we had begun to believe that God did, in fact, *speak* to those who had a *mind* to listen.

His *voice* came to us in the same invisible way in which radio and television signals arrive at a receiver appliance. We can't see these waves but we know they exist because we turn a dial and find them; result...*proof positive*!

In God's case, the same invisible signal can be picked up by the receptive mind that is tuned to that input. When the words are a directive, then the listener obeys; result...*proof positive*?

Well, that depends. Let's explore my experience. I don't suggest it is anything more than an example, a *leap of faith over a giant obstacle.*

"Well Paul," I replied after a brief pause.

"We will pray about it and let you know." I didn't want to immediately react; this needed time to fully grasp the implications.

"I want a credit on your TV show."
"Jesus without compromise."

These were words we had *heard*, not with physical ears but inside our head or heart. They had made perfect sense and we had eventually obeyed. Thus, for us, they had become *proof positive.*

The way I thought about this was colored by our recent understanding of having received a miracle that had been scientifically qualified as such and we now had lived within that context for over a year. Therefore, although we understood their concern for an apparent intrusion in their cash flow system, we also had our concern about *compromise.*

If we took it off the credits, were we in a form of disobedience...and did that matter?

We prayed and sought counsel from people we knew to be wise. We were overwhelmingly advised that our very small "credit" was, in fact, no threat or even a possible example that might lead others to greater exposure. It was one second for one verse and the verses were not chosen for any coded or secret manipulation that might cause harm to anyone. It was additionally suggested that just possibly there might be some spiritual warfare behind this complaint! Since the cash flow impact was so slight as to be unreasonable, there remained the possibility that this was the *enemy* trying to stamp out a *spark* that was glimmering in darkness where it had been put for some unknown or unknowable purpose.

It was this that we came to believe.

"Paul, it's Graham and Treena," I announced, "about the scripture credit."

"Oh yes...thanks for getting back...so what do we do?" He asked cheerfully.

"We have prayed and sought counsel in this, and we feel that the verses are there because..."

It was there that I hesitated. How could I explain it to him? Even as I rehearsed the words in my head they sounded so lame?

"...because it is required of us in our new relationship with God." There, it was spoken out!

"So, I see." Paul was now the one searching for words.

"You are refusing to take the credit off?" He asked.

"Well, refuse is a tough way of putting it." I replied.

"Let's say that I would be grateful if they could understand our position," I added.

"I really don't think they are willing to do that," he countered.

"Then what can we do?" I tried to at least gain him as an ally.

"Nothing much," he ventured slowly. "If we refuse, they could take *us* off the air." He was using our plurality to make his point abundantly clear.

So, there it was. We take the "free plug for God" down or they would take us off the air. Being back on air was helping to repair our financial situation, and the exposure was making all the other opportunities happen. We had even, during this very period, received a letter of intent concerning a healthy fast food franchise that could be called "The Galloping Gourmet." We had responded positively and had a date set for late May to visit with bankers in Toronto to move the idea forward.

But, all of this depended upon my on-air exposure. What if I was taken off?

We had sought wisdom from our friends; now it was time to seek it from God. Boy, did we need a word to help us overcome this obstacle! The only *words* we received, we read in scripture, when describing the "word of wisdom from above." Tucked into a list of attributes, it has the words...pure, peace loving, gentle at all times, and willing to yield to others...James 3:17 (NLT).

It reminded us of the famous *love* chapter in 1 Corinthians 13:4–5..."Love does not insist on its own way." (ESV)

Added together, it seemed to be a perfectly reasonable Biblical response to our present problem.

After all, for the same set of reasons we had stopped pursuing the pornography issue with the Rocky Road denomination, yet, had that not resulted in the magazines refilling all the shelves that had been emptied?

So...where was the *proof positive* in that outcome? Had it been right to be "willing to yield to others" and not insist on our own way? If this was spiritual warfare, it certainly did not look like it was the way to win?

I called Paul back over a week later.

"We've done some more praying and we want to keep the credit where it is –please." I added softly.

"You can't win."

He was now clearly concerned, but he promised to let our distributor know. Our distributor was the largest advertising agency in the world at that time. Let me simply call them GFS for "gray flannel suit" after the movie of the same name with Gregory Peck that was made in 1955. The GFS apparently saw our program as more important to their cash flow from the concerns of one albeit important television station in Chicago.

Paul called us up with the news.

"Good news Graham, the agency has told me that you can keep your credits." He was obviously delighted and we were literally beside ourselves with joy.

We paraphrased scripture to read...

"Greater is He that is in us, than he that is in...Madison Avenue" (replacing the word *world!*)

We continued at our own swift pace and our time to visit the banks in Toronto arrived about the same time we were scheduled to record another series of "Take Kerr," complete with its subliminal messages and its obvious credits. As it happened, we had reconnected with some old associates with whom we had worked in our New Zealand days.

Charles and Angela (his wife) had become good friends during the time that he had become the manager of the enormously successful Maori Hi Five...a group that traveled worldwide to much acclaim. Charles and Angela were now living in Las Vegas, and Angela was very ill with a crippling form of arthritis that had forced her to bed with a "disintegrating spine."

We had learned that an extraordinary couple, Charles and Frances Hunter, would be in Toronto at the same time as our appointment with the bankers for the proposed restaurant franchise.

Charles and Frances called themselves the "Happy Hunters" and had achieved considerable attention as "miracle workers," that being one of the gifts/abilities of the Holy Spirit. Their meetings drew hundreds, even thousands, and many claimed that they had received *healing*.

We decided to go early and attend one of their meetings in order to pray for Angela and see if we could ask the Hunters to "agree with us" for a miracle for her.

We arrived very early at their venue, an old converted church theater with a distinctly round shape and upper level seating in two almost "C" shaped tiers. We sat, inadvertently, in the area reserved for the choir. I seemed to be making my choral entrances a habit –shades of the Ottawa "snowy" arrival! When it came time to be moved the ushers noticed who we were and reported our presence backstage to the Hunters. Charles and Frances were blissfully unaware of our existence as celebrities, but nonetheless invited us to join them on stage and to "encourage the audience with your stories."

This we were now practiced at doing and we agreed since it got us closer to them for the Angela prayer.

The church was packed and every seat was taken, all the way up into what theater people call..."the gods."

During a time of quite robust worship Treena suddenly fell over.

"Treena's fainted." I grabbed Frances' arm anxiously.

"No, no," she replied. "She's just been "slain in the Spirit of God."

"What's that?" I asked, by no means comforted by her explanation.

"You give up the ability to remain standing, your knees give way and you fall into a time of great comfort."

I studied Treena's face. She was breathing easily, her eyes were shut and a small smile touched her lips. She looked entirely peaceful.

"Do you want to lie down too?" Frances asked.

Not on your life, I thought, *in front of all these people...no way! A platoon of Marines couldn't get me on my back!*

Frances came toward me and broke a phial of powerful incense close to my face. I went down without the slightest struggle and hit the stage as though it was a bath filled with goose feathers. I was not, however, comfortable or at peace. The stage had been lined with a hedge of potted chrysanthemums. I couldn't get up, there was pressure that seemed to come with the aroma, but I was able to inch my way closer to the flowering "hedge."

It was through this green border that I could see the audience...but they could not see much of me! I watched with amazement as almost everyone on the ground level of that church, several hundred people fell as though a hand had gently brushed over them from right to left...starting in the front and finishing in the rear.

There were shouts amid the praise worship and all "heaven seemed to break loose."

The pressure on my chest lifted and I got to my feet.

Charles Hunter took my hands in his and said...

"Holy Spirit, anoint these hands for your purposes."

He then added excitedly...

"Go amongst the people and bless them."

"How do I do that?" I shouted, in order to be heard over the din.

"You touch them and say...Holy Spirit, come upon these people. That's all they need to hear, it's not about you or them."

I chose to take the stairs to "the gods," the upper level as far away as possible from the "battleground" below.

The musicians played on...mostly a melody-laden song that kept repeating the word "alleluia."

Finding a pew of about fourteen people, holding hands and singing, I took the raised right hand of a man with thick glasses whose eyes were closed...lost in worship?

"Holy Spirit, come upon these people," I said, rather self-consciously.

Immediately the entire row fell over!

Totally shocked at the sight...I was both alarmed and then hugely pleased...as though I had actually received a powerfully *obvious* gift. I went looking for another pew; or really any one person that looked promisingly "lost in worship." There were many, but not one responded to my increasingly strident cries.

"It's not about you, or them."

Within a very short time I had learned a really big lesson that would help me to avoid a common enough temptation.

Nothing was up to me!

I took Treena to dinner that night and we discussed the extraordinary experiences. I got to the aromatic capsule part, which had got me down on the stage, and she seemed to question its use.

By way of *proof positive*, I extended my tie across the table for her to smell for herself...something I do not do, actually have never done, in any kind of restaurant.

The tie was still highly aromatic.

"I can't smell a thing," she replied.

I followed up on this strange manifestation and was told by the Hunters, and others, that no aroma had been used and that, in fact, they never came closer than 2 to 3 feet, and... *nobody* could sense the now evaporating aroma.

I can never forget that fragrance. In all our global travels, I had never, ever smelled anything even remotely similar.

Is this how heaven smells?

Please join us in the *Reflective Readers Club*
www.grahamkerr.com/rrc

Rite of Passage Forty-Seven: "The Missing Credit"

I sensed it first and this was quite a change since my hen had always been the one who caught the scent of our destination before me. It had been lessened by a sudden rushing inflow to one side, a kind of break in the bank.

For a short while, it almost overwhelmed our choice, do we go straight ahead, or veer off to the entry of this new flow of water?

It didn't last long and then the fragrance returned, even stronger than it ever had been. We swam on and left the turbulence behind.

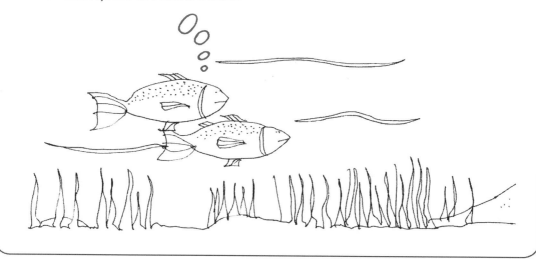

An Understanding

Rivers are not without their tributaries, those that leave on their way downstream and those that join in their downward rush. This joining had been with a major stream whose waters had come down from the hills on both sides. The Clackamas River is a large tributary of the Willamette whose faster and clearer waters join about a mile or two below Oregon City's Willamette Falls. It also has a run of spring Chinook that return up it to spawn. It did not carry the natal McKenzie River aromas and actually diluted the flow of the Willamette to such an extent that it had become confusing. They turned back toward the falls, but with both doubt and hope...

1976 to 1977
I am forty two to forty three years old

I was quite shaken by our time in Toronto with the Hunters.

I had become comfortable with our own miracle and increasingly at ease with the way that our financial wellspring was being restored by one commercial success after another. I was also delighted that the television series (Take Kerr) and the companion books (The New Seasoning –1976, and The Love Feast –1978) were helping people to begin to make some real changes in their day-to-day food choices.

In my research and development with Ann Collier I had found many quite innovative ways of retaining good taste yet reducing the, to me, obvious risks coming from saturated fats and refined (or manufactured) carbohydrates. My choices were mostly made to avoid the risks, rather than focus upon flavor. It was not entirely wise; however. It's hard to make a 180-degree turn without some degree of error.

I had packed my bags with another sixty five carefully scripted and rehearsed episodes, and left for the Toronto visit and then on to Ottawa to record. That was before the Hunters and the unknown fragrance. We were so influenced by that experience that we agreed to accompany them to their next event in Montreal, which meant an early flight and a cancellation of The Galloping Gourmet franchised restaurant meeting with the bankers. This, I might add, was not well received but then, as I said at the time, "it's only money." Montreal was not a repeat performance. It was about as normal as a miracle healing service is likely to be! The next day we drove to Ottawa and began to set up for the next series of "Take Kerr."

This is when Mr. GFS (gray flannel suit) arrived on the set direct from Madison Avenue.

"Mr. Kerr." He addressed me quite formally.

"I have come to ask you to remove the credits, with the scripture verses, from this new series."

I was quite shocked. "But, I was told that you had agreed to their retention."

"Well, that was provisional –until you had had the time to reconsider and prepare for this series." He waved his arms to encompass the whole set.

"I see you are ready to roll and you've done all the development and scripts...so" he smiled thinly..."let's be reasonable and get on with the show."

He gathered up his briefcase and made for the studio door, where I caught up with him.

"Please understand, I don't want to appear unreasonable or unappreciative I love doing these programs. All I want is just *one second* to recognize the source of my creativity." I tried to keep my voice down and avoid any sense of pleading but it was what I was feeling!

"Surely," he replied, somewhat frustrated, "you wouldn't just throw away all this preparation for just a one second credit!"

"Well, I suspect there will always be a use for what I have done elsewhere." I replied.

He stood still, looking me straight in the eyes, his jaw clamped shut so tightly that his cheek muscles twitched.

"Alright then...have your little God thing...if you must." With that he turned and strode out of the studio.

Round two was over and we appeared to have won that as well?

During our time in Ottawa we visited our chiropractor's church, which happened to be our first formal Pentecostal experience. As always in this story, its actual denominational name (or flavor) isn't necessary...let's call it Rum Raisin. We had, until now, attended main line flavors that adopted worship services where there were few surprises and no interruptions; everything was proper, decent and in order. For this to happen, which was certainly "biblical," there was also a minor problem to overcome. Scripture also says that we should "not despise prophecy" and also should not "quench the Spirit." In an orderly service a prophetic word might be seen to be "out of order"...even destructive of order itself. To actually let it be known that such an utterance was not expected to take place, could be seen by some, as "quenching the Spirit."

The Pentecostal Church had long been known for permitting prophecy and other verbal manifestations of the Spirit, as well as quite robust worship songs complete with clapping and raised hands, with arms fully extended.

The Charismatic Movement had allowed some of those activities to spill over into main-line flavors where they had received a somewhat chilly reception.

Our chiropractor's church was not one of these. They were wholeheartedly enthusiastic about their faith, and their very freedom was infectious.

We loved it.

Then Treena, who had always taken the lead in our spiritual life experiences, began to sing in the Spirit. It was a lovely melody filled with the Latin-sounding words she used as her "prayer language."

She had a beautiful soprano...that began softly and then gained volume until it filled the sanctuary quite as captivating in sound as I had experienced with my scent of heaven.

As I listened in awe at its beauty, I began to see a vision that completely surrounded me. I was transported to *another place* as real as the church that we could also see physically.

I was free enough in that environment to open my mouth and speak out quite loudly what it was that I was *seeing*.

"I see a canyon, with limestone cliffs rising high on both sides. The way ahead is narrow and winding. The path beneath is sandy and blown by the wind that "moans" through the rocks on either side.

As the wind blows it disturbs the sand and I see tiny spears of green –crocus before they flower.

Now I see our feet, they are bare. Where they tread water wells up in little pools fed by springs.

The canyon opens to a small pond where Stickleback reeds grow in abundance. A deer is by the pool, unafraid of us.

I see us from behind now. We are naked. We hold hands.

We arrive at the end of the canyon. A huge cliff bars our way. On the very top of the cliff is an angel holding a giant sword that is on fire.

The angel raises the sword on high and with a mighty blow brings it down hard on the canyon's edge.

The flames spill off the sword and become a stream of blue, clear water that flows like gossamer silk, billows down toward our feet.

We step upon the waters and climb up toward the rim of the canyon into great shards of brilliant light."

The vision and my description stopped abruptly.

Author's Note: I should like you, before you come to any conclusion about this "happening," to read the account in Isaiah 35 and to receive my absolute assurance in the full "fear of the Lord" that I had never set eyes on this passage before this time of worship. Then please read it again. I shall not attempt to explain it further.

Following this very scary moment (*scary* because it entailed speaking out in the middle of a service with something that was way beyond anything I had ever experienced) I was literally shaking in my boots! The Pastor immediately called the entire congregation forward and explained that they had just "heard from God through two of his servants." I have no memory of other words he spoke.

That was the very first time that we had experienced the gift/ability of tongues and their interpretation.

We were to go on to use these gifts over a period of forty years; perhaps less than twelve times. This was not a treasured public utterance that would become an anticipated "performance," but rather one that always came unexpectedly and with considerable "fear of the Lord." Even when we practiced the gifts in private, we knew that we stood on the threshold of "taking the Lord's name in vain".

We completed the series (with its full credits) and returned home to Maryland to start work on the next sixty five episodes.

"Take Kerr" (pronounced "care") was getting some interesting press. It had begun before the *Government White Paper on Nutrition Goals* that was issued in 1977–1978, and I felt deeply confirmed in the direction the program had taken. It dovetailed exactly with the goals described which included a reduction in saturated fat, an increase in whole food carbohydrates (unrefined), a reduction in sodium (salt), and an increase in both soluble and insoluble fiber. Every single episode dealt as creatively as I knew how with each of these major goals. Because the program was only four minutes long, there was no room for storytelling or film inserts, or jumping over *anything*. There was also no audience. It was back to the camera as my sole viewer.

I loved doing this because I had nothing to distract me and everything I did was so new that it felt exhilarating, even life changing for so many viewers who I thought of as being *at risk*. I wanted people to try my ideas for their sake, not mine.

It was not entirely altruistic. There were the books that contained the ideas and branded equipment that I used but ratings no longer were a concern since our episodes were mostly used as "fillers" in many different time slots of magazine-styled shows. I was being measured by the apparent rightness of the encapsulated idea. In a sense, it was a taste of things to come when the worldwide web would pick up the speed of information delivery without the need for *entertainment.*

Television back in 1976 was still limited to four or five major channels in each marketplace and therefore gained sizeable enough audiences for advertisers to actually measure the consumer response to their messages. My show moved product, so regardless of their unknown ratings, my sponsors, which now included major supermarkets, were enthusiastic supporters. We were *on a roll* and things were changing for the better.

In the midst of all this change one moment stands out in stark relief.

We were watching a dinnertime episode of "Law and Order" in which a villain hauls off and punches someone in the face. It was most realistic; so realistic that I actually recoiled and almost fainted.

In the past, Treena and I had had a habit of going to shocker movies where creatures suddenly emerged from black swamp waters, so I had been pretty well inoculated against such tricks. Why, then, did a well delivered (and edited) punch have such a profound and memorable affect? The only answer I can find is that my mind had begun to change; all things were becoming new and even violent acts had a fresh sense of being seen as though for the first time and therefore profoundly shocking. Since our entertainment world is so full of shocking violence my mind has now adapted and my reactions became normalized. I do regret this loss of innocence and occasionally reach for the remote and put such naked aggression back where it belongs...a *fade to black*.

"Daddy, did you do your tomato paste browning idea in the last series?" Tess had been watching one of our "Take Kerr" series on a local channel.

"Yes...why do you ask?"

"Well, there's no scripture credit at the end."

"Should be...we had one for every episode."

I called Paul in New York to see what was going on.

"Graham...yes...er...we know." He was hesitant.

"You know...what?" I replied cautiously.

"The scriptures are no longer on the show." He replied.

"Why not?"

"Well, you know that we had had complaints through the GFS Agency..."

"Yes, I know; we got their permission up in Canada." I interrupted.

"They were not happy and well –we all felt we should not rock the boat at that time. We rather hoped that, by the time they went to air, you would be less concerned, that you would..." he added carefully, "...have come to your senses."

There followed a time of silence.

"So you did...what?" I questioned softly.

"We edited out the scriptures from the new series and all the others." He added, almost nervously.

"I see." Again, the silence.

"And what if I have not come to my senses?" I spoke quite slowly, trying to get my emotions under control.

"We can't put them back!" Paul blustered.

"Why not –I didn't agree –so why not?"

"Because they'll take you...er...us...off the air...that's why not." He was now urgent.

"So, maybe it's time for me to go?" I replied.

Paul offered to go back and talk *once more* to the good folks at GFS (who hadn't initiated the complaint in the first place) and see if the credits could be replaced.

The answer was totally unexpected.

"They have agreed to replace all the credits." Paul announced.

"Wonderful, I'm surprised but so pleased." I continued.

"In return they want you to agree to not make any further reference to your *private* faith in the public marketplace."

I was to trade my right to free speech for a one-second credit. It made no sense whatsoever.

"Paul..." I was playing for time.

"Paul...I will pray with Treena and get back to you."

"Graham...I haven't wanted to bother you with my situation but I must now tell you; my son is extremely ill in the hospital, costing over $300 a day (in 1976 dollars). I have invested unwisely and lost a great deal in the recession." He paused.

"If you insist on this and won't *compromise* we may go bankrupt and all the good people here will be out of work because of your decision. So," he added strongly, "remember all who have helped you to succeed when you pray..." Click.

Please join us in the Reflective Readers Club
www.grahamkerr.com/rrc

Rite of Passage Forty-Eight:
"A Cry For Justice"

Following the other salmon, both like us and the smaller ones, we began to sense tumult in the waters when they turned white and pressed against us. There is a dim recollection of a life once lived when this was the norm, but it has been years ago.

The encounters with narrower and faster water increase our energy and determination to fight against it. If we keep going we know there will be some peaceful places where we can rest, there always has been...so...why not now?

Oh ho! Here we go! Boy...this is the roughest so far...hang in there. I'm pushed sideways and catch a glimpse of my hen just behind. There's that twinkle in her eyes...she's actually enjoying it...so...whee!...push on baby...this is a big one!

An Understanding

They are now passing through the lower Clackamas River where it has greatly narrowed from the expanses of the Willamette and Columbia. The increasing gradient includes rapids of white water between the quiet pools. It is white water that big Chinook are well adapted to overcome for long distances. It's a combination of sheer muscle weight and stored energy in Omega 3's that provide the ability to go against such a concentrated flow for long distances...one that has no respite, no backwaters, no deep pools in which to rest. It's either keep going...or fail!

Author's Note: We are about to enter a major event, one that may easily stretch your ability to understand, as it will mine as I put pencil to paper.

I commit, before I write a word, to seek out both the truth and the motivations that lead up to the decisions that gave rise to such major changes of personal understanding.

1976
I am forty two years old

During our travels, we had met Bill and Marilyn Baer who had a Foundation that cared for orphaned children in the rust belt northern states of the United States. They were visiting us at home during my recent phone calls with Paul in New York. Bill and Marilyn agreed to join with us in prayer as we set out to understand how we might begin to try to assemble scrambled thoughts into some form of prayerful petition.

Paul had specifically and strongly voiced his request that we remember all those who had helped us to succeed over the years since the time we had met in Sydney back in 1967. It was now 1976. Nine years had passed and there was no doubt that we would never have been sitting in this great house with all our security and ongoing opportunities had it not been for Paul, Wilbur and their team. So our prayer began by doing what he had asked. We spoke out words of thanksgiving for each person that we knew by name and for their labors on our behalf.

Paul had almost shouted with urgency in his last request before which he had tried to explain his personal financial vulnerability. He had often expressed how he could see how much Treena and I had benefited by our newfound faith, and how impressed and grateful it made him feel.

And yet...! *There was the obstacle* the need to compromise with the television industry that had seen the Scripture verses as some kind of threat to their commercial well being?

We poured out these understandings as one would turn jigsaw puzzle pieces color side up and look for the straight edges of what we knew to be *facts*.

Paul's urgency took on what I would later come to understand as a *cry for justice!* He needed me to know that, from *his point of view*, our insistence upon a one-second scripture just didn't make any sense when set against a cancellation of an ongoing successful contract and the almost certain demise of his production company. His voice had been strident, almost shouting but it wasn't a threat and not manipulative, it was a *cry for justice!*

As we prayed, it was the issue of justice that emerged with clarity. Paul had not changed, we had. We had both signed an agreement and it was we who were changing the nature of that contract by having transferred our primary life-intent from financial survival and security to one in which we had begun to seek guidance beyond our physical senses.

Why then, should it be Paul who would be seriously affected by our unwillingness to compromise?

This we found ourselves expressing in prayer because it was clearly a straight-edged *fact.*

It was then that our verbalized petition (or one-sided debate) ended with a nonverbal but clearly heard question...

"What is it that they want?" Asked the pre-voice.

"They want cash flow." I replied.

"What is it that you want?"

"To know you better." I replied again.

"Then give them the money and follow me."

That was the full extent of the discussion, nothing more, no scriptures, no visions, just that final guidance in eight simple, completely unambiguous words.

I spoke out the complete exchange to Bill, Marilyn and my beloved Treena, asking for them to help me to accept what was, for me, an immediately devastating conclusion.

What was being presented, should I wish to know God better, was that I relinquish all that we had worked so hard to achieve within the last nine years; hundreds of TV shows, radio programs, books, advertising fees, a potential restaurant chain, royalties on branded food and equipment; even the name "Galloping Gourmet" itself. All of which could provide Paul's company with the cash flow it needed, at least in the short-term, to survive.

You remember that we had, like Paul, made unwise investments in the 1973 through 1975 recession and had been rapidly rebuilding our sense of security. Now all this would be gone and with it the means of any known recovery. The reality of the proposal began to weigh upon me and its enormity stirred up a sense of overwhelming sadness that slid into self-pity. I began to cry, I would lose everything I relied upon! There remained quite a long period of silence while I struggled with my emotions.

I turned to Treena.

"What do you think...is this God speaking?" I asked.

"Yes, I believe it is." Treena replied simply.

I looked to Bill and Marilyn. They simply nodded their heads.

This had all begun with my argument back in 1975 that God didn't actually speak directly to individuals. I had then heard the words "the true face of Satan is the compromiser."

We had adopted the slogan "live for Jesus without compromise."

Then there was the half-shaved face and the words "I want a credit on your TV show," and the collision of those words at Cornell that resulted in the replacement of their credit with the scriptures, this being followed by the television industry and its back-and-forth insistence on the credit's removal. From beginning to end, it was over one year, our first year of faith. SO...the big question was the same as it was in the beginning.

Does God actually speak directly to individuals?

If the answer was "yes," and if that answer was somehow measurable by the ongoing outcome of obedience to that guidance, then I was going to have to either turn aside from those unspoken but heard words and compromise, remove the scriptures, be quiet about my faith...and survive.

OR –I was to obey and simply transfer my sense of security to Him and as a result, to know Him better?

Later that same day I wrote a simple one-page letter, without the need for a lawyer, in which I relinquished my rights, royalties, and outstanding payments then due. The name "Galloping Gourmet" as a brand and all that might flow from its future use. Also, I listed ten books and their royalties.

I had no way of putting a price on this action; a good deal would depend upon what they would do with the opportunity but, of course, it would lack the immediacy of my ongoing presence on the screen with new programs.

We sealed and posted the letter.

That evening Paul called.

"So, have you made your decision yet?" He asked.

"Yes, we have." I replied quietly.

"What is it?" He was quite tense.

"We will resign from all ongoing contracts." I explained.

"I told you; that will ruin me." He cried out desperately.

"No...I don't think so." I then explained how we had prayed and what we believed to be God's reply and that we had a letter in the post.

Silence again...this was now an almost routine experience.

"Is this Christianity?" He asked very softly.

"Paul, I can't really say. I've only been a Christian for a year but what I do know is that if you believe that God actually speaks to individuals and that you have received a *word*, then that word is to be obeyed, so that is really all that we have done."

Paul later told me that, following the call, he had not known what else to do in his relief, other than get down on his knees in his New York office and in some personal way; reach out for God.

Is there no limit to which God will not go in his unending desire to be reconciled with all his creation?

It was then that I had an unusual visual experience. I saw myself as somewhat larger than life, standing with feet well apart on an ice flow. A deep crack spread across the ice right between my feet. It was separating a sizeable acre or so of ice from that which was firmly embedded in a landmass.

I did my best to keep the two together, but the current that moved South...prevailed. I had to get onto the landmass, or choose the smaller breakaway ice. I knew that in more southern waters, the moving flow would gradually melt; yet I knew that I would prefer to move. I moved my right foot to join my left and began to drift South.

Some would call our response to Paul's "cry for justice" quite out of proportion. Why give up *everything* after so little reflection?

It's a good observation and calls for a more detailed response. So, let's flashback to some earlier events that operate as a kind of fish ladder that allows salmon to get around a dam and continue upstream in a series of more easily attained mini-jumps.

The issue itself of the Scripture-based TV credit was played out over a series of small obstacles that gave us the opportunity to gently and respectfully explain why we found it difficult to compromise. Each time that we appeared to prevail seemed to strengthen our resolve.

Interspersed between the challenges were a series of other prayer opportunities, each of which had *measurable* results...

The first came with the long, hot, humid East Coast summer. Our vast house with its poor insulation required an equally robust air conditioning unit. It died and we had a real comfort emergency on our hands. The repairmen arrived just before Treena set out in a brilliant white outfit to play tennis. She cheerfully greeted the two burly appliance men and thanked them profusely for coming. She had made them sweet iced tea in a jug surrounded by ice in a small cooler.

Two hours later she returned to find the men sweating heavily and more than a little bothered by the machine's unwillingness to restart.

"Goodness!" Treena exclaimed as brightly as she had when she had left. "Isn't it going yet? Oh dear!"

The sweet tea was drained, the ice had melted, and the good guys were now behaving like bad guys.

They simply grunted.

"Have you laid hands on it...and prayed?" She asked.

I would have cheerfully gone into hiding to avoid being associated with her in anyway. This was not the way to treat two well-meaning, extremely frustrated repairmen. This time they didn't even grunt...they just looked at her in her spotless whites and then at me who was mid-cringe.

It was not a happy stare.

"So..." Treena continued, completely unaware of the angelic turf she had trodden upon. "How does it normally start?"

They pointed at a small green button.

Treena moved over, stepped carefully through the tools and laid her hand on the air conditioner.

"Now Lord...you know how hot it is and how these DEAR men have worked so hard... and how much we would be grateful for your cool breeze as it was in the Garden of Eden and your time with Adam...so please heal this button."

With that she pressed the green button.

It started and ran all that summer without a hitch.

When the repairmen departed that day they thanked Treena for the iced tea and, in a much more respectful way, they actually thanked her for her prayer.

As for me, they simply gave me that same passing stare.

This was another round for Treena and her willingness to...pray and not because it would "look good" to those watching, but because she just saw this as a perfectly obvious solution when the normal wasn't working.

I began to wonder if there was, in fact, another set of circumstances that prevailed that were invisible to our human senses but yet were assessable by our spiritual senses when we used our *other* set of ears and eyes. To go from the obvious to the least expected had been a *leap of faith* that I had been unwilling to take. I had now seen at least two examples, as a kind of flash of silver. I resolved that, in the future, I would not be left out. I would, at the very least, agree with her prayerful leaps of faith.

It is because of these acts of willingness that I had been able to face the straight-edged facts of faith and justice and believed that we should put our money where our mouth was and…

"Live for Jesus without compromise."

Please join us in the Reflective Readers Club
www.grahamkerr.com/rrc

Rite of Passage Forty-Nine: "Galloping Gourmet Sells All!"

At the top of one of these tumults came another choice as we faced a fork in the river. One way, or the other?

The scent that had always led us was no longer there. Not since backtracking from the impassable wall of water have we had that familiarity to guide us. What slight familiarity of scent remained was shared by both streams. We chose to go on the side of my scar (he doesn't know his left from his right, but can't forget the wound caused by the hook).

It is the narrower of the two streams, its flow even faster and with more closely spaced tumult than the other. I feel almost comfortable, yet with a slight feeling of apprehension that hadn't been there before.

An Understanding

After readapting to the faster waters of the lower Clackamas River they face another "fork in the road." They go left and head upstream into the mountains where the waters carry a good deal of the same signature materials found in their birth river. Despite their Willamette entries being over 100 miles apart, the Clackamas and their home McKenzie River both have Cascade Mountain origins on the east side of the Willamette basin.

This can sometimes be the reason why some wild salmon wind up in rivers that are not their birthplace. Indeed it has to be so; otherwise, without some straying (typically about five percent of salmon), there would be no way to replace populations that may have been depleted or entirely eliminated by volcanic eruptions, glaciations, or cataclysmic floods. For instance, some 15,000 years ago during the repetitive Missoula Flood events, the lower Willamette Valley was covered with 400 feet of water. Entire populations of Columbia River salmon were lost or displaced —only to return thereafter in many instances thanks to straying.

This was not, however, the choice our Chinook had made and was, as a result, the cause of their apprehension. Their instincts continued to inform them that this was not their intended destination. What were they to do?

Our two salmon have gone up a significant tributary of the lower Clackamas River, Eagle Creek, that has rushing waters and waterfalls.

1977
I am forty three years old

The deal was done and immediately the entire cash flow from our work was redirected to our producers.

There had been a time immediately following the prayer and the formal relinquishment letter, that we had experienced a splendid sense of *freedom*. Our choice had severed over thirty four contracts. There were no ongoing obligations to perform, no deadlines, no more times away from home and the children.

We were free!

That was, until it became clear that we were still obligated. There were the bills to be paid, school fees; the house needed paint, the grass needed, whatever grass needed!

I had earlier felt, following my call for a personal miracle, that I didn't own anything, but rather *it* owned me; that I was a slave to my circumstances, yet I had kept on working in order to rebuild my confidence in the future.

Now I wasn't working so how could I keep it all going?

I couldn't, and I had known it and that had been the source of my sadness and self-pity.

We owned the house outright, the boat hadn't yet sold and we had all kinds of personal stuff that we had accumulated over the years, so we were not without some net worth, it was just that none of it was *liquid* and there was suddenly no cash flow!

We began meeting as a family to talk about what we needed to do. Our son Andy had to leave the costly boarding school at Westtown. We decided to have an auction sale and to put the house and the boat up for urgent sale.

Where then should we live?

This brought us back to those eight words that had prompted this outcome.

"Then give them the money and follow me."

Follow...where?

We decided that this should be our primary focus. We needed to sell things to meet our immediate needs but first and foremost we needed to find the *right path* to take.

Prayer was the only solution; we needed to *hear!*

Within the tumult of choices and financial uncertainty there was now a *buffeting* rather than a peaceful trusting. The eight words became the one thing we could trust; everything else was suspect, especially my own *bright ideas!*

In the midst of the prayer huddle we spent time being thankful for all that had happened to us over the past year. Treena and I were especially grateful about our being reunited in such a warm, affectionate and forgiving way. This was so strong that it led us to want the same healing for other couples we knew, and had known, over the years. The idea began to grow. Could we establish a place somewhere where desperately unhappy couples facing divorce could come to give God the opportunity to heal and reunite them as he had done for us? The more we prayed, the stronger the idea became.

We began to discuss this with folks who still attended our Tuesday night gatherings and began to meet as a group with those who shared our vision. We were not alone, and the enthusiasm was infectious.

We believed that it should be *a place apart* so that couples would have some distance to travel to leave their broken worlds behind them.

We eventually found a remote parcel of land, about four hundred acres, down the road from Wolcott to Steamboat Springs on the western slopes of the Colorado Mountains just west of Vail, the ski resort. There was one established simple house and plenty of land that could be developed as a small village. We decided to put out a *fleece*, a listing of all that was needed and if the listing was completely "yes" then that would be our confirmation. Most of the list was perfectly reasonable, practical and logical; only one random item bordered on the religious fringe.

I had *seen* in prayer, myself taking up a large bow and arrow and aiming the tip at Castle Rock, a prominent peak to the west of the property and releasing it to fly over and into the grass slopes some hundred yards or so from the house.

I then *heard* our instruction...

"Where the arrow lands, dig down and you will discover a spring that will be a constant supply of water. That shall be as a sign for you."

Over time, almost the entire list of prerequisites was met including the purchase loan, secured by a lien upon our unsold house in the Chesapeake. We were delighted with the obvious progress and set about designing cottages built with logs in the shape of a cross. The foot of the cross was a river stone fireplace with a table and two love seats at either side, they doubled for sitting and eating, and followed the design we had for the big boat saloon. The top of the "cross" was the front door with a storm entrance for wet clothes, leading into the main room through another door. The left "cross" was a four-poster bedroom. The right was a sunken bathtub looking out over the mountains. A very simple kitchen was in the main "upright" of the cross.

In our exuberance, we went on to plan for a hub-come-meeting-room that we would call "The Nest," where couples could gather to celebrate and, if they wished, be baptized together in a specially designed baptistery fed by warm water that gushed out of a rock. By now we had the bit firmly between our teeth and a really detailed budget that seemed possible.

All we needed now was...cash!

For this, we needed to sell the boat, the house and...the stuff.

Our prayers shifted to the necessary auction and this is where it became sticky.

We believed we *heard* in prayer that we were to obtain the services of a professional auctioneer and that he would donate his services entirely. That would be a sign that he was the right one for the job!

That proved much easier *said* than done!

I began going down a listing of ten noted auction houses in Maryland. One after the other were delighted to be of service in our "estate sale" and were prepared to donate ten percent to the "charity" of our choosing. When it came to the extremely humbling moment of asking that their entire services be pro bono, their response was neither polite nor long-winded. In most cases it was a simple "click" as they placed the receiver back in its cradle; with some force in one case.

Having exhausted both the list and myself, I was left with "Agricultural Auctioneers"... one of whom said he would stop by to see what we had.

He arrived in an old pickup, dressed in jeans, windbreaker and a rather nice Harris Tweed felt driving cap.

I showed him around, pointing out that everything he saw would be offered, all our clothes except warm stuff for the mountains and all jewelry, tapes, books, cookware, boats, cars, including awards, gold medal and a huge library, then all the furniture and drapes, garden equipment...the lot!

He was clearly impressed and actually enthusiastic.

Then came the dreaded moment when I asked that he do all of this for...*nothing*.

"How can you ask me to do that?" He was incredulous.

"Well...it's how God told us to be sure that it would be the right man for the job," I explained.

"God...spoke to...you?" He was clearly out of his comfort zone.

"Well...yes...yes..." I added as firmly as I could.

"Mmmm." He paused for a moment.

"Well...he hasn't spoken to me." With that, he pulled his cap firmly down by the peak and walked out. I went upstairs to give Treena the bad news and glanced out of the second floor window into the parking circle. He had reached his pickup and stopped, then removed his fashionable cap, scratched his head, jammed the cap back on and strode back over the gravel to our front door.

I went back downstairs to greet him.

He stood there for a moment and then said quite defiantly...

"God just spoke to me!"

We now had our promised auctioneer, but it wasn't the end of our *tumult*.

We *again* felt that we heard additional instructions and here I am ready to concede that the waters may have become muddied by a degree of self. I laid down two conditions. The first was that my name not be used in any advertising. I did not want to *profit* from my past "celebrity." We had changed and I wanted to leave all *that* behind us. The second was that none of the awards, cups, gold medal and citations were to be sold. All these were past idols for which I had almost sacrificed my family in my zeal for recognition.

"All these will go out in the trash," I announced, with perhaps a degree of self-righteousness?

After some considerable argument; I prevailed and we advertised locally an "Estate Sale," with a plethora of nautical and household furniture, cars, boats, etc. There was a footnote telling interested parties to collect a map at a well known bridge between 8 a.m. and noon on the auction day.

The editor of our local newspaper happened to see this unusual announcement and asked his bookkeeper who had placed it. That's when my name surfaced and the headline on page one "Galloping Gourmet Sells All!"

Locust Grove—
the Garage Sale

We were flooded with fans and other dear people who came to pick over our past excesses and walk off with some amazing buys.

We had no reserve prices for anything, including the twelve place settings from the world famous restaurants, the Waterford crystal, Sheffield silver and on and on; a matching pair of Laser sailboats, a power boat with water skis, our Volvo and Treena's specially equipped Pinto.

Furs, gold bracelets, sextant, on and on to over fifty suits and countless classic tapes.

On and on, until it was all gone, everything we had except for a few useful clothes that fitted into four or five suitcases.

We had purchased three Jeeps for the long trek to Colorado and our sole remaining "stuff" was loaded; complete with the days takings, which almost totaled $40,000 for what could have cost us at least $200,000 when new? It would just be enough to get us started in ministry if we were really careful; no more room for excess. This was lean if not mean.

Before we left our home and our past on that day, our very friendly trash collector had agreed to stop by and pick up anything that was left over.

"How did it go," he inquired.

"Just fine, not much left, only those sacks over there; we cleaned up the rest," I replied, almost exhausted. Treena joined me at the door and gave Sam a goodbye hug.

We watched as he lifted the plastic bags into his truck and we distinctly heard a faint metallic clink as some cup collided with perhaps the gold medal from Frankfurt?

He started the truck, waved goodbye and our past with its temptations and treasures gradually drove down the long drive into the fall evening.

We were ready to leave and to follow, but one important issue remained. What to do with our 71-foot ocean racing yacht that we were mooring in an Oxford shipyard. We had advertised extensively and put her with a yacht brokerage company but as yet, not a single bite. It was, after all, a recession; so nobody seemed to want to invest in such a luxury.

Then, as though it came from heaven itself, we received a call from a private buyer who had just stumbled across "Treena" when visiting Oxford on a vacation.

Would we please be available for a test sail as soon as possible…

We delayed our departure, staying at a local hotel and were more than willing to show off the beautiful boat that had been our home for over two years.

The buyer was impressed and immediately made us an offer.

He explained that he had no cash, but he did have something far more valuable. He offered us shares in a company with "great plans" that was about to "go public" in what he called an I.P.O., or initial public offering.

You may recall that we had already experienced a serious financial loss in a not too dissimilar venture and this, coupled with the fact that the potential buyer drove a stretch Mercedes Limousine, not unlike the ones used for important weddings, made us, to say the least, hesitant.

It was, however, the lack of cash that sealed the issue for us; so we thanked him and wished him well with his I.P.O.

Later we learned that his company had "gone public" and had done better than even he had expected. Had we taken his offer we would eventually have received several million dollars.

We decided, that day, to commission "Treena" in the yacht chartering business and locate her in Antigua in the Antilles, on the eastern edge of the Caribbean.

Had we sold "Treena" to Sprint we might never have gone through what awaited us in the Colorado Mountains and the pathways that were leading us very much upstream against overwhelming odds.

Please join us in the Reflective Readers Club
www.grahamkerr.com/rrc

Rite of Passage Fifty: "A Mountain Hideaway?"

For some time now the river banks have been closing in and with that closure there is much less space. In fact, it is getting a trifle crowded, especially for my present size and weight. My hen isn't far behind me when compared to the great many smaller ones that are almost like us during our entry to this fork.

We have become aware that there is a bundling of these smaller ones over to one side of the river where they seem to have picked up a familiar scent, at least, for them? We have come to follow them up some sort of staircase near the edges of turbulent walls of water, miniatures of the one that had stopped us at the larger water now far downstream. There is nothing familiar.

We stopped going forward to watch a whole shoal of them leave the main stream of water into a narrow little entryway. They simply and suddenly disappeared, leaving us with much more space to continue our journey in relative peace. In fact, we are now nearly alone...

An Understanding

The higher they go up Eagle Creek the narrower it becomes and the more fish for each cubic foot of water. The smaller fish are winter-run steelhead.

The narrow entryway leads these steelhead to a hatchery where they were reared in concrete ponds for a year and then released to make their downstream migration to the ocean two years before. Rather than protect the habitat as needed for wild salmon, their space is altered *or eliminated in the belief that hatcheries can compensate for such loss. However, after more than 130 years of hatchery history on the West Coast, it has become apparent that hatcheries are unable to come even close to compensating for wild fish losses. They are also now known to further contribute to wild fish losses...all in all, a situation leading to further salmon depletions unless something is changed.*

From the perspective of our two wild salmon, they avoid the risk of entering the narrow hatchery passageway. They continue upstream, having passed two waterfalls downstream of the hatchery where fish ladders were built around them. Eagle Creek is not noted as a spring Chinook stream, and with the disappearance of the hatchery steelhead they are for the first time largely without other salmon company.

1976
I am forty two years old

Shortly after our arrival in the Colorado Mountains at "Rejoice" (the name we had given to our planned village) we were invited to visit the 700 Club that was just one year away from launching its CBN Satellite Service. We were very impressed by the cohosts, Pat Robertson and Ben Kinchlow. The format was simple, and the studio quite ordinary. The extraordinary part was the small circular prayer room with old painted pews surrounding a wooden cross that hung from the ceiling. I had not, until the visit to that room, ever felt such a strong *presence* of the divine. After the recording, Pat and Ben kindly drove us to the airport for our flight back to Denver.

It was after saying a warm farewell that an idea lodged in my mind. It was so strong and so urgent, and we felt so moved by Pat Robertson's friendly nature that I ran back outside the terminal to pass it on to Pat, face to face.

"A dollar bill is not a fishing license for man."

It wasn't up to me to try to understand, only to pass it on to someone I liked and respected. It must have meant something to Pat, because he later wrote to me with a word for me that was to mean a great deal...but later on.

"You are hiding up in the mountains. You need to get down into the plains where the people are hurting."

Had I been able to accept it as a true word in season and not as some kind of response to what he might have seen to be a criticism of his work, then we might have at least prayed about it...but we didn't. Instead we labored, and I do mean *labored,* day after day moving earth to lay a water system at least eight feet deep and driving huge nails into larger logs. Yet it was fun and we loved the challenge because we had such high hopes for the couples who would come to have their marriages healed; just as ours had been.

When we had exhausted our cash supply from the auction sale, things were looking bleak.

It was at that needful moment that we received an offer for our home. It was still in the recession and the offer was almost exactly what we needed to pay off the bank loans for the mountain property. But, there still wasn't any cash and the cost of keeping our boat in Antigua was eating us alive.

We received a visit from a charming Christian who had heard about our intentions and came all the way out from his New York office to see for himself.

"I just love what you are doing here, it is so needed with almost fifty percent of all Christian marriages ending in divorce." He shared our enthusiasm and we were hugely encouraged.

"So how much do you need to finish the building and begin to minister?" He asked, while opening a lovely leather folder to make notes with a Mont Blanc pen. With my past associations with appearances, one tends to notice these things!

"About $20,000 would do it." I explained, and offered my very detailed budget notes from a spiral bound school notebook.

"How about $2 million?" He responded with an encouraging smile?

"With your name and reputation, the obvious need and this lovely place (he waved his arm to encompass the valley and the mountains), why, $2 million would be a snap!"

"But...er...we don't need $2 million." I explained haltingly, somewhat appalled by the very idea of so much money.

Our very charming friend, it turned out, was a fundraiser for mostly but not exclusively, Christian endeavors, including church buildings.

His services would be paid for out of the funds raised. They added up to only "twenty percent of the eventual offering," he explained.

I quickly did the math. Twenty percent of $20,000 was $400, and $400,000 if we had gone for his proposal. He was not really interested in our need, and we were not interested in his.

Shortly after his visit it got extremely cold and there was almost no snow. The earth froze deep down without its snow cover and our river froze so that no water came into our valley.

"shoot the arrow and where it lands, dig down and there you will find a spring"

I had never fulfilled that *fringe religious* requirement in our prayer list to be checked off before deciding to come up to the mountains from the plains *"where the people are hurting."*

I was becoming increasingly aware of the necessity to take *real* time and pay *real* attention to *everything* that might offer us direction as we set out to "follow and know God better!"

We spent the last of our money on trucking in water, followed by an invitation to share, as a whole family, at Pastor Charles Blaire's church in Denver. On our return, we found that all our carpets and appliances for the cottages had been stolen.

We were now in serious trouble.

"You are hiding in the mountains, get down in the plains where the people are hurting."

This was clearly a failure on my behalf to hear. I had obviously failed; this had always been my idea, no doubt logical, no doubt inspirational, no doubt needed but, without doubt, it was all my idea and would never have happened if I had only...*listened.*

As if we were being watched from on high our boat finally sold, again in a down market at a considerable loss but enough to allow us to recompense our daughter Tess and her husband Joe for their investment in the building of their own house in the Village. We were also able to pass on the ministry of "Rejoice" and a large parcel of land to a couple who had joined with us to provide a measure of qualified professional counseling. They did continue the basic idea which eventually moved to Florida and for years did some special work, with restored marriages.

So all was not lost.

Before we decided to leave we wrote to all the eighty four large charismatically inclined churches that had asked us to come and speak; asking if they might be prepared to help us to survive.

We received three replies.

One said that they were pleased to see God was dealing with us, "His disciplines those he loves."

Another sent us their change of address.

The third offered to pray for us; for which we were grateful.

We received no financial support and since we had invested pretty well all our assets in the business of ministry, it was now time to quite simply go...*somewhere!*

We were back with the only certain direction that we had received, those eight words...

"Then give them the money and follow me!"

If indeed this was God speaking and we had begun to follow, then I had to admit to having taken a willful wrong turn by doing my own thing and not just getting on with following!

It was at that *precise* moment that a past contact in Palm Springs, California, called to find out how we were doing with the building of the village. He was a professional, familiar with such development work. I explained what had happened and admitted our financial situation as well as my perception of personal failure.

"Come and stay with me, I have the room. I know we would love to help." He was both charming and understanding, even loving.

This invitation gave us somewhere to go and a roof over our heads. I took this to be an answer to prayer and we rented a small U-Haul van, packed all our worldly goods in it and took off for California.

We arrived at about the same time that our kind hosts had become involved in a house church movement that had begun back on the East Coast. The way it was described to us was that the then widespread Charismatic movement had become a little like a large, bright red London double-decker bus, filled with exuberant worshipers loudly praising God. The bus was going rapidly downhill in the Rocky Mountains and had lost its brakes. On the back open platform of the bus a small band of *men* were getting a huge anchor ready to drop off the back. It was secured to the bus with chains. The purpose was to slow the bus down and save the *movement* from an awful accident with massive loss of "spiritual life."

They proposed to do this "anchoring" with one basic premise...*Discipleship.* However, they added on two other words...with *submission* and *authority.* This allowed for a formal hierarchy where each and every member was submitted to the authority of someone else.

Small groups formed under an appointed Shepherd, who in this town, had *covering* provided by his Shepherd.

One very clear issue was addressed from the very beginning. There would be no Shepherdesses!

Women were, in part, the reason why they saw the Charismatic double-decker bus was out-of-control. Each wife was to be in submission first of all to her own husband, and each husband was to do his best to see that this was so.

Under normal circumstances we would never have become involved, but these were not exactly normal times for us. We were virtually penniless; we had no dwelling place of our own and I was concerned that this had all happened because I hadn't listened carefully and then obeyed. It was all my fault and I wanted *desperately* to avoid making another mistake with whatever was left of our lives. I chose to get out from under this load and get our kind host to carry it. Let him listen for me and we would somehow find the way we should go. I have no doubt whatsoever that our hosts were good, well-intentioned people, at least in the beginning. The problems arose when we were in disagreement and didn't feel that we should do as "suggested"; which had almost become "commanded."

As an example, our Shepherd had a digestive problem and had received a "colonic lavage" as treatment. He felt so "revived" that he told his small flock, that included us, to have the same treatment.

Authors Note: For the record, a "colonic lavage" was rather like being hooked up to what looked like a small gas pump that "hosed" ones bowels in a continuous soapy enema. Not exactly a fun experience.

I chose not to and was told "something toxic is dripping on our relationship." Given the nature of the treatment, this was a rare choice of words!

This was followed swiftly by an observation that Treena was not properly in submission to my authority.

OUCH!

It was Treena that had so radiantly lived out her new faith *without words or persuasion* that had got my spiritual attention in the first place. We shared and always have and continue to share every decision about our family's lives and directions; this did not sit well but for them it was an absolute.

Our son Andy had decided, entirely on his own, to join "Youth with a Mission" (YWAM) in Kona, Hawaii, for *their* Discipleship Training School (DTS). He returned after several months a completely transformed radiant young man who, it seemed, had been taught how to *hear God's voice.*

This had been our intent on leaving our old life...when we felt that God had questioned us as to our intent, our answer had been...

"To know you better."

This now appeared to be our answer. Could we, at forty three years of age, join *Youth with a Mission?*

Once again, there was an immediate answer. The eldership of YWAM were themselves growing older and saw the need to include folks over forty in their program; we would be able to join their very first DTS for this age group.

There was, of course, one immediate hurdle...

CASH!

Once again an amazing; almost miraculous provision?

When I had signed over all books, television and radio programs to our producers, I had listed each book and completely forgotten one title that had simply not sold; it was easily overlooked!

"The Complete Galloping Gourmet Cookbook" was the compilation I wrote during the time that we built our boat "TREENA" in Poole Dorset. It ran over five hundred pages and weighed almost four pounds; we called it "The Door Stop." It sold initially at $35...well... sold is hardly an appropriate term; let's just call it by the culinary term...*drizzled!*

It was about this neglected book that our old agent, Wilbur, called.

"I have had an offer from a publisher to reprint and reissue your big blue book, for which you still own the rights. They are offering an advance of $250,000."

...pause..."Hello...are you still there?"

Please join us in the *Reflective Readers Club*
www.grahamkerr.com/rrc

Rite of Passage Fifty-One: "Retracing our Steps"

There were more fine bubbles in the water again and I wondered what new challenge was facing us. I was feeling just a little tired, especially because I had recently lost the scent that had led us...well...I actually lost it awhile back, but kept on going. Since I was doing the leading now, my hen simply followed rather than taking over the lead as she had done on several previous occasions.

We came around a bend in the river and there it was, a huge flat wall with a torrent of white water coming over the top.

I swam up to the dry part of the wall looking for any kind of opening, then back and under the torrent but still no way to go around or over.

Had the scent been there I would have kept on and on, back and forth, but it wasn't and so the urgency was now missing. I turned and looked at my hen. She looked as listless as I had now become.

I had taken the wrong river; it seemed right but now it was proven wrong. We had to find the scent again and never lose it!

An Understanding

When smaller tributaries spill into a larger river they can often carry much the same mineral and organic materials and almost mimic the true scent of the original birth river. This had led our pair up first one wrong river and then another tributary stream until they encounter an impassable waterfall on Eagle Creek.

They must then, having searched, turn around and for a short period retrace their journey by going back downstream.

1978 to 1980
I am forty four to forty six years old

The advanced royalties for my one remaining book saved our lives. We had gone as far as we were able, used all our assets and had no home or place of our own and no income.

We had a roof over our heads; however, it had come at quite a price...*submission with authority*. We had handed over our freedom in order to hear through another man, and we had granted that man the authority to insist that we obey *him!*

It really was like in my early Army service. Someone in authority was deciding what we would do and then ordered us to do it. We had to obey!

Treena can trace her family roots back to the "Queen" of the Romani Gypsies. She has also been grafted into French, Irish and Dutch stock; all of which are at least moderately opinionated people! Treena has never lacked a voice and throughout our entire relationship could be described best as "spunky." Our Shepherd who, from memory, had been married five times might be thought to have had some brushes with "spunky" women. How could the idea that they be silently submissive to their husbands have found a receptive home in his mindset?

The clash was inevitable.

The advanced royalty check was our *exodus from Egypt*. Our departure, as it happened, almost coincided with the entire movement's implosion due to unwillingness of one of the original leaders to submit to the authority of his "covering." It all fell apart like a house of cards and was seen as yet another example of a desire to control other people's private lives in order to somehow protect God's reputation?

We were to find a house in the old part of Palm Springs, almost halfway between Kirk Douglas and Liberace, as we awaited the development of the Senior D.T.S. at YWAM (Youth with a Mission) in Kona, Hawaii.

Following our descent from the mountains to the desert, I had taken up my pen and wooden spoon again and written a sequel to the "New Seasoning" for Simon & Schuster and Random House. It was eventually named the "Love Feast" and was published in 1978.

It sought to find a way to select, cook and eat in a more natural, less risky manner and I spent many, many months trying to understand what might be doing us harm. That was my focus...*harm*. If I could just deal with the negatives and get them off the table, then only the positives might remain? I am amazed, looking back, that our editors didn't suggest that it be toned down a bit. I spent all my energy attacking almost everything from the obvious saturated fats all the way through multiple refining processes to artificial colors and their apparent affect on hyperactivity.

This thoroughly negative appraisal was played out in the way I chose to put food on our own table. Gone were the gourmet dinners with friends and family. Our table groaned under a relatively colorless assortment of non-fat, no sugar added, low sodium, high fiber foods that were collectively good for our bowels and quite often began with "B," brown rice, brewer's yeast, black beans, bulgur wheat...

Our son Andy observed that while I was preoccupied with bowels neither he, nor his friends at school gave them a second thought. Our daughter Kareena added, "it used to be such fun at the table...but now it's...so..." she searched for but couldn't find an apt word. If she had called it "grazing on the backside of the moon" it just might have got my attention but I was at full flood and couldn't be stopped at home or away. Until...

I had been reading about nitrosamines that are possibly synthesized in the digestive tract by residual nitrite ions and secondary amines. I put the book down and walked from my study to the kitchen where Treena was making a box lunch for our son Andy. She held in her hand a slice of bologna...the very lunchmeat that contained these "carcinogenic, mutagenic and teratogenic" toxic substances.

"You're not putting that on our son's sandwiches." I pointed sternly with a preacher's finger at the limp pink luncheon meat. My darling, the love of my youth, the direct descendant of the Romani Gypsies with other volatile people's gene pools added...

Erupted!

She flung the bologna in my general direction. For a brief moment in time it seemed like a Frisbee as it flew across the kitchen and landed at my feet. She then proceeded to do what is hard to replicate; she *dealt* the rest of the pack like a dealer in Las Vegas. They, too, wound up on the floor nicely separated from each other. During this slight of hand she announced in her impressive stage voice...for the neighbors to hear...

"There is NOTHING left in this world to eat...nothing, nothing, nothing!"

She accompanied this outburst by swiftly turning to an open pantry where she selected cans, jars and packets at random, heaving them into an open trash bin.

My primary concern during this extraordinary demonstration was to protect whatever reputation I thought I might have retained as a well-known gourmet in our otherwise quiet star-studded neighborhood.

"Hush...hush," I pleaded, my finger replaced by open palms splayed out in supplication.

"I have an idea." I tried to make myself heard over the tumult.

"What's that!" Treena demanded.

"We will have two menus at each meal," I suggested, "one for you and the kids, the other for me. You all eat whatever you like...I'll stay with what I know."

"Fine, fine, FINE! Treena was in complete agreement. And so it began.

Since I cooked, it was up to me to make up the second meal, which I did for the next eight years until...well, I'll get to that later on.

What I had done was to create very hard to accept lifestyle choices for my family. To them it looked like *rules*. To me, it represented *solutions*.

When presented with hard and fast rules, it can often cause *rebellion*. The usual way of putting down a rebellion is to seek for a *compromise*. This I had now done. How much better it would have been had I started out with creative choices complete with understanding. This piece of wisdom had yet to arrive.

You may well gather from this brief rebellion that Treena was not exactly a pushover and that she was, as a result, a fairly easy target for the male-only shepherding movement. Our time under authority concluded when our Shepherd conducted a "Pigs in the Parlor" styled deliverance on Treena and tape recorded the session secretly in order to discuss it with his "covering authority." That broke almost all of the absolute basics of small group ethics and practice. As a direct result we were well motivated to seek after God by literally *any other means* but theirs, no matter how well intentioned they might have been!

We had already applied and had been accepted, for the older folk's discipleship school in Kona, Hawaii, and in September 1978 we had another garage sale and left Palm Springs for the fabled Pacific Islands.

The YWAM (Youth with a Mission) base in Kona on the big island of Hawaii was an older hotel converted into a relatively small instructional center. There were several rooms with baths attached. A central open-air dining room, a pretty ordinary kitchen designed to feed two hundred and that was about it. Not exactly the romantic image of ocean views and manicured lawns under swaying palm trees.

We had arrived early and had settled into one of the rooms to await the course commencement. The course was led by Loren and Darlene Cunningham who, not unlike Bill Gates of

Microsoft, had begun YWAM in a California garage in 1960. Loren had *seen* the world from a distance and observed waves of young people literally rippling over the whole earth.

The young ones were being trained to "know God and make Him known."

It really was as simple as that.

I remember during our time in Sydney, Australia, that Prince Phillip (of the UK) visited a university in New South Wales and was greatly encouraged by what he saw as unrivaled youthful enthusiasm that could easily change the world. He then added "but why does this so easily evaporate after about 25 years of age?"

You can account for YWAM's ministry since 1960 by looking at it as Loren had in his early "vision of youthful waves." It now has a volunteer staff of over 20,000 and trains thousands of short-term missionaries each year who go off to "make God known" in over 1,500 locations in at least187 countries.

The energy behind such a "movement" comes from the youthful enthusiasm of its grass roots; the kind of *"all things are possible"* attitude that continues to inspire the leaders; who are still going for it in their seventies and early eighties.

Our great desire, when we had come to know ourselves as being Christian, was "to know God better." We had seen how our normally stubborn teenaged son had been wonderfully changed by his D.T.S. in Kona and we were very eager to embrace the notion that we might, by attending, get to know God, and to *clearly* learn how to hear his *voice* for ourselves.

Our training included doing various domestic duties on the base. This helped to reduce school costs and allowed all of us to be of service to each other. Everyone tended to be selected or offer their talents in areas where they felt they could make a difference.

Guess where I wound up?

We were, at that time, feeding four hundred students and staff every day, from the small 200-person kitchen. On my first day I joined about twelve *volunteers* around a large central island workstation upon which was heaped the raw provisions for that day's evening meal.

The Chef in charge was Mike Barger, a slim, sandy haired young man who had done a two-month baking course in the U.S. Army. These were his entire qualifications...well...not really! He was a deeply committed, absolutely reliable young man who consistently did his very best day after day having a dozen or so completely unskilled workers, very few of them coming for more than five days in a row!

Under any other set of circumstances it would have been a nightmare!

I found Mike and his team gathered around its central island prep table. He invited me to join them.

I was very much aware that all of them knew that I had had a worldwide audience of many millions and could be said to be, as a result, a reasonably famous "Chef." His crew made room for me and took me by the hands. I was now linked with them as Mike led us in prayer.

"Oh Lord, just look at all this fine food you have provided." It actually looked somewhat tired and rather sparse.

"We thank you for it and for each other." He glanced around and smiled sheepishly in my direction.

"We ask that you bless the work of our hands so that as we prepare this food it blesses and pleases those who will eat it tonight. We pray these things in Jesus name."

In all my years in the kitchen, that now exceeded thirty, I had never witnessed such a gathering or felt so influenced to do my best. When he finished, even the food seemed to have perked up.

I can easily credit Mike for a great deal of the benefit I received from YWAM. He never led a class but he certainly lived his role as a servant-leader who worked diligently for the common good. I wanted to be like him. He was a flash of silver!

The other huge benefit that I derived came from a visiting teacher who used up his entire one-hour session with just one minute of instruction in the form of a question...

"If you are, as it says in Galatians 2:20, *crucified with Christ,* how is this possible? Go away and use the hour to come to your own conclusion. *You* need to have the answer. You don't need to report it to *me.*"

With that, he dismissed us...and left!

I set out to imagine a large wooden cross with Jesus hanging there. I wondered if it was my role to take the place of the thieves who were indeed "crucified with Christ." I deserved the death he suffered because of all the pain I had selfishly caused and for which I had been forgiven.

"There is therefore no condemnation" (Romans 8:1)...*so why am I crucified?*

Surely, in a practical sense I cannot be put up on his cross first, or for that matter, over or on him...equally repugnant to even consider. It was then that I walked around the back of my imaginary cross and found...me!

I was firmly nailed in place, hidden from all observation. I was dressed in a fine Prince of Wales check suit, white shirt with French cuffs and links, my old school tie, and perfectly polished shoes. My hair was well groomed; I had a suntan face and a wide welcoming smile.

I cried out. "Oh Lord, that is frightful –awful...what does it mean?"

I received that inward-sounding voice in answer.

"You have brought your sins to me and been forgiven. What you see now is yourself as you would most want to be seen...and admired. If you leave that where it is then your old self will have been finally crucified with me..."

"Come now...follow me..."

Please join us in the Reflective Readers Club
www.grahamkerr.com/rrc

Rite of Passage Fifty-Two:
"Back to School Again"

We had turned around when we couldn't find our way past the big wall and the high white waters, and for the first time in our journey since the big waters...we were going with the flow.

We learned as we went, as we had done so many years ago. This time we were trying to catch the scent once again...the true scent that would lead us back home.

An Understanding

The two salmon, having sensed their error, are now traveling back down Eagle Creek and the Clackamas River toward the Willamette River —their true upper watershed destination that their inherent guidance system is programmed for. Downstream travel can be rapid, as much as 30 miles in a day or more as found in steelhead that can survive spawning and return to the ocean once again. Although Chinook, Coho, Sockeye, Pink, and Chum salmon all die after spawning, straying can result in their need to make adult downstream travels to find their true destinations that are presumably at a similar speed.

1978 to 1980
I am forty four to forty six years old

The normal sequence of the Discipleship Training School, or DTS, is three months in the classroom followed by three months in the *field*; a place beyond our normal culture where we might assist others as *waves* whose basic purpose was to "make God known." I never made it out there because of the immediate need on the Kona base. Amongst many issues that were urgent were the kitchen and the daily requirement to...eat!

I therefore found myself as the "Director of Food Services" with full authority to do what I could within an extremely tight budget. Mike Barger remained at my side and I was joined by several really remarkable young and youngish people who all wanted to help to make things a little better.

The YWAM culture is based upon a universal agreement to be of service to one another and then to the world, as we might feel led...a kind of spiritual Peace Corps. In a very few cases some of us had come with enough financial worth to be self-sustaining for at least a few years. By far the largest number were younger or less advantaged who had been funded by parents, other family, friends and, in many cases, by church congregations or individual members under the budget heading of "Missions."

Every YWAM–er is responsible for somehow raising their own support and so therefore the idea that these folks are "knowing God and then making Him known throughout the world" is a clear incentive to contribute. What is less clear is when that short-term mission is over and the individual begins to join a base as a staff member...perhaps in the kitchen. It is true that without such volunteers there would have to be a salaried staff and, as a result, the school fees would begin to mount and become restrictive.

The way I saw it was that I was helping those who were serving *outward*, and my behind the front lines work was of somewhat equal value in terms of meeting human needs.

I say *somewhat* because I was, once again, in a culinary staff position and I had wrestled with this *status* issue since I had first served others back in my parent's hotel in 1948. That had been followed by the "fate worse than death," which was my father's expression for the British Army Catering Corp. Then the Royal New Zealand Air Force and the clear awareness that the pilots were the *real* Air Force and my role was way down the pecking order.

So, here I was yet again, only this time the pilots were frontline missionaries in sometimes quite dangerous places and here was I cooking on the Big Island of Hawaii within sound of the surf under a bright blue sky!

Fortunately there was a continuous stream of truly wonderful teachers from all over the world; so widespread that the base swiftly morphed into the University of the Nations whose influence and campus outreach has now been felt in over a hundred nations.

I organized the food as best I could and in between this daily task I attended lectures and continued to be fed spiritually as a result. It was at one of these lectures that the amazing Joy Dawson spoke. Joy was the forerunner of a stream of women who were anointed to teach and who had won the respect of men and women who, as a result, had sidestepped the Biblical instruction that required "women to be silent in church."

Joy had spent her early years in New Zealand where, as a housewife, she had begun to construct "sermons" over a fourteen-year period without having anyone to listen to her...other than her family and a few friends. Fortunately, she was discovered by Loren Cunningham in his early days as YWAM's founder and released to teach along with his encouragement.

Joy was forceful and utterly confident, even to the point of being quite outrageous yet always within Biblical truth.

It was during her lecture on, I believe, "the pursuit of peace," that she uttered a sentence that was to change my life.

"If you are stretched thin, it could be that you are shallow." In just twelve words, she had nailed me!

When road crews have to work at night on highways they wear bright orange jackets with white reflective tape. It's hard to miss them, and that's for everyone's safety. The same can be said for *celebrity*, except that my outfit was who I appeared to be and it was other folks who dressed me up in orange and the tape that reflected my past occupation on worldwide television. I was somehow different and nothing I tried to do was able to distance me from the "Galloping Gourmet" who was now doing the food for YWAM, Kona.

I did the food. I arranged a breakfast buffet of whole grains and fruit and yogurt, which gained the title "bird seed."

For one very odd season when our location had no money I invented and served a dish that was called Manna that used an emergency store of lentils, rice powder and chard for over thirty days. It was actually quite nourishing but looked as though a regiment of Marines had washed their fatigues in it (the color...you understand?).

In addition, I was involved in teaching both on base and with Treena on a worldwide YWAM circuit and other events on campus.

I was stretched thin and Joy's message helped me to see that who I used to be had almost *nothing* to do with who I was now. This excellent word was followed soon after by another direct thought that came to me in a time of prayer. Again, it was inwardly felt rather than audible.

"Do a small thing and do it well until it's done."

The two fit neatly together and had I paid attention to them would have made the world of a difference to the rest of our lives. They did, in the brief time that followed; which meant that I was both willing and able to receive a vision that was to provide a clear understanding as to what many people described as a "calling."

I had become aware of a basic obstacle in YWAM's style of outreach. You may recall that each team member, or YWAM–er, was supported as an individual who, as a result, was taught how to "know God and make him known." This method of application was called short-term missions, usually three months in duration. With limited funds the outreach was usually one-on-one encounters accompanied by team worship and drama in public places –a kind of Salvation Army street corner concert with personal sharing to follow, all quite low cost and often truly life-changing. When confronted by the longer term needs of better food and drinkable water, sanitation, etc., there was only so much that could be achieved with so little time and money.

By this time, my understanding about the need for better overall nutrition and especially the benefit of eating plant foods had now become a personal passion. I could see just how much good could be done amongst the most impoverished people on the planet and how all this youthful enthusiasm might be harnessed for such a needy cause. The obstacle was, to say the least; obvious, it was consistent, long-term cash flow. In YWAM that didn't exist and, as a result perhaps, there were fewer people who had that "calling."

I began to pray about what I called a "two-handed Gospel" (or good news) which presented the story about Jesus and what he had said and done that was such good news and with the other hand offered both material assistance and direct help and understanding to individual poor people, so that they could provide for their own family's needs.

This strong desire was meshed with not being "stretched thin," and doing a "small thing well until it was done" and my personal need for removing the celebrity "reflective jacket." The result was a detailed vision that I received one cloudy afternoon sitting alone at one of the dining tables in the open courtyard in Kailua-Kona, Hawaii.

I had a pencil in hand and typing paper, and it began to come in pictures that I eventually had rendered for you to see and share with me now...

The Vision

Author's Note: We have many dear Christian friends who are well convinced and perfectly content with the idea that "prophecies" and similar communications ceased when the Scriptures were completed by the Book of Revelation. The verse they understand to say this is found in 1 Corinthians 13:8 *"Love never fails. But where there are prophecies, they will cease; where there are tongues, they will be stilled; where there is knowledge, it will pass away."* Our intent is not, by any means, to argue with the interpretation, or to offer anything to countermand this belief. We fully understand its roots come from indiscriminate additions that have generally weakened the strength of the words contained within the "approved" Scriptures.

I will now introduce what I "received" in Kailua-Kona during this Discipleship Training Period; a period set aside to learn how one might hear God's voice, not so much as seeking *new words* as coming to a faithful understanding of what has already been recorded in Scriptures.

My attitude, as I sat in the empty dining room, was focused upon my concern for the mission within which I served. How could I practice what I considered to be the whole Gospel...the *Gospel of Two Hands* that carried the Good News of Salvation through Jesus and God's provision for men to provide for their families or, if you like, the message of social justice.

If they were dovetailed together they might best show how we might love God and our neighbor, and indeed ourselves, *with all our heart, soul, mind and strength*?

It was with this *desire of my heart* that I was waiting for an understanding. The vision came first in pictures that I drew. Then came a description of the pictures, and that was followed by what was meant by the understood picture.

I shall therefore lay it out as it was received, and let you be the one who discerns whether or not this was "self-generated" or could have been divinely inspired.

In the text version you see a pencil drawing. In the audio you have my description of that sketch.

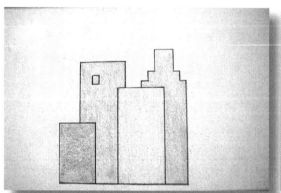

A city skyline with one window:
This is Manhattan, New York City. The window is a corner office of a Senior Executive. He has read of a mission to serve the hungry and poor in Calcutta, India, and is about to sign a check. He pauses to look out at the view up Madison Avenue towards Central Park.

An Indian woman with stick-thin child:
He sees "beyond the view" to the need itself. The Mother and child are in desperate circumstances. He is moved by compassion for them.

Barbed wire obscures the need:

Suddenly, a roll of barbed wire unravels between him and the mother and child. He sees this as his monetary gift being "ripped off" by administrative and other costs before it reaches the need itself.

Regretfully, he puts the cap back on his pen and doesn't contribute.

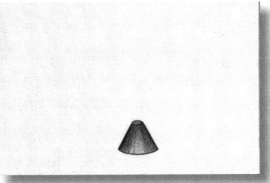

A cone-shaped wooden model:

This I understood to be a model for the way in which the contribution could have been made. The model represented a local church.

A ball bearing on the model:

The model had a concave top that perfectly fits a large ball bearing.

I saw this as a church that was devoted to "lifting up Jesus Christ" as its primary mission.

I saw Jesus as the ball bearing (when ball bearings are used in moving parts they make everything run smoothly...when lubricated (anointed?)

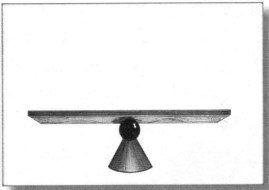

A plank perfectly balanced on the ball bearing:

God has a balanced view of all of his creation. His loving-care is impartial.

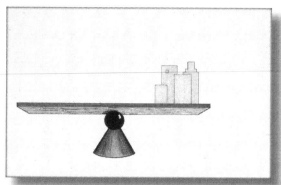

One man in all of New York City:
God was deeply grieved over the one man in the entire city who had not been blessed by giving.

The mother and child on the other end of the plank:
God was equally moved by the unmet need in Calcutta.

The Executive and the mother and child separated by barbed wire:
God was brokenhearted by what was causing his blessings to be frustrated. He gives both for the rich and the poor in equal measure.

The wooden model once again:
I understood that I was being shown that the local church was God's remedy.

A man carries a "box" to a bus:
There was provision of some kind of instruction and understanding in that box.

A second man carries a saucepan to the bus:
The Church sends out teams to meet practical needs that aid understanding about nourishment and delight.

The two-man team and bus and New York City:
The team goes to the advantaged to explain how best to have a life of compassion and service.

Two men with simple tools:
The local church also sends out teams to provide understanding on self-sufficiency and resilience. They receive their funding to do so from the generosity and compassion released by the work of the first team.

Two men and a palm tree:
The second team goes to the impoverished everywhere.

There is no end to human need and no end to the ways in which modern Christians can provide God's planned solutions…that can lead to personal resilience.

The entire picture was now completed:
This, then, was God's answer to the needs that will always be with us.

I immediately took this to those who taught me and they gave it their approval. They suggested that I take it to the YWAM bases worldwide and see what they may think about its application.

In high hopes, we set forth!

Please join us in the Reflective Readers Club
www.grahamkerr.com/rrc

Rite of Passage Fifty-Three: "The Flood"

As we made our way back downstream in search of our real scent, it began to make small circles on the brightness above. It had done this often, but this time it was different.

The circles went deeper and wider and didn't come and go...they never stopped!

The waters around us seemed wider and much swifter, which I didn't mind because we would reach our special scented waters sooner.

But it didn't stop, even when it became dark above. The waters rose to the top of the banks and even above those and we had to swim hard to stay as much in the center as possible.

I seem to have lost the scent altogether. There is a dark brown in the water and many new, strange scents.

I'm troubled...we don't know which way to turn or even when.

An Understanding

Our gallant pair of fish, having turned back downstream are looking for the true aroma of their birth river.

It began to rain, and rained hard and continuously, even overnight. The river bursts its banks and begins to flood...drawing lots of "new" aromas to muddy the now swiftly running river. All this tumult has now obscured the scent of their natal river to which they are drawn with such passionate, consistent determination.

Although such storms and floods are relatively rare in late March, heavy spring rainfall seems to be an increasing trend in the Pacific Northwest. A potential result of what has come to be called "climate change", or global warming.

1980
I am forty six years old

Filled with such high hopes, we set forth on a worldwide journey to communicate the vision that had been approved by senior servant leaders in YWAM, Kailua-Kona, Hawaii. We were to encounter a wonderfully warm welcome wherever we traveled. YWAM had Darlene Cunningham's God-given gift of hospitality at its core. Visitors and lecturers were cared for in an almost exuberant fashion; with every little need thought of carefully in advance.

At each base, the leadership listened and went over my drawings. When they were satisfied, they allowed us to talk to the base as a whole. At no place were we denied access to the multiple locations and people who were committed to the simple task of "knowing God and making him known."

We returned to our small home in Hawaii greatly encouraged, at least, for a while.

The mission had grown rapidly worldwide because of its willingness to be waves of young people with the simple message that Jesus had come for the express purpose of making forgiveness possible for people who had somehow caused pain or ruin by their actions; providing that they made it plain to all those who knew them or of them, that they had put all their troublesome behavior behind them and chosen to lead a life that resulted in the common good.

This was often referred to as "repenting for one's sins and receiving forgiveness".

Depending upon the culture concerned, the more lengthy explanation of Jesus' time on earth was perhaps better able to be understood in the long term?

This "good news" was what YWAM was used to delivering in many face-to-face encounters throughout the world. There is, perhaps, for the committed Christian, nothing that is so truly wonderful as being used to provide that communication and seeing it wholeheartedly received. It's quite rightly referred to as a *great blessing* for both individuals because of its *eternal* significance and the *immediate* opportunity to begin a whole new way of living the life one has been given.

My vision was understood by everyone...however, it didn't appear to fit into short-term missions. For the vision to work, it would take at least a three-year commitment (it takes such a time to plant even a simple abundant garden). Three years was too much for young people to grasp when compared to their highly effective ministry that was ongoing and blessing thousands every year.

There was also one other obstacle. We were talking *simple lifestyle* whilst living in Hawaii. Hawaii, to most people, is a splendid subtropical tourist paradise where, if you need a banana, you go and pick one in your garden. You don't have heating bills; the list of advantages for less complicated living is almost endless.

"It's pretty easy for you but try that in upper New York State," they would reply.

For these two reasons alone, and perhaps the constant celebrity christian question that would usually remain unsaid, we got almost no takers. I say almost, because there was an extremely charismatic young couple in Salem, Oregon, whose family, as well as themselves, understood and wanted to help it happen.

We left Hawaii and moved into an old trailer home in a pasture just outside Oregon's capital city in 1980. We were able to sell our home in Hawaii quickly and to design and commission a small home for ourselves in the midst of that same pasture.

At least the Hawaiian limitation had been removed from the global resistance to what we now called Operation L.O.R.D. –which stood for Long Range Development. The missing "O" was filled in with the world as depicted from space.

Before long our house was up, we had moved in and we had begun to assemble a great team of young people who understood the vision and whose families and friends were prepared to support them in their desires to make it a success.

We began to dream it into being, using our whole team's imagination. Scripture does speak of a time when young men will see visions and old men will dream dreams. At 46 years of age, I was almost at the midpoint and as the oldest person available and the visionary I became, with Treena at my side, the default servant leader.

Oh, how we prayed, planned and even pleaded for the support we needed to create mini-farms for the absolute poor, and to do so with funds provided by advantaged people who were able to convert "habits that harmed them into resources that might heal others."

It was so alarmingly *logical* and reasonable. Surely it would be a solution for those who lived in abject poverty without hope?

We designed a one-acre unit with technical help from John Jeavons whose Biointensive Workshop had begun eight years earlier. On this single acre we envisioned three small dwellings raised on stilts to enable the "crawl space" to be used for small animals such as rabbits.

Each dwelling sat on 1/4 acre roughly 52 feet by 52 feet. By allowing three of these mini-plots to one acre it left nearly four hundred square feet for common walkways and a shared area for composting, etc.

Certainly, this is as small as one could possibly go to provide the slightest benefit, but it was designed to be managed by the owner's family members while (usually) the man was working in the plantation. By including small animals and even a tilapia fish pond under the dwelling it was possible to barter for the essential cereal crops that couldn't be grown in such limited conditions.

Our hope was that with some on-location coaching, it might provide sufficient income to allow the owners to buy the land over a ten-year period.

It was all *just* feasible and we built a model unit on the agricultural fairgrounds in Belize with some help from the Weyerhaeuser Foundation. This work was greatly impacted by a prior visit to Dominica in the Lesser Antilles of the Caribbean.

I had led a small team to that small island immediately after the 1979 Hurricane David. David was a Force Five hurricane with wind speeds of up to 175 miles per hour.

Little Dominica suffered 56 deaths and 180 injured. Eighty percent of all the wooden homes were destroyed, seventy five percent were homeless. Rivers became destructive torrents bursting their banks and eroding farmland completely. All power lines were ripped away and subsistence crops were mostly destroyed.

All of this took place on August 29, 1979. Our team arrived in mid September. In the immediate aftermath they were recycling bandages and the only painkillers were aspirin.

It was a desperate situation and there was so little that we could do in the midst of so much need but there was much to learn.

Of significance to my life was the meeting we had with a French Biodynamic Agron-omist whose name, as best I can recall, was Gregoire (if you, as my reader, recall his full name I will be most grateful).

He had a low-to-the ground farm surrounded by a well-built rock wall. Almost all his organic crops survived and, as a result, he was able to provide for his neighbors in the first days of chaos and ruin.

His example has remained firmly in my mind ever since. He

Our first "implant" in Belize

had the hindsight to locate his farm on a hillside that could not be washed away by flooding rivers. He had worked the poor soil –banking beds with rock walls. He had chosen nourishing plants to grow; such as collard greens.

The man had planted for a storm yet, none had hit the island since 1930, and there was virtually no preparation made for one.

I wonder to what degree our world is ready for a succession of hugely disruptive events, of a scale that goes well beyond whatever reasonable precautions are being made?

It was these ten days spent in a tent (receiving over eighty mosquito bites...is that a sign of obsessive/compulsive behavior?) without any clean water or electricity; that helped me to plan ahead to meet situations that met those kinds of disruption.

Our little farm in Belize had been born with the Dominican disaster in mind.

It was these experiences that landed me an invitation to attend the the Hoddesdon Conference held in the United Kingdom under the leadership of John Stott who was the one-time Anglican "pastor" of All Souls Church in Langham Place in London. The Reverend Stott was an extremely influential churchman over many years in post World War II.

The Lausanne Committee was meeting to consider how evangelically-minded Christians might choose to live "simple" lifestyles in order to show, with clarity, how determined they were in their desire that, at the very least, all the world should be able to hear the story and intentions of Jesus' life on earth and then to make their choice based upon a "reasonably consistent witness."

The Committee met from March 17th to March 21st in 1980 at the High Leigh Conference Center, which is about seventeen miles north of London. John Stott let me know that I was to be an observer and therefore was not to speak...at all!

I watched, suitably muted and listened to a great throng of Theologians who debated the issue over four intense days. The paper labeled LOP20 "An Evangelical Commitment to Simple Lifestyle" can be found at http://www.lausanne.org. It is fourteen pages long and well worth reading.

I was, however, at the time, almost completely baffled by the ebb and flow of the debate. It was like one of the torrential rivers of Dominica bursting its banks, but this time with a flood of well-meaning words from men and women from all over the world.

Upon completion of the paper, John Stott drew me aside...

"The BBC World Service wants to do a program about our meeting here," he explained.

"Jolly good show," I replied, having become quite British during my otherwise muted participation.

"Yes...well ummm...I'd like you to go down and do the interview." He appeared otherwise to be sane.

"Me?" I exclaimed. "But, you said I was to be silent."

"Yes, of course, but the BBC needs a communicator and Theologians are not necessarily good communicators...especially (he added with a faint smile) in about four minutes!"

Four minutes to cover fourteen pages of close typed theology.

OUCH!

"John, with all due respect, —are you sure about this?"

"Do you read the Bible?" This was his immediate, somewhat stern, rejoinder.

"Of course...yes."

"Do you recall that passage where they may be called before magistrates and were not to be concerned...just to open their mouth and the Lord would fill it?"

"You mean you just want me to...open my mouth at a BBC interview?"

"Precisely." With that, he left me with my feelings of...well...*open rebellion* might be a good term to use. How could he possibly suggest such a thing and run the risk of putting a six-year Christian in such an impossible situation!

I left for London that afternoon and entered the hallowed halls of the venerable BBC in Langham Place...right next door to John Stott's old church.

I was greeted with great warmth by a North of England interviewer who clapped me on the back.

"This is such an honor, my mum and I used to watch your Galloping Gourmet together... it was such great fun."

He went on to let me know that we would be going...

"Live...worldwide in five minutes...when the red light goes on."

He then chattered away about my past while I was wondering what on earth would happen when I simply...opened my mouth to let...to let...the Lord...fill it with about three hundred words that might make sense...somewhere.

The light went on and my friendly Northern chappie morphed into a Southern England County accented BBC type.

"We have in the studio today Graham Cur (his mispronunciation) who has been with God (drawn out) for the past week.

"So, what is God saying?"

I sat there and opened my mouth...

Please join us in the Reflective Readers Club

www.grahamkerr.com/rrc

Rite of Passage Fifty-Four: "Resilience"

It's white water time...back to that big white wall of water from which we had previously been diverted. There is no avoiding that this is our true way. I need to find the less frothy way up and I swim back and forth looking for some location where the wall may be lowest or less steep. Poking my head above the frothing water I found what seemed a low point. I turn round to offer the first leap to my hen. I am unaware of how a few humans practice good manners, in my case it has gradually become natural.

She dives deep, turns and swims slowly through the tumbling force of the falling waters. She breaks the surface and looks upward at the downpour as it froths white around her. She is looking at the clear air beyond and gauging the effort required.

I love the way she does this; it's her measured approach that has finally cured me of making an impulsive dash at every obstacle.

Then in a sudden flash she drives powerfully from the rocky bottom through the swirling water —breaks the surface with a final great swish of her tail and begins to fly through the air, just touching and thrashing onward and upward, it's a splendid sight.

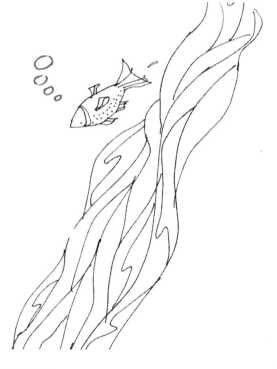

And then...she seems to falter...the very tip of the waters catch her and as she struggles it gains control, she slows and then arching over she falls back with a huge crash against a large worn boulder. Held there in the torrent for a gasping moment she weakly shrugs herself into the pool and moving to one side, lies quietly, with her head inclined downward, her lovely eyes closed. I swim quickly to her side and lie quietly with her, our fins touch.

An Understanding

The two salmon have returned once again to the great falls of the Willamette at Oregon City. It is now April with the flow of the river subsiding after the heavy March rain. The falls remain a great obstacle that seemingly no fish could overcome. Although a ladder has been constructed around it. In this case, the recent high water brought a large log downstream that lodged at the ladder entry in a way that prevented fish from finding it.

Chinook in their prime condition, can leap as high as twelve feet, but in order to achieve this remarkable feat they must find a combination of currents beneath the falls to enable a maximum leap and threads of flowing water breaking over the falls that they can swim up to extend the maximum height; even a few feet more. Both fish have examined the falls by poking their heads out of the water to better determine a route. This is often done several times to orient themselves to what seems the best leaping location.

Our Chinook hen has counted the cost; she had, like an Olympian athlete...gone through the motions that she would eventually take, then she went for it with everything she had in her...and she almost made it, only to fall back in a bruising tumble onto a rock just beneath the surface.

Now she is stunned and disoriented and needs her natural resilience to bring healing and the renewed confidence to try once more.

1980 to 1982
I am forty six to forty eight years old

I am in the BBC about to speak live on their worldwide service. I have no idea what I am to say...

I opened my mouth and since nothing came out...I shut it and almost panicked.

Then I saw in one brilliant, mind-filling moment a full screen picture of an Army boot stepping onto parade ground gravel, followed by its mate...left, right, left, right.

I reopened my mouth to ask my BBC interviewer a question.

"Were you ever in the Army?" Startled by my odd way of responding to his enquiry on what God had been saying to a conference of Evangelical Christian Theologians, he replied...

"Yes."

"Did you ever have a drill instructor who shouted, "by the left quick march?" By this time my mind and mouth were beginning to catch up with the swiftly moving pictures that I was now seeing.

"Yeeees." He had drawn out his reply as though wondering if he had a live-to-air problem on his hands.

"Well…that's it, you see." I smiled encouragingly, which is hard to perceive on radio.

"You mean God (he drew it out again) said, "by the left quick march?" He was right on the borderline of scoffing.

"Yes indeed." I now understood as I spoke only a word or two ahead of my mouth, but it came swiftly and with great confidence.

"You see," I explained, "the left foot is the story about Jesus Christ, why he came, what he said and did, and its result for mankind…it's called the Gospel."

I hurried on.

"The right foot is social justice, what some call liberal or humanitarian…or when action is taken to help a man to make provision for his own family."

"Alright…so how does it work?" He seemed a little more interested.

"Well, if one simply told the Jesus story it would mean that I would keep on putting my left foot forward and dragging my right (social justice) foot behind me." I smiled again.

"It's what I call a prosthetic (as in artificial limb) witness." It was the first time I had used a pun to explain theology…of any kind.

He got it and actually laughed at the play on words.

"Of course," I added, "it works the other way as well. If you keep putting the right foot of social justice first, then you are left with dragging the Gospel of Jesus Christ behind."

"Better, by far, to quite simply walk and become consistently involved in both."

We spent the remaining two or three minutes having a very warm chat about converting personal habits that might be harmful (like smoking) into resources that might be healing, like providing for widows and orphans and people without hope.

We parted warmly; his northern accent back in its proper place.

I returned directly to High Leigh and sought out John Stott, who was packing to leave.

"I'm back." I announced brightly.

"Where from?" He enquired.

"Er…the BBC…World Service," I added for effect.

"Oh yes." He continued to fold clothes into his bag.

"Don't you want to know how it went?" I asked.

"Mmm…so?" He didn't look up.

"Well…" I then launched into a quite enthusiastic account of my time of revelation… boots and all.

He stopped packing, turned around and looked at me thoughtfully.

"You appear to be quite pleased with yourself."

"Well…yes…but it's really so amazing…to just open my mouth…and, as you said…God filled it…I mean…!"

"Precisely, God filled it, just don't forget that."

He added his remaining roll of socks and snapped the suitcase shut.

Somewhat smarting over the lack of encouragement from a man whom I greatly admired, I went out for a brisk walk into town with Christian Futurist, Tom Sine. I mentioned my still fresh experience with the BBC and he responded with the enthusiasm that I wished had come from John Stott, so much so that I could almost hear once again those early whispered words...

"Such a good little boy, see how he's folded his clothes."

Within one hour I received two great lessons.

- If God appears to have used you be careful not to think too highly of yourself. Do not treat such words or actions as belonging to you and only repeat them in their complete context.

- By all means, seek to have the word or action confirmed by godly men or women, but seek confirmation rather than approval.

We returned to our new small home in the Pacific Northwest to some extremely disturbing news.

Our secretary was no longer available. She had been instructed not to speak to us and when we tried to reach her; our calls were unanswered. We then discovered that all the financial assistance we had received that was designated for use in the ongoing Belize project had been frozen.

When I began to seek some reason for these disruptions, I was told that the Base Leadership Team would be meeting with me to answer both questions and explain my actions and theirs. It seems to have become a boring cliché because it has been so overused in purple patch writing but the feeling of iced water in the midsection of one's body...was entirely accurate.

I hadn't the slightest idea what this might mean, and why such action was being undertaken.

My calls to our charismatically friendly leader went unanswered.

Since nobody was speaking, I went directly to the North American Director of YWAM (a kind of benign Bishop).

He also had no idea what was taking place, but suggested that I attend the meeting and for the most part, if not all, to listen but remain silent.

I attended the meeting that night with my mutually muted mate. (I simply can't resist alliterations.) We sat in a circle with five of the leadership team of young men; all of whom were roughly half our age. The leader himself was absent.

The meeting began with several probes about my motives for being in ministry and conducting the model farm in Belize. This involved more statements than questions and appeared to be leading to some conclusion that they had reached. Their eventual questions were so obscure and even sketchily defined that I was unable to answer what I could not even begin to understand.

At last it was clearly stated. In the opinion of the leadership it was my intention to take over the entire base and use it for my express purposes. I resisted the impulse to somehow laugh it off because it was so patently absurd but then these young men were so obviously serious that I did my best to remain as muted as possible, thanked them for their time and left.

Within a day or two the North American Director arrived and conducted his own enquiry.

He was, at heart, a peacemaker; as indeed his unenviable role required. He sought to quench the flames, or perhaps better put, to separate the opposing parties.

"In the best interest of the common good," he proposed carefully, "we think it best that the issues related to the entire ministry emphasis...be clearly defined and then separated."

He went on with great care and concern for us specifically.

"The base leader will be removed from his post and will be traveling with a senior YWAM leader, under his direct oversight until further notice."

"We suggest, in order to avoid any and all potential division, that you move Operation Lord, complete with all its financial and team support, to the base in Tacoma, Washington, where I have their assurance you would receive a warm welcome."

And so the apparently warring participants were separated but never reconciled.

I have no idea to this day what lay at the root of this dislocation, and after over thirty six years there has been no attempt to either explain or provide understanding.

I have, of course, given some time to conjecture and can only arrive at the baggage I continue to carry as a one-time celebrity. When someone who has had a major audience undertakes anything on a smaller scale, they do so with the added weight and attention that was once due them, even though it was left far behind. Amongst numerous examples of people far above and beyond my brief brush with fame is the sublime example of Saul of Tarsus who became the Apostle Paul. Clearly, he could never be free from his past reputation no matter how profound was his change.

I was given the opportunity to invite the Operation Lord team to remain at the base, or to come with us to Tacoma. The entire team, other than our "muted" secretary, agreed to the move.

Our recently built home was purchased from us at its actual cost and within days we were on our way. We had to leave the Belize project unfinished, which we all deeply regretted at the time and still do. We also left the Operation Lord gardens where we had done our practical "bio intensive" training.

Tacoma, under the very warm leadership of Denny and Dodie Gunderson, was in an urban setting and possessed no land or access to land.

In our prayers, where we tried to make sense of this "waterfall" experience we began to accept that our work until that date was to create a solution for those who had been left out; for the poor and those often without hope.

But that was only half of the vision. To be balanced we now needed to see how we could reach those who were advantaged and who needed somehow to be compassionately connected to the disadvantaged.

The Scripture says…

"And we know that in all things God works for the good of those who love him, who have been called according to his purpose." Romans 8:28

Had all this taken place to remind us that there are two parts to almost every positive solution?

In our move to Tacoma we had left behind an embryo farm for those left out and had arrived with a vision to serve those who lived in the midst of a life that was so abundant that it might, in part, be a physical, emotional and spiritual hindrance.

It was during this transition that Treena and I made a trip across the Cascade Mountains to Wenatchee during which we entered into a word game as we tried to fit whatever we had understood so far into our brand new circumstance.

As we drove carefully through snow and ice, we slowly added our edited words…until we arrived at…

"Habits that harm can become resources that heal."

It was another simple eight-word statement about what could happen; not what would take place. This wasn't prophecy; it was just a logical fact of life!

From this understanding, we found ourselves with an even smaller description…"Double Benefit." When set alongside the habits that harm the double benefit could be seen as one in which the advantaged and the disadvantaged were both able to benefit.

There would be less harm to one and healing for the other.

It went just one stage further on that slow, slippery, freezing mountain top journey, we came to the conclusion that when combined these lifestyle actions would upgrade the quality of life which we would come to refer to as Q.O.L.

Please join us in the Reflective Readers Club
www.grahamkerr.com/rrc

Rite of Passage Fifty-Five: "Sidetracked for a Season"

My hen continued to gain strength but it was slow going and she was in no shape to leap the tall white waters that stood in our way. We knew we had to follow the scent but her bruising had made it impossible for the time being.

Very gently we dropped back downstream into the depths of the great pool below the falls that promised some peace and quiet where my mate could heal and regain her confidence.

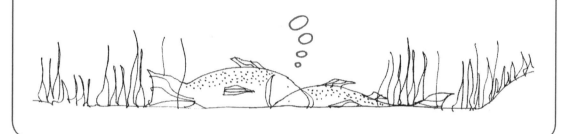

An Understanding

The female Chinook had taken quite a bruising in the fall upon the rock shelf that jutted out just beneath the surface concealed by the foam of the falls. She was sufficiently weakened that she couldn't make another attempt at the falls that stood in the way up the natal river anytime soon. In this case it was just as well, the river was still subsiding from the high flow after the rainfall and would become increasingly passable for the salmon a month later.

1981
I am forty seven years old

Author's Note: It's time for another brief aside with you, dear reader. I hesitate to settle another metaphor upon your reading or listening "shoulders," but I suspect that it is either needed, or will be...as we proceed over the next thirty three years together.

As you know by now, I am a sailor with over 30,000 miles under my keel. I prefer to sail by wind power alone. Quite often the wind would blow directly from the direction in which I wanted to travel. Sailors call this wind "on the nose." By pulling every sail in tight and turning the bow some thirty five degrees away from the wind it is possible to make progress along what is called a rhumb line (This is a pencil track that goes directly from point A to point B. By "tacking" back and forth across the line in thirty five to forty degree zigzags.)

To the casual observer it often looks odd, since the yacht may appear to be heading directly for rocks if the passage being made is up a narrow estuary with the wind "on the nose!" The only way to avoid this sometimes tiresome and uncomfortable (but to some, exhilarating) experience is to lower the headsails, center the mainsail (or even drop it), turn on the engine and follow the rhumb line on its direct path to your destination.

What was now clear to me was that we were in such a situation "spiritually". We were aware that there was now a destination or purpose for our lives but that there was a stiff wind of resistance blowing on our nose.

We could either drop our sails and motor by using proven worldly methods, or continue to tack back and forth "as the Lord might lead."

It seemed to us that these apparent "on course" angles of sail were allowing us some depth of understanding that we might have otherwise missed if we had simply ploughed ahead under our own steam.

This understanding has grown over the years as the back and forth progression unfolded. One thing you will see is that we never, ever, let go of the *rhumb line vision* we had received in Kona, Hawaii.

Now, let's get on with our often "odd" journey...upstream, on purpose, with the wind on our nose!

When we were first "invited" to transfer to Tacoma in Washington State we drove up to get an idea of what might be in store for us.

It was a very wet and windy day in which the paper mill odor was being directed into the city. It is called the "Tacoma Aroma" by its inhabitants (it has lessened over the years).

As we drove up dark gray rain-swept odorous streets we passed a vast red brick church on our left. Its roadside board announced that it was the First Presbyterian Church of Tacoma, Dr. Albert Lindsey, Pastor. At one time in our short Christian journey we had heard Presbyterians refer to themselves as "God's frozen chosen."

I laughingly spoke it out, "boy, bet there are a bunch of frozen chosen in there."

Suddenly on that windy, rain slicked street I completely lost control of our car and we wound up sideways across the pedestrian pavement.

"What on earth are you doing?" Treena shouted, clutching at the dashboard.

"I just...I just lost it." I was bewildered at the suddenness of the movement.

I was shaking as we got back on the road. I parked. We prayed.

It was the sternest-ever encounter I've had or would have (so far) with God who I now firmly believed could speak directly to our hearts, if not to our ears.

"How dare you speak such disapproving words about any part of My Body...you will attend that church and see the error of your ways."

That was it. Treena agreed that it was a direct command to change course. Acting upon that one rebuke, we needed no further prompting to move to Tacoma. We attended that church for the next seven years, enough time for most of our 74 trillion cells to complete one cycle and for our attitude to change!

At some time in our first year, back in Easton, Maryland, we had received another unusual message.

"You will attempt to understand the various reasons why My Body calls itself by so many names. You will study their individual doctrines and dogmas and for a brief time you may think you understand but you will never retain that understanding."

For a season we thought we understood about John Calvin and his early thoughts that guided the Reformed Church Movement. The teachings appeared to be biblical in their very nature and only controversial in areas where no absolute answers seemed possible. In time, all the garnish dropped away, as had been promised and we entered into the vein of gold that becomes evident (when looked for) in every denomination.

That vein was made up of some very ordinary people in very ordinary jobs and pastimes who loved God and each other in a truly extraordinary way that was neither legalistic or self-righteous...rather, their behavior was, for us, a flash of silver as they applied their personal faith to the day-by-day pressures of living...with the wind on their nose!

Dr. Albert Lindsey (the Senior Minister) was a great bible scholar and one who had been brought up in the faith to allow few if any "personal relationships" among his current congregation. To do so would have run the risk of becoming *partial.*

I asked Dr. Lindsey if I might introduce my ideas on the Double Benefit and how they might somehow compassionately connect members of the congregation to those in great need through the Missions Committee.

He took me to a small southern-facing but somewhat shaded garden on the Church grounds and walked me around its narrow red brick path.

"Now," he spoke carefully yet sternly.

"Can you find a space for another plant to grow?" He gestured to the tightly packed Evergreen shrubs where there appeared to be no colorful relief. It was, to say the least, *dense.* "No Pastor, I cannot," I replied.

"Precisely." With that he left me amongst the inedible but tidy garden.

Dr. Lindsey was to retire directly to heaven shortly after our encounter, and the new interim minister was rather more accepting of the "colorful" opportunity that was being proposed.

Treena and I were given the great privilege of conducting a thirteen-week Sunday school class that we called "The Creative Lifestyle Group." Our primary goal was to take a full three months to *count the cost of commitment.*

We took, as our Biblical text, Luke 14:28–29

"Suppose one of you wants to build a tower. Won't you first sit down and estimate the cost to see if you have enough money to complete it? For if you lay the foundation and are not able to finish it, everyone who sees it will ridicule you saying...this person began to build and was not able to finish...vs35...whoever has ears to hear, let them hear!"

Our opening rationale, with about twenty eight class members, five of whom were elders, was that we should avoid beginning anything that we were not able to finish.

I took the word I had heard in my own life and suggested that we all accept it as our attitude. *"Do a small thing and do it well until it's done"*

We all agreed that we would attend, listen, question and pray and when we thought we were ready we would make a very personal, very private, commitment.

And they exceeded our expectations: They gave themselves first of all to the Lord, and then by the will of God also to us. 2 Corinthians 8:5

Treena first taught about the inner hindrances that often prevented outward actions, and I spoke about lifestyle choices in which we might choose to spend less time and resources in ways that might do us harm.

The idea was that we might all *count the cost* of making a creative lifestyle change BEFORE WE ATTEMPTED TO DO SO. In this way we hoped to avoid what I had begun to call "Fickle Funding" in which we were often giving to causes that offered the greatest promise of godly performance, which in some sense began to look like a competitive marketplace in which opportunities to give had the high gloss and manipulation of Madison Avenue.

Such short-term funding sometimes wound up with incomplete *towers* that resulted in ridicule.

We met in the Gold Room in the church annex, an area often used for small memorial services, so it was with great joy that, in such sober surroundings, we completed the series with every member having made their own private commitment.

One of the class volunteered to be the receiver and recorder of the money released by lifestyle choices so that this was handled correctly by the church and appropriate tax receipts given.

None of us, apart from this silent one, had the slightest clue what anyone else was giving. Our goal was to do something between us that might somehow help someone out of their sense of *hopelessness*.

Author's Note: It would be very time consuming to provide here all the teaching that was covered. If you would want to know of the content, please let us know. www. grahamkerr.com.

The class, having committed *first to the Lord*, needed to know what was *the will of God*. We agreed to pray for discernment and received the location from *National Geographic Magazine* who in 1984 had an extended piece on the orphans of Brazil.

We were all touched, not by *a mission sales pitch*, but by the plight of over two million children living on the streets in this emerging nation, where the promise was bright for some of the advantaged and hopeless for others –like the least of these little ones. Using the money already collected, we sent two young YWAM men to spy out the land. They reported back about an orphanage in Belo Horizonte, just north of Rio de Janeiro in northeast Brazil.

It took several weeks to count the cost, but having done so in the light of our understanding, we applied to the Missions Committee for their approval and in due time (and in good orderly Presbyterian style) we commissioned the two Operation L.O.R.D. graduates as our missionaries to Brazil.

Thus began a work with all the zigzags of a sailboat with the wind on-the-nose that was continuously funded, in part, by the Creative Lifestyle Group members (including Treena and myself) for over twenty years.

It was during this time of outreach to the disadvantaged by the advantaged that I was helped to further understand the *sequence of the spirit*.

I awakened early one morning with a distinct, almost audible, phrase...

"It is not a system it is a sequence."

By this I came to know that all my elaborate, almost obsessive-compulsive "listings" of actions needed could be swept up in only three words.

I was helped to see this by Tim Kleefeld, my administrative right hand man, who we came to love as though he was a part of our own family.

"You need to get your vision down to three words." He suggested, which as it happened was the way many sermons were constructed at First Presbyterian Church of Tacoma!

After much trial, error and team prayer, we arrived at three words.

Compassion – Commitment – Consistency, which for pretty obvious reasons we chose to call...

C³

It really was a sequence and no longer a system. We had been led to Brazil by *compassion* for the orphans who were hopeless. We had *committed* to give out of our lifestyle changes for at least three years, and we had made that *commitment "first to the Lord and to Brazil as the specific will of God."* That only left us with one other action...

To keep on turning up! (Consistent!)

Our goal, in the beginning, was to do *"a small thing and do it well until it was done."* This we know we accomplished because orphans were provided with hope.

We didn't build anything that lasted as an edifice. We planted seeds in small gardens in places of extreme poverty and within these gardens we found the good soil of good little hearts that needed to know they were loved. So often, especially in the modern fundraising business, there are declarations of intent that have quite large goals and confident assessments of success. When they fail...it is a shame!

We never had any sense of the need for great achievement. All we needed to know was that somewhere, somehow our very personal changes were of benefit to someone.

Jesus said...

"Truly I tell you, whatever you did for one of the least of these brothers and sisters of mine, you did for me." Matthew 25:40

Surely in the grand scheme of things this is enough?

Please join us in the Reflective Readers Club
www.grahamkerr.com/rrc

Rite of Passage Fifty-Six: "Replication?"

I felt full and had been for some time. It was the sense of being replete following a large and varied meal of smaller ones than me, those that I had always regarded as food.

Both my hen and I are considerably larger than the very small ones like us that we meet going downstream in the opposite direction.

In the big waters these little ones would have made an interesting snack but now I just didn't have room for them.

What overwhelms me now is the certainty that, if I can reach my birthplace, I might somehow contribute to more like me and my hen. We held within us the future of fish-kind!

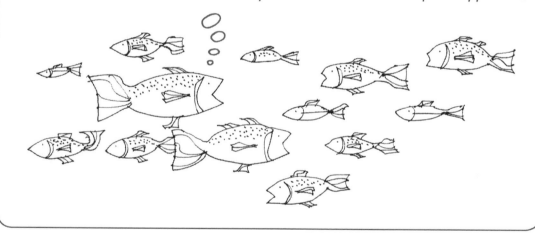

An Understanding

In our male Chinook there was a multiplication of the milt, which would fertilize the hen's eggs.

In both fish, the space taken up by eggs and milt pressed back upon the stomach and resulted in a type of human bariatric surgery outcome in which the stomach size is markedly reduced. Along with their stomach reduction has come the replacement of body functions from predominantly that of feeding and avoiding death to that of but one dominant driver —reproduction that will actually result in death. Their future is strictly that of their progeny thereafter.

Our Chinook are now six years old and a year older than most of their Chinook cohorts and much larger as a result.

They are aware of this "in-filling" and somehow understand that together they represent the resilience of their species.

1984
I am now fifty years old

Science has a wonderful way of dismissing early experiments by calling them *anecdotal.*

"Anecdotes are useless precisely because they may point to idiosyncratic responses."

The word *idiosyncratic* used in this quote means individualistic, peculiar or unique.

This was certainly the case with the *compassionate connection* that had taken place between our advantaged Creative Lifestyle Group and the disadvantaged orphans in Brazil. It was individualistic, peculiar and unique. As such, it could also be called perhaps, *miraculous*?

We had seen twenty eight adults living in the midst of the world's most abundant economy, deliberately (having carefully weighed the outcome) lessening their consumption in order to share the difference with orphaned children they might never meet who lived in an extremely poor location several thousand miles to their south.

Furthermore, they had undertaken to do this *consistently* for at least three years and to continue until there might be evidence that the specific *small thing* had been done *well.*

Youth With A Mission (YWAM), with whom Treena and I had now served six years, is never short of big goals. It is typically awash with the youthful enthusiasm that knows no real bounds. Even at fifty years old I was not immune to their contagious thinking. Here was I, in the midst of an *anecdotal* happening that needed to be replicated in order to be proven as...possible.

I sat down in our small home in west Tacoma and imagined what would happen if advantaged people converted habits that somehow hindered them into resources that would be used to heal those in desperate circumstances. It was the year 1984, two years before Bill Gates met his future wife Melinda and ten years before the couple launched their own philanthropic organization that would focus a great deal of attention upon the *least of the little ones.* I had, of course, not the slightest idea what they would go on to do with their "double benefit" giving. All I could do was to measure what a very ordinary family might achieve and then do the math and multiply its effect worldwide to achieve what has now been done, in part, by Bill and Melinda.

It was staggering in its promise; the world could be a better place...if only...?

I took my extrapolation math to Davis and Annette Weyerhaeuser who had themselves blazed a trail for people like the Gates to follow.

Davis agreed that the basic vision and even its goals were logical. "The only obstacle," he observed, looking up from my global spreadsheet, "is the local church."

"But," I countered, "see what has been done even here in your own home town."

"Oh, I see it and applaud you and them for it," he responded carefully.

"But, can it be replicated?"

I thought that it could and I argued strenuously with them for the opportunity to prove it. The Weyerhaeuser Foundation provided several small grants that helped us develop what we called the "Quality of Life Display Center," in downtown Tacoma, a few hundred yards south of the First Presbyterian Church.

We set to work to build the data and the teaching aids as well as a center where visitors could come to see how such a movement was both possible and practical. Its layout followed my earlier New Zealand Food and Wine Display Center in Wellington, New Zealand.

It was in these glorious visionary days that I met the then young filmmaker Michael Lineau, and with him and his future wife Shari, we made a series of videos that we called The Double Benefit that addressed, in an entertaining manner, the changes that we could make in our daily lifestyle choices that would help us to achieve better overall health.

A major hospital chain wanted to use these lifestyle prompts to assist their postoperative patients in their rehab programs and to help the patient's family to better appreciate the changes that needed to be made in order to reduce the possibility of a relapse.

The immediate usefulness of this service was derailed by the Mother Superior of the Catholic-based hospitals when she decided to elope with the Bishop; charmingly romantic but regrettably not exactly politically correct.

The Mother Superior CEO had been our most enthusiastic supporter so, in the house-cleaning that ensued, we found ourselves swept up with others and set out for collection.

It had taken a full year to research, script, produce and film. Treena both produced and appeared, as she had done in the Galloping Gourmet.

It was enormous fun and the production values were way ahead of their time.

In the early 1980s, when we were in our formative stage, the interest rate charged by some banks on a thirty year mortgage was 18.45 percent. This kind of inflation was having a strong ripple effect through the entire nation and that included the church. It was especially hard on those new "vibrant" congregations that had invested heavily, taking out large loans for new buildings or renovations. These churches were amongst those with whom we had relationships over the years and who had previously heard about our "Double Benefit" message. The result was pretty obvious. Their cost of doing ministry had risen along with the interest rates and many very well meaning folks were wondering how to make ends meet and pay their own bills; let alone make changes to meet the needs of those they might never meet.

Our dear friends Davis and Annette were proven correct. Our obstacle was the local church, and their obstacle was the economy. We suffered from too large a vision and too small a bank account, not at all an unusual experience at any time but especially so in those troublesome days.

We were greatly blessed by those who had been our early supporters, who hung in with us but became fewer and farther between. In the end I received a simple torn off sheet from a spiral bound pocket-sized notebook.

It read:

We wish to advise you that we will no longer be supporting your QOL Center.
Sincerely,
The Missions Committee

That was it plain and simple, and so that one pledge of $25 a month became our final revelation that God had, in very real terms, closed the financial door.

Our very bright, very committed team met together to hear the news and to pray about what might come next. We eventually understood that finances really mean very little in knowing the will of God. It is a standard way of measuring the world but it means much less in God's Kingdom since it is simply a way of watching things *pass away*. The Kingdom was to ponder what was *to come* and why.

Each team member eventually made plans to depart and go where they felt God was leading them. There were those who were bewildered for a season, but in time all of us came to understand the words.

"And we know that in all things God works for the good of those who love him, who have been called according to his purpose". Romans 8:28

It was at this precise moment in August 1987 that Treena had a stroke; she was just 53 years old.

I got the call as I was packing up my QOL Center desk.

"Your wife is in the emergency room at St. Joseph's Hospital. She's had a stroke."

I drove to the hospital thumping the wheel and crying out..."why, why, why!"

But of course I didn't have to ask, the reason was obvious. It went all the way back to 1979 in Palm Springs and my classic *compromise* in the face of her rebellion over my very legalistic menu options for the family.

I had offered to cook two menus, one for the family, the other for myself and whoever wanted to join in my quest for better health! Treena had opted for her continued enjoyment of such foods as bacon, cheese, eggs and meat, and a range of refined starches. Eight years had gone by and now here was the result! I was to learn that strict rules will often cause *rebellion*, and that can result in a *compromise* that may well end with the very opposite of the original intention.

Two neurosurgeons were convinced that a stroke had taken place and offered as proof a series of wildly differing ultrasound readings of her carotid arteries. They had begun in the high eighty percent and fallen to an acceptable twenty percent.

Treena, of course, was able to explain it all away as another *miracle* and since she had no medical insurance we were released that day and admonished to…

"Take it easy and try a baby aspirin."

I should explain our position with regard to health insurance.

Back in our early charismatic days with the Happy Hunters and our own Tuesday night gatherings we had seen many "happenings" that we could only describe as unusual enough to merit the classification of miracle. There were no scientific follow-ups; we were simply too delighted to even consider a plausible alternative. As a direct result, coupled with our severely depleted financial situation, we chose to "go-it-alone" and rely upon faith to take the place of insurance. Treena's "cerebral brush" was simply another confirmation that we were apparently still on the right track.

For several years we had been able to husband our advance for our big blue book and had adopted a very simple lifestyle. We had received no personal financial support during our nine-year missionary season; all the funds I raised went directly to the ministry itself. We were now left with our small house and a large mortgage. We also had a very small mission's outreach in Brazil and an enduring vision for the Double Benefit.

How exactly were we to respond?

We were back at the junction of another river in our journey upstream.

We understood our purpose; but which way should we go?

In 1987 YWAM decided to offer its worldwide leadership a special school called the LTS (Leadership Training School) in Kailua, Kona, Hawaii, under the leadership of Earl Pitts, a former IBM executive, who insisted that business and religion could coexist within certain reasonable guidelines.

We joined that school in September 1987 to see what we could learn from such an important source. It was during this three month intensive instruction that I shared with Joy Dawson, who was one of our teachers, my earlier life changing moment under her 1978 class on prayer.

You said, "If you are stretched thin, it could be that you are shallow."

"I never said that." Joy was as certain as always.

"You did, I still have my notebook," I replied with equal certainty, well...almost equal.

We took my notes, found the class date and located the audiotape.

She never said it; she had touched on being too busy to hear but she never said what I had written down! Did this confirm that God does, in fact, speak to us even in the midst of a teaching, sermon or even primetime television news?

Treena later came up with some scientific research that suggested that we can comprehend up to four hundred words per minute, yet usually only speak at about one hundred twenty five words.

This left a gap of two hundred seventy five words —a gap during which we might think about what was being said or even, perhaps, for God to speak?

It was then at the crossroads of all this worldly and spiritual activity that Treena suffered a heart attack...

Please join us in the Reflective Readers Club
www.grahamkerr.com/rrc

Rite of Passage Fifty-Seven: "Up, Up and Away"

At last the quiet depths of the pool had provided the needed healing. We had been some distance downstream at the bottom of a great eddy current. Ready now, we again approached the turbulence of water and there it was, almost the same as we had left it... the torrents of white water that we had failed to leap.

I say "almost" because it did seem less forceful, especially at one point as I once again peeked above the surface to better view this great wall of water. Many more like us were gathered in great numbers in the pool with dozens hurling their bodies upward, most to fall back.

At our last attempt I could now see why I had let my hen go first. Had I not done so and she had still fallen, I would not have been there during her healing. So once again I held back as she went through her pre-leap routine even more carefully than she had the previous time. Once, twice, three times she peaked upwards at the falls moving slightly back and forth with each peak.

Suddenly she burst through the frothing waters and its rush with such power and purpose that she disappeared in a flash of silver!

She's done it! Gone!

There is only me. I found her last point of takeoff and held the image of her leap in my mind. I could smell the old scent once again, so much stronger. Now it's my turn. I sped to the brightness and the white fury above. I broke clear; in front and close were the falling waters. I was alone in the air with rushing waters all around me —higher, and higher.

At the apex of the leap I bent my body sideways and dug my tail into the rush of water trying to drive me back. In that hanging instant with that great force trying to push me backward, I pushed hard, my tail working as it never had before, the feeling of my great strength and vigor pouring through me.

I held my own against the force of the streaming water up the wall's vertical lip, gained on it — and suddenly it lessened and I drove ahead with unexpected ease through the diminishing speed of the shallows until it began to deepen.

I caught that flash again —just ahead. It was my hen.

We had done it...together we had done it! We were back in our stream and the white water was behind us.

An Understanding

Willamette Falls is one of several famed waterfalls of the Columbia basin that salmon historically overcame in their former great abundance. It is also the site of one of the earliest Euro-American settlements in the Old West. Oregon City was established by the Hudson Bay Company in 1829 and by 1844 was considered the first city west of the Rocky Mountains.

Willamette Falls is shown in the introduction to this book...here it is again!

In the picture we can see two Chinook salmon beginning their attempt to climb the falls.

Their ability to do so depends upon the season which itself provides just the right amount of water flowing downriver.

Too much rain or snowmelt, and the current is far too strong going over the falls for salmon to overcome. Too little flow of water, and there isn't enough surface water over the rocks to provide passage and/or the height of the falls can no longer be overcome as the surface level of the pool below drops. The fish ladder, first carved out of the falls by settlers in the 1880s, would have made passage easier if the blockage had not occurred in the case of our story.

Each year there may be a three to four week "opening" when the waters are just right — generally in May or early June. Our Chinook, by taking off downstream, had returned still a little too early, but the injury sustained by the hen resulted in a healing at exactly the right time for our two salmon to overcome the obstacle of the falls just as their ancestors had 150 years ago.

For everything there is a season!

1987
I am fifty three years old

It had begun with a deep back pain just below her shoulder blades. At first we put it down to our sleeping accommodations in which we had opted for a loft that was served by a vertical ladder of a dozen or so rungs.

The pain persisted and migrated to the chest. I insisted that we go immediately to our local hospital. An EKG was done and an IV started. The pain grew more severe. The doctor drew me aside into the corridor.

"She is having a heart attack; the EKG is all over the place..." He looked at me seriously. "She may not make it," he added as he took a firm grip of my arm.

"We need to get her airlifted to Honolulu where they can more accurately assess and respond."

By this time I was surrounded by our fellow leaders who prayed for Treena and me.

Treena was sedated and had the oxygen mask and the IV in place. A portable EKG was added and we were off to the airport in the same ambulance.

The airlift used a fully equipped small two-engine plane that bumped its way into Honolulu International Airport in pretty good time.

I sat by her side and held her hand, which from time to time closed gently upon mine as if to reassure me that all was well. So like her. During that brief flight we both made a major lifestyle decision. Mine was to try to understand how I could delight her, but do her less harm. It was everything that I had taught others but that I had agreed not to do with her!

There *had* to be a way to nourish and delight and I would find it. It would now be my #1 job!

I found out much later that Treena was also thinking that she needed to do what I was teaching others to do and not be put at such apparent risk. We had both decided within that thirty minute flight to engage in a creative change that might somehow repair the damage already done and to use every means to allow the body to become more naturally resilient.

The rest of that day was a blur of white-coated antiseptic activity. An angiogram was performed and our Japanese cardiologist (doctor "got-your-car-keys"; his way of helping us to pronounce his name) showed me, and our son Andy who had joined us in the hospital, the x-ray film that had been taken. He indicated where an area on the heart, the size of a silver dollar, had "deadened" and several points at which arteries were narrowed.

"Treena is a quadruple heart bypass candidate," he explained.

"Before we undertake such an action, there is a protocol to follow."

He went on to explain that since there was no immediate need to operate, there was time to see what could be done by using lifestyle changes alone.

"Let's give it three months and see what progress you can make without surgery or medication." He made suggestions and then handed me several folders, which described the actions we could take.

They mostly described what *not* to eat using lists of practically everything that Treena loved to eat. It looked almost like my Palm Springs legalistic diet, the one that had caused her earlier rebellion! There were other more positive ideas, all using much more plant food than we had ever consumed. There was also an exercise plan that would use up almost one hour in our already overcrowded day.

Treena remained in the hospital for two days and our bill was $14,000 including the air ambulance. We had no insurance and very little savings. We left with the bill and Treena's cholesterol test. Her total cholesterol was 365, one point for each day of the year, a number to remember!

Our great friends and supporters, Annette and Davis Weyerhaeuser, had heard about Treena's heart attack and sent her a get well card with a brief P.S. that read...

"You take care of what you can of the hospital costs and let us take care of the rest."

We were totally amazed at their loving generosity and our faith level went through the roof with gratitude. When we eventually came back to earth we immediately began investing in health insurance, which a high-risk pool in Washington State made possible. In retrospect, we were never *instructed* to go it alone. I suspect it was one of several times in which I presumed upon God and that He would be unconditionally on my side in all things, if I lived by faith *alone*!

We returned to a new accommodation that had no ladders to climb and began to continue with the LTS classes coupled with a completely new lifestyle.

I was considerably shaken by Treena's experience, especially since both her parents had died young from heart disease. We had an apparent reprieve and I wanted to make the most of it as soon as possible.

I had begun my career with food in my father's hotel where fine dining was the focus. My hotel school reinforced that idea with a decided French twist. I had gone on and on looking for, and consuming, elegant rich dishes in our time as the Galloping Gourmet. It was in 1971 with the traffic accident and the sudden understanding that came hand in hand with the seasickness, that I had searched for an alternative style that would do less harm.

In doing so I managed to regard the fine food of my past as somehow *indulgent* and potentially risky. My early answer was to remove everything that looked like it might do harm. As an example, let me show you how I chose to deal with chocolate.

I *loved* chocolate, especially Cadbury's Fruit and Nut. Such sweetness, such texture, such pure pleasure! When the wrapper began to show the nutritional facts, the calories and fats contained in my favorite sized bar became all too apparent a risk! We had, just prior to my investigation, been given a large double-decker box of Belgium chocolates. I began to lift the edge of the top layer carefully and consume the lower layer and thus put off Treena's criticism that I was an addict. Of course the day came when the last two of the top layer were shared between us and the empty tray was removed to reveal...from memory there were only four left.

In an effort to defend myself I purchased a long bar of Kit Kat, the kind that is sold in movie theaters. I broke it up into fingers and put it in a plastic bag and laid it on an upper shelf in the freezer. I had written on the bag the initials R.M. and the number #2; R.M. stood for what I thought might be "reasonable and moderate" for me to consume in one day.

In two days the frozen fingers had gone and I had proven to *myself*, let alone Treena, that I was an addict. I knew what was reasonable but I couldn't control myself; so I lacked self-control to the extent that I just "couldn't help myself."

I needed no further understanding. I simply cut out chocolate in the same way that I had stopped smoking...*completely*! It was 1987 and not one piece of chocolate of any kind passed my lips until 2000. I'll tell you what happened when we reach that point in the story.

Chocolate was only one small element in my broad sweeping earlier legalism; butter, cream, bacon, corn-fed fattened meats, all luncheon meats and sausage...need I really go on?

Not only did I not consume these foods but I also began to think of them as *evil* or at least bad. From there it was fairly easy to call the people that served them at least *irresponsible* and harmful to the common good! This was my state of mind when I sat down to try to find a lifestyle that might, this time, actually work for Treena.

It was a huge help to have her *willing* to be part of the experiment. She described her willingness as her way of, "letting you know that I love you...for caring for me."

My search began with an acronym that I posted on our refrigerator door. It spelled out...

T.A.C.T.
TASTE, AROMA, COLOR, TEXTURE

I knew from almost thirty years of hands-on experience that these four words best explained what we *loved* about the food we ate.

I asked Treena to sit quietly and list every single ingredient that she really *loved* that could be placed under each of these words. It didn't really matter if the food item was repeated across all four, and it certainly didn't matter if she judged them as "too rich, too sweet, or too salty." Everything was to be listed as *loved*.

When the four hundred food entries had been made, I asked her to make up another list of the foods she really didn't like. I now held in my hand her *preferences*, what she *loved*, and what she preferred never to eat.

This was how I began to *reinvent the wheel* of her daily food choices.

It was actually pretty simple. I halved the amount of each risky food, those with saturated fat, refined carbohydrates such as sugar, sodas, pastry and high sodium. I didn't eliminate *anything*, just cut it in half. The 8-ounce steak became 4-ounce, the dozen (or more) French fries became 6 only, the 1/8th slice of pie became 1/16th, and ice cream went from 1 cup to 1/2 cup.

I made up the vacated plate space with plant foods that she *loved*, a broiled beefsteak tomato with the steak, French fries made with sweet potatoes and nutmeg-seasoned steamed kale, fresh fruits and low fat vanilla yogurt with the ice cream and pie. My very first assembly of her preferences into one complete meal was greeted with profound suspicion.

"I can't eat THAT," she exclaimed in horror.

"Oh yes you can," I assured her.

And so we began to select for ourselves a whole new way of living and eating, one that was far better suited to our well-being *and* our enjoyment. Right in the midst of all this change came the letter that was once again to change our course heading but not our intent.

Please join us in the Reflective Readers Club
www.grahamkerr.com/rrc

Rite of Passage Fifty-Eight: "The Penultimate Plan"

Time for a breath! What an incredible experience that was. We were both over the white wall of water and had sped to the far side, near the bank full of green things that offered shade.

Was this to be our last great effort? I certainly hoped so because it had taken all the strength I had to make that leap and I was amazed that my hen had also managed it so well.

We lay alongside each other, fins just touching in a deep pool thinking about our eventual destination and sensing now more powerfully than ever...the scent of our birthplace.

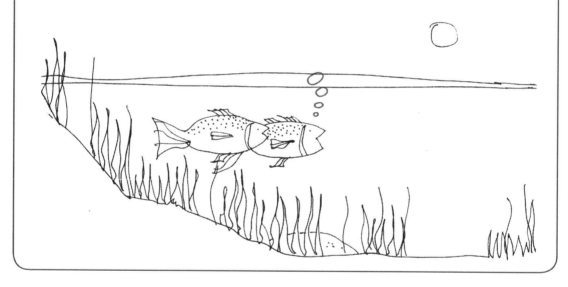

An Understanding

Their great leaps had carried them over the falls and directly upstream and over to the banks where the current lessens and often provides a back eddy with a deepened pool worn out of the tree-fringed banks.

Here they rest after the great obstacle before continuing to move closer to their ultimate destination, the redds in which they had received life upstream in the McKenzie River.

1988/1990
I am fifty four to fifty six years old

In the midst of rehab following Treena's heart attack and while still in the Leadership Training School (LTS) in the University of the Nations at Kailua, Kona in Hawaii, we received a letter that would, once again, offer a change of direction.

Just prior to its arrival we were being taught, under Earl Pitts' direction, that there were several areas of human endeavor that were responsible for "molding the minds" of our generation. Amongst these "mind molders" were family, business, religion, arts and entertainment, media, education and government. This idea, also called the Seven Mountains, was an understanding that came separately to Loren Cunningham, Bill Bright, the founder of Campus Crusade and Francis Schaeffer, who had been touching on much the same message for several years.

Loren and Bill Bright met in Colorado in 1975 to discuss their respective understanding and their combined message began to find a life of its own.

At the time that we were to hear it in Hawaii, it was already twelve years old and had gained strength. Basically, it was a modified tent-making concept taken from the Apostle Paul's willingness to make tents in order to support himself as a missionary/apostle to the early church.

It also echoed a paragraph from the first of Paul's letters to the earlier church, in this case to the new believers in a small fishing village in the far north of the Aegean Sea that is now called Thessaloniki.

"...make it your ambition to lead a quiet life: You should mind your own business and work with your hands, just as we told you, so that your daily life may win the respect of outsiders and so that you will not be dependent on anybody." 1 Thessalonians 4:11–12

This was *exactly* how I had interpreted the teaching that I was hearing from our former IBM executive who had considerable personal experience in the business field. What I loved about the idea was two-fold; first of all was the "winning of respect of outsiders" who, in another translation, are referred to as "those who do not believe as you believe."

This suggested to me that there may be a level of trust built upon a *measured* performance of an easily seen task that might lead to a willingness to communicate that went beyond the more *set apart* environment of a church service or Sunday school class.

The second and profoundly interesting point was the final nine words...

"...so that you will not be dependent on anybody."

This, as you now know, was a gray area for us since our *work* with Operation LORD/ The Q.O.L Center and the Double Benefit would have been impossible without outside support. Also, there was our very recent experience with the support we had received in paying Treena's hospital bills!

Of course, any time anyone in full time service (as we were) received a single dollar from a donor, there was an immediate prayer of gratitude... "first to the Lord, and then to the donor."

What the Seven Mountains/Mind Molders were suggesting was that there were other perfectly valid and necessary occupations within which the good news of the coming Kingdom of God could become a welcome benefit to all concerned. It would also mean that one could be financially rewarded while with "gentleness and respect" we continued to make our life's purpose known. It was with this happy engagement with scriptural truth that we received a letter, which seemed, as a result, to be extraordinary timing!

The letter came from a film company in New Zealand that had done some good work over many years. What they wanted Treena and I to consider was to come to New Zealand early in January of 1988 and make a series of video episodes to be sold to the Japanese VCR market as a means of encouraging their people to take the plunge and visit New Zealand for both its spectacular scenery and "wonderful fresh food."

What an invitation, especially at a time when we had closed down and disbanded our "full time service" in Tacoma, Washington and were now in a holding pattern following Treena's stroke and heart attack. We were wondering what was to come next!

Now here was something we could do and do well. We would also be paid and it would mean spending the rest of the winter in New Zealand's summer; a lovely thought!

We had always looked back to our time in New Zealand with fondness, both for her people and as a truly wonderful place to live in relative peace and security. We immediately took the letter to Loren Cunningham. He, in turn, shared it with the other leaders; all of whom thought it fitted brilliantly with the Seven Mountains/Mind Molders concept and were unanimous in their approval to "go ahead."

I shared the opportunity with one of my old associates with whom I had some contact, Wilbur Friefeld, who had remained my literary agent with nothing at all to do since 1978. Wilbur leapt at the idea and suggested it be shot in Beta Cam (the highest quality tape system in use in 1987) so that we could use the footage on television as well as VCR tape. I forwarded this suggestion to Bruce Reynolds in New Zealand and we entered into a remarkable season of our lives, one in which the past success of the "Galloping Gourmet" predisposed a great many people to believe that lightening can, indeed, strike twice!

Neither Treena nor I were in full agreement with the upgrade suggested by Wilbur. The whole idea of a return to television was an anathema to us, something to be almost hated because of its past ability to utterly rule our lives to the exclusion of our children and close friends.

On the other hand, there were these Seven Mountains/Mind Molders and the vision we had had back in 1978 that had become "The Double Benefit." Surely, we reasoned, we now know what can be done to "convert habits that harm into resources that heal!" We had made a useful and entertaining video series on the subject and now stood on the threshold of reaching way *beyond* ourselves into the mind-molding media of the day.

Was this an open door, one where we had proven gifts complete with understanding and even possibly a divinely inspired visionary purpose?

To say that we prayed hard would be a classic understatement. Even so, we had *no clear word* to encourage us beyond the enthusiastic agreement of our more experienced servant leaders who truthfully knew almost nothing about the modern television media. Bruce Reynolds suggested a modest fee for the series, one in which we would receive $400 for each episode with all our expenses paid. In return we would produce, write, develop, and perform. This would provide us with $5,200 for about six weeks of work.

If there had been a worldly temptation to return to television it was certainly not a financial one. Perhaps it was a pleasant vacation in a sun-drenched beautiful land or even the opportunity to be a blessing to a land that had given us our first break with success?

In the end it was probably a combination of all these coupled with the very strong encouragement of everyone who had gathered about the proposed project. I was overwhelmed by other people's confidence that I could, once again, succeed. I agreed to do the thirteen episodes *only*.

We called the show "Simply Marvelous" and designed it to begin with Treena on a search for a key ingredient in the recipe, a local food or seafood that she would harvest or catch on location from the top of the North Island to the bottom of the South Island, a total of 1,000 miles. I would then prepare two meals on location for the farmers or fisherman in their own

homes, using their produce. One meal would be for their family, the other for their friends. In this way we blended day-to-day food with that better suited for hospitality.

In both cases, the recipes were created to nourish delight and do less harm. It was the core purpose of the "Double Benefit" at work in the arts and entertainment and media *mountains*.

All our hosts were Christians and each had a simple story to tell about a *measureable* way in which their personal faith had been respected by those who "did not believe as they believed." These brief vignettes were added at the conclusion of each show without any attention being brought to their Christian belief itself.

We completed the kitchen demonstrations in a converted warehouse that had no air conditioning. The set was often at or above 100 degrees. We used ice cold face cloths between frequent breaks.

Wilbur took the series to New York as a pilot and came back with a predictable response.

"They won't look at anything less than 39 episodes and would prefer 195!"

This was precisely what we had feared, and while we were quite firm in saying "no," the fact was that we had been paid $5,000 by people we really loved who were about to lose thousands more if we didn't at least go the other mile.

Brideshead Revisited Estate

Could this be called "dependent upon...?"

We agreed and in something of a rush we set up a tour of the British Isles to make up the remaining twenty nine! The budget climbed to over $1 million (New Zealand). We filmed at the "Brideshead Revisited" estate as well as castles and cottages, another great experience was had with our splendid crew and hosts.

The funding had come from a Christian publishing house in New Zealand who had already reasoned that my performance was worthy of investment; once again looking over my shoulder at my past, rather than at my quite different present?

Each program extolled the "virtue" of restraint and reasonable moderation in all things. The Galloping Gourmet had celebrated the pure joy of excess. There was no question or doubt which was the more entertaining!

Wilbur went off once again in search of a sponsor and came back empty-handed. The million dollars began to earn interest as six months of work lay waiting for an audience. When cash flow appears to be at risk, everything begins to change quite rapidly.

Since the idea to upgrade to Beta Cam had come from our side, it was entirely reasonable that we were to become, to some extent, responsible for the apparent failure. It really didn't matter that we had been reluctant or that our share in the costs were miniscule.

Lightening hadn't struck twice. That's all that mattered.

As the film company contemplated a bankruptcy, an offer was made to take over the company and the debt. Our contract was part of the deal and we were passed on as *goods and chattel* in the process to a man who had several years earlier wanted to put us back on television. We had at that time politely said no but now we had become *dependent*...or at least obligated to help to find a solution for our well-intentioned "mind molding" media adventure.

Our life became a series of dominoes, one falling onto another. The driving force of that sequence was cash flow. The expectation was that "the next program will bail out the last." Each time, a new set of players would arrive and cluster about my past persona in search of profit. We agreed to one series after another in the hope that such a profit would eventually transpire and that we would be *free* from obligation or, as was now the case, *dependency.*

Dominoes have two sides; one with

With John Bowen university president of Johnson & Wales University. And more recently Chancellor of the University

numbers and one is blank. While everyone else was preoccupied with the side that added up, we were still pursuing the idea of "habits that harm can become resources that heal." We had no team or ministry to support. We simply tried to reinvent the wheel with content that might somehow help someone to make wiser choices with their daily food and, as a result, find wellness as Treena and I and our family had found in our private lives.

During the period of 1987 to 2004 we made almost one thousand separate shows and episode inserts. Each and every program was an exercise in shifting the emphasis from risk to benefit. We even called the overall method "Mini-Max" for minimum risk, maximum flavor (or enjoyment).

Nobody who counted the domino dots were ever pleased and we lived in the shadow of their disappointment as though all of it was...our fault!

During these seventeen years in which I consistently underperformed in the financial sector, I grew in my understanding of what really good food was all about. I taught at the CIA (Culinary Institute of America) and at Johnson Wales University. I received an Honorary Doctorate in Culinary Nutrition from Johnson & Wales.

There were several other events and much positive recognition that all added up in my mind as...*respect!*

It was this immense benefit to my sense of self-worth that almost offset the huge disappointment suffered by those who counted the dots on the dominoes and to whom I continued to feel responsible.

Eventually that tension had to snap and it was heartbreaking!

Please join us in the Reflective Readers Club
www.grahamkerr.com/rrc

Rite of Passage Fifty-Nine: "The Irritant"

We are at peace, at last, and my hen would become quite frisky; her lovely eyes seemed to wink mischievously now and again.

The waters of our new stream had become shallow and there were white water times; each easy enough to overcome. There were also some deep quiet green pools overhung with many tall green things.

It was in one of those still waters that a bright red, winged snack dropped on the brightness right above my head. It was one of those that I enjoyed eating on my way downstream many, many brightnesses ago before the big waters. I wasn't hungry for anything. I always felt full these days but memories die hard and I could almost feel the fluttering wriggle of its texture in my mouth...

Then it flew away, only to alight again on the brightness above.

I snapped in impatience, not hunger and shut my mouth on it; disappointing...it didn't flutter!

Suddenly I felt a sharp jolt in my jaw, which sparked another old memory of the time in the big waters when I had been pulled about by something beyond myself along with the same pain.

I flung myself to one side and the other. I thrashed my tail and leapt high above the brightness...in an instant the pulling stopped and the pain lessened. The snack remained; it had no taste, only a sharp bite of its own.

Once again I was free but constantly reminded of the cost of irritation.

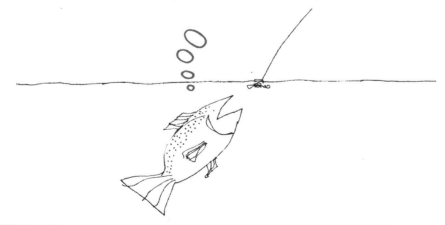

An Understanding

Our Chinooks had grown accustomed to their easygoing Willamette River and had spent long hours in the back flowing eddies and deep green pools that were well shaded by close growing trees. But on entry to their home McKenzie River they found that it was of a shallower and faster water nature with remarkable clarity. No place like home. But with the arrival the male's guard was down and a dim memory of having eaten aquatic insects compelled him to respond in a most unusual way for an adult spring Chinook salmon nearing its spawning grounds — especially one of his age and great size.

The flying insect was a lure...a dry fly tied by an expert fisherman who was fly-fishing in the deep-set pools of the McKenzie noted for its red-sided rainbow trout.

The fly dropped repetitively on the pool's surface until our salmon snapped at it with impatience and swallowed the fly. For a brief moment he was hooked and responded with the full vigor of our mature male Chinook's near sixty pound weight. In that violent maneuver he snapped the fine filament with ease and was free. The fly, with its bright hook, remained buried in his jaw, leaving a nasty taste in his mouth...but he was free!

The fisherman left the river with a story that he could get no one to believe with his arms spread as far as he could extend them to represent his lost fish.

1990 to 1995
I am fifty six to sixty one years old

Hippocrates, who lived some four hundred years before Christ, the so-called "father of medicine" wrote...

"Let food be thy medicine, and let medicine be thy food."

Fresh Foodies were now clearly concerned about the cause and effect of eating and in particular the consumption of certain ingredients.

I was by no means the first to attempt to bring foodies and fresh foodies together but I was amongst a very few who attempted to do this within the entertainment media. Please remember that, way back in the early 1960's in New Zealand Treena had called me "the most unutterably boring man in the world." I had always striven, since that date, not to repeat that fatal flaw in communicating. The Food Network graciously tipped their hat to Treena when they said "you made our network possible by combining entertainment and food with a live audience."

Our great obstacle was with that live audience and in a series that we made with the Mary Tyler Moore studios in 1990 called "Graham Kerr," we set out to take segments from the old Galloping Gourmet in which I had made excessive use of butter, cream, brandy, etc., and suggested ways of decreasing the risk by adding high flavored foods and some new techniques that were designed to increase sensual enjoyment.

We called this Mini-Max for minimize risk, maximize flavor.

It was not an easy exercise at any time in the production, especially hard when, in repeated edited segments of my old persona, I was throwing in a huge hunk of butter to the enormous delight of my previous audience and then to be followed by me using in its place a carefully measured tablespoon of olive oil.

Audiences can remain relatively unmoved by reasonable and moderate behavior.

We took the position that *flat out enthusiasm and passion* can trump excessive portions and unwise content.

To some degree the hard work and commitment paid off but it couldn't rise fast enough to meet the very arbitrary levels of audience ratings that the contract had specified. The show, after its initial one hundred seventy episodes, found its way onto the Discovery Channel where it played six days a week in multiple reruns.

During each show I had a segment where I showed on a robotic instrument called Max how I had switched one food for another in order to *lighten up*, and then on a large drafting board (that I had used in the 1970's for "Take Kerr" on CNN), I showed the fine points of what could be achieved by such a switch in what I called "the numbers."

The reason why we used our old shows was to avoid appearing critical of *anyone* else. Better

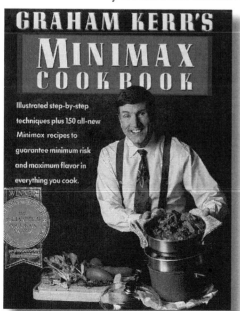

to admit to earlier excess and try to make amends? It was a constant learning curve with the ever-present hard "numbers" and audience tasting of the dish – keeping me ever focused upon less risk and more flavor. When the regular commercial network audience couldn't meet the requested level of cash flow that had been projected, we switched over to PBS and a smaller budget with no audience.

I continued to strive for the "Double Benefit" ethic and was enormously helped by Susan Butler as my Senior Food Associate from that season onward. During one such season of twenty six episodes she was undergoing chemotherapy for breast cancer at the same time as doing the behind-the-scenes preparations for the on-camera finishing that I would do.

No greater commitment had I ever known!

I had also entered into a fine relationship with a publishing editor, John Duff, who worked with me over many, many books –again, an obvious commitment of very creative time and talent.

I also came to know and dearly love Julia Child; not withstanding the fact that our culinary pathways led in almost exactly the opposite direction. Julia, once she had met Treena, remarked, "now I know why you cook like that for your Treena, so go ahead... and I'll cook for my butter friends."

We had an annual "act" at the International Association of Culinary Professions (I.A.C.P.) at which we presented the awards. I, at Julia's insistence, wore my kilt with its green velvet, silver buttoned dinner jacket, silver sporran, etc., and Julia wore her customary pants suit.

This gave her the opportunity to announce "you can see who wears the pants around here!"

With our good friend Susan Butler

We did have several good moments together but none as priceless as a minor competition with a simple French sauce in which, without knowing it, she had shaken far too much cayenne pepper.

She tasted my low risk version and declared it "not bad...here, taste mine." She spooned her high-octane sauce into my mouth. I choked on its vivid heat.

Searching for *anything* to say, I managed to splutter...

"I think, as an Englishman, I've just been violated."

She responded as quick as a flash...

"Really, I wouldn't have thought it would have been so easy!"

We loved dear Julia and miss her love of good food and a good life. Eventually the Food Network played our old shows back-to-back in the middle of the night for insomniac hedonists.

On the outside, all appeared to be well, but on the inside it was one failed fiscal effort after another and no matter how well received we were, the lack of profit had sharpened areas of disagreement to the snapping point.

Demands were made upon the conclusion of the contract, which we had determined should coincide with my 60th birthday in 1994. We found, however, that the actual copies of the contract had been changed to 1995 without our approval and we had missed the date change.

For six years, starting in 1988 to 1994, I had done the best I knew how to do a small thing and do it well until it was done. Treena and I, as a result, were stretched thin and shallow.

We desperately wanted it all to end and to know that we had done our best. Now the contract was saying...*another year*, and we had signed it without seeing the fine print.

Author's Note: When cash flow is the primary goal of a business association, there will usually be winners and losers, success and failure and while ego may easily enter into such a balance, it is seldom the basis of litigation.

If relationships can be kept intact and communications kept open, then there should be no need for the courts to intervene. When one side is strictly cash flow and the other less than partially so, then that very *purpose* difference can be a vulnerable link that through constant *irritation* can snap apart.

In 1987 we had entered into a contract with Bruce Reynolds who we both admired and respected, and still do. Our initial failure with "Simply Marvelous" led to another party taking over that contract. We had previously said "no" to this individual, yet now he was our business partner.

We had widely differing goals. On the one hand, he was driven by a desire to succeed in the media business, especially in television. The end product of such an ambition would become a personal fortune?

Treena and I, on the other hand, had only agreed to keep on keeping on –in order to see that our early investors had their money returned to them, with interest; if possible. In addition, we were eager to see if our message of moderation resulting in better health might reach those whose excessive consumption was putting them at risk.

It was the Manhattan end of the 1978 vision we had received in Kona and, as such, was our primary motivation. From day one we had decided that we should receive just enough recompense to cover our living expenses, which remained moderate.

Our primary goal was to *endure* the pressures of the media until my 60th birthday on January 22, 1994. Not unlike our plans to sail around the world after the Galloping Gourmet, we had planned to sail up the Inside Passage from Seattle to Glacier Bay, and back, a journey of 2,400 miles.

To some degree, we counted off the days as 1988 became 1993 and had purchased an older 36 foot Nonsuch sailboat to practice ahead of the adventure. It was early in 1993 that we discovered that the extremely carefully negotiated contract between ourselves with all the amendments carefully checked had been retyped and had had that one very small change made that had apparently escaped *everyone's* attention...1994 had been changed to 1995. We had all signed a deal that had extended our partnership by one full year.

Since the 60th birthday date had been well known by everyone as the conclusion, this *new* date took us all by surprise. Our partner agreed that it had "somehow been changed by someone." He explained, however, that he would never be able to explain to his board that the contract would have to be terminated "one year ahead of the schedule."

This was a huge disappointment and yet it seemed to be an unsolvable mystery how the four had become five. So, in the interest of both parties, I agreed to make another TV series for 1994 and a companion book. I also agreed to their management representation (with its shared revenue) for the entire "extra" year. We would, as a result, be able to leave as planned on our awesome adventure to Glacier Bay and back between May and October of 1994.

It was October 18, 1993, that we discovered that our partner was now demanding that he receive twenty percent of all our future business revenue that had anything to do with food and health. He claimed that he had made such a career possible and therefore co-owned the mark "Mini-Max." It was that little red fly that had landed many, many times on our daily lives that caused me to lose it and snap! The moment that I began legal proceedings to challenge this demand, I was hooked, and began to be led where I did not want to go.

We were assured that the twenty percent in perpetuity was "utterly ridiculous" and "would never fly in any court of law."

Further, we were told that all the hourly legal fees and expenses would be recovered in the eventual settlement, which we would unquestionably win.

The battle was eventually short and bloody in a court of arbitration in which the arbitrator, after only one day of hearings, said, "I see no real reason to bring this case." He instructed the attorneys to "arrive at a settlement right now," and adjourned the meeting for a long lunch.

A deal was done. We were totally released; there would be no twenty percent. We were free...

What also transpired was that our partner was found to be bankrupt and couldn't pay anything toward our expenses, which had reached $96,000 in lawyers' fees and $25,000 in expenses.

This final result of our cash flow dominated relationship was that neither party left the contract with a cash profit of any kind. The filament had broken, but the lure remained for a long time as a bad taste in the mouth and an ongoing pain to remind me of the high cost of *impatience* coupled with a growing preoccupation with money.

Please join us in the Reflective Readers Club
www.grahamkerr.com/rrc

Rite of Passage Sixty: "Pulling a U-Turn"

This was my second encounter with being pulled in a direction that I didn't want to go. There was lingering pain and a/ mouthful of inedible roughness. A very thin clear weed trailed from my jaw and was unshakable.

I felt so close to my goal, less whitewater and much stronger scent and yet I was shaken by the sudden tugging. Could I continue to have these trials and still survive?

I had to survive! We had to make it! We had no choice but once again to take the plunge as we had done in the big waters, surely the end was in sight?

An Understanding

Having relived the experience of being "hooked," our salmon is aware of the freedom but constantly reminded of the pressures of being led about when the fly fisherman had begun to reel him in.

The fly-covered hook remained in his mouth and jaw and the filament line trailed behind him and would continue to do so for the rest of his life.

They have encountered a great many dangerous obstacles and time after time overcome each one. Their history combined with the flavor-filled waters provide the tenacity to keep on going upstream on purpose.

1994
I am sixty years old

Before the conflict in the arbitration courts with our production partner, I had been joined by our son Andy who at that time was serving as an associate Pastor in a large church near Seattle.

Andy was willing to help me through the transition between being a solo innovator/performer and a complete one man business band or was that better seen as...*brand?*

It was wonderful to be free at last, but were we? Certainly the business was now entirely ours but it came complete with all the trappings that included a huge legal debt.

Our extremely well meaning lawyer had assured us that his fees and our expenses would be fully met by the other side, which indeed might well have happened had not the other side declared themselves to be bankrupt. The legal costs were all ours now and they were staggering.

When we surveyed the net result of six years of full time production the answer was that nobody had gained anything!

Andy and I regarded the complete failure with a sense that together, as family only, we could surely succeed. Really, we had no alternative other than to join our protagonist in bankruptcy, and this, at least for us, was another of those fates worse than death!

We set out along with Treena to reinvent the way we did business and were greatly helped by a remarkable opportunity to travel around the world on the newly refitted QE II (Queen

Elizabeth), the Cunard liner of regal design. Treena and I would be the on-board lecturers. I would deal with lifestyle issues concerning food and well being, and Treena would be Poet in Residence and read from her work to fellow passengers in the bars and at afternoon tea.

We had agreed to use this worldwide trip to film and do research for a new television series we had planned called "The Gathering Place," that we would make, as before, in Canada. The Cunard Lines saw this as an ongoing opportunity for public relations and we saw it

For a time all was bleak for us as Father and Son

as splendid, all expenses paid, on location research. We would, in addition to the series, have yet another companion cookbook which, this time, we would self-publish. We were now on our way to a whole new business model!

Back in 1988, following the "Simply Marvelous" filming in New Zealand, when we began "Graham Kerr," we had decided to add suspenders (braces in Brit talk) in order to clearly set my new direction toward well-being apart from my galloping past.

I now set out to add a triumphant *nautical beard* to somehow signal another fork in the road and also blend in as a "jolly-sea-going chappy."

The trouble with all this newness is that it appeared to take our audience by surprise.

I've often thought of it as being like the opening titles of the "Beverly Hillbillies" in which Jed Clampett drives his family down Rodeo Drive in Beverly Hills en route to their "better life". All their possessions, including Granny, are piled onto an old trunk and tied in place. Had they pulled a U-turn, at what looked like 30 miles per hour, without slowing down, the overladen truck would have overturned and all their prize belongings would have been ruined.

We had pulled just such a U-turn in our productions without slowing down!

When one is saddled with a huge debt and an immediate need to stay afloat, there is an almost complete preoccupation with cash flow. I no longer had that *other purpose*, the one in which I had so strongly invested myself since 1979 in Kailua, Kona. The idea that "habits that harmed could become resources that healed" had been shifted to the extreme back burner of my intent. I continued with the outward appearance of better health through better culinary choices, but first and foremost came the essential need for *cash flow*.

Andy and I did the very best we could and to some extent it did work. We were honest and transparent and best of all we never ever spoke ill of our past partners.

We had paid our legal bills by obtaining a large line of credit with our very gracious local bank, but the interest rate was eating us alive and we were unable to see any real progress. We cut our losses and sold what we could. Andy went back to his life as a missionary and Treena and I made a very long slow "U-turn" as I shaved off my beard and quietly, without any fanfare, retreated back downstream in our search for our old *sense of purpose* that might still somehow matter?

1978

It was after our initial DTS in Kailua, Kona, Hawaii, that we were in prayer together. Out of nowhere came the desire to pray for David and Norma Jean Mainse, a lovely Canadian couple who hosted a remarkably tinsel-free Christian TV talk show called "100 Huntley Street." As we prayed we sensed they were exhausted and needing a time together to be restored.

I called David at his Toronto number. We had met them briefly during our earlier travels.

"David...how are you and Norma Jean?" I asked.

"Fine, just fine." He replied brightly.

"Oh," I hesitated.

"I guess I got it wrong...we felt, in prayer, that you were both exhausted and needed us to fill in to give you a break."

"Oh Lord...oh my...oh." He almost wept in gratitude.

And so we flew to Toronto and served as hosts while they had their time apart.

I need to add here, very briefly, that it was during their short respite that they allowed us to introduce an unusual idea that lasted for several seasons. We suggested that a well-respected Bible scholar mark up on a chalkboard the scriptural basis for all the guests' comments... either in support, or even to gently offer another viewpoint. We did this in order to avoid aiding or abetting some well-meaning, but nonetheless non-Biblical, ideas that sometimes surface in these public forums.

Author's Note: This will seem like a distraction in our story; however, you are about to see how our early availability caused an amazing consequence after a gap of eight fruitless years. It seems essential for me to explain this in scriptural terms..."*At this present time, your abundance being a supply for their (David and Norma Jean) need, so that their abundance also may become a supply for your (Graham and Treena) need, that there may be equality.*" 2 Corinthians 8:14 (NASB)

In 1978 Treena and I were invited to go up again, this time to 100 Huntley Street's new studio, now called Crossroads Communications, just outside Toronto in Canada. During our visit we appeared on the new 100 Huntley Street and also made one culinary demonstration and lecture to a large invited studio audience. It was following these exposures that we got a call from their General Manager, Wendall Wilkes, a charming Messianic Jew who had a decidedly entrepreneurial side to his personality.

"Graham, we'd like you and Treena to consider making your "Gathering Place" series with us right here in our studios." He was quite certain and uncharacteristically brief.

My immediate reaction was..."Oh dear, off we go again...another Christian production who can't get their eyes off the old Galloping Gourmet success; would they never learn?"

I was about to say just that when he continued, "We believe that what you have to say about habits that harm becoming resources that heal needs to be heard and we want to help you to say it."

This had to be an answer to prayer. Their primary reason to produce would reconnect me with my purpose; like a salmon rejoining its natal river? I leapt at the chance. Just when everything we had tried to do had gone nowhere, here was an opportunity to get back in line and erase the word *failure* from our thoughts of the future.

Wendall set about creating a budget and finding the needed investors whom we duly met and who sincerely agreed with the main purpose for the show.

As part of the budget Wendall asked me to decide between either a 40 percent ownership of all the profits and associated merchandising, books, etc., or a one-time clean-cut buyout of all my rights in everything in perpetuity. The not exactly biblical idea of "a bird in the hand is worth two in the bush" came immediately to mind.

A secondary thought was that with a one-time remuneration we might be less cash flow conscious about the program in the future. This might result in our purpose taking precedent over the long-term financial success of the exposure. We had some serious debt and a largely unmet mortgage and very little ongoing commercial income...so?

We decided to opt for the buyout and were faithfully reimbursed for our research, scripting, performing and merchandising availability as we recorded twice nightly before a live audience on Mondays, Wednesdays, and Fridays.

When all was said (and cooked) and done we had one hundred thirty episodes in the can and enough money after taxes to pay off all our debt including the mortgage on our house, with a wee bit left over. In five months of recording and almost two years of effort we had managed to literally leap over our sense of hopelessness and to do so with the power that comes with real purpose to make a difference.

Our preoccupation with the...*buck* had stopped there!

That wasn't all that the program provided. We decided to build each show around a lifestyle choice that would, in part, provide a sense of wellbeing for our viewers. We recruited Chavanne Hanson, RD. a delightful registered dietitian who we had met during Treena's early days following her heart attack. We had remained in touch and worked together on many projects.

We developed a list of need to know issues to be covered by the 130 episodes such as, for example, what is HDL (high density lipoprotein) and why is it good and how to get more. We would then match the need to know with a well-known and highly respected scientist who, in many cases, was a medical doctor who taught at leading universities in North America. We asked each expert guest to touch on only three issues that explained how the viewer's need could be met in very simple terms.

I then matched their suggestions to a dish, which I had designed to illustrate how the viewer could make a practical application. After an initial interview at a small dining table,

I then left the guest to watch the demonstration and then eat the finished dish along with a member from the audience. During their tasting time I then wrote up the numbers that resulted from the culinary changes I had made. The guest would then comment on both the science and the senses of the dish presented.

At the very end of the show I did a short, one-minute windup in which I told how the research and experimental work had helped me to make a better specific choice about my life and how it might help others.

I wish I could tell you that it had become the huge success that everyone knew it would be but it wasn't.

The major reason for its limited success, which indeed it did have, was its length. It had to be one hour because of the need to communicate in sufficient depth to be fully understood.

Over my entire career as a public/media communicator I have had numerous opportunities to be interviewed on TV news/magazine styled shows worldwide. Over time I've seen the duration progressively reduced to apparently match the attention span of the average audience member.

I see it as skipping a flat stone over a still lake to see how many times it can touch down before it sinks and is forgotten. In other words, how do I make a lasting impression with those remaining ripples on the surface of the viewer's mind? Better, I reasoned, to skip the flat stone (of a good idea) across a flat, small inlet so that it could reach the beach and be found by another communicator who might pick it up and skip it on.

Our one hundred thirty skipping stones are now on DVD and are just as valid and just as able to *reach the beach* —because they remain long enough to matter.

Please join us in the Reflective Readers Club
www.grahamkerr.com/rrc

Rite of Passage Sixty-One: "Walking in the Light"

Everything is so familiar. I know I've been here before and yet it's all just beyond my memory. I know I had been small and had gone with the waters, not against them. Everything had been so amazingly new in those early days. This was close to where I met my hen, when our fins had first touched.

The brightness above became shaded and then dull, the sparkle left the clear waters and I recalled the really tough times. They were so hard to forget. If I had to do it all over, would there be a change?

Slowly the drabness passed and everything was filled once again with abundant life. The grey times were well behind us; only the promise of new life lay ahead.

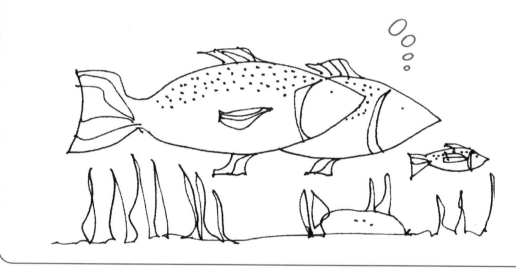

An Understanding

Our Chinook has suffered so many setbacks and continued, in spite of them all, to keep on going. He can remember, in brief flashes, both good and bad times...but always the way ahead was filled with purpose and the energy to endure until the glorious end. It felt as though it was full of light.

1999 to 2004
I am sixty five to seventy years old

The Gathering Place television series was safely in the can and its early test market ratings in Montreal were exciting; they proved there was an immediate public interest in wellness achieved by making wise and creative choices.

Andy went ahead and gathered a great team of editors and book designers, and together we crafted a truly handsome, beautifully illustrated and formatted hardcover book that covered the first thirteen ports of call in our QE II around the world research trip.

It was immediately following its publications that we had begun to experience the pushback from an industry that simply couldn't bend their minds around the idea of a one-hour food program.

We tried and tried so hard to explain that there was an enormous need to convey a deeper understanding of the creative choices that were offered to steer a healthy course between the rocks and hard places of the modern commercial culture.

In the end we were forced to edit the programs down to half an hour format used by PBS (Public Broadcasting Service) in the U.S.

I hated doing this. It compressed the great information and the persuasive passion of my guests into a lukewarm message that sounded right on the surface, but it didn't make it to the beach to be picked up and passed on!

There was just the possibility that the U.K. television world might understand the need and solution —so we combined a trip back to our birthplace to promote the idea and also film inserts for the Biography TV program that had decided to add to their collection with one about the two of us in their celebrity series.

I chose the opportunity to make things right with my friend Maitre Chef de Cuisines Silvano Trompetto at the Savoy Hotel in London. You may recall how relieved I had been that this great chef had not remembered that I had never been a commis in training in his kitchens. It had been an innocent enough conceit that I had blurted out in a gathering in a small town in New Zealand in my mid twenties and it had followed me in the media record of my life.

I had never felt that I needed to set the record straight because Chef Trompetto thought that I had begun in his kitchen at the Savoy in London, so why not simply go with it since nobody knew the truth –except me?

The problem now was the idea of *walking in the light*. I needed to tell my friend –the truth.

I checked into the Savoy and asked for a small inside room. My name surfaced in their records and the Duty Manager appeared.

"Mr. Kerr, sir, welcome back." He wore a frock coat, striped pants and had a pearl gray silk tie...but no red carnation.

"Good to be back." I smiled a little self-consciously.

"You asked for an inside room...a small one?"

"Yes."

"But sir, please, since you began your professional life with us; let me offer you the Chaplin Suite."

I protested, he insisted, and I found myself in the grand suite that overlooked the Thames awaiting the arrival of the Maitre Chef des Cuisines, my friend..."Tromps."

"Graham, my dear friend how good to see you; Treena, your most lovely wife, is she well?"

We exchanged the usual pleasantries...

"Tromps...I've come on a very embarrassing mission," I explained hesitantly.

"Yes...yes...so please do share it." He leaned forward.

"Well, I've become a Christian since we last met," I started.

"Capital...good show...I am too, go to Mass every morning." He beamed his approval.

"I'm trying to walk in the light...and need to confess to you...a lie that I've told about you."

He sat quietly; his smile had softened.

"I never worked in your kitchen –I lied about it a long time ago and well –I never did." I finished, almost out of breath.

"Well, of course you didn't." He replied heartily.

I almost shouted in surprise..."You knew?"

"Yes, of course I did...I assumed that at one stage it had suited you to know me. When you came into my kitchen with the BBC cameras it suited me to know you."

We laughed together, didn't touch the fruit or the champagne and became friends at last without a shadow.

I was free...indeed.

If that freedom wasn't enough, there followed another great release.

As part of the Biography filming, they wanted me to revisit my old school, where I had been beaten as a child of ten. I met, once again, my school chum John Collard who traveled with us for two days while shooting. It was during this time that I stood in front of our old apartment in Cromwell Road Home and said...

"We lived here until my father returned from the war and then I was immediately sent to boarding school."

"That's not true," blustered my friend John.

The camera stopped and all eyes were on the two of us.

"Excuse me...er...John?" I was both confused and a little upset by this almost rude interruption.

"Your father came home and you were a family for at least two years."

This directly contradicted my very early recollection of my time of abuse at school. Somehow I had added 2 + 2 and made it 5 and had blamed my father for the distress of those years.

It wasn't actually he who had been a distant dad —it was more that I had been a distant son...all the way through his entire life. I had lived within my confused memory of that time for far too many years, and now he was gone and reconciliation was beyond reach. Almost immediately I started to recall snatches of times when he had made a valiant attempt with me. Warm and wonderful moments that flooded in to take the place of the "jolly good chap" that he had been to others but not to me.

Not true...not true.

This had already been an important visit to our birthplace, but it wasn't over yet.

We stayed for a week in London, in a small boutique hotel in Kensington, not far from Harrods. Sunday came around and I asked the Hall Porter if he knew of a local church that was "on fire."

"On fire Sir I hadn't heard...is it serious?"

"No, no, no, not literally on fire, just spiritually." I hastened to soften his obvious concern.

"Oh, yes sir...well, you see...I 'ave to work on Sundays so..." He trailed off as though a solution had arrived.

"We 'ave a telephonist who 'as a big cross 'round her neck...she might know."

We went backstage and found a tiny lady with a very big cross.

"You mean a church what is really going for it?" She asked.

"Yes..."

"You mean where they clap their 'ands?"

"Well...that would be a start!"

"There's one out at Clapham, no pun intended." She gave me a shy smile.

"Is there anything closer?" I asked.

" 'ave you tried the yellow pages?"

Unlikely that I would find a church listed under an "on fire" heading but nonetheless I took her advice and that's when I found it.

All Souls Langham Place, right next to the BBC. It was the church at which Rev. John Stott had served for many years. The Anglican evangelical who had told me to go on BBC World Service and just open my mouth allowing God to fill it! How could I ever forget!

I called their number and found out that the Rev. Stott was speaking that very night.

The service was good, the message fine and just as we were about to be dismissed a stalwart lady in a yellow twin set with Lisle stockings and a tweed skirt took the microphone at the lectern.

"Before we dismiss, a quick reminder." She had a crisp, very county English accent that blended perfectly with her outfit.

"All those who have heard from God this week, please meet in the Narthex for a cup of tea."

Now this was different. In twenty eight years of attending multiple flavors of churches I had never heard such an announcement. I went to the gathering where a welcome cup of strong British tea was served in thick white mugs. There were about twenty people chatting quietly with each other. Some were quite old, others looked like students, one Asian, another African. One couple sat behind a small table taking down notes on ruled cards.

I found the lady who had made this announcement.

"Would you mind telling me what's happening here?" I asked.

"Why certainly –it's such good fun you know." She replied, with a lovely sense of enthusiasm.

"Do you...er...perhaps believe that God still speaks to people...mmm...personally, as in one-on-one?"

"I do...yes."

"Capital!" It was a buzzword at that time in the U.K. like the well used "brilliant" that was to follow.

"Well, you see..." She hurried on.

"All these dear people have somehow heard what they thought might have been God speaking during the past week. We take down the gist of the idea...in some cases it's written out word for word and stored in a card index system and given a generic heading...such as widows or HIV or hunger.

Then we put anyone who has heard something that falls under these headings in touch with the others. They gather together in one mind and heart and often do something that obeys what they have heard." She paused briefly to take a breath.

"The other day we had a stockbroker who heard God on the top deck of a bright red double decker bus." She laughed delightedly...

"What do you think of that?"

Well, I thought it was...well, capital –splendid, even brilliant but most of all I thought it was God.

I found out later that there had been almost one hundred outreach projects that had been birthed within those gatherings of tea drinking tweed-jacketed...British enthusiasts.

I completely understood the passionate declaration by many deeply committed Christians that the Bible was enough; no need to be told anything more. If we just did what it said we *would* find God's will for our lives.

I absolutely agree.

However, I was not prepared to say with equal conviction that God would never speak again to anyone about anything especially when it agreed, or at least didn't contradict, what was contained in the Bible.

I had asked for a "church on fire." I had found one and had had my faith renewed by this thoroughly charming example right next to the British Broadcasting Corporation, one of the greatest message centers of the world.

Please join us in the Reflective Readers Club
www.grahamkerr.com/rrc

Rite of Passage Sixty-Two:
"Topless in Tennessee"

We have regained strength and purpose after our rest and after darkness followed brightness several times, we again worked upstream —confused at one point by a great wall of water until finding a small stream of odd smooth steps around it. And then there was the easy swim through a place without current. The breadth around, above, and below us seemed almost like briefly returning to travels long past my short memory.

But now we seemed truly home. The aroma of where we came from so long ago has led us to a point where it no longer compels us to go further.

The waters with strikingly blue clarity are now shallow and filled with fine bubbles and little clumps of white froth. There was a stretch of white water ahead which we easily overcame, but then the aroma of familiarity weakened. We turned back to where the scent seemed strongest...

An Understanding

After resting for several days in recovery from the fly fisherman encounter, they were on their way again and shortly came to Leaburg Dam. It would be impassable if not for a fish ladder around it. The ladders took them to the reservoir behind with an easy swim through its calm *and deep expanse until again meeting the uninhibited McKenzie River, noted for its swift waters and lovely blue clarity.*

Their natural guidance system at this time is dominated by their remarkable sense of smell that has detected the exact location of the gravel riffle of their birth. However, they could not know this exactly until passing it. They went through a swift shallow stretch beyond it before turning back to where the scent of their incubation grounds.

2004 to 2006
I am seventy to seventy two years old

Our recording sessions in Canada for the Gathering Place television series and our agreement to be bought out of all our rights and residuals had provided us with sufficient funds to pay off our legal debts and the mortgage on our home on Camano Island.

For a short while we made a series of radio and television announcements in support of a local grocery chain and a fresh food packaging concept. Both had agreed to do their best to reduce risk and enhance flavor and enjoyment for their customers.

Our support/endorsement was meant to further my commitment to see things happen in the day-to-day commercial food world, and do less harm. In neither case did our joint efforts succeed and so *once again* I realized that the vision and word I had received back in 1978 was still completely appropriate, at least for my life.

"Do a small thing and do it well until it's done."

Commercial announcements by and large are designed to increase consumption at a specific business and, as a result, to increase profits and/or survival in the hugely competitive marketplace.

As such it promotes cash flow and success is usually measured simply in dollars and cents.

There was, however, a very small breakthrough during this time that suggested a simple idea called "5 a day." It referred to a fairly well funded message to eat more fruits and vegetables and was aimed at going from 2 servings (each about 100 grams) to 5 servings which could weigh in at about 16 ounces of store-weighed produce.

I did over four hundred public service announcements for fresh produce, each of which was about 70 seconds long. They were played during local newscasts.

"Do a small thing and do it well until it's done."?

During this series I worked with very gifted communicators from a major advertising agency, the Center for Disease Control and the American Diabetes Association who sat in at every recording session. We called them Hear, See and Speak...no evil!

I did all the research; testing and presentation with my long time associate Suzanne Butler.

It did seem to work, although frankly it's hard to measure in the grand scheme of things. I think that it played a small part in the increased use of fresh produce by many chefs from 2010 onward? The one thing it did do was help me to truly understand the value of plant foods in our own daily menu planning. It was a great start that was taking me in a new direction.

Each late summer, usually in September after Labor Day, Treena and I would take off in our small sailboat to "pothole" around the San Juan Islands. Basically we cruised, mostly very slowly under sail and dropped our anchor in relatively quiet and protected bays. These were lovely times of retreat from the often stressful production times from 1995 onward.

In 2003 this ended. We were coming into the marina at the Port of Sidney on Vancouver Island in the midst of a sharp choppy sea and a brisk breeze. Treena, as usual, was putting out our bumpers before docking. I was on the wheel watching her. She hung onto the safety line; she almost went overboard before catching her balance. In that moment I heard the voice again, *"it's now time to stop sailing."*

We docked that day and prayed together for confirmation. We had done almost six thousand miles in this *place apart* over the past decade.

It had been our deep hole or back eddy in the rapids of life; was it really time to let it go?

That day we went ashore and visited a famous local bookstore and returned to "Dovetail" with a bag full of books and magazines on recreational vehicles. Our voyage wasn't over yet but we were planning to do our next trip on a land yacht.

Author's Note: Way back in 1971–1972 we had done 24,000 miles in our much larger sailboat "Treena." I suggested to you then, that in the interest of brevity, we would offer a separate account of that adventure.

I now want to do the same about the RV trip during which we traveled 42,000 miles in just over two years (2004–2006). Please let us know if you want to have this covered elsewhere?

We took our time to understand what this might mean. We sold the Camano house and began to plan for a new, more radical dwelling in Mount Vernon, Washington. Radical because we wanted to convert what we had learned about space utilization on our 71 foot long, 18 foot beam "Treena" where seven of us had lived for two years at sea. Could we take 71 feet by 18 feet, about 1300 square feet if expressed as a rectangle and have it become a creative space for our final dwelling? We chose a local architect, Dan Nelson of Designs Northwest, to help us with the planning during which we chose to live aboard our 36 footer in the Anacortes Marina.

It took just on two years to plan the place we would come to name "Nonsuch Cottage" that overlooks the famous Skagit Valley. Every single inch was measured. What did we need to have to live in less space but with a sense of spaciousness. Could we have a home that, at times, felt like a boat and yet didn't try to look like one?

I come from a long line of successful British and Scottish architects and something of those genes were in my blood. I loved working with Treena and Dan to craft our cottage-sized future to include the time when we might need wheelchairs to get about.

We moved into our "odd" dwelling place on December 4, 2000, in the midst of the "hanging chad" debacle over the votes in Florida for President Bush.

We had arrived in our well-planned penultimate resting place. We were convinced that if we were to move, it would have to be feet first!

In September 2004, immediately after Labor Day we began our two-year *land yacht* experience.

This time it wasn't so much a gentle cruise with quiet, protected bays as joining a stream of metal rushing down roadways en route to yet another crowded RV camping ground...or "resort." I had never driven a vehicle larger than a U-Haul and our 38 foot Discovery diesel with its 14 foot tow car and its attachment exceeded 52 feet overall!

Treena and I took an RV driving course and attended a very well organized conference that gave us at least a theoretical understanding.

We were not without a purpose and rather hoped that we could combine a pure vacation-like adventure with an opportunity to pass on what we felt had been given concerning creative lifestyle choices. A Christian church consulting group offered to put us in touch with the "top 100 growing churches of the U.S. and Canada." So that we could arrange our tour to connect with these "dots" and so "spread the word on the double benefit" that we were now calling "OUTDULGENCE."

This felt rather too much like our earliest tour of big churches back in 1975 when our faith had been newly minted. We opted instead for a highways and byways approach in which we would follow some kind of geographic sequence during which we would mark off 250 to 300 miles and see where we might wind up.

At each stopover we asked permission to invite our fellow campers to come to a gathering to hear about and then discuss the idea of "habits that harm can become resources that heal."

In a very real sense we became a community of like-minded people who parked their vehicles, put out chairs, cooked a meal and then visited from one "porch" to the next on an evening walk.

These were real people living beyond their normal day-to-day distractions. For us it was literally a "God send" to be able to propose and sometimes try to defend, our position. I won some and lost some, and spent two years soaking into the United States of America as we shared our story of change with an increasing depth of understanding to middle income Americans, justly, in most cases, representing the "salt of the earth." Treena was happy, so was I; we were making friends with real people with very few examples of conspicuous consumption, at least not in the camping grounds where we stayed.

By the end of year one we were convinced that this was the place for us to be and we put our beloved "Nonsuch Cottage" up for sale, having found a couple to rent it until we might be ready to return. We found a park in Phoenix, Arizona, that had many single and doublewide mobile homes as well as a few open slots for travelers like us. We parked for a time to enjoy their sunny winter weather and began to look at the doublewide units as a possible home. It was during this time that I began to realize that my lifelong preoccupation with outward appearances had changed. Gone was the frock coat, striped trousers and gray silk tie (the carnation had long since been left behind).

These mobile homes were well constructed, slightly larger than our "cottage" at home and vastly less expensive in all respects.

If we relinquished our outward-appearance home, we would have funds that we could invest in other people's lives when we saw the obvious needs that surrounded us. As we continued on our journey we kept our eyes open and our cottage on the market.

We should have been a little more wide-eyed!

In the Fall of 2006 in October we had spent a great time with our elder daughter Tessa and husband Scott at their home in Anderson, South Carolina. We had been rained out in a planned gathering at a local RV campground where the management had fixed our "poster" on an old rusty dumpster.

We should have taken this more to heart but at the time we thought it just plain funny.

The very next day we set off for Harrison, Tennessee, where our youngest daughter Kareena lived. It was on that road in a city called Cleveland, Tennessee, that our lives changed once again.

We approached the city on Route 64 that eventually got us to the junction of Lynden Avenue SE and Inman Street E.

Our early model GPS had decided to go blank and I was somewhat distracted as we sat at the traffic light wondering which way to go.

The light turned green and I decided to go straight across.

Suddenly the road disappeared down an extremely sharp, short hill. My eyes were fixed on this rapid descent; so much so that I missed a very large sign on a railroad overpass that read "10 feet 6 inch clearance." Under normal circumstances we reached 11 feet 6 inches.

The hill finally leveled out as we moved quite slowly under the railroad lines.

The noise was deafening and for a few brief moments –continuous –as was the sense that we had been slowed down by…something.

I said nothing, neither did Treena; I simply sat there and steered.

We had, of course, run into the bridge, a good solid well-constructed immovable object. In our case it was the forward air conditioning unit that made the initial contact. It had been ripped free from its restraints only to meet and firmly embrace its sister aft unit, which also found freedom. One large bent bolt had trapped over 100 pounds of newly united metal in the back panel of the RV where it hung directly over the tow car.

Before we could say a word, there was a beep from behind. A small red pickup signaled with its lights and we pulled over and were approached by a pleasant looking man in a plaid shirt and jeans.

"Hi…" He looked up and introduced himself.

"My name is Corky and I'm the Assistant Fire Marshall. Do y'all know you've got an air conditioner hangin' over your tow car?"

"I rather thought so," I replied lamely.

"Would y'all like to find a place to park?" He enquired helpfully.

"Sure." I followed him to a gas station that had room for us to inspect the damage.

The first air conditioner, having embraced the second, had then been collectively crushed down into the roof and had ripped a gaping hole before coming to rest in the aft panel.

We had, in one remarkable moment, managed to own perhaps the world's first convertible RV!

We had been keeping our eyes open for a suitable place to live!

Had I truly kept my eyes open that day we might have kept going. We didn't. At just on 42,000 miles our adventure had ended and we, unlike Sleepless in Seattle, had become Topless in Tennessee.

Please join us in the *Reflective Readers Club*

www.grahamkerr.com/rrc

Rite of Passage Sixty-Three: "Community"

Never before had we ever had such a powerful awareness of our birth river; the scent was overwhelming. We are here, and it is strangely exciting and yet...peaceful?

Our entire lives had been filled with daily challenges that now seemed to be missing; was this true or would there be other unforeseen obstacles in our path?

For the moment at least I was content to lay alongside my hen behind a giant rock that had helped to create the quiet, deep pool in which we now floated. Just above us is a long shallow gravel reach that beckons.

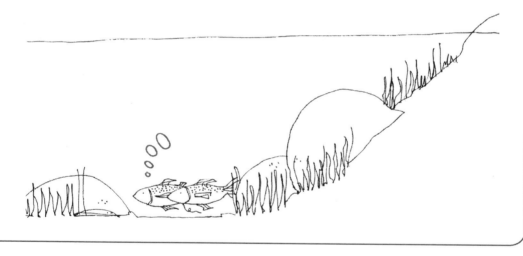

2006 to 2009
I am seventy two to seventy five years old

Back in 2005, in the midst of our road trip we stayed awhile to celebrate our 50th wedding anniversary at the Texas Hill Country town of Kerrville.

It was here that Treena had begun to have repeated chest pains that led eventually to the heart bypass that our cardiologist "Dr. get-your-car-keys" had predicted back in 1987. We had managed to go eighteen years before such an event became necessary.

It was another time when I waited, this time with Andy and Kareena who had flown in to be there for support. Unlike the cancer scare in 1971, this time I was not alone. This time I was with family and my faith. It was very different and yet also somewhat the same. I still cried out for her healing with a great deal of emotion. The thought of losing her was overwhelming yet there was a peace that is described as being "beyond understanding" that allowed sleep to eventually provide relief.

Our surgeon, in his post-operation consultation, told me...

"I held your wife's heart in my hand...and " He seemed to search for the right words, "it is as though she has a flame burning in it."

We recuperated in our RV amongst some of the dearest Texans we have ever met. Once again, we had attended a local church with its own distinct flavor that we thoroughly enjoyed. We even tried to find a manufactured home and site by the river and settle down. The site we had found was eventually unavailable and we took this as a sign to move on.

It was shortly after this that we encountered the low bridge in Tennessee and our return *home* to Washington State.

Treena now had three strikes against her medical record. The stroke and heart attack in 1987 and now the triple bypass in 2005. With that kind of a pre-existing pattern it was not easy to obtain insurance. We did, of course, have Medicare, but the rest was unattainable. Well, not so in the State of Washington that had, as some other States, a high risk health insurance pool that had the unusual acronym WSHP, that to us was short for worship!

WSHP was funded by premiums and an assessment on the health insurers in Washington State.

This merger of commercial and social provision that was called a "pool" became a wakeup call for me as I looked, once again, at the value of community, especially when things looked bleak. We were home again and our community greeted us with open arms, open hearts and a compassionate awareness of our personal needs.

Much as we loved our sending out church, they had upgraded their sound equipment and the result was a percussion wave that caused vertigo, at least for me with my considerable hearing loss since my early British Army days.

We left in search of a small, quiet church that was close to our home and might, as a result, include our immediate neighbors. Its denominational *flavor* was new to us, but it had a long and interesting history that had blended evangelism and social action and that combination appealed. It was also small and quiet. On my very first visit I sniffed the air and said to myself...

"Smells like an old person's church," to which I felt that voice again say "So?"

This was 2007 and I was 74 but obviously unwilling to admit to that as beyond middle age!

We were surrounded by splendid, kind people who were well settled and quietly content. We felt we had come home and it was a deep pool.

2008

The stock market/investment banking bubble finally burst on September 29, 2008, having slid rapidly downhill all that year. From its high to its low the stock market had lost fifty percent of its value in only eighteen months.

We were a part of that "adjustment." Our small, but relatively costly, house lost a good deal of its value, and a previously agreed upon sale to a Master Builder who loved everything about it fell through.

We had planned on a move downtown to a modest corner house in a quiet neighborhood, and a direct result would be the release of a good deal of money that we might then use to somehow benefit our neighbors.

When the sale fell through I was devastated because I had become concerned about being observed as speaking a *creative lifestyle* that shared with others in need, yet living in a small house with a fabulous view and a somewhat exotic design. Would this somehow be used against us by the ever-present cadre of cynics?

I started to step up my prayers for the house to sell, even at a distressed price. When my prayers turned to pleading I got one of my most audible responses...

"You seem to think that I am pacing up and down in my Throne Room fretting over my inability to meet certain needs in your community and wondering when the funds from your house will arrive!"

"I would remind you that I do not need your apparent sacrifice. I am perfectly able to afford doing what I think is best at precisely the right time for everyone.

"NOW...receive your house for the gift that it has always been, live in it with celebration –it comes without shadow or turning!"

The words were firmly enough delivered that I promptly began to forget about moving. It was, once again, a reminder of my preoccupation with my outward appearance –would it never end?

The Biblical word *blessed* can also be interpreted as *happy*. The immediate community that surrounded us and our church was neither happy nor blessed; it was actually quite depressed and bewildered. The big question for ourselves at this time was –does happiness or blessedness depend upon the economy?

The airwaves were filled with gloom and doom and so it was hard to feel anything like... happy. And yet there was that same emotional disconnect that I had had when Treena had gone in for the heart bypass. On the surface there was deeply felt concern, both for her and what it might be like without her...a kind of self-focused pity party; but then there was that peaceful safety net that kept me from the hard landing of despondency.

Now here it was again. I was leading in self-interest. What would happen if everything were to collapse?

It was then that the basic trust factor cut in –we actually had a personal ongoing *relationship* rather than a religion, and that allowed us to feel *secure* regardless of whatever took place.

I didn't have a plan by which we could survive as a family. We had enough dry goods to make it for perhaps a month but that would be it. So it wasn't material self-sufficiency, it was more a matter of *resilience*. There simply had to be a way *upstream* no matter what the obstacles might be!

This state of peace was so *out there* that I began to wonder what Treena and I could do to somehow be a blessing (or provide a sense of happiness) to our neighbors through our church. Could we find any means to communicate this level of trust and confidence that we were experiencing in a God that was so much more reliable and loving than the upsetting manipulations of the economy?

I simply didn't have any idea of what this might mean so I went to an "Elder" of the church, Larry Ashby, who I admired for his mix of good humor, lack of religiosity and above all, his consistency. He was, in a word –*reliable.* Together we pieced together, with Treena, an idea to call the entire church to prayerfully seek an answer.

We had some experience with the prayer gatherings in YWAM and at other churches, and could see how sometimes it was easy to become influenced by those with strong settled opinions and sometimes hidden agendas. In an effort to clear the decks of self-interest we set out to meet for eight weeks on Wednesday nights and to ask eight questions of God and each other.

Since it was the economic crisis of 2008 that had prompted this concern, and given my pretty consistent use of metaphors, it occurred to me that 2008 could be seen as the black ball in the game of pool. If one inadvertently "pots" the black ball out of sequence then the entire game is lost. Was this what had happened in our banking mortgage world –had the 2008 bubble brought the entire economy to the very brink of the pocket of a massive depression where a single false move might tip it into a complete collapse?

I had titled the gathering "Getting out from behind the ate ball." The use of "ate" in place of "eight" was almost getting out of hand.

The eight questions were summed up with eight words all ending in *ate!*

Compassion*ate*, Evalu*ate*, Innov*ate*, Educ*ate*, Motiv*ate*, Facilit*ate*, Consolid*ate* and Celebr*ate!*

It hadn't started out that way but with a bit of tweaking that's how it ended up. As it happened, it made a lot more sense than I had expected. Look at each question with me just for a moment, and think of your own community and its state of happiness when you take economic influence out of the picture.

Are we, as a global people –the entire human race, suffering from a High Risk Spiritual Health disorder where we respond immediately to good or bad news by feeling either *blessed* or *bewildered,* both without the safety net of ongoing trust?

Here were our questions:

1. **Compassionate.** What has broken and causes us to strongly desire to resolve the harm done?
2. **Evaluate.** Why did it break?
3. **Innovate.** What can be done that's new?
4. **Educate (communicate).** How can we communicate with clarity?
5. **Motivate.** How can others be encouraged to assist with the solution?
6. **Facilitate.** Who is already committed to help and how can we help them?
7. **Consolidate.** How can we strengthen our resolve to be consistent?
8. **Celebrate.** How can we gather to say "thank you" and "well done?"

We are now living in a pragmatic age, one that is seemingly able to measure just about anything and, as a result, have pretty convincing statistics to prove whatever they have to suggest.

That is, until we get to faith, because faith in its purest form is *beyond measurement* because it believes in things that are unseen. I can say that I love God until I'm blue in the face (I know, I've tried it!) but that isn't going to convince a pure pragmatist...

"Prove it!" They say with perfectly reasonable common sense on their side.

It isn't until the complete commandment is added that measurements can begin.

The whole deal that Jesus announced when asked to provide the greatest commandment of them all was:

"Love the Lord your God with all your heart and with all your strength and with all your mind; and love your neighbors as yourself. (Luke 10:27, Matthew 22:37–40, Mark 12:30, Luke 10:27.)

It is when we love our neighbors as we love ourselves that faith can be measured by even casual, and in some cases, cynical observers.

How then could Treena and I in the midst of our small congregation be measured by our pragmatic age...as reliable witnesses when we say, "I believe that when Jesus said that he was speaking the truth, that he was in fact doing so."

We met week after week and did our best to pray without hidden agendas getting in the way.

It was a little easier for me, as its servant leader, because I was suffering from an intense form of vertigo at that time that prevented me from standing up, and in some cases, from driving.

I was almost out of it and so what I could add was not reinforced by any level of charismatic behavior.

When the two months of meetings were up we were left with a startlingly simple agenda for action.

1. Help people to eat with greater wisdom, especially plant foods.
2. Help people to plant their own edible backyard gardens.
3. Help people to do this for and with their neighbors.

Roughly one quarter of all the adults signed up to see that this was accomplished and we set out as the Garden Gate Group (G3) to do what we could. It wasn't meant to be the exclusive task to be undertaken but it was meant to be measureable. It had to be *seen to be believed*.

Churches are pretty good at raising money and enthusiasm to build things. I call it the "edifice complex" and I fit right into that opportunity, and along with a faithful team, gave both money and time to see it up and running.

It did both in 2009 and continues until today.

But did it become a "blessing" to our community? Did it somehow communicate to those who were at high risk in their economy-dependent lives?

That is so hard to measure, except in one very well documented case...

Mine.

I set out to do exactly what we had collectively heard. I would be careful how we consumed *everything* and especially plant foods. I would grow my own; something I had never been able to do. In fact, I'd never met a plant I couldn't kill! I would also gather together with others who gardened in order to learn from them and, if possible, to be an encouragement.

My whole life changed following that "Ate Ball" time.

I had come back full circle to the point in Salem, Oregon, where I had felt "called" to plant small edible gardens amongst communities that had great needs. At that time back in 1980, my measurement of "need" was mostly physical –hunger and malnutrition.

Now it was to go way *beyond* that to the greatest need the world has ever experienced... survival of our species, indeed, of the planet itself.

Please join us in the Reflective Readers Club
www.grahamkerr.com/rrc

Rite of Passage Sixty-Four: "Return to the Redd"

The relief of finding a quiet place, one filled with the promise of aromas of our birthplace, was wonderful and peaceful but it wasn't long before inner stirrings drew us to the otherwise dangerous shallows of the gravel riffle just upstream of our secure pool.

It had been some time since I had thought of casting an admiring glance at my hen, or thinking about one in return.

The truth was that we carried the scars of time and close calls, yet her eyes were just the same as always and now and again they actually helped me to see myself through them.

It wasn't so far upstream when we became aware of others just like us and the occasional youngster who seemed attracted to the birthing time and had to be chased off by us older guys.

My hen found a bed of large gravel, just the right size, and the waters rippled nicely. She began to sweep them aside to make a shallow depression using her powerful tail.

I kept watch and snapped at any precocious intruder, occasionally chasing one downstream.

Her time, and mine, had come. She dug deeply creating almost a little pond in the swifter current and now dropped down into it and began to shiver and then shake her stream of eggs free from her body.

I lay alongside her —our fins touching as they had so long ago.

Once again I felt that deep movement within, but this time it built until I, too, shook to my scales with the emotions of fulfilling the purpose for my entire life.

We moved and then moved again from bed to bed, our growing emptiness replaced by a greater peace than we had ever known.

Exhausted, we continued to just press against the river and each other as we swept the gravel back in place to cover our precious eggs and milt.

Our job was done, our task complete, we had achieved, and in time new life would come.

We floated for a while, quite close, while resilience slowly ebbed. We ceased to struggle and were gently carried to the banks, to our resting place.

An Understanding

It is early September. Their six year journey is almost over. They recovered from the fly fisher and found the home waters of their ancestors.

During this time, the hen's eggs had matured and she was ready to spawn.

After their rest in the pool they moved up into the shallow riffle from which they themselves had come.

Other younger males, called Jacks, were also present and drawn to the spawning grounds by some instinct for which they were unprepared. They met fierce resistance by their now aged and hook-toothed elders.

The female finds clean gravel stones and a ripple of good water free from grit or mud and sweeps out a bed called a redd in which to lay her eggs. Some fish will prepare up to seven and distribute the eggs amongst each of these.

When the eggs are released and the milt settled upon them, both fish display a great deal of almost violent movement, mouths frozen open in the ecstasy of procreation.

Empty of eggs and milt, they may float nearby for several hours keeping watch over the future of their species until, exhausted by the effort, they finally die.

Their once powerful and resilient bodies then continue to provide life-sustaining nourishment to the animals and birds of the forest and even the trees themselves that, in season, clap their hands in respect and gratitude for a job well done.

2009
Five Levels Of Awareness

I had spent rather too many of my years in a state of envy, personal ambition, competition and judgment of others.

Eventually, at least in my case, most of this *me* centeredness had begun to pass away. The further upstream I went, the less I observed the need to beat someone else to the punch, or even to move ahead by using someone else as a stepping stone. I did have an increasing sense of purpose and just enough energy to keep me going. Doing anything truly *big* had ceased to be an ambition, but completing a *small* thing had become my passionate purpose.

This began in 2009 with the two gardens; one at our church, the other in my backyard.

Both had needed serious input, both in the soil and in my limited understanding.

The soil was mostly clay and stones and so perhaps was what I needed to know in order to grow anything? *I needed a lot of nourishment!*

The most important leap I took toward this improvement was to understand that my gardens needed my time and attention.

Up until this revelation I had often said publicly...

"What is the point of slowing down to smell the roses when I blew the petals off on my way past."

We had adopted the words "Galloping Gourmet" not just because of outward activity, but also due to the inward unrest caused by the ever-present demand for *attention* that drives all forms of media.

At home I had a small greenhouse built as job one, followed by grass killing and tilling and nourishing; all ready for seed.

I was helped at every single stage by new friends who had gardened for almost as many years as I had cooked. I loved these people, Charlie Yaw, Scott Titus and Deb Mitchel, the list would go on and on because my need to know was almost without limit. At each level I recorded every word of advice on tape filmed by our old and dear friend Michael Lienau with whom I had worked since 1980. We wound up with over seventeen hours of new footage that documented my scrubby patch of dandelion ridden lawn's transition to 450 square feet of intensive biodynamic edible garden.

At the same time I wrote a book "Growing At The Speed Of Life". It covered my first year in my first garden and explored what it meant to actually *have* to slow down to match the way that nature unfolds and, for the most part, can't be rushed.

My garden overlooks an Interstate Highway about two miles away, always flooded with both cars and sixteen-wheelers back and forth –to and fro. It occurred to me one day, while thinning out a bed of carrots, with the distant roar of traffic, that life was like that, like the hustle on the highway.

As a child, when I got my first bicycle, I had ridden it behind the Baker's Van and thrilled to the way it had created the *draft* that had carried me along, almost without effort.

I thought of this as I watched a giant double truck doing at least sixty miles an hour. Had I in modern times exchanged the bakers van for the huge transport. Thirty miles an hour to sixty; was I being spurred along, unable to go where I wanted at a speed that I knew was dangerous? Was the truck the economy and were we, in the United States, working harder for longer hours in order to live at a *consuming speed* that was damaging our quality of life, even that of our planet?

At that moment, I began to "smell the roses"

My second *awareness* came from the basil seeds I had sown under Master Gardener Bev Mitchell's direction in the greenhouse. For six days I had visited "them." Not a peep, nothing stirred. I began to see this as evidence of my own brown thumb syndrome!

On the seventh day (with apologies to Genesis) I opened the door and there "they" were, a long line of tiny green leaves, one of which still had a grain of soil balanced on its sturdy little head.

"Good morning everyone." I cried out loud and hearing my own voice clapped my hands over my mouth with embarrassment. I had actually talked to a row of seedlings as if they could understand! They might not have understood but they were alive and so was I, and with that I understood that we were somehow *connected*.

At that moment I became an environmentalist

The third *awareness* followed swiftly.

I had planted a tomato start called a Russian Paste that I had eaten with great pleasure over a year prior at a function on Orcas Island.

It had the perfect balance of sweet and sour with a lovely geranium type fragrance.

I awaited its blossom, its tiny green fruit and its blushing arrival into maturity. It took time but it matched my early basil planting perfectly.

In June they were both ready for –me!

I had a fine Balsamic vinegar left over from a trip to Bologna years before, sea salt and freshly ground black peppercorns. I was ready to combine the Russian Paste with its bright green neighbors –drizzled with balsamic, dusted with salt and pepper.

Yes!

At the moment of approaching gastronomic bliss, I heard *that* voice again.

"Share it with your neighbor."

I ignored it, plucked the tomato from its vine and held it ready for the knife.

"Share it with your neighbor." This time the voice was firmer and louder.

I obeyed, and lined a small basket with basil leaves and settled the perfect tomato in their midst.

I carried it next door to our neighbor who I scarcely knew.

I knocked on the door and she opened it.

"This is for you." I smiled and handed over the basket.

"This is the first tomato I've ever grown," I explained.

"It's a gift –for you." I wasn't trying to earn a special brownie point for a sacrificed gift –I was just being a proud parent!

"Thank you," she said without a smile.

"Thank you!" Was that all she could muster for such a splendid gift?

"Is there something wrong?" I asked.

"My mother has just passed," she replied sadly.

I went to get Treena and came back to wrap our arms around the lady who had moved in next door.

At that moment we became neighbors

I had to wait until the harvest in that great local growing year of 2009 to discover the fourth *awareness*.

From the time that I had begun to cook in the Roebuck Hotel in Sussex (UK) until 2009, close to my 77th birthday, I had cooked just about everything that anyone had grown –worldwide.

I had never grown anything (apart from the odd herb) that I had ever cooked. Each plant that I harvested was a revelation.

To grow, plants had needed me. Now, for me to continue to *grow*, I needed them. We were connected in our respective lifestyles; we needed each other, together we were *resilient*, we were *naturally connected*. It was that partnership in purpose that led me to begin to eat with added discernment. I savored each bite, and admired the colors, textures and aromas.

At that moment I became an intentional eater.

Being aware of both nourishment and delight, in that order. My cooking ability improved along with a more simple creativity. Years before I had coined the phrase...

"Food least handled is best liked."

and

"Get to your food fast before someone gets there first."

I was now able to fully apply both, with *real* understanding.

When the gardening book came out, complete with my new understandings, I was asked onto Rachel Ray's television talk show in New York City. I had a very good time and found her refreshingly easy to talk to.

Her website resounded with some very warm comments about the appearance, and she very kindly invited me to return...at her

Photo Credit RachaelRayShow.com

expense. I was to appear with Mario Batali, Sara Moulton and Guy Fieri. I was to come on last...as some kind of finale.

It was not as refreshing but it still came complete with a smaller storm of requests for me to "return to television...where you are still a star."

I returned to my hotel room following the show in an extremely despondent mood.

I actually kicked the furniture as I had done when I had earned just over a million dollars back in Ottawa in 1970. This was thirty years later and almost exactly the same feeling. The difference this time was that I wanted to know why I felt so discouraged when so many had been so encouraging. This time I could ask the question and even believe, in my distress, that I could get an answer.

It was along with the answer that I came to my fifth and final (at this time) *awareness*.

The familiar "voice" was gentle.

"Come with me to the beach in Oregon in the early morning on a cloudless day and stand, facing the ocean with the rising sun at your back."

"I am now going to show you your whole life span in just one day."

I stood in my hotel room and faced due West across the Hudson River from thirty eight stories high, at least two thousand miles away from Cannon Beach and imagined myself standing on the firm sand.

"Feel the sun on your back; now see how long your shadow is, it reaches all the way across the beach into the sea. When you were young you saw there was no end to what you might achieve in the Oceans of Opportunity."

My mind fled backward through the years of ambition and its cost.

"But notice, as the sun rises and the years go by, that your shadow retreats toward you until at 40 and halfway, the shadow disappears in a pool at your feet."

"You are now in the evening of your life, the sun has dipped toward the horizon and has reflected across the sea in a pathway of gold."

I was reminded of streets paved with gold in the coming Kingdom.

"See where your shadow is now —it's behind you stretching into the dunes."

"Yes," I said, "I see this, but please answer me...why do I feel so discouraged?"

"You have been asked to go back on television and repeat what you once did successfully. To do so, you will have to take your eyes off the Ocean of Eternity, turn around and walk back in your old shadow."

"Now pick up a stick and write in the sand the letters E. G. G. S. This has been given to you to speak out while there is yet still light. They spell eat, grow, gather and share. You have learned these things as you went downstream, around the Oceans of Opportunity, and finally upstream for this specific purpose."

I saw myself carving out these letters in the sand.

"But do not build an edifice, or a business —you know what happens when the tide comes in to a sandcastle."

"Yes but," I replied quickly, "but these letters will also disappear."

"Look over your shoulder, see all the people walking on the beach, they will see the letters and wonder what they mean. Your work is to help answer that question."

I became, at that moment, a focused witness of all I had seen and heard throughout my whole life and began to set it all down for you to read and hopefully to understand.

The sun is now setting and the pathway of gold is more brilliant. The tide is coming in, just touching the letters in the sand.

There is still time to work while there is still light.

Please join us in the Reflective Readers Club
www.grahamkerr.com/rrc

Epilogue

It is said that every metaphor eventually runs out.

Our two Chinook have successfully completed their life cycle of seven years. Their eggs and milt provide for the miracle of new life already beginning under a blanket of small stones and washed by clear, cold water. Their once long and lovely silver bodies have supplied nourishment for small animals and birds —even tiny microscopic life forms.

In turn the trees also receive marine nitrates that can be found in trace amounts in their foliage.

Resilient even beyond their very active lives, they provide a true template for an enduring future, were it not for man.

Treena and I live on in the twilight of our lives. We have found *a place of peace* for the days we have left in our tree-strewn valley.

Yet we, like the salmon, are not content with our deep quiet pool carved out by the living waters flowing around the secure rock of our faith. For as long as there is life, there is a race to be run with perseverance, one that we want to finish well.

In doing so, we hope to display some sense of the salmon's resilience, what we are now calling **The Stamp of the Salmon** that might allow others like us to see what might be done to bring healing to our troubled times.

We have learned how...

To EAT *intentionally*, using mostly plant foods.

To GROW *our own edible plants* in the backyard and beyond with an eye to the ecology and environment that connects us to them.

Original Painting by David McCall Johnston

To GATHER *with our neighbors* in our small community and consider what we can do together for the common good.

To SHARE *with those less fortunate* so that they may receive sufficient inner resilience for their upstream journey to a better future.

So, I wondered, what could a *better future* look like, not just for ourselves but also for those we now call neighbors?

Climate change has become a political football with science its active partner, on both sides. Does it mean that our planet is at risk and our behavior is the cause?

I know that individual behavior is both cause and effect for our individual health and wellbeing because many experts say that as much as eighty percent of our chronic diseases are self-inflicted.

If *we* are the canary in the coal mine, could this mean that the world is now at risk for the same reason, the intervention of man that somehow goes against the natural resilience that was the original design intention?

This takes me on a journey of faith back to the garden and God's original design for man to eat from it and then multiply (its resilient affect) throughout the whole earth.

My small gardens have become, for me, tiny Edens. A gentle reminder of a loving God who continues to provide the very best for all that He created because *everything is –connected.*

My idea then of a better future is a conscious return to resilience, the natural sequence of ongoing life.

It is this strong desire that continues to urge me to go upstream on purpose, one in which Treena and I can creatively eat, grow, gather and share under his ever-watchful care and, by doing so, we can go *beyond our immediate self interest.*

"Upstreaming"…beyond immediate self interest

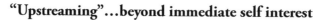

Image by © Thomas Kitchin & Victoria Hurst/First Light/Corbis.jpg

LABOR DAY 7 SEPTEMBER 2015.
"The Last Word"

"Flash of Silver…the leap that changed my world" and TREENA'S new book of poetry were both completed, ready for the printer, on Labor Day 2015. We looked at each other and smiled at two jobs that we felt we had done quite well.

"It is finished!" we cried in unison.

The very next day Treena was scheduled for minor day surgery from which we expected she would recover rapidly enough to celebrate our 60th wedding anniversary with all our children on September 22.

Sadly, this was not to be.

It began with a simple infection that became full-blown pneumonia that was so rapid that a ventilator was used to help her breathe whilst the antibiotics did their work.

The prognosis was mixed and we had to consider two tracks to the future.

In one we would choose a day and time with a very tender and loving palliative care team, and gather about her as they removed the support ventilator and then watch as she went to "sleep" (see 1 Thessalonians 4:14 NIV)

On the other path she would pull through and be able, after a couple of days rehab, to return home. Hour by hour we wrestled with what would Treena want. We were all trying to live beyond our own immediate interest, which was powerfully wanting her to live.

On the morning of 16 September she took the decision into her own hands and awakened out of her drug assisted sleep and yanked the tube out of her throat…breathing on her own after a full three days on the machine.

Within a couple of hours she was able to speak and then began a 36 hour gift of radiant life to everyone who entered her room; family, friends, nurses, doctors, janitorial staff, not one single soul was overlooked...she chatted, smiled, hugged, sat up and made us all laugh with her infectious joy.

At one point she announced, without any hesitation, "I'm going to have tea and eggs with Jesus!" She was clearly excited about the prospect.

She was interested in all our lives, wanting the best for us and recalling some small issues that were really personal and hardly pressing...yet wonderfully warming to have had her remember us so individually.

She left nobody out. She lived in that splendid outgoing giving of herself until the last hour, with only 30 minutes sleep in that day and a half of happiness. What a gift!

As the reader of our story you will have become aware of most of the ways in which she lived her life. It was not an easy journey but she certainly lived it to the full and her not being by my side has opened up an enormous space.

I am writing this just one week after her final breath and my emotions are still both raw and unpredictable. She called me "The bestest husband in all the world". That was her opinion so I didn't argue...she was, for me, the love of my life and will remain in that place forever.

Not exactly a Hollywood ending but then, we were not exactly a Hollywood couple.

It's enough for us that the leaves of the trees may clap their hands as we both close the book on this Rite Of Passage we call human life.

"We are not human beings having a spiritual experience, we are spiritual beings having a human experience". Pierre Teilhard de Chardin

Graham Kerr,
Nonsuch Cottage
Mount Vernon, Washington
United States.
24 September 2015.

27463381R00232

Made in the USA
San Bernardino, CA
13 December 2015